Thinking Things Through

General Editors
Graham Slater and C. S. Rodd

12. The Holy Spirit

Thinking Things Through

Thinking Things Through

12. The Holy Spirit

Graham Slater

 EPWORTH

British Library Cataloguing in Publication data

A catalogue record for this book is available
from the British Library

0-7162-0582-3

First published in 2005
by Epworth Press
4 John Wesley Road
Werrington
Peterborough PE4 6ZP

Printed and bound in Great Britain by
Biddles Ltd, www.biddles.co.uk

Contents

General Introduction

The great Swiss theologian, Hans Küng, has said that his aim in all his writings is to enable his readers to hold their faith with confidence and not with a bad conscience. This new series, prompted by the conviction that Christians need to think through their faith but often lack appropriate help in so doing, has a similar aim. Moreover, the assistance that it seeks to offer is related to another conviction: that many church members need persuading that theologians are concerned in any way with their problems and that theology can be at all relevant to their lives.

In such a situation, it is essential, we are sure, to begin with life and with church life. Only in that way can we be confident that we are dealing with grassroots issues. Plainly, however, it is not enough to identify the questions where they arise; we must also indicate the sources of help, if not of all the answers, in as non-technical a way as possible.

In some volumes, these tasks will be tackled in sequence; in others, they will be interwoven. Whatever the precise format, however, our hope is that through this interaction, difficulties will be faced, fears dispelled, open discussion promoted, and faith informed and strengthened.

The books can be either read by individuals on their own or used in groups. We hope that the questions at the end of each chapter will be useful both as a check that the text has been understood and as a spur to reflection and discussion.

This book is the last in the 12-volume series.

GRAHAM SLATER AND C. S. RODD

Introduction

Looking back, I am inclined to think that I have spent as much time pondering how to write this book as actually writing it. Needless to say, there are several reasons for this. In the first place, almost every previous writer stresses that the subject bristles with difficulties, and Wolfhart Pannenberg (*The Apostles' Creed in the Light of Today's Questions*, SCM Press, 1972) makes the point with his usual thoroughness. Moreover, since 1972 both theology and church life have been powerfully affected by Charismatic Renewal, and it is difficult to know how to handle the sharp disagreements about its present influence and long-term value. Lastly, though it is impossible within the format of this series to tackle the whole range of questions which clamour for attention, some way of indicating the significance of what has been left out needs to be found.

In the event, I have been anxious to identify the questions that bother ordinary folk and not to over-face my House Group with issues which could quite properly concern others. At the same time, while acknowledging the recent influence of Charismatic Renewal, I have tried to do justice to a wider ecclesiastical and theological context. For though before 1950 the doctrine of the Holy Spirit did not claim the attention which it has received since, it was never totally neglected, in devotion or theological reflection. In short, the reality of the Holy Spirit was not discovered and interpreted, though it may have been widely rediscovered and reinterpreted, in my lifetime.

As the last chapter bears witness, now that the work is done three quotations linger in my mind: '. . . in point of fact, the Holy Spirit is the Person of the Trinity with whom we are most constantly in conscious contact' (William Temple, *Christian Faith and Life*, SCM Press, 1931); the Holy Spirit is 'the shy member of the Trinity' (F. D. Bruner and W. Hordern, *The Holy Spirit – Shy Member of the Trinity*, Augsburg, 1984); 'There is no more intimate friend of common sense than the Holy Spirit' (Karl Barth, *Dogmatics in Outline*, SCM Press, 1949). I find the first challenging, the second humbling and the third reassuring. I hope that the following pages will explain why.

All hymns quoted in the text are taken from *Hymns and Psalms, a Methodist and Ecumenical Hymnbook* (Methodist Publishing House, 1983).

This is the last volume in the *Thinking Things Through* series, and I offer my warmest thanks to my co-editor, Cyril Rodd, for his kindly and generous help over the past eight years. I could not have wished for a more congenial, knowledgeable and efficient colleague.

GRAHAM SLATER

Part 1

The House Group

1

Getting Started

Bill's role in the House Group was important but difficult to describe. He wasn't the 'leader' – the word sounded too formal, granted the relaxed ethos which the group favoured – but he was the kind of person to whom others turned for help. And at this moment he was struggling with a particularly tricky request.

For the group had decided that, during the next session, it would explore 'The Holy Spirit'. This sounded a good idea – perhaps a very good idea – at the time, and when Bill had been asked to suggest an approach to the subject, he had readily agreed to see what he could do. But the more that he thought about the task, the more problems it seemed to pose.

Bill reflected, for example, that the Holy Spirit is relevant to all the topics so far covered in the *Thinking Things Through* series! But plainly it was unrealistic to attempt, in a few meetings, to trace exactly how. Moreover, Christian understanding of the Holy Spirit is bound up, historically, with the formulation of the doctrine of the Trinity. It seemed unlikely, however, that the group would want, at least initially, to address so technical a topic.

Why then had 'The Holy Spirit' been chosen? A number of factors, Bill decided, were probably at work. The group members were aware that, in their own congregation and in other churches, there was a wide range of views about the nature and importance of the Holy Spirit. They recognised, too, that these convictions manifested themselves in differing styles of worship, types of spirituality and patterns of church life. At the same time, they were unsure why such disagreements arose and how, if at all, they could be resolved.

Moreover, in their own desire to be better Christians, they were anxious, so far as Bill could judge, to clarify their ideas about how God works in the world and how his present help is made available to believers. But the questions remained: Could a feasible approach be devised? Could a manageable agenda be created?

At this point, Bill wondered whether his minister knew of a suitable book. To his disappointment, he was told that, though some excellent works had appeared in recent years – James Dunn's *Jesus and the Spirit* (SCM Press, 1975), G. W. H. Lampe's *God as Spirit* (Oxford University Press, 1977), John V. Taylor's *The Go-Between God* (SCM Press, 1972), John McIntyre's *The Shape of Pneumatology* (T&T Clark, 1997), and Yves Congar's three volumes entitled *I Believe in the Holy Spirit* (Geoffrey Chapman, 1986) were mentioned – none of them were likely to meet the House Group's needs.

What other options were there? As Bill began to feel that there might not be any, a sentence floated into his mind: 'Most Christians get their theology from hymns.' He couldn't remember where he had read that, but it suggested a first step. He would get word to his friends in the House Group, asking them to look at the section about the Holy Spirit – in, for example, *Hymns and Psalms, a Methodist and Ecumenical Hymnbook* (Methodist Publishing House, 1983) – and to be prepared at the first meeting to share what was most interesting or puzzling or challenging in what they found there. In this way, the particular interests and concerns of the group should quickly become apparent.

Bill was sure that, in the light of what emerged, the group members would have ideas of their own about how to go further.

2

First Impressions

The first meeting of the new session proved very lively, for all the right reasons.

It was clear from the start that the members were intrigued by the method that Bill had suggested. Fred, who liked to get down to the basics, was the spokesman. 'Why', he asked, 'have you suggested that we start with hymns? Why not the Bible?'

'Well', Bill replied, 'I was searching for a starting point which would be familiar and accessible. Having looked at several books about the Holy Spirit, I learned that the Bible contains a vast amount of relevant material which doesn't fit neatly into a clear pattern. It seemed likely therefore that a direct approach to the biblical evidence could prove bewildering.'

'I take the point,' said Fred. 'But I still want to know: why hymns?'

'For several reasons,' Bill explained. 'First, hymns offer not speculation or argument but testimony. In other words, they reveal what their writers have proved in experience about the deep things of God. Second, the continuing popularity of some of the oldest hymns suggests that they focus on essentials and can help us to do the same. Third, it seems likely that, since most of the hymns are reworkings of biblical ideas, they can point us to key passages of Scripture.

'In short, my choice of hymns was not meant to question the fundamental importance of Scripture but rather to offer a way of identifying and beginning to understand the most important things that it tells us about the Holy Spirit.'

To Bill's relief, the group members were persuaded by his explanation, and he was able to move the conversation on. 'What caught your attention', he asked, 'when you looked at the relevant hymns?'

Fred, true to form, focused on how the Holy Spirit was first received by the Church. 'I noticed', he said, 'that there are numerous echoes of the two New Testament accounts, in John 20 and Acts 2, of how the Spirit was "given": by Jesus "breathing" on his disciples or by an experience described in terms of wind and fire. One hymn, indeed, seems to combine both images, speaking of "The Breath of God in power/Like Wind and roaring flame". Can we know, I ask myself, what really happened? And how important is such knowledge today?'

Mary, who is a great reader and is fascinated by language, pointed out the way in which 'fire' is used to link the Holy Spirit with a wide range of experiences: the quickening of new life, purification, inspiration, enlightenment, possession of the glow of God's presence and being filled with love. 'It seems to me', she said, 'that, in studying the Holy Spirit, we shall need to be particularly alert to the special ways in which language is used in religious contexts. And I, for one, am looking forward to what we will discover.'

John, who is very methodical and likes to tackle one thing at a time, noted that some hymns explore a single aspect of the Spirit's work. 'Born by the Holy Spirit's breath', for example, expounds the message of Romans 8, 'Come Holy Ghost, our hearts inspire' focuses on enlightenment and 'Come down, O love divine' concentrates on the work of divine love in the life of a Christian. 'Why', he asked, 'have these particular themes been selected and how are they related to each other?'

Helen, by contrast, was attracted by the way in which some hymns try to provide a comprehensive picture. 'Gracious Spirit, dwell with me', she pointed out, goes on to list the Spirit's other qualities – being truthful, silent, mighty and holy; and 'Holy Spirit, truth divine' adds verses on divine love, power, right, peace and joy. 'How complete a picture', she enquired, 'do these characteristics provide?'

Bill, for his part, had been reflecting about the references to sevenfold gifts, sevenfold energy and sevenfold mystical dowry, on the one hand, and the unspecified 'lovely tempers, fruits of grace', on the other. 'I assume', he said, 'that the gifts are those mentioned in Romans 12 and 1 Corinthians 12 and that the fruits are those listed in Galatians 5. But I'm still puzzled by the distinction between "gifts" and "fruits".'

Angela, who always strikes a practical note, had spotted that most of the hymns about fellowship focus on Christ joining believers by his grace. The Benediction, by contrast, speaks of 'the fellowship of the Holy Spirit'. She wondered, therefore, why – fellowship being something that we all crave for our churches – there aren't more hymns like 'O Holy Spirit, Lord of grace', with its plea:

> As thou in bond of love dost join
>   The Father and the Son,
> So fill us all with mutual love,
>   And knit our hearts in one.

Lest the group should immediately fall into animated discussion of any or all of these fascinating questions, Bill reminded them of the need to plan ahead. 'Thank you', he said, 'for this useful preliminary survey. In the light of what we have already discovered, how do you want to proceed?'

'I share Fred's desire to know more about how the Spirit was first given', said John, 'but I suspect that we may need help where the accounts in John 20 and Acts 2 are concerned. Perhaps this could be a topic – perhaps one of several? – about which Tony, our minister, could be consulted in due course. Meanwhile, I think that we should discuss the meaning of "Holy Spirit". After all, we all know that "Holy Ghost" has nothing to do with haunting! But we may not be at all clear about what "Holy Ghost/Spirit" does mean and how he/it is received today.'

'I'm sure', said Angela, 'that that is a good idea, and I'll be glad to introduce a discussion on those lines next week – indeed, I can immediately think of a hymn that may help us.' 'And what hymn is that?' was the chorused response. 'You must come and find out,' was Angela's teasing reply.

7

And with that the group dispersed, with appetites whetted for what lay ahead.

Questions for discussion

1. Look at the hymns on the Holy Spirit in the hymn-book that you regularly use. Can you spot anything significant that the members of the House Group have missed?

2. When the nature of the Holy Spirit is explored next week, what will you be most anxious to contribute to the discussion?

3. If you had to pick a hymn to stimulate and inform discussion of the Holy Spirit, what would your choice be, and how would you justify it?

3

Life and Love

A week later Angela was proved right: her choice of hymn –
'Breathe on me, Breath of God' by Edwin Hatch (1835–89) –
triggered a whole evening's discussion.

The hymn appealed to her, she explained, by the simplicity and
directness of its language. In four short verses it covers four central
Christian beliefs: new life in Christ, the God-given capacity to
love, growth in holiness and the assurance of a place in God's
eternity. Not only so: it uses the image of the 'breath of God',
prompting connections with important biblical passages – for
example, the Genesis account of creation, Ezekiel's episode of the
re-animation of the dry bones, and Jesus' gift of the Holy Spirit to
the disciples in John 20.22. And from this point the close relation
in Scripture between 'breath' and 'wind' and the use of both as
symbols of God's unobtrusive but powerful activity in the world
and in human life can easily be grasped.

'I can see', said Fred, 'the importance of the link between life,
love and the Holy Spirit, and I can understand that the stress on
"love" as the key characteristic of the Christian life chimes in with
Paul's teaching, especially in 1 Corinthians 13, which many feel is
a theological portrait of Jesus himself. I can also appreciate that,
because there are many kinds of wind, from the fierce scirocco to
the soothing evening breeze, "wind/breath" provides a helpful way
of speaking about a wide range of divine activities. But I'm still
anxious to learn more about how the Spirit – the Spirit which
makes love possible – is "received", especially today.'

'I suppose', replied John, 'that two possible answers can be
given. Some would say that the Spirit is given through baptism,
while others opt for its reception along with the faith which the
impact of the gospel triggers.

'The first view can be found in the Baptismal Service of the 1662
Book of Common Prayer. It depends, of course, on a very strong
view of original sin. The child to be baptised is judged to have been

conceived and born in sin and to be in need of regeneration through baptism in order to become a member of the Church and to enter the kingdom of God. The congregation, therefore, is asked to pray that, through baptism, God will give the child the Holy Spirit so that he/she may be born again and become an heir of everlasting salvation.

'The second view builds not on baptismal regeneration but on the unique impact of the gospel. Take, for example, Isaac Watts's "When I survey the wondrous cross" with its affirmation "Love so amazing, so divine/Demands my life, my soul, my all", or Charles Wesley's "What shall I render to my God/For all his mercy's store" with its response "I'll take the gifts he has bestowed/and humbly ask for more", or F. Pratt Green's "Lord, we have come at your own invitation" with its concluding prayer "Help us to make these decisions that bind us,/Lord, to yourself, in obedience and joy". In and through such responses the individual comes to faith and the Holy Spirit is "received".'

At this point, Bill had a simpler suggestion to make. 'As I looked at the hymns about the Holy Spirit,' he volunteered, 'I noticed how many were requests for the gift of the Spirit. I realise, of course, that at this point we hit a difficulty. Is the Spirit given with the gift of faith or subsequently? The Pentecostalists, I know, see baptism in the Spirit as an experience distinct from the reception of faith, and that view depends on some detailed biblical interpretation with which we may need help from our minister. It also involves a particular understanding of how the reception of the Spirit can be verified, and that too merits separate attention. Leaving all that aside, however, it seems reasonable to identify the reception of the Spirit as an answer to prayer.'

Mary wanted to take the conversation in another direction. 'It sounds to me', she chipped in, 'as though coming to faith, being born again, learning to love God and neighbour and receiving the Holy Spirit are four different ways of referring to the same experience. And I'm very interested in the language being used. How far, for example, does the Fourth Gospel's reference to Jesus "breathing" on his disciples relate to the fact that his exemplary love must have "inspired" them?'

Not pausing to attempt an answer to this question, Helen also moved into new territory. 'To think of the disciples meeting together after the death and resurrection of Jesus', she reflected, 'is to be reminded of the old saying about Christianity being caught as well as taught. In other words, when the disciples reflected together on the character and teaching of Jesus, they would have been reminded of his Spirit and affected by it. And, in the light of this fact, it comes as no surprise that the Spirit was "given", apparently, to a group – either the disciples or "all the believers" – and not to an individual. It would have been possible for anyone impressed by the preaching of the apostles to "receive" – or to "catch" – the Spirit as they joined the fellowship of believers.'

The other members of the group didn't want to be drawn into such speculations. They were anxious, rather, to explore the full range of the Spirit's activities. It became clear, in fact, that the potential agenda for the next few weeks was rapidly outgrowing what could be tackled, and someone needed to assess the situation and make some realistic proposals. Bill stepped into the breach. 'As I see it,' he said, 'Angela's choice of hymn has helped us to do three things: to remind ourselves of why the creed describes the Holy Spirit as "the Lord, the giver of life" and why "love" is so central to Christian living; to speculate on how the Spirit was first "given" and to explore how it is still "given" today; and to decide what is going to be possible in future meetings.

'At the same time, I believe, we have made some progress in our understanding of "Spirit language". We have been enabled, for example, to see that it points to the activity of God in his world, in creation and re-creation. We haven't, it is true, touched on the work of the Spirit in our lives before we come to faith, but we have recognised that, when we hear the gospel and respond, we "receive" the Spirit and begin consciously to co-operate with him. But we have still to explore how the worship of our churches can be enriched; how our communion with God can be strengthened and developed; how God's guidance can be experienced; how we can be equipped for mission and service; how we can be confident in our faith; and whether and in what sense, we, like the disciples, can receive "power".'

'I think', said John, 'that we should turn immediately to the activity of the Spirit in the life of our own congregation. Perhaps, therefore, "Worship and the Sacraments" should be first on our list and, if you like, I'll start us off next week.' At this point, it was unanimously agreed that the time had come for a well-earned cup of tea.

Questions for discussion

1. The chapter claims that Holy Spirit refers to 'God's unobtrusive but powerful activity in the world and in human life'. Work out why you feel that this definition does or does not go far enough.

2. How do you think that the Spirit (a) was first 'received' and (b) is still 'received'?

3. Bill suggests what seems to him the most important topics to explore next. Does his list correspond with your priorities? If not, explain what alterations you would make and why.

In this and the following five weeks, it may be useful to undertake an additional task. Try using the opportunity to look more carefully than perhaps you have ever done before not only at the hymn chosen by the House Group member but also at any similar hymns which you can locate. You may be surprised – in every sense of the word! – by what you discover.

4

Worship and Sacraments

'Angela's choice of a hymn proved so creative', said John, 'that I decided to use one myself – "Holy Spirit, hear us;/Help us while we sing" by W. H. Parker (1845–1929).'

'This hymn appeals to me', he went on, 'in much the same way as Angela's choice did to her: the language is simple and the requests – for help in singing, praying, reading the Bible, and choosing what is right – are basically important. I need constantly to be reminded of the overall aim of becoming "more like Jesus", even though I find "gentle, pure and kind" a limited description of his character.

'At the same time, this hymn, by contrast with the one we looked at last week, expresses a corporate request – "hear us", "help us", "prompt us", etc. And it is important to bear in mind what Helen noted in the accounts of the first "gift" of the Spirit: the recipients are a group – and a worshipping, learning group at that.'

'But people in our own day have been singing that hymn for years,' said practical Angela, 'and nothing much seems to have happened. We still hear complaints about the dullness and deadness of worship. Why should this be the case? Is the Holy Spirit falling down on the job? Or are his efforts being blocked somehow?'

'It could be', said Fred, 'that many people have never experienced true worship and that they don't understand what their part in it should be. So the key question becomes: Do they come to worship with minds and hearts prepared and expecting from God what they most need to receive?'

'I suppose', added Helen, 'that you could put much the same point in another way. Many people have heard a lot about "fellowship" but they have never experienced it. In other words, they have never sensed that togetherness that arises from shared faith and mutual acceptance. For them the sentiments of Charles Wesley's hymn "All praise to our redeeming Lord" will therefore be largely unintelligible. For others, by contrast, that hymn will speak eloquently of the foundations on which the richest worship rests.'

'What you all seem to be saying in slightly different ways', Bill suggested, 'is that if "dead" worship is all that people have experienced, they don't know either what they are missing or what it is appropriate to expect. So there is a blockage. How do we think that it can be cleared?'

In response to Bill's question, the members of the group shared their experience. There is, they decided, no universal solution. But they could identify how, in different circumstances, worship had been transformed. In one church, a preacher's ability to bring the Bible alive had revolutionised the congregation's expectations. In another, the influence of a House Group had healed relationships and made it possible for worship to be offered by a united fellowship. In another, a young music teacher had formed a choir whose joyful singing had filled the worship with new life. In yet another, a Youth Group that had visited Taizé had offered liberating contributions from a style of worship never before experienced. And so on.

Fred summed up where the conversation was going: 'As I see it, we're back again with "life", and perhaps we should again link it with "love". I'm sure that you all remember the last verse of "Come, Holy Spirit, heavenly Dove" – "Come, shed abroad the Saviour's love/And that shall kindle ours". In other words, it is only as the love of Christ is presented to us – through preaching or fellowship or worship – that we begin to come alive ourselves and to glimpse what is possible in all areas of Christian activity.'

'But can we be a little more specific', asked Mary, 'about the activities mentioned in the hymn that John chose – singing, praying, reading the Bible and choosing what is right? Where in them do we see the assistance of the Holy Spirit?'

Once again the group members shared their experiences. They agreed that Isaac Watts was right: if our hymns are to be more than 'formal songs', our hearts need to be kindled by the Saviour's love – and that can only be a work of the Holy Spirit. They also agreed that Christians need help in prayer, as in all aspects of life, and that it is therefore reassuring that, thanks to the presence of the Holy Spirit, communication with God can take place even when words fail us. Finally, they agreed that we need help, help which the Holy Spirit provides, in understanding the Bible, whether reading it ourselves or hearing it read.

'And don't forget', Mary interjected, 'something most important which the hymn doesn't mention – the preaching. It isn't enough that the preacher understands the Bible – he/she must have the kind of insight that can be communicated helpfully to a congregation. And that often comes in a very complex fashion, involving, like all creative activity, both conscious and unconscious processes. And when the sermon is preached the result can be remarkable: both the preacher and the hearers can recognise that, in a mysterious way, human words have become the vehicle of God's Word.'

'There are two other important things', added John, 'which the hymn doesn't mention – the sacraments. And here I detect a certain amount of ambiguity in some modern liturgies. We have already heard, at an earlier meeting, about the *BCP* service of baptism, which enshrines the view that baptism effects regeneration. And we all know that the Wesleys had a similarly high view of Holy Communion: see, for example, Charles Wesley's hymn "Come, Holy Ghost, thine influence shed" with the lines "Thy life infuse into the bread, Thy power into the wine". Today, however, the focus tends to be not on the elements but on the total significance of the liturgy. So, in the new *Methodist Worship Book* we find a prayer in the baptismal service which reads: "Pour out your Holy Spirit that those baptised in this water may die to sin, be raised with Christ and be born to new life in the family of your church." Does this prayer expect an instant effect or ask for an eventual outcome? Similarly, in the service of the Holy Communion we find "Pour out your Holy Spirit that these gifts of bread and wine may be to us the body and blood of Christ." We are told: "This standard *epiclesis* is a deliberately ambiguous sentence which does not preclude our believing what Charles Wesley believed but does not absolutely require that we should."'

'My guess is', John concluded, 'that there is here a cluster of problems about the nature of a sacrament. Does baptism, for example, do more than convey a status, i.e. a place within the family of Christ's people? And is the Holy Communion more than a visual presentation of the gospel and of the possibility of feeding on Christ in our hearts by faith and with thanksgiving? If, in both cases, more is involved, what is it and how can it be conceptualised?'

Mary was quick to respond. 'I take your point, and I understand the importance of your question. But I haven't a clue how to begin to answer it. And I'm not sure that it would be fair to face Tony with it. Perhaps we can only leave it to the professional theologians.'

At this point, Bill decided that summing up was in order! 'We've covered a great deal of ground,' he said, 'but one thing should probably be mentioned in conclusion. The music in our churches has changed greatly in recent years. Many congregations now prefer a band to an organ to accompany singing and use worship songs as much as traditional hymns. In addition, participation in worship has become physically more expressive, and it is widely believed that in these ways what was previously dead has come to life. We must look later, I am convinced, at the assumptions on which this claim is based, probably after our minister has explained the ways in which "Baptism in the Holy Spirit" has been understood and what, for many, its implications for worship are felt to be.

'It is perhaps enough, here and now, to register firmly and gratefully that our discussion tonight has illustrated the creative role of the Holy Spirit in all aspects of worship. For Christians, after all, the whole of life involves interaction – not only with their physical environment and their fellow human beings but also with God. At no time, therefore, are they alone and when they meet for worship, as in all other circumstances, God's loving support and stimulus are available to them.

'And I would like to suggest that we leave "choosing what is right" to our next meeting, when the topic can be "Guidance". Do we have a volunteer to open the discussion?'

Mary's offer was accepted without hesitation!

Questions for discussion

1. What, for you, are the chief marks of the presence of the Holy Spirit in worship?

2. Why is prayer offered for the special activity of the Holy Spirit in the sacraments?

3. How can we know whether the Holy Spirit can still achieve more through preaching than through any other activity?

5

Guidance

Mary's decision to use 'Captain of Israel's host and Guide/Of all that seek the land above' by Charles Wesley (1707–88) to introduce this session surprised no one. It is, after all, one of the most famous two-verse hymns in the history of hymnody, and it focuses admirably on several key issues.

Mary began by quoting the second verse in full:

> By thine unerring Spirit led
> We shall not in the desert stray;
> We shall not full direction need,
> Nor miss our providential way;
> As far from danger as from fear
> While love, almighty love, is near.

'I don't need to tell you', she continued, 'that this hymn draws a parallel between the people of Israel wandering in the desert and the New Israel, the members of the Christian Church, wandering through life. Like the Jews of old, the hymn maintains, Christians of every age require guidance or "full direction". They need, in other words, to find the route that God desires for them – their "providential way" – and they can be confident of the leadership of God's "unerring Spirit" and of the protection of his ever-present love.

'I looked for help in expanding this theme,' Mary added, 'and I found it in a couple of books that my dad left me. From a theological dictionary I made the acquaintance of a distinction between general and special providence; and from a book by Dr Sangster, entitled *God does guide us* (Hodder & Stoughton, 1934), I learned something about the ways in which guidance is provided. At the same time, it occurred to me that there could be important differences between the ways in which individuals and groups are guided to specific courses of action. Where, among these lines of thought, would you like to start?'

'I read that book of Sangster's myself,' said Bill. 'It was a long time ago, and I seem to recall that at the time he was greatly influenced by Moral Re-Armament. Consequently, the book is chiefly concerned with guidance given to the individual and stresses the key importance of a daily "quiet time" in the whole process. As I remember, Sangster also stresses the complexity of the process by which guidance is received – through circumstances, reason, the Bible and fellowship – and the ever-open possibility of being mistaken.'

'Ought we, then, to look at those channels through which guidance can come before going further?' asked Fred. Mary explained that she couldn't recall the details of Dr Sangster's argument but that it shouldn't be too difficult to produce their own examples. So they did. For guidance through circumstances: Albert Schweitzer finding a missionary magazine, left on his desk by his cleaning lady – an occurrence which pointed him to service in Africa. For guidance through a reason: a man rejecting an apparently irresistible job, because he wasn't convinced by the reasons for accepting it which he offered himself. For guidance through the Bible: St Augustine's conversion being triggered by his reading of Romans 13.13–14. And for guidance through fellowship: John Wesley recommending that Methodists should, in fellowship, tell each other their faults 'home and plain'.

Then the discussion moved on. 'I was sufficiently interested in guidance about corporate decisions,' John revealed, 'to do a bit of research on that intriguing phrase in Acts 15: "it has seemed good to the Holy Spirit and to us". The reference is to the decision at the Council of Jerusalem about the terms on which Gentiles should be allowed to join the Church, and scholars offer a wide range of elucidatory comment. One, for example, simply notes that the link between this corporate decision and the Holy Spirit is unique, while another points out that it is unclear how the conclusion was reached, but clear that Paul seems to have disagreed with it! A third mentions that, though Luke's references to the Holy Spirit may appear routine, in this case an explicit mention is probably justified, while a fourth stresses that a genuine desire to reach a correct decision seems to have proved as influential as a vision or a word of prophecy could have done. I have to say that I found this last comment – which amounts to the claim that honest debate produced a genuine consensus for which the Holy Spirit can properly be credited – very convincing. At the same time, I have to acknowledge that on other occasions guidance was received through visions – see, for example, Acts 16 (Paul's vision of a man from Macedonia).'

Helen, meanwhile, was itching to talk about 'providence'. 'I take it', she said, 'that "general providence" refers to (for example) the regularity of the seasons and "special providence" to (for example) prophets receiving inspired insights into difficult situations. But I'm puzzled by the expression "our providential way". Does it assume a certain view of omnipotence as total control and a consequent view of the will of God as the realisation, in every circumstance, of a single pre-determined goal? If so, does this view take either the difficulty of discerning God's guidance or the need to respect human free will sufficiently seriously?

'At the same time, I find it difficult to formulate an alternative view, though I think that I can see some of the elements it would have to contain. It would have to relate closely, in the first place, to the role of the best kind of human parent – anxious to commend certain values to their child but not wishing to prescribe exactly what they should do in relation either to career choices or other matters. Such a parent will be delighted with any decisions taken freely, honestly and responsibly, on the grounds that, in some way difficult to grasp, they will enrich human life. At the same time, such a parent will combat irresponsible behaviour, not with force but with loving concern and the persuasive power of example. In the light of this analogy, discerning and doing the will of God will be more a matter of living in a certain spirit than hitting a divinely decided target. And even what, objectively regarded, may appear "mistakes" can be fruitful.'

'There may be a related problem', Fred chimed in, 'with the

expression "As far from danger as from fear/While love, almighty love, is near". Everything turns, I suppose, on whether we are thinking about immediate circumstances or ultimate results. We all know that Christians are not magically protected in this life from sorrow, fear and suffering, but it can be argued that God's love, being inexhaustible, is able to protect from ultimate disaster. In the end, therefore, those who put their trust in God have nothing to fear.'

At this point, Mary felt a need to check whether she had understood the wide-ranging discussion. 'It seems to me', she began, 'that we accept that "guidance" is needed and that there is plenty of Christian testimony that it has been, and can be, received. Such guidance is related to the idea that God is working his purpose out and involving men and women in the process. So his "providential care" is manifested in the regularity of the seasons and in the guidance he affords to individuals and groups desiring to do his will. This does not mean, however, that either individuals or groups are excused from thinking through what needs to be done. Rather, the Holy Spirit can work though honest reflection – that is, reflection which acknowledges the many channels through which guidance can come: circumstances, reason, Bible and fellowship – to produce individual clarity and group consensus. And even if, with hindsight, a decision may be seen to be "wrong", it can become a positive factor in the realisation of God's purposes.'

The group were grateful for this succinct summary, but wondered to what topic it naturally led them. 'It seems to me', said Helen, 'that where the Church is concerned "guidance" is crucial both for the life of fellowship and for the work of mission. Why don't we tackle these topics in turn?'

'Good idea', said Fred, and volunteered to introduce 'Fellowship' next time.

Questions for discussion

1. Have you ever been aware of 'guidance'? If so, how was it given? If not, how have you made key decisions?

2. What tests will help you decide whether what appears to be 'guidance' is genuine?

3. How do William Cowper's lines: 'Behind a frowning providence/He hides a smiling face' relate to what this chapter has said about 'providence'?

6

Fellowship

'When I tell you that I have chosen "All praise to our redeeming Lord" by Charles Wesley (1707–88) as the starting point for this session,' said Fred, 'I can foresee that you will have two reactions: first, that it contains no explicit reference to the Holy Spirit and, second, that it seems guilty, at times, of more than a little exaggeration.

'The first reaction can be easily dealt with. It relates, of course, to something that Angela noted at our first meeting. She wondered why the hymns on fellowship are focused on Christ to the exclusion of the Holy Spirit. The answer is that they are focused on Christ, but not to the exclusion of the Holy Spirit. From the beginning, Christian theologians refused to regard the activity of the persons of the Trinity as mutually exclusive. A particular function could be associated with a particular person, but the whole Godhead, they were convinced, would always be involved. At the same time, it must be stressed that, since Christian faith is faith in Christ as saviour, it is natural that the fellowship of believers should be centred on him: hence my choice of hymn.

'It's the fourth verse that may seem exaggerated: "Ev'n now we think and speak the same/And cordially agree;/Concentred all through Jesu's name,/In perfect harmony." Most of us, I suspect, have yet to come across a congregation which exhibits such a shining example; and we recall that in the New Testament such goals are set – for example, in the opening verses of Philippians 2 – but rarely realised. So is Charles Wesley being a little naïve? Is he carried away by his experience of the Evangelical Revival? Can we really believe in the existence of "perfect harmony"?

'We have to remember, I suppose, that the hymn was written in a situation in which unexpectedly wonderful things happened every day and over-assessment was almost pardonable. Perhaps John Wesley, while accepting that relationships had been transformed by conversion, would have waited longer than his brother to see whether they were sustained at their new level!'

At this point, Bill interrupted, anxious to underline the scarcely credible. 'What is just as amazing,' he said, 'though in this case certainly true, is the fact that Jews and Gentiles, slaves and freemen, men and women all found a place within the fellowship of the New Testament Church. Their common dependence on grace united them in a unique way and enabled them, as Charles Wesley's hymn spells out, to build each other up, to appreciate each other's gifts, to share an unspeakable joy and peace and to go forward hopefully.'

Mary, fascinated as always by language, immediately underlined this train of thought. She pointed out the number of Greek words in the New Testament reflecting togetherness, both variations on the word for 'fellowship' and compounds of the preposition 'with': so, Christians share in Christ's death, life, suffering, etc. and they refer to each other as fellow-prisoners, servants, workers, etc. Finally, she quoted C. E. B. Cranfield, who put the matter in a nutshell: 'Characteristic of the church was a togetherness far deeper than any mere camaraderie.'

Then it was Angela's turn to sound a typically practical note. 'In the early days of Methodism, as Charles Wesley's hymn bears witness, these characteristics of fellowship in the early Church were replicated. But it seems to me that, as time went by, the Class Meetings and Band Meetings ran into difficulties, and I wonder why. Band Meetings, of course, were small groups concentrating on growth in holiness, and perhaps that was too narrow a focus. And the Class Meetings, groups devoted to mutual support in the Christian life, became formalised as members found it difficult, when called upon to share what the Lord had done for them in the previous week, to discern anything fresh to report. Fortunately, in this "House Group", as such gatherings are now called, we manage to avoid these pitfalls by constantly looking at familiar themes from new angles: in other words, though the sharing of experience is not neglected, we try to practise "life-long learning" to keep our faith fresh. And all of us, far from being totally dependent on what the House Group can provide, are involved in other aspects of church life. And I'm sure that that balance is important. But – and this is the question to which I have been working round – have we lost anything along the way? How does our "fellowship" compare with that recorded in the New Testament?'

'At this point', said John, 'we begin to touch upon a question that will come up in other contexts as well: How far, and in what sense, is the life of the early Church normative? Or, to put the matter in another way, is it possible to see change and development – in doctrine, for example, and in the Church's organisation and self-understanding – not just as something to be grudgingly accepted but as something to be embraced thankfully and enthusiastically?

'This does not mean, I hasten to add, that we have nothing to learn from our forebears in the faith. But it may mean that we have to focus on fundamental attitudes rather than specific beliefs or practices. So, at their best, the early Christians were clearly deeply committed, mutually supportive, courageous in their witness and open to the guidance of the Spirit in their personal and congregational lives. If, therefore, we are giving ourselves a spiritual check-up, these are probably the characteristics on which we should concentrate.'

'I can see', said Helen, 'that, by this yardstick, there may well be a case for allocating more time at our meetings to prayer. Certainly the New Testament letters give a major attention to the need to pray at all times. But just because it would have been impossible for the early Christians to engage, as we do, in theological exploration, it would be a mistake, I'm quite sure, to play it down now.'

'What is clearly of key importance', added Fred, 'is the general ambience not just of the House Groups but of the worshipping congregation. The sense of belonging together may be specially nurtured in the smaller groups, but unless the congregation's overall sense of fellowship is enhanced, they are not contributing all that they can and should.'

'We have come', Bill announced, 'to the very edge of "Mission", and I'll gladly introduce it next week. But before we finish tonight's meeting, it seems right to thank God for the fellowship which is so important to us in this group.' So they prayed together, as only those can who are entirely comfortable with each other.

Question for discussion

1. How can fellowship best be fostered today?

2. In what ways is fellowship in the modern Church bound to be different from what the New Testament describes?

3. How can House Groups maintain their vitality and freshness?

7

Mission

'During my lifetime', Bill began – and the group, recognising that he was falling into reminiscent mode, gave a teasing cheer! Undeterred, Bill began again: 'During my lifetime, I have noted a shift in the language which we use about Christian "outreach".

'When I was a lad, we talked of "evangelism" and, from time to time, churches held evangelical "campaigns". If I had been asked to choose a hymn on tonight's subject in those days, I would probably have plumped for "Go forth and tell, O Church of God awake". After all, the Church's task, to judge by the New Testament, seemed very straightforward. At the end of Luke's Gospel, for example, Jesus promises, immediately before the Ascension, that his followers will receive power for the task of preaching the message of repentance and forgiveness to all nations; and at the beginning of Acts, the promise is fulfilled and Peter preaches the first Christian sermon.

'I recognise, of course, that the ethos of my youth was still influenced by the "revivalism" that had characterised evangelical churches during the nineteenth century, and I will be grateful if our minister can provide some background information on "revival" and "revivalism". Nowadays, however, we speak not of "evangelism" but of "mission", which includes evangelism but refers, in addition, to Christian service in the broadest terms. So my present choice is "The Church of Christ, in every age" by Fred Pratt Green (1903–2001) with its repeated emphasis on the Servant Church. The final verse puts things in a nutshell:

> We have no mission but to serve
> In full obedience to our Lord:
> To care for all without reserve,
> And spread his liberating Word.

'The first verse, in my view, is equally important but for a different reason: it underlines the need for adaptability, and raises questions about how, and in what sense, the New Testament contains a blueprint for the Church for all time:

> The Church of Christ, in every age
> Beset by change but Spirit-led,
> Must claim and test its heritage
> And keep on rising from the dead.'

Helen made the first contribution to discussion. 'I suppose', she conjectured, 'that more people today are conscious of being "beset by change" than of being "Spirit-led". I can see, however, that the shift from "evangelism" to "mission" could have both religious and secular roots. On the one hand, Jesus did more than preach – his total concern for human beings was expressed in preaching and healing. On the other hand, the social sciences have underlined that human wellbeing depends on an appropriate environment as well as wholesome values. So the focus on "mission" rather than "evangelism" seems doubly justified.'

'It isn't clear, however, that most people have grasped the implications of this shift.' The group looked quizzically at John, who had contributed this tantalising remark, and he responded at length! 'I was thinking', he said, 'about the qualities which, from each perspective, the Church regards as important. If, for example, the stress is on evangelism, the key figures will be, as in the early Church, "apostles, prophets, evangelists", to whom will be added, as an ordained ministry develops, "pastors and teachers". If, on the other hand, the stress is on "mission", the emphasis will be on a broader range of contributors, culminating eventually in talk of "every member ministry".

'I know, of course, that I must be careful at this point, because there is a sense in which, from the beginning, ordinary Christians were evangelists who, by their love and example, won others for Christ. I know too that the involvement of every member in mission doesn't render the special contribution of ministers unimportant. But I still want to maintain that the concept of mission offers a perspective within which more people can see themselves as able to make a significant contribution.

'If the church is called to serve humankind in all its complexity, the gifts needed will be much wider in scope than those listed in the New Testament. But they too will be gifts of the Spirit! We have already seen, in discussing fellowship, the early focus on those qualities which built up the Church and we have become aware, as we perhaps had never done before, of the complex ties which bound the early Christians to Christ and to one another. Needless to say, those bonds continue to be vitally important – and we need to beware that, in our desire to serve our needy neighbour, whoever he or she may be, we do not neglect our Christian neighbour, on whose support the full expression of mission depends. As so often, Charles Wesley expresses the point admirably:

> Never from thy service move,
> Needful to each other prove,
> Use the grace on each bestowed,
> Tempered by the art of God.'

'I can think of two other hymns', said Mary, 'that illustrate what John has just said. First, Philip Doddridge's "The Saviour, when to heaven he rose" stresses the role of pastors, as successors of the apostles. Their varied gifts derive from Christ and he protects them "midst all the rage of hell". Equally importantly, "unborn churches by their care/Shall rise and flourish large and fair" and pastors and people shall shout Jesus' praise. The stress here is very much on the leadership role of the minister.

'On the other hand, Richard Jones's "Come, all who look to Christ today" emphasises the need for the whole Christian community to be involved in mission, sharing in Christ's living way, finding new powers of brotherhood, seeking the common good, pressing beyond the truths already shared, bringing together the rich stores of the past, exploring old visions and praying for more, "since God delights to meet fresh needs". The stress here is on the

openness of the future and the possibility of growth and development – which must involve the discovery of new gifts to meet new
situations.'

'And that', Helen remarked, 'helps to answer my question. You
may remember that I wondered about the hymns that list aspects
of the Spirit's work. "How complete are they?" I asked. "How
complete can they be?" I now realise that, in each age, different
selections have been made as different needs have been met. But at
no stage are we offered what claims to be a complete list.

'The same is true of the gifts of the Spirit. There was no complete
list in New Testament times, and any list we may compile must be
open-ended. Moreover, just as in New Testament times, the test for
what is included must be what builds the Church for service and
sustains it in its mission.'

The group then fell into general conversation, reflecting on the
need to preserve a balance within any congregation between
enriching worship and loving involvement in every aspect of community life. And as they spoke of unsuspected talents developing
in both spheres and of the notion of 'vocation' – what it is and how
it is identified – they realised that here was another sphere of the
Spirit's activity about which they could profitably consult their
minister.

They also realised that there was an important topic, closely
related to mission, which they hadn't tackled. According to Acts,
the Holy Spirit gave the disciples/apostles confidence to preach
and heal in Jesus' name. So 'Assurance' needed to be next on
their agenda, and Helen volunteered to introduce it. And beyond
'assurance' lurked the question of the 'power' which fuelled the
mission of the early Church. What exactly did that key word refer
to? It was decided that so central a topic could best be addressed by
a joint effort! Everyone therefore promised to start thinking about
it and to be ready to contribute their ideas at the last meeting of the
session.

Questions for discussion

1. Has 'mission' replaced 'evangelism' in the thinking of the congregation to which you belong? If so, with what results? If not, why not?

2. What gifts have been unlocked in your life through involvement in the Church's mission and service?

3. How easy/difficult do you find it to share Jesus' vision of a world full of possibilities rather than riddled with problems?

8

Assurance

'I opted to introduce this session', said Helen, 'because, not being a very confident person myself, I'm a bit suspicious of those who are "assured", especially where religion is concerned. At the same time, I'm anxious to discuss the issue and, as a starting point, I have chosen two hymns: one –"Blessed assurance, Jesus is mine" by Frances Jane van Alstyne (1820–1915) – represents the position against which I tend to react; and the other – "When our confidence is shaken" by Fred Pratt Green (1903–2001) – speaks very much to my condition.

'I was encouraged, I'm bound to say, to discover that John Wesley, having first thought that assurance was essential to salvation, later concluded that, though desirable and to be generally expected, it wasn't vital. I don't want to get bogged down in the details of his two sermons on 'The Witness of the Spirit' (dated 1746 and 1767), but rather to start from the two hymns I have chosen.

'The first seems to refer to a self-authenticating religious experience. Having submitted to her Saviour, Jesus, the author knows perfect delight and is perfectly at rest, because she is filled with his goodness and lost in his love. I confess that I find such a testimony to unshadowed bliss bewildering. For me, as apparently for Fred Pratt Green, faith is still maturing, thanks not least to life's hard times, and with a long way still to go. And I will be grateful for any light you can shed on these questions.'

'I find it significant', Fred observed, 'that the section of the hymn-book from which these two hymns are taken is headed "Faith and Confidence", and I feel more comfortable talking about "confidence" than about "assurance". For "assurance" has overtones of "absolute certainty", whereas "confidence" indicates an attitude which, though justifiable, cannot be absolutely proved. I am reminded, in fact, of a book of essays entitled *Is Christianity Credible?* (Epworth Press, 1981). As I recall, the 12 distinguished contributors spent some time debating what the question meant, but in the end the issue was: Does Christian faith require a blind leap or can it be supported by rational argument? I believe that it can be so supported and that therefore it is possible to be confident, as Christians, without being totally assured.'

'What I find remarkable', said Mary, 'is that Fred Pratt Green's hymn directly addresses the subject of "doubt" and, in particular, its possible value. He focuses on three situations: the freezing impact on faith of impersonal solar systems; the struggle to pray when belief is almost impossible; and the cost of going beyond sympathy to the drudgery of caring for others. In every case, faith must rebuild, mature or die.'

'I seem to recall', John chipped in, 'some debates in the 1960s about the religious education of children. The argument started, as far as I remember, from the claim that children were brought up on views of God which later proved unconvincing. It was therefore essential, it was argued, to make as sure as possible that inadequate ideas were not absorbed in early life, so avoiding the pain of rethinking later what God is like or abandoning religion altogether. It sounds, however, as though some would maintain that such adjustments are unavoidable and, if rightly faced, beneficial, since they can contribute to the maturing of faith. I suspect, therefore, that forewarning is vital if doubt is to be handled positively rather than suffered helplessly. And you could say that such forewarning is precisely what Fred Pratt Green is offering.'

'I am very anxious', said Angela, 'that we don't overplay the difficulties in belief. I can acknowledge, of course, the agony that lies behind a hymn like William Cowper's "God moves in a mysterious way/His wonders to perform". For Cowper, I know, went through agonies of doubt and depression, and for much of his life he was a "fearful saint" more conscious of the "frowning providence" and clouds which filled him with dread than of God's "smiling face". But in the end he was sure that blind unbelief was sure to err and that God's purposes would ripen fast. Not only so: I feel that Tate and Brady's hymn, "Through all the changing scenes

33

of life", probably speaks to less tortured souls than Cowper, especially in the verse:

> O make but trial of his love;
>   Experience will decide
> How blest are they, and only they,
>   Who in his truth confide.

'I am assuming, needless to say, that "experience" is here used in its widest sense – to cover the experience of believing, of sharing in Christian fellowship, of playing one's part in the Church's mission and service, of enjoying moments when God is very real, etc. etc.'

Bill had been looking very thoughtful, and everyone was wondering what he would eventually say. They now discovered. 'I am very concerned', he said, 'about how easily assurance can turn into dogmatism, and my anxieties have not been eased by the TV documentary "God is Black". The programme traced the rise of fundamentalist Christianity in the Anglican Church in Africa, and more specifically in Nigeria, and went on to reflect on the implications of its dogmatic stance for the future of the worldwide Anglican Communion. It also focused, alarmingly, on the tensions between evangelical and liberal approaches to the Christian faith in Great Britain, stressing that attitudes to homosexuality reveal very clearly what has become a battle for the soul of Anglicanism. Finally, it offered a warning about the growing influence of megachurches, run like secular corporations and based on a "reward" theology (Give generously to God and he will reward you many times over!).

'It is difficult to assess the argument of this programme in detail, but it affords a timely warning of the dangerous influence of religious fundamentalism – of Christian and other kinds – in our world. In my view, those who are truly confident will not feel a need to impose their understanding of faith on others or to make it the subject of a hard sell; rather, they will let their example speak for itself, while always being willing to give a reason for the faith that is in them. So confidence is combined with love and tolerance, and not with dogmatism and control.'

Helen was quick to respond. 'I suppose', she said, 'that in this context it is important to pinpoint the reason for my adverse reaction to "Blessed assurance! Jesus is mine!" I feel, on the one hand, that "Jesus is mine" tells only half the story, and not necessarily the important half: contrast "I am his, and he is mine" (in *MHB* 443, verse 2); and, on the other hand, that talk of "perfect submission" lacks an important element which "grateful obedience" would supply. In other words, I find that, in this hymn, the depiction of the character of Jesus and of the nature of our relationship with him leaves a lot to be desired.'

'It seems to me,' added Mary, 'that we have moved close to our final topic, "power". People "submit" to power in its most obvious sense; and therefore if you "receive" power, you can expect others to submit to you. On the other hand, from the Christian perspective, love is the most powerful quality in the universe, and love elicits a response of joy and gratitude. I'm sure that we shall have a stimulating time trying to sort out the concepts used in this area – but only if everyone does their homework!'

The group dutifully nodded their agreement, and went home with serious intent.

Questions for discussion

1. If 'experience' is the key to confidence, 'obedience' must be the key to experience. Can you point to a specific way in which the Holy Spirit helped you to get started on the Christian life?

2. The books in this series aim to help Christians 'to hold their faith with confidence and not with a bad conscience'. Where the present volume is concerned, how important is this aim, and how successfully is it achieved?

3. Indicate your reasons for regarding wrestling with doubt as either a strengthening or a distressing experience.

9

Power

'Since we last met,' Mary announced, 'I've discovered something very interesting. When William Barclay produced his *A New Testament Wordbook* in 1955 the word *dunamis*/power wasn't included. Today, however, we hear a lot about it, and a Charismatic magazine even bears that title. But what does it mean?'

'I suspect', said Fred, 'that it is very easy to be misled by modern usage. I'm thinking, of course, of our preoccupation with politics and with the threat from dictators who exercise absolute power. But, as far as I can discover from Bible dictionaries, 'power', when used of God, is never capricious but is always determined in the Old Testament by his righteousness and in the New Testament by his love. I've also discovered that the family of words within which "dunamis" is the noun refers basically to ability or capacity.

'Putting these two pieces of information together, I judge that when the disciples "received power" at Pentecost, their experience was not dissimilar from that of Jesus at his baptism and of the disciples when they were sent out on mission. The chief difference, needless to say, was that after Pentecost the disciples were enabled to bear witness to Jesus and his resurrection rather than to the good news of the kingdom. And the fact that they were able to do so was very remarkable: it involved the transformation of a group of fearful and confused individuals into a confident community. But such a transformation was not a work of naked power, nor did it equip them to exercise such power. Rather, all that the disciples were enabled to do revealed the same characteristics as we see in the ministry of Jesus himself.'

'I wonder', Angela tentatively suggested, 'whether we could collect some biblical passages that illustrate in more detail how God's special power was at work in the early Christian communities. It is clear, for example, that the first disciples could not have preached and healed in their own strength, and Paul records – I'm thinking of 2 Corinthians 12.7ff. – how he had to learn that he would never be able to rely on his own natural fitness. God's word to him was "My grace is all you need, for my power is strongest when you are weak." '

Helen was quick to make a contribution of the same kind. 'I would like to offer Ephesians 3.14ff. It contains, first of all, a very rich prayer indeed. The author asks that the Ephesian Christians may be enabled by the Spirit to be strong in their inner selves, that they may have their roots and foundations in love and that they may be able to understand the breadth, length, height and depth of Christ's love. And to these requests is added a familiar but remarkable doxology to the God who, by his power working in us, can do more than we can ever ask or think.

'The passage prompts me to reflect on the power of the preached word which first brought the Ephesian Christians to faith and on the ability to love God and neighbour which it triggered. I am then led to reflect on the power of Christian love to hold together the early congregations and to maintain their concerns for an unbelieving world, despite persecution and other kinds of hostility. And, as a result, I am convinced that the "power" which the Holy Spirit brought came in an amazing range of forms, all of them controlled by God's love for the world and focused on the creation and strengthening of communities of believers which expressed that love.'

'It's worth reminding ourselves', said John, 'that as the first Christians began to realise the power of love, in the cross of Christ, in the resurrection and even, through the gift of the Spirit, in their own lives, they realised that a special word – *agape* – was needed. And so the New Testament proceeds from Paul's "God proves his love for us in that while we were still sinners Christ died for us" to John's "God loved the world so much that he gave his only son" and 1 John's "God is love". Similarly, the New Testament moves from Paul's "the love of Christ urges us on" to John's "Those who have my commandments and keep them are those who love me" to 1 John's "Beloved, let us love another, because love is from God".'

Mary was quick to follow up this contribution by a shift of focus.

'In addition to this key term of "love",' she stressed, 'we must note the role of "truth", especially in the Fourth Gospel. We are told there that those who continue in Jesus' word will know the truth and the truth will make them free; we are also told that when the Spirit of truth comes he will guide the disciples into all truth. Here is clear evidence that, in the early Church, when eyes were opened to see the truth as it is in Jesus Christ, such discernment was a liberating experience. In other words knowledge of the truth which Jesus embodied had the power to free people from their sins and enable them to enter into what John called "eternal life".'

'We seem', Bill commented, 'to have come full circle. We began these meetings by exploring what it meant to call the Holy Spirit "the Lord, the giver of life", and we are ending with John's concept of "eternal life". And I, for one, am particularly grateful for this last session. There can be little doubt that recently the concept of "power", understood in a very simplistic way, has been unfortunately dominant in some theological circles. And while the original reference in Acts may well refer primarily, as Mary pointed out, to bearing oral testimony, performing miracles and generally behaving with authority, adequate understanding of the role of the Holy Spirit required, as we have begun to discover, many other concepts.

'But we cannot say that our coverage of the Holy Spirit in these meetings has been at all adequate unless we mention another one. Although the whole Godhead is involved in the redemption of the world, the Holy Spirit has, from the first, been especially associated with "sanctification". Like the related terms "saint" and "holiness", "sanctification" has for most people an over-serious and perhaps even a depressing air. But there is no reason why it should. It is, after all, a kind of umbrella term under which the various aspects of the Holy Spirit's activity nestle comfortably.

'The Spirit is involved in the transformation of individuals from what they are into what God always intended that they should be. And the topics that we have discussed highlight different aspects of that transforming process. In the world as we know it, life – and

38

the Christian life – is characterised by ups and downs. But when shared with a committed Christian congregation, united in fellowship, enriched by worship, guided and sustained in mission and confident in the divine love which has begun a good work in them and in the world, that special growth which is not our achievement but God's gracious gift will assuredly take place. When "sanctification" is spelled out in this way, it can be seen in its true light: not as dull and repressive but as uniquely life-giving and life fulfilling.'

The group were delighted that Bill had been able to provide this ending to their sessions, and they told him so. But they didn't stay long after their cup of tea. They all felt a need – as they discovered when they compared notes later – to reflect quietly about the path that they had traced together and to prepare themselves for Tony's contributions in the weeks ahead.

Questions for discussion

1. Where do you think that you have personally seen the Holy Spirit most powerfully at work?

2. In the light of widespread disagreements within and between Christian churches, what sense can you make of the claim that the Holy Spirit would guide believers into all truth?

3. How would you begin to explain the joys of the Christian life to someone who had never belonged to the kind of 'committed Christian congregation' that Bill described?

10

Unfinished Business

In the discussions so far recorded in this book, a number of questions have arisen, most of which await answers to be attempted in Part 2.

Three, however, have already been addressed almost incidentally:

Helen, for example, wondered at the outset how complete a picture was afforded by hymns which listed characteristic activities of the Holy Spirit. During the discussion in Chapter 7, she decided that no such selection was complete and that any list compiled today would also have to be open-ended.

Angela, who had asked why the hymns about fellowship focused on Jesus rather than the Holy Spirit, also found an answer, this time during the discussion in Chapter 6. She learned that, according to traditional Trinitarian thought, the focus on Christ did not exclude the involvement of the Holy Spirit.

Finally, Mary was anxious to know what it meant that on the day of Pentecost the disciples 'received power', and the discussion in Chapter 9 addressed that issue.

All but one of the remaining questions were specifically referred to Tony, the minister of the church to which the House Group belonged, and can be conveniently listed here:

1. Can you provide some background information about the notions of spirit and Holy Spirit? (John)

2. Can we know what happened at Pentecost? And how important is such knowledge today? (Fred)

3. What is 'baptism in the Holy Spirit' and what do many see as its implications for worship? (Bill)

4. What is the difference between gifts of the Spirit and fruits of the Spirit? (Bill)

5. What is a 'vocation' and how is it tested? (The group)

6. Can you please provide some background information about revival and revivalism? (Bill)

One question remains and can perhaps be answered in the final summary: Why did hymn writers devote whole hymns to Romans 8, enlightenment and love and how are these themes related to each other? (John)

Part 2

Thinking Through the Issues

Introduction

Bill contacted the minister, Tony, and asked for his help.

Tony was very willing to speak on the questions that had arisen in the House Group's discussions, provided that he was not expected to produce clear-cut 'answers'. 'It's impossible', he said, 'to be absolutely clear when thinking about the active presence of God in the world, and I can't promise to resolve any of the difficulties that you have come across. What I can do, however – and this may be of some value in the business of learning to live with questions – is to offer some information, supply some perspectives and make some connections.'

Bill indicated that the group would be grateful for any light that could be shed, and it was agreed that Tony should speak at the next six meetings. What follows is a summary of what he said.

11

Spirit and Spirits

The discussion recorded in Chapter 4 established that talk of 'spirit/s' seems to have derived from reflection on 'wind' and 'breath': both curiously intangible but symbols of power and life. From such a beginning there emerged the general conviction that what happened in the world was not totally explicable in terms of visible causes and that it was essential for men and women to relate appropriately to the 'spirits', good and bad, by which their lives were constantly affected.

When some of these spiritual realities were personalised as 'gods' and even, as in the case of biblical religion, conceived as characteristics of 'the one true God', the lesser spirits remained. If they were regarded as beneficent, they could be depicted as 'angels', i.e. messengers of God; if they were held to be agents of wickedness, they could be identified as 'fallen angels'. And the ministry of Jesus is understood against this background: on the one hand, angels come and minister to him after he has been tempted by the devil; on the other hand, his vision of Satan falling like lightning from heaven is a sign of the effectiveness of the mission of the 72 disciples.

For most people, therefore, to live in the ancient world was to feel surrounded by spirits and, as a result, to expend a lot of energy either procuring their favour or combating their influence. And Christians shared this world-view, with one massive exception. For their thinking was controlled by the fact that Jesus' warfare with evil spirits had been crowned by his victory on the cross over 'principalities and powers'. At the same time, however, they recognised that, if the ultimate issue was no longer in doubt, battles had still to be fought.

They rejoiced, therefore, that they were now equipped with the whole armour of God (see Ephesians 6.10ff.) and could face the foe with confidence.

But there is a problem here. Whatever may have been the case in the past, we today have difficulties with the notions of spirits, both good and bad, holy and unholy. Where the Holy Spirit is concerned, for example, we are puzzled to understand what calling him a 'person' of the Trinity really means. And where evil spirits are concerned, we are hesitant, knowing that mental illness can be successfully treated by drugs, to ascribe them to demon possession.

At the end of the day, however, it is difficult to separate problems with the Holy Spirit from difficulties with the basic notion of 'God'. For 'Spirit' is not only used of a person of the Trinity but also of God's distinctive nature: as the Fourth Gospel says, 'God is Spirit' (John 4.12). And many people today find it difficult, if not impossible, to conceive of a reality 'wholly other' than what our senses perceive but living and active within the world.

The question of the 'evil spirits' is also problematical. From one point of view, it would seem natural, against the background of our scientific culture, to dismiss the notion out of hand. After all, the idea of the devil has been so caricatured as to be quite incredible. On the other hand, if we look at world history, there seem to be grounds for a more careful approach. In 2004, for example, there were several programmes on TV analysing the rise of Nazism, on the one hand, and the collapse of Communism on the other. Who, in the light of the evidence thus presented, can deny that 'the spirit of Nazism' and the 'spirit of Communism' were experienced realities of frightening power and seemingly irresistible impact. And is there not evidence, in the scandals associated with big business, of companies being enveloped by a spirit of deceit and ruthless greed?

How then is the influence of such evil spirits to be combated? What does it mean that the Christian warfare is not with human beings but with evil spiritual realities (Ephesians 6.12)? The passage which follows about the 'armour of God' provides a clue. The Christian is exhorted to accept the helmet of salvation and the word of God as the sword which the Spirit gives. In other words, it is through the initial impact of the Word of God that individuals receive the Holy Spirit and are enabled to attack evil in the light of its truth. Moreover, as Christians worship and serve together, the life of their congregations is characterised by the Spirit of Christ and influences all who come into contact with them. It is not to be thought, of course, that the lives of all Church members are transformed in a moment or that the corporate life of the churches is perfect. Rather, wherever the gospel is preached and the sacraments celebrated, the Spirit can work in and through men, women and children. And as they fight injustice wherever it is found, they will be combating not just human wrongdoing but the mysterious forces that can so easily control human life.

Four footnotes may be helpful. First, not too many years ago the zeal and commitment of Communists used to be contrasted with the lukewarmness of many Christians. Strange as it may seem, small groups were a feature of both movements, but Communist cells seemed to generate more informed enthusiasm than church fellowships. Since those days, we have seen, in the case of Communism, an eclipse of a certain kind of idealism by other spirits which it was scarcely aware would pose a threat and was not equipped to handle. And, for reasons that need not be enumerated, a similar explanation could be offered for the decline of the churches in Great Britain.

Second, we must beware of rejecting too easily the notion of spirits which can damage our own lives from within. In his Epworth Commentary on *Ephesians*, Larry Kreitzer refers to the film 'Platoon', which tells of the experiences of a young American soldier, Chris Taylor, during the war in Vietnam. No details of the terror, violence and agony of warfare are glossed over, and Taylor is wounded in a last bloody encounter. As he is carried to the plane that will take him home, a voice-over conveys his thoughts: 'I think now, looking back, we did not fight the enemy. We fought ourselves, and the enemy was in us.' That may not be the whole truth, but it is certainly part of the truth, and it warns us how circumstances can disturb within us what can be described as 'evil spirits'.

Third, I recently came across an article by Dr Rowan Williams entitled 'Confronting the untamed spirits'. It both describes one of Dr Williams's favourite spots in Wales, the site of Llantony Priory, and spells out why monks chose to settle in such a place. They were driven, he explains, 'by a conviction that they had to go and confront the ambiguous, possibly demonic, presence that inhabited a waste place and claim it for the gospel, make it inhabited by other kinds of presence.' Such places, he therefore claims, are characterised by two sorts of density: 'the tangle of old forces and struggles . . . and the abiding density of prayer including it and transfiguring it'.

The final point is closely related. The Christian life is rarely plain sailing, for individuals or for congregations. There is need, therefore, for constant vigilance, underlined by the stress on prayer in Ephesians 6. The use of the whole armour of God must be backed by prayer for God's help: 'Pray on every occasion as the Spirit leads. For this reason, keep alert and never give up; pray always for all people. And pray also for me.' Such an attitude of prayerfulness is a token of openness to all that God has to offer and a willingness to do all that he may ask us to do. It is a sign of the prompting of God's Spirit and of a human desire to grow in grace.

Questions for discussion

1. Do you find it helpful to see the cross as a victory over evil spirits? If so, what spirits do you have in mind? And in what sense was the victory 'final'?

2. Whether we explain them in 'spirit' terms or not, which attitudes are most damaging and most difficult to deal with in Church life today?

3. In what ways do you see the Holy Spirit at work in the Church to which you belong and in your own life?

12

Historical Background

You did not request the contents of this chapter, but I am convinced of its relevance to the subject as a whole and to the questions that you have raised. For Christian thinking about the Holy Spirit, like Christian thinking about everything else, has a history. In other words, different questions have emerged and different aspects of the subject have been tackled at different times. What this means is that, broadly speaking, Christian theologians were first preoccupied with the significance of the Holy Spirit for their understanding of God and, later, turned their attention to the full range of his activities in the world. We will look briefly at both phases of this development.

A: The earliest Christians were vividly aware that, as a result of the ministry of Jesus, a new era had dawned, and they struggled to describe and to understand what had happened and was happening.

'Spirit/Holy Spirit' provided them with a primary category of interpretation. They discerned that Jesus was the long-expected Messiah and that in his birth, baptism and resurrection and in his preaching, teaching and healing God's Spirit was at work. Moreover, they recognised that, following his resurrection, Jesus was able to 'give' that same Spirit to all who believed in him, thus creating a new people of God, commissioned to spread the good news of salvation to the world. Again, they saw the Holy Spirit at work not only in guiding and empowering the Church's mission but also in inspiring its worship and transforming the lives of its members.

The place of the Spirit in the life of Jesus was spelled out in the first three Gospels, and Acts, Paul's letters and John's Gospel covered other aspects of his work. Thereafter theologians entered first into vigorous debate about the person of Christ and then turned their attention to the nature of the Holy Spirit and his relationship to the Godhead. The eventual result was the formulation of the doctrine of the Trinity – 'God in three persons, blessed Trinity', as the hymn puts it. This position, we have to understand, was reached in different places by different routes: theologians in the East started with the three persons and had problems about their unity, while those in the West started with the unity of God and had difficulty in saying how he was also three. Both groups struggled to explain what 'person' meant in this context. The word certainly didn't mean 'individual centre of consciousness' as it does in modern speech, and Augustine said that he only used it because, if he didn't, he would be unable to say anything about the subject!

As it happens, Augustine's chief contribution – his idea of the Holy Spirit as the bond of love between Father and Son – dominated theology for a thousand years. Indeed, it initiated a shift of attention: the focus on the inner life of God suggested, first, that the Holy Spirit was also the soul of the Church and, later, that it was the source of the individual's inner life. This line of thinking was crowned by the stress, deriving from the fundamental insights of the Reformation, on the Holy Spirit representing Christ, conveying forgiveness and providing illumination and renewal to the believer.

Three stages can be discerned in the subsequent development of Protestant theology. In the first, a tension may be detected between Scripture and Christian experience as the primary material for theological reflection – a tension which was initially resolved in favour of experience as interpreted by Liberal Theology. In the second, there was a reaction, led by Karl Barth, who stressed the uniqueness of Scripture and the centrality of Christ. And in the third, various forms of Liberation Theology were developed, and various assessments were made of the practical and theological significance of the Charismatic Movement.

We will look at the Charismatic Movement later. It is enough for now to make a simple but important point. The twentieth century was also marked by a renewed interest in the nature of the Church and a growing pre-occupation with eschatology, and both these developments had a significant effect on thinking about the Holy Spirit. What follows will prepare the ground for a brief explanation of this terse utterance!

B: Against the background already provided, it is instructive to look at six examples of how twentieth-century theologians have approached the doctrine of the Holy Spirit. In each case, the material has been taken from popular works of Christian theology which were highly valued when they first appeared.

1. William Temple's *Christian Faith and Life* (SCM Press, 1931) consists of eight addresses delivered during a mission to Oxford University. Chapter 6, entitled 'The Holy Spirit in Life', begins from the fact that, for the believer in God, the work of the Spirit can be discerned in the process of evolution, the evidence of progress in history, and the experience of the claims of truth, beauty and goodness in human life. Temple's main point, however, is that the individual becomes uniquely aware of the reality of the Spirit through the influence of Jesus Christ on his life. 'Jesus is not only the revelation of the Spirit; He is the source of that Spirit to us.' 'You cannot know the power of the Holy Spirit in its fullness except by the companionship of Jesus Christ.' It is thus crucially important for everyone to discipline their lives in such a way that in worship, thought and action they are brought back constantly to the remembrance and companionship of Jesus Christ. 'Upon that everything else depends, for if the inward life is not sound, you cannot do much with the outer.' If, on the other hand, the inward life is sound, individuals will be able to trace the operation of the Spirit in the whole field of nature and history and to make their own contributions to the realisation of God's purposes as they discover and pursue their own vocations.

2. J. S. Whale's *Christian Doctrine* (Cambridge University Press, 1941) reproduces and slightly expands eight Open Lectures delivered at Cambridge University in 1940. By contrast with Temple, who concentrates on the individual's experience of the Spirit, Whale incorporates his treatment of the Holy Spirit in a

lecture on the Church. This does not mean that he underestimates the importance of personal experience. Rather, he values it highly, but only in its proper context, as indicated by the following quotations: 'For all its sovereign individuality, the self exists only in a community of selves.' 'Though an intensely personal matter, faith is never a purely private matter.' 'To be saved (by Christ) is to be incorporated into the new community, his church, of which he is not so much Founder as Foundation.' 'In short, the Christian life is not accidentally but necessarily corporate, always and everywhere. It is so by its very nature as the body of Christ.' 'The New Testament describes the life of this society as life in the Spirit.' Whale is very conscious that Christian theology has often failed to hold together the corporate/communal and the individual/personal aspects of human life and of the Christian life, and that both Catholic institutionalism and Protestant individualism distort the true nature of the Church. He himself emphasises that the Church is more and other than an earthly society which, at the same time, takes institutional form and is committed to share its inner 'new life' with the whole creation.

3. Karl Barth's *Dogmatics in Outline* (SCM Press, 1949) reproduces lectures on the Apostles' Creed delivered at Bonn University in the summer of 1946. By this time, Barth was well known for his theology of the Word – that is, for his conviction that our ability to know God and to live as his children is totally dependent on the revelation in Jesus Christ. At that point in German history, however, it hardly seemed advisable, granted the demands of post-war reconstruction, to underline human limitations; unless, of course, you had confidence – the kind of confidence that Barth did have – in the utter reliability of God's grace. In the chapter on the Holy Spirit, therefore, Barth focuses on freedom and on Jesus Christ as the source of true freedom, citing Paul: 'Where the Spirit of the Lord is, there is freedom.' His position can, in fact, be summarised in four quotations: 'What matters here is simply belonging to Jesus Christ.' 'The Holy Spirit is the Spirit of Jesus Christ.' 'Christians are those breathed on by Jesus Christ.' 'What

is involved is the participation of man in the word and work of Christ.' In short, 'we do not "have" this freedom; it is again and again given to us by God', with the result that we become hearers of his word and responsible, grateful and hopeful people. And this is as great a miracle as the birth of Christ or the creation of the world.

4. Alec Vidler's *Christian Belief* (SCM Press, 1950) consists of Open Lectures given at Cambridge in 1949. It is characterised by his own brand of robust common sense, admirably exemplified by what he says about Pentecost, to which we shall turn later. For the moment our attention will be focused on this general approach to the Holy Spirit. The relevant chapter is divided into three parts: in the first, he characterises the work of the Spirit after Pentecost – it became inward instead of outward, permanent instead of spasmodic, corporate instead of individual, and universal instead of national; in the second, he describes the Spirit's work as the interpreter of Christ; and in the third, he indicates how the Spirit harmonises individual personalities and unifies groups, works like an acid on all complacency and fortifies by humbling. Two points are of particular interest: the insistence that, in the New Testament, the primary work of the Spirit is to create and sustain a common or corporate life, and the observation that, also in the New Testament, Christians do not pray for the coming of the Spirit but gladly recall that he is 'the present and permanent source of their life'.

5. Wolfhart Pannenberg's *The Apostles' Creed in the Light of Today's Questions* (SCM Press, 1972) consists of a series of Open Lectures given several times from 1965 at Munich University. Pannenberg is primarily concerned to challenge the common assumption that the Spirit is the God-given guarantee of religious certainty. Such a view, he holds, does scant justice, on the one hand, to the power of God's Word to make its own unique impact and, on the other hand, to the fact that until God's purpose is fulfilled, faith must be exposed to the uncertainty of the future – which the believer believes will be God's, though this cannot be proved. In the Bible, certainly, the Spirit is not seen as the source

of supernatural knowledge but as the source of life, both physical life and the new life which appeared in Jesus. 'The Spirit is the present reality of God, the mode of the presence of the God of Jesus, whose power and kingdom has still to come, yet has already come to us in the sending of Jesus.' And its primary expression is the Christian's ability to love.

6. Jürgen Moltmann's *The Source of Life* (SCM Press, 1977) consists of lectures and addresses on the theme of his major academic work *The Spirit of Life* (SCM Press, 1992). For our purposes, the key chapter is Chapter II, entitled 'The Holy Spirit and the Theology of Life'. It is divided into two parts, the first dealing with the biblical evidence and the second with the mission of the Holy Spirit today. When the Holy Spirit – that is, God himself – is present in us, Moltmann affirms, our lives become 'wholly living from within'. And how is this possible? Thanks to the life, death and resurrection of Jesus: 'The Christ sent in the Spirit becomes Christ the sender of the Spirit.' 'The presence of Christ in appearances became the presence of Christ in the Spirit, because in Christ's appearances the Spirit was already present.' Therefore, 'to recognize the risen Christ and to experience the energies of our own rebirth in the Spirit of the resurrection are one.' Jesus, then, brought new life, not a new religion into the world, and it follows that our traditional understanding of mission – in terms of the Christian *imperium*, Christian civilisation or the religious values of the Western World – has been couched in terms which are evidently too narrow. What Moltmann calls 'The Spirit's wave of salvation' covers, in fact, the renewal of God's people, of all living things and of the earth itself. In short, mission is the invitation to God's future and to hope for the new creation of all things.

How then does the work of these six theologians relate to the focus on the Church and eschatology that I mentioned earlier?

It may well be that Temple's attention to individual experience in his discussion of the Holy Spirit is explained, at least in part, by the fact that he was preaching at a mission, i.e. for individual commitment. He certainly goes on in the next chapter to speak about the Church or 'The Christian Society', as he called it. But his immediate aim may not offer a complete explanation. His academic background in philosophy, and especially in that philosophy which underlines the individual's awareness of values as crucial to his understanding of ultimate reality, may be even more influential.

Whale, by contrast, is clearly reacting strongly from what he sees as the betrayal, in some Protestant circles, of the stress on the Church in the work of Luther and Calvin. Indeed, he describes himself as a Congregationalist minister 'who stands proudly in the Reformed tradition of Genevan High Churchmanship'; and he insists that: 'The thought of the New Testament about redemption is as much corporate and communal, as it is individual and personal. This two-fold truth is the key to the Christian doctrine of the Church.'

Vidler's position is very similar. He stresses that the Holy Spirit cannot be imparted to individuals in isolation. 'To receive the Holy Spirit is to be drawn out of isolation into the fellowship of the common life of the body of Christ . . . Here, if anywhere, it is true that things have to be shared in order to be fully possessed.'

Barth, as we have seen, focuses attention on the impact of the Word, and especially of the preached Word, on the individual believer. The Spirit is given as that Word is received in faith. For Barth, in fact, the Church means the local congregation, where the gospel is preached and the sacraments are celebrated. In so far as all such congregations have something in common, the word 'church' can have a wider reference. But the crucial work of the Holy Spirit is focused on the local congregation, where the Word is communicated and faith is prompted and preserved.

When we turn to Pannenberg and Moltmann we sense that theology is operating in a new key. What is happening, in fact, is that the biblical view of history is being taken seriously. For the biblical writers, history is going somewhere: God is working his purpose out as year succeeds to year. And both Pannenberg and

Moltmann see God involving men and women, through the work of his Spirit, in the transformation of the world as it is into the world as God intends it to be. But they see the realisation of God's goal in different terms: for Pannenberg it will provide incontrovertible evidence of the reality of God; for Moltmann it will fulfil the promises in which God has already revealed himself.

It is hoped that this brief survey of the ways in which major trends in theology have affected our understanding of the Holy Spirit has provided an illuminating background to the discussion of particular questions which follows.

Questions for discussion

1. Has this brief historical survey raised questions which you would like to pursue? If so, are there other sources of help – perhaps individuals with the necessary expertise or courses arranged by a university extra-mural department – which you could, and perhaps should, make use of?

2. Can a weak Church effectively mediate the reality of the Holy Spirit? If not, how can individuals be made aware of the possibility and importance of 'receiving' the Spirit?

3. On what grounds is it reasonable, granted the present world situation, to claim that the Holy Spirit is involved in the transformation of all creation?

13

Pentecost: Birthday of the Church?

When you shared your 'First Impressions', Fred asked whether we can know how and when the Spirit was given to the first Christians and whether such knowledge is important for us. He had in mind, I assume, that there are two accounts in the New Testament – in John 20 and Acts 2 – and was wondering how they are related. He was also doubtless asking himself whether these episodes provide any clue to the way in which the Spirit is 'received' today.

Everything turns, needless to say, on what kind of literature we think that we are dealing with, on the one hand, and on how we assess contemporary religious experience, on the other.

There was a time, for example, when scholars believed that if you wanted historical information, you went to the first three Gospels, but if you wanted theological insight, you turned to John. Today, by contrast, it is generally agreed that all the Gospels are theological documents, and that there is more history in John than had previously been thought. Even so, there can be no doubt that John is a more complex document than the first three Gospels. In other words, even if John knew the traditions preserved in the other Gospels, he has clearly translated their material into a new and very different idiom. As a result, it is very difficult to be sure that any episode is quite what it seems. It is true, of course, that Jesus seems to have acted in ways that reflected popular assumptions. The healing of the man born blind in John 9.6, for example, involves the use of mud (i.e. spittle plus dust) after the manner of village healers. Why then should not Jesus have tapped into other convictions – namely, those associated with creation in Genesis and the giving of life to dry bones in Ezekiel – when he breathed on the disciples, thereby 'giving' them the Holy Spirit? On the other hand, why should not John have devised the episode to express his deepest beliefs about the fact that Jesus did not leave his disciples comfortless? After all, even so apparently straight-forward an event as the healing of the man born blind is treated by John as deeply symbolic: the one who heals him is the light of the world.

The same kind of problems face us when we turn to Acts. Some people are deeply influenced by the fact that it is Luke's second volume and that in the first he stresses the painstaking historical research that he has undertaken. On the strength of this, they assume that the Pentecost story in Acts is to be regarded as historically reliable. Certainly, the Pentecostalists, from what is in practice a fundamentalist stance, regard the account of the gift of the Spirit in Acts 2 as straightforward history. Others, however, see the account, like everything else in Acts, as stylised and controlled by a particular theological position. From this perspective, Acts 2 can be described as a 'set piece', i.e. as a dramatic depiction of the worldwide mission of the Church and of the resources on which it could draw in fulfilling it.

Dr Alec Vidler – and I promised earlier a glimpse of his observations – seems to take up a middle position, seeing Acts 2 as depicting an event, but a heavily interpreted one. He regards, for example, the temporary phenomena of rushing wind, tongues of fire, etc. as unimportant compared with the 'permanent transformation of human life that then began'; and he sees the speech in diverse languages as symbolic of the fact that henceforth 'it will be the work of the Holy Spirit to convey the good news of Christ to all nations and to enable all men to hear about the wonderful works of God.' At the same time, Vidler acknowledges that, in addition to the permanent transformation, the outpouring of the Spirit resulted in what he calls 'a temporary effervescence', typified by 'speaking in tongues', and his next comment reflects the temper of his times rather than ours. 'St Paul', he says, 'who knew all about it put this phenomenon in its right place (which he valued indeed more than we are likely to do) and firmly rebuked those who treated it as the thing that really mattered.'

But we must move on. For it is important to note that the later chapters in Acts reflect a situation in which conversion, baptism and reception of the Holy Spirit are all jumbled together. In other words, there seems no one occasion and no one method by which the Spirit is received. Rather, whenever and wherever individuals hear and believe that the Spirit has been promised, the Spirit can be – and is – received.

And that would still seem to be the case today. But we must be careful in spelling out exactly what this involves. I remember, for example, a film from the days when religious films and evangelism through the use of religious films were very popular. It was called 'The Promise' and told of a young social worker dealing with ex-offenders. He tried hard but met with little success. His predecessor, however, had been wonderfully effective in the job. Why? Because he drew on the Spirit's help in all that he did. Once the young man accepted that the promise of the Spirit was for him too, all went well. Or, at least, that is my memory of the situation. We all know, however, that life is often more complicated than that. The presence of the Spirit does not always bring success, but it can enable conscientious persistence in all circumstances, coupled with a hopeful demeanour.

In short, openness to the Spirit is bound up with that positive attitude which holds that for God and for the person of faith all things are possible. Such a statement may sound an exaggeration, but it prevents people being trapped within what is thought of as 'realism' but is in fact 'defeatism'. It prompts everyone, in fact, to take another look at the world and ask themselves whether 'doom and gloom' is justified or whether, as Brian Wren puts it,

> Still (Christ's) Spirit leads the fight,
> Seeing wrong and setting right:
> God in Christ has come to stay;
> We can see his power today.

It seems then that the Christian Church does not have a single, identifiable 'birthday'. Rather, there was a period in which, in a variety of places and circumstances, a new community began to be created, united by a shared faith in Jesus Christ and empowered by the Holy Spirit to witness, in word and deed, to the truth of the gospel.

Questions for discussion

1. How did you understand John 20 and Acts 2 before reading this chapter? Do you now see things differently? If so, why? If not, why not?

2. How does your reading of the two biblical passages affect your understanding of the reception of the Holy Spirit today?

3. 'To receive the Holy Spirit is to be drawn out of isolation into the common life of the body of Christ . . . Here, if anywhere, it is true that things have to be shared in order to be fully possessed' (A. R. Vidler). Discuss.

14

Baptism in the Holy Spirit

The denomination known as 'Pentecostalism' began in the early years of the twentieth century. Fifty years later, the movement within the major denominations known as 'Charismatic Renewal' emerged. How are the two related?

Basically, those involved in Charismatic Renewal have revitalised their own Christian discipleship by adopting teaching and devotional practices from Pentecostalism. In this process, 'baptism in the Holy Spirit' is of key importance in that it is shorthand for three fundamental convictions.

First, it offers a particular interpretation of seven New Testament texts:

Acts	2.1–4: Pentecost
	2.38: The converts at Pentecost
	8.4–25: Converts at Samaria
	9.1–29: Paul's experience
	10–11: Cornelius's household
	19.1–7: The disciples at Ephesus
Mark	1.9–11: Baptism of Jesus

On the basis of this evidence, a case is presented for a two-stage entry into the fullness of Christian faith. First comes the gift of faith, which is sufficient for salvation; but then, as individuals grow in faith, an experience of being filled by the Spirit can be granted to them and they can begin to reveal spiritual gifts.

Second, the most significant of these gifts is 'speaking in tongues', though there is disagreement about whether it is essential or merely desirable. Either way, it is believed to offer evidence that a person has been baptised in the Spirit. Speaking in tongues, it should be added, should be distinguished from speaking in other languages. The latter seems to be what Acts associates with the day of Pentecost, while the former (i.e. speaking in no known language), appears to lie at the heart of Paul's pastoral concerns in 1 Corinthians 12–14.

Third, 'speaking in tongues' is only one of the gifts listed in 1 Corinthians 12.8–10, and Pentecostalist teaching insists that the use of all such gifts is still essential to the worship life of a Christian congregation. For such a position it is therefore important to identify the precise character of the gifts, described in the Good News Bible translation as messages full of wisdom and knowledge, faith, the power to heal and to work miracles, the ability to speak God's message, skill in distinguishing true spiritual gifts from false, speaking in strange tongues and interpreting such utterances.

As we have seen, there are problems with all three elements in this theological package. First, it is difficult to discern a clear pattern in Acts according to which it is possible to separate baptism in the Holy Spirit from the gift of faith and, in addition, it seems strange to think of the Spirit being given a little at a time. Second, the importance given to 'speaking in tongues' appears at variance with Paul's estimate of its place in the life of a congregation. And, finally, there are problems associated with the listings of gifts in the New Testament, none of which seem complete or obviously superior to the others and all of which may need reviewing in the light of our present understanding of the life and mission of the Church.

We should note, however, that despite their stress on these unusual – they would say, supernatural – gifts, charismatic Christians do not deny the importance of those marks of Christian maturity known as the fruits of the Spirit, of the illumination which the Spirit brings (John 14.26, 16.8–15) or of the love, peace, power and joy which the Spirit bestows.

On the other hand, there can be no doubt that this cluster of convictions, which 'baptism in the Holy Spirit' represents, has had a profound effect on the character of some churches of all denominations. Many services of worship have, as a result, become livelier and more participatory. But, as we have seen, a number of exegetical and theological weaknesses must be set in the balance on the other side.

Important questions are thus raised in two areas: Church organisation and Christian education. Where the first is concerned, a friend recently suggested to me that the Charismatic Renewal movement is more significant for its stress on the contribution of every member's God-given gifts than for its concentration on 'supernatural' gifts in particular. If this is true – and I think that there is an element of truth in it – it is important to ponder the possible results of stimulating and developing the 'natural' talents of every member. In other words, if conversion results – as we have every reason to suppose that it does – in a refocusing of personality and a commitment to new goals and an awareness of personal potential, all aided and abetted by the sense of togetherness which we have noted in the discussion of 'fellowship', there seems no reason why a different kind of transformation of Church life cannot be achieved. Indeed, to judge from recent debates about the nature of ministry, circumstances would indicate that such a change is urgently needed. In many parts of our own country, and perhaps even more in other areas of the world, the shortage of ordained clergy has prompted radical proposals for Church reorganisation, variously referred to as collaborative ministry, team ministry or every member ministry.

But if some of the ideas being considered are to stand any chance at all, Christian education in the churches has to be carried to a new level. In my own experience, whenever and wherever such education is offered, it meets with an eager response, and this fact probably indicates two things: how little education has hitherto been taking place and how much many people are desperately missing it. At the same time, we must be very careful about the way in which Christian education is talked about. For some folk have had a very bad experience of formal education and therefore shrink from education of any kind. Moreover, the tendency of educational establishments to stress the formal qualifications which courses yield can also be a mixed blessing. For some people a certificate can be an irresistible attraction, for others a potent dissuasive. The aim of the kind of education I have in mind is to convince people that genuine faith should yield a desire to realise their overall potential; not to fulfil personal ambition but to be the best that they can in God's service. For such folk, life-long learning will depend upon bringing an alert and intelligent interest to everything that they undertake, and their Christian education will need to give them the encouragement and confidence that they require to get started – and to keep going.

Come to think of it, this House Group and these sessions arising from it are examples of the kind of thing I'm talking about! But they are only one form that the enterprise could take. There is plenty of room for imaginative experiment in the light of particular needs and particular situations. But all would need to start from deep convictions of the rich potential of each human being and of the gracious co-operation of the Holy Spirit in its realisation.

Questions for discussion

1. Why, in your view, has Charismatic Renewal proved so attractive to many people?

2. In what ways has Charismatic Renewal's concentration on supernatural gifts affected our valuation of natural gifts?

3. What kind of education is most needed if the church is to continue to fulfil its mission?

15

Gifts, Fruit and Vocation

Bill, you will recall, indicated at the outset that he was puzzled by the distinction between 'spiritual gifts' and 'fruit of the Spirit', and later the whole group indicated that they would appreciate some help in understanding how the assessment of 'gifts and graces' relates to the discernment of 'vocation'.

Where the first question is concerned, it probably seems, at first glance, that a simple distinction can be made. For it is clearly indicated in 1 Corinthians 12 that 'gifts' are specific to individuals, whereas the 'fruit' listed in Galatians 5 – love, joy, peace, patience, kindness, goodness, faithfulness, humility and self-control – are qualities which all Christians may be expected to manifest. But there is a problem: the discussion of gifts in 1 Corinthians culminates in an affirmation of the supreme importance of faith, hope and love. Is 'love', then, both a fruit and a gift? Or does this cluster of special values constitute 'a more excellent way', meaning a framework for assessing the 'more important gifts' from those listed in 1 Corinthians 12? For we must remember that Paul is trying to sort out an apparent conflict of 'gifts'. He wants to stress the importance of preaching the gospel message in ordinary speech, but without dismissing the value of 'speaking in tongues', primarily for personal devotion. And he is working in a context that lacks a clear conceptuality for discussing the issues. In other words, both 'gifts' and 'fruit' refer to the results of openness to the gospel and to the Holy Spirit, but there is no clear demarcation between individual capacities and general qualities.

It is also difficult to discern how special gifts are thought to relate to the emergence of 'hidden talents'. We can think, for example, of all kinds of situations in which an individual begins to show hitherto unsuspected qualities. It may be that a student with an abysmal academic record is fired by the discovery of the subject that will be his life's work, or a young woman with no business experience masterminds a family firm on the sudden death of her father, or a young man previously content to live for the day commits himself wholeheartedly to the work of a Relief Organisation. In each case, even those who know them best are surprised by their performance. But were the gifts that they reveal 'new' or were they always there, but hidden until triggered by circumstances?

And what of the person who comes to Christian faith? It will be helpful at this point to draw on the work of John V. Taylor. His book *The Go-Between God* (SCM Press, 1972) is a classic with a somewhat complex argument. Fortunately, however, the basic insight on which it builds is beautifully stated in the first of five mission addresses delivered at Oxford University in 1986 and published under the title *A Matter of Life and Death*. Taylor was travelling by train from Oxford to London on a lovely summer evening. He found himself deeply moved by the countryside through which he was passing, and he could only describe the experience in terms of a mutual communication or exchange taking place which did not originate entirely in himself. Then the penny dropped: 'This is how God acts upon human beings, maybe upon all created things, working from within, making them more aware.'

And, we may add, as they become more aware, they become more alive. There is thus a sense in which the only 'gift' which is 'received' is the Holy Spirit. As Taylor says, it has been at work anonymously in all our lives from the start, but we need to welcome its influence: 'We cannot switch it on, this new aliveness, just because we feel ready for it . . . You simply ask for it; ask and wait trustfully; and let yourself come alive.' And as you respond to life as it unfolds for you, you become more aware of your potential and realise it in faithful service. Such, at any rate, seems a reasonable scenario.

We should not forget, however, that through most of Christian history there has been a debate about the relationship between nature and grace. Protestants have tended to emphasise the radical change involved in conversion and new birth, whereas Catholics have resorted to the adage that grace does not destroy nature but perfects it. I have tried to suggest that both are right and both shall have prizes. Coming to faith does involve revolutionary changes, but the new person is still, in a very real sense, the same person. Moreover, if conversion is crucially important in re-ordering more harmoniously, through the new relationship with God, the elements in a personality, circumstances may still limit what can be realised in a single lifetime. It is thus possible to conceive of the same person developing different 'gifts' in different circumstances or at different times, while revealing throughout identical personal qualities.

But what about the second question that was raised? Suppose that, at some point, an individual feels 'called to a particular piece of full-time Christian service, as a layworker or deacon or presbyter? How should the Church react to that conviction? Should it accept the claim at its face value? Or should it feel constrained to check it out?

There can be no doubt that, quite properly, each denomination has devised a method of assessing such a 'call'. I say 'quite properly' because experience has shown that human nature is very complex, and there can be no guarantee that every person making such a profession has interpreted the situation correctly. In many, perhaps most cases, the Holy Spirit may have been at work enabling a person to discern their 'vocation'. But in others an individual may have been influenced, often without realising it, by factors such as frustration with their present work, a desire for personal recognition or an over-estimation of their own abilities.

In such a situation, an objective assessment of every candidate has to be sought, and information is gathered from various tests and interviews and from referees within and outside the Church. And the testing process does not end with admission to training.

This is not the time to look, in detail, at the standards that are applied. Obviously, 'gifts and graces' are important, as are mental and physical healthiness, sincerity, teachability and maturity and all who are involved in the assessment process are given guidance about the appropriate criteria. But there is a sense in which the key factor is sanctified common sense. In other words, men and women of faith and experience are invited to use their practical wisdom to discern whether a call is genuine. It is difficult and demanding work but, in and through it all, the Holy Spirit may be seen at work. For the Spirit does not short-circuit our natural abilities but focuses and energises them to forward God's work.

Questions for discussion

1. Make lists of the 'gifts' and 'fruit' which, in your view, are most important in today's Church. Do your lists differ from those in the New Testament? If so, why? If not, why not?

2. What 'gifts' have you received/developed since becoming a Christian?

3. How can anyone know whether 'discernment' is a self-authenticating gift of the Spirit?

16

Revival, Revivalism and the Coming of the Kingdom

During the discussion on 'Mission', Bill requested some information about 'Revival' and 'Revivalism', and I have presumed to add
'The Coming of the Kingdom'. I hope that the relationship
between all three topics will become clear as we go along.

If you live at a time when church life is anything but vibrant but
know of times when things have been very different, you will
be inclined to ask God to 'revive' or 'renew' his Church: hence
hymns like 'Revive thy work, O Lord' in the nineteenth century
and 'Lord, thy Church on earth is seeking/Thy renewal from
above' in the twentieth. Moreover, if you live in the middle of a
revival, you will be inclined to see what is happening around you
as the prelude to the fulfilment of God's purpose, the final coming
of the kingdom of God. Thus, in the middle of the Evangelical
Revival of the eighteenth century, Charles Wesley can write:

> Lo, the promise of a shower
> Drops already from above;
> But the Lord will shortly pour
> All the Spirit of his love!

If and when your prayer is answered, you will acknowledge
that God has acted to forward his purpose and you will be deeply
grateful. In other words, you will see the onset of revival as entirely
in God's hands, a gift given in his own good time. Such indeed must
have been the prevailing view when the Great Awakening occurred
in the American colonies in the eighteenth century. But the key
figures in that revival may not have grasped the significance of
their own contribution. Jonathan Edwards, for example, made a
significant contribution by his choice of themes – 'Sinners in the
hands of an angry God' was perhaps the most memorable example
– and by the language which he used to preach about them. Hardly
surprisingly, in the nineteenth century others took things into their

71

own hands, studying the methods by which revivals could be promoted and putting them vigorously into practice, the most conspicuous proponent of modern 'revivalism' being Charles Grandison Finney. In the twentieth century, the fundamentalistic and tasteless practice of 'Billy' Sunday led to a marked decline in revivalism until Billy Graham gave the approach a new lease of life.

Our main concern, however, is not with 'revivalism's' techniques but with its theological assumptions. The belief that 'revivals' can be 'engineered', for example, is clearly very dangerous: it opens the door to the kind of exploitation and manipulation of which twentieth-century American Church history provides many illustrations. But more seriously it presents a distorted picture of the work of the Holy Spirit. Dr Thomas Smail in his book *The Giving Gift* (Hodder & Stoughton, 1988) makes the point very forcefully – 'The revivalist picture of the Spirit as merely occasional visitor to the church in its day of renewal with long periods of absence in between is nothing more than a parody and travesty of Church history' – and adds some interesting supportive reflections.

In the natural world, what looks dead in winter bursts into life in spring, just as in history hidden movements in the medieval Church precede the surging life of the Reformation. Similarly, where the ministry of Jesus is concerned, 'the Spirit who is openly at work in the resurrection is just as much secretly at work at the cross'. In general, 'the church is never so dead as to have no promise and foretaste of new life within it; the church is never so alive as to have no danger of decline and dissolution'. And through it all the Spirit continues his converting and sanctifying work.

But how are we to conceive of the End of this process of redemption? That is the 64,000 dollar question! And since the emergence of a preoccupation with eschatology not just in the sects but in the theological mainstream, it has been high on the theological agenda. We have already touched upon this matter in surveying the approach of Pannenberg and Moltmann in Chapter 12, but now a little more needs to be said.

72

The key problem is one of interpretation, especially where the language used in the New Testament to refer to the fulfilment of God's purpose is concerned. Take 'the kingdom of God', for example. Some scholars find it difficult to give a precise meaning to the term, while others are sharply divided into two camps. One group holds that the kingdom came with the ministry of Jesus, while the other sees the kingdom as still to come at some unspecified time in the future. Moreover, the final coming of the kingdom is referred to in very figurative language, and it is difficult to decide whether the event is the culmination of ordinary history or the inauguration of an entirely new creation. Yet again, although the final consummation is regarded as a mystery, there is widespread agreement that the resurrection of Jesus provides a crucial clue to its character, and the dawning of the era of the Holy Spirit is seen as a pointer to the fact that, though we cannot build the new Jerusalem, we can make a contribution to its arrival. In other words, if God is working his purpose out as history unfolds, then in every post-resurrection age Christians can have a God-given share in its realisation.

Inevitably, in all these matters it is very difficult to be at all precise. But it is remarkable that an academic preoccupation with 'apocalyptic', i.e. the often other-worldly ideas about the consummation of God's purpose, should have led to a lively involvement with Liberation Theology – the Third World approach which stresses the need for Christians to pursue this-worldly justice through every social and political channel.

In this particular context, then, preoccupation with the End is seen as non-problematical – and indeed as providing a spur for highly relevant social action. Others, however, have found 'apocalyptic' and all its works to be a barrier to the contemporary communication of the gospel. Rudolf Bultmann, for example, thinks that the language of the kingdom refers to the experience of the individual rather than to events within or beyond history. Thus, for him, the kingdom comes when a person comes to faith. In a similar way, C. H. Dodd is content to live by the gospel in all circumstances, recognising that we have no knowledge of what the future may or may not hold, for humanity as a whole or for us as individuals. For him, the important thing is that, thanks to the gospel, anyone may now know fullness of life.

To take the language of the kingdom literally and see its final coming as imminent, by contrast, can produce strange reactions. It seems, in fact, that much missionary activity in the nineteenth century may have been motivated by a desire to make as many converts as possible before the kingdom came, the Lord returned and evangelism was no longer relevant.

I would want myself to argue that the universal activity of the Holy Spirit is fundamental to the mission of the Church. I would also want to stress a corollary of this conviction: namely, that renewal, revival, transformation are everywhere possible and that Christians are justified in facing every situation hopefully. I would acknowledge, however, that thanks to human freedom, the gospel is often rejected and that, if and when it is, Christians need not be impatient or become discouraged. For the resurrection offers assurance that God's purpose of love can never ultimately be defeated.

Questions for discussion

1. List the possible reasons – good and bad – behind the yearning for 'revival'?

2. What kind of arguments can be formulated for and against the view that 'revivalism' misrepresents God?

3. How do you understand the language which the New Testament uses about the End?

17

Drawing the Threads Together

This book is not an attempt to relate a view of the Holy Spirit which had already been worked out to the activities of a fictional House Group. Rather, the activities of the House Group have provided a framework for exploring issues which are important for any theology of the Holy Spirit. It may be helpful, therefore, to spell out the picture which has started to emerge.

We began with the fact that the early Christians lived in a spirit-filled world. Some spirits were good, others were bad, and each kind could be known by their fruits.

Moreover, Jewish thinking – and that included the thinking of Jesus – was dominated by an eschatological perspective. In other words, there was a widespread belief that history was going somewhere. There might be disagreement about the precise character of the End – would it be within the world as we know it or in the context of a new creation? – but it was coming. Not only so: specific events were crucial in indicating its character and hastening its coming. What happened as a result of the death and resurrection of Jesus and led to the emergence of the Christian Church was such an event or series of events.

We have seen reason to doubt, however, whether the Church had a specific birthday. Rather, wherever the gospel was first preached it made a unique impact and led to a unique experience, namely, the reception of the Holy Spirit. This was not a second event within the life of faith but an element in the birth of faith itself. It led to the emergence of spiritual gifts which enriched the worship and fellowship of the first congregations. Several lists of these gifts appear in the New Testament but none can be regarded as complete or as a blueprint for what may be expected in all future generations.

What is crucial is that conversion leads to new life and that, within this new life, all kinds of talents, many hitherto unsuspected, begin to emerge. In recent years, it has been customary, in many

Christian circles, to focus attention on the 'supernatural' gifts listed in the New Testament. It may well be important, however, granted the present understanding of mission, to look to the development of 'natural' abilities, triggered by the Holy Spirit as a consequence of an individual's response to the gospel in faith. For there can be no conflict between the purpose of the Holy Spirit in creation and in re-creation. And our natural abilities are as much God-given as any gifts listed in the New Testament.

Moreover, the use of natural gifts and the application of common sense can be seen to be crucially important in two contexts which we have discussed. First, we noticed that the decisions of the Jerusalem Council (*c*. 48 CE) seem to have depended on discussion rather than supernatural revelations. In other words, the Holy Spirit worked through the normal process of human reflection. Second, when decisions are taken about candidates for the ministry, sober reflection and what we described as 'sanctified common sense' prove themselves, under God, to be valid means of discerning what is right.

Absolute certainty, however, is never achievable, but 'experience' in the widest sense – that is to say, what is learned from the full range of relationships and activities in which faith is expressed and supported – provides grounds for the kind of confidence which is very necessary today. Such confidence is a far cry from dogmatism, and it involves tolerance and respect. Above all, it is grounded in an optimism of grace – in other words, a conviction that God is at work in his world and that therefore things often thought impossible become possible.

We saw, at the beginning, that in understanding the work of the Holy Spirit 'life' and 'love' are key categories. To be 'alive' in the Christian sense is to be alert and sensitive and involved, responding positively to changing circumstances and always eager to learn. Our churches, therefore, must not only play their part in bringing people alive by communicating the gospel but also sustain that new life in every possible way. If this goal is to be realised, Christians will need to discern the presence of God in the whole of life – hence William Temple's comment about the Holy Spirit being the Person of the Trinity 'with whom we are most conscious of being constantly in contact'. They will need, too, to see that the Spirit is not to be identified with the striking and unusual – hence Bruner and Hordern's remark about the Holy Spirit being 'the shy member of the Trinity'. Finally, they will need to trust what God has given them by creation – hence Karl Barth's comment about the Holy Spirit being 'the intimate friend of commonsense'.

And what about 'love'? We can only love because God has first loved us. And to love, in the Christian sense, is to be concerned about others in the deepest possible way, no matter what the cost. This demands courage and persistence, but also sensitivity and sympathy and imagination; and it presupposes at least the beginnings of deliverance from self-centredness and of entry into the freedom of the children of God. Needless to say, there will be resistance to this way of love, both within the believer and outside – which brings us to the meaning of New Testament language about evil spirits, principalities and powers, etc. We illustrated this from experience of 'the spirit of Nazism', and it is instructive that a recent obituary of Sir Stuart Hampshire reported that his work with Army Intelligence as an interrogator of Nazi officers, especially the Gestapo commander Ernst Kaltenbrunner, 'led to his insistence, rare among twentieth-century philosophers, on the reality of evil'. It is not recorded, however, whether Hampshire saw the way of suffering love as, in the end, the only way to combat such evil.

Against this background, it is easy to see why hymn writers chose the themes cited in our one outstanding question. Timothy Dudley-Smith in 'Born by the Holy Spirit's breath' uses Romans 8 to trace our life of faith from new birth to sharing in the likeness of Christ in glory, sustained throughout by the conviction that nothing can separate us from the love of Christ. Charles Wesley in 'Spirit of faith, come down,/Reveal the things of God' starts from the need of believers for enlightenment but ends with a prayer that all the world may be helped to believe. Finally, Christopher Wordsworth in 'Gracious Spirit, Holy Ghost', inspired by 1 Corinthians 13, affirms that he, like his fellow believers, is most 'covetous' of the gift of 'holy, heavenly love'. Three key themes are here closely related: confidence in Christ linking with commitment to mission and with recognition of a need for God's help in fulfilling the command to love.

Finally, a word about Chapter 12: Historical Background. It attempts two tasks: first, to provide an indication of what one may describe as non-charismatic approaches to the Holy Spirit; and second, to illustrate how every treatment of the Holy Spirit is affected by an overall theological approach. If, in addition, it entices readers to explore the theological hinterland to which it points, that will be very satisfying to one for whom Temple was an early hero and Moltmann is still a bit of a puzzle!

Further Reading

Many, perhaps most, of the books listed below are out of print.
They are chosen, however, because of their enduring interest, and
because libraries should be able to help you to see copies.

1. *Historical*

Walter Hollenweger, *The Pentecostals* (SCM Press, 1972).

The standard work: Part I is historical, outlining the development
of Pentecostalism in America, Brazil, South Africa and Europe;
Part II deals with Pentecostalist belief and practice, allocating 30
pages to the Doctrine of the Spirit.

Simon Tugwell, Peter Hocken, George Every and John Orme
Mills, *New Heaven? New Earth? An Encounter with Pentecostalism* (Darton, Longman & Todd, 1976).

A useful example of early responses to Pentecostalism by four
Roman Catholic scholars.

David F. Wells, *God the Evangelist: How the Holy Spirit Works to
Bring Men and Women to Faith* (Eerdmans/Paternoster, 1987).

A response to issues raised by Pentecostalism from an international conference of Evangelicals.

2. *Biblical*

Michael Ramsey, *Holy Spirit: A Biblical Study* (SPCK, 1977).
William Barclay, *The Promise of the Spirit* (Epworth Press, 1960).

Two surveys of the biblical material, written with the engaging
clarity which one always expects from these authors.

3. *Theological*

F. A. Cockin, *God in Action* (Pelican, 1961).

I include this elderly volume because it reflects the temper of the time when it was written and locates theological questions about the Holy Spirit in a wide intellectual setting.

J. E. Fison, *Fire Upon the Earth* (Edinburgh House, 1958).

A sample of the work of an Anglican theologian whose contribution should not be forgotten.

George S. Hendry, *The Holy Spirit in Christian Theology* (SCM Press, 1965).

A stimulating pre-Charismatic discussion of seven topical questions about the Holy Spirit by a distinguished American theologian.

Alasdair Heron, *The Holy Spirit: The Holy Spirit in the Bible, in the History of Christian Thought and in Recent Theology* (Marshall, Morgan and Scott, 1983).

As the subtitle indicates, this book attempts a great deal and sometimes becomes too compressed for easy understanding. But no volume I know covers so much ground.

G. W. H. Lampe, *God as Spirit* (Oxford University Press, 1977).

Professor Lampe argues that many theological puzzles can be resolved if the Holy Spirit is understood not as a third person of the Trinity but as God himself in personal relationship with his creation.

The book is dedicated to the memory of C. E. Raven, who wrote extensively on the Holy Spirit in the 1920s: see F. W. Dillistone, *Charles Raven: Naturalist, Historian and Theologian* (Hodder & Stoughton, 1975), especially ch. 7.

Jürgen Moltmann, *The Source of Life: The Holy Spirit and the Theology of Life* (SCM Press, 1997).

A series of lectures attempting to express in a more popular idiom what is set out academically in Moltmann's *The Spirit of Life* (SCM Press, 1991).

John V. Taylor, *The Go-Between God: The Holy Spirit and the Christian Mission* (SCM Press, 1972).

A complex but creative and widely influential book. Do not expect to be able to read it quickly.

belong to this church, but does so not in the far more dubious
sense implied in speaking of particular churches belonging to
the larger whole. The church is indicated by these three papers
here, for all its inner ... and visibility, the invisible story are
committed to it ... it ... through human ... is seldom ... on the
father and master only in the ... by his ... Christ is here
incorporated into the ... community, the church, of which he is
not ... but Founder as Foundation ... In short, the Christian life
is not accidentally but necessarily corporate, always and ...
where ... as it ... ... as the Body of Christ. The ...
Testament describing the life of this ... ... in the Spirit.
While it very conscious that Christian theology too often failed to
hold together the ... ... the individual and the individualistic ...
aspects of this new life ... of the Christian life ... that both
Catholic Institutionalism and Protestant Individualism distort the
true nature of the Church. He himself emphasises that the Church
is body and other, but a freely social ... which, at the same time,
takes institutional form and is committed to share its new life
with the whole creation.

Karl Barth's *Dogmatik von Ausgabe* (SCM Press, 1949) reproduces lectures on the Apostles' Creed delivered at ... the university in the summer of 1946. By this time, Barth was so taken up
in his theology of the Word — that is, by his conviction that our
ability to know God and to ... ... children is totally dependent
on the revelation in Jesus Christ. All that is not in Christian ...
however, it readily seemed advisable to ... the demands of
post war ... his critique of human limitations; unless of
course you find confidence — the kind of confidence that Barth ...
found — in the utter reliability of ... in his ... In the chapter on the
Holy Spirit he ... With Paul ... as liberator and on Jesus
Christ as the source bringing freedom, citing one: "Where the Spirit
of the Lord is, there is freedom." He ... on, but on how he
continued in this quotation ... Wine matters here is simply
... ... to desire ... The ... ... Spirit ... Jesus
Christ — Christianity once breathed as ... Jesus Christ ... Whatever

Contents

Figures

Abbreviations

AIWRS	Arctic International Wildlife Range Society
ANCSA	Alaska Native Claims Settlement Act
ANWB	Netherlands Tourist Association (Algemene Nederlandse Wielrijdersbond)
COPE	Committee for Original Peoples' Entitlement, Canada
DIAND	Canadian Department of Indian Affairs and Northern Development
FAO	Food and Agriculture Organization of the United Nations
IFAW	International Foundation for Animal Welfare
ICC	Inuit Circumpolar Conference
IUCN	International Union for the Conservation of Nature and Natural Resources
MAB	Man and the Biosphere
NGO	Nongovernmental Organization
NWPSC	National Wilderness Park Steering Committee
SPCA	Society for the Prevention of Cruelty to Animals
SPFE	Society for the Preservation of the (Wild) Fauna of the Empire
UNCED	United Nations Conference on the Environment and Development, Rio de Janeiro 1992
UNEP	United Nations Environment Programme
UNESCO	United Nations Educational, Scientific and Cultural Organisation
WNBR	World Network of Biosphere Reserves
WSSD	World Summit on Sustainable Development
WWF	World Wide Fund for Nature
ZGF	Zoologische Gesellschaft Frankfurt

Acknowledgements

This volume originated in a conference, 'National Parks in Transnational Historical Perspective', held at the German Historical Institute, Washington, DC. The editors are grateful to director Hartmut Berghoff and the GHI staff for their hospitality and professional help with the organization of the conference; to all participants who enriched the discussions, and especially to Jane Carruthers, Catherine A. Christen, Uwe Lübken, Christof Mauch, John M. McNeill and Karen Oslund, who have inspired and stimulated the conference as chairs and commentators. The introduction to this volume has benefitted greatly from the critical feedback received in the Research Colloquium at the Rachel Carson Centre in Munich, while the constructive suggestions from three anonymous referees have proved extremely helpful to refine the argument of single chapters as well as improve the coherence of the volume. All contributors are to be thanked for their cooperation, encouragement, enthusiasm and untiring commitment to the project over the last years. The editors are equally indebted to Patricia Hongler and Franziska Hupfer at ETH Zurich, Sven Borchardt, Katharina Niederau and Gabriel Schimmeroth at the University of Mannheim and Melissa Spinelli, Lauren Weiss and Ann Przyzycki DeVita at Berghahn Publishers, who have been invaluable in their assistance with proofreading, copy editing and compiling the index. Finally, we are most grateful to the series editors for their continuous support of the book project and their decision to include the volume in the 'The Environment in History: International Perspectives' series.

Towards a Global History of National Parks

Bernhard Gissibl, Sabine Höhler and Patrick Kupper

National parks and related forms of protected areas have been the most important tool of nature conservation since the late nineteenth century. Ever since the United States invented the label of a 'national park' to preserve the natural wonders of Yellowstone in 1872, the idea of confining 'nature' to a 'park' and assigning it the status of a national heritage has been transferred to a wide and diverse range of political, social and ecological settings. At the moment of this writing, national governments have officially assigned some degree of protection to around 130,000 areas, i.e. almost 13 per cent of the global land mass in 2010.[1] The increase of protected areas in both number and geographical extent has been nothing but staggering over the last few decades, and there is no end foreseeable to this boom.

Judged merely by their impressive extension in size and number, parks and protected areas appear to have been a phenomenal success. However, the past performance of protected areas casts doubt on such an optimistic outlook. Bill Adams, one of the foremost experts in conservation history, states that the '20th century saw conservation's creation but nature's decline'.[2] Although the International Union for the Conservation of Nature and Natural Resources (IUCN) hails protected areas as 'the world's most cost effective tool for biodiversity conservation',[3] they have apparently been unable to bring a halt to the rampant loss of biodiversity. According to the same organization, the current species extinction rate is estimated 'between 1,000 and 10,000 times higher than it would naturally be'.[4] Conservation biologists routinely blame the apparent failure of protected areas to safeguard global biodiversity on their fragmented geography and lack of coherence. Today's protected areas would neither encompass all biodiversity 'hotspots' nor even the most representative biomes of each continent. Parks and protected areas are more akin to thousands of isolated islands of conservation in a global sea of continuing transformation and degradation of land, nature and ecosystems. As it seems, the efforts to harness ever-changing dynamic ecological systems within rigid boundaries have turned out to be as futile as nailing the infamous jelly to the wall.[5]

This volume is premised upon the assumption that the blatant discord between the enthusiastic appraisal of protected areas as the most successful instrument of nature conservation on the one hand, and their questionable ecological performance on the other, is a result of the history and *political* ecology of the worldwide proliferation of protected areas. The contributions assembled here take the national park, in many respects the most important conservation trade mark in history, as a vantage point to navigate through the bewildering variety of past and present conservation categories and concepts. They study the transfer, implementation and adaptation of the national park, both as idea and as label, in a variety of political, social and ecological settings. Altogether, they show that the much-deplored lack of ecological interconnectivity in today's global landscape of conservation is a consequence of the peculiar political, cultural and social conditions and connections that moulded the national park idea since the late nineteenth century. The patchy global geography of conservation is a consequence of the very malleability and adaptability that characterized and actually enabled the global spread of the national park idea.

National parks are, of course, a well-established theme in environmental history. This volume adopts a fresh perspective in that it confronts parks with the perspectives and sensibilities of recent debates in transnational and global history. Environmental historians' understanding of park making, we believe, could greatly benefit from the conceptual repertoire offered by global history. Vice versa, environmental history offers a promising field of study for historians interested in the emergence of global connectivities. National parks are more adequately understood as 'transnational parks': globalized localities that owe their establishment to transnational processes of learning, pressure, support and exchange. Interpreting national parks in global historical perspective, while undeniably part of the 'urgent intellectual project' of a 'closer integration of world history and environmental history',[6] should by no means be equated with an encyclopaedic world history of national parks or protected areas.[7] The contributions assembled here are exemplary rather than comprehensive. Major areas and biomes of the globe are not or only cursorily covered. By adopting a global perspective on exemplary cases and localities this volume seeks to identify as concretely as possible the mechanics, actors and institutions that fostered the transfer of an environmental idea that, by its very name and nature, was characterized by territorial and conceptual closure.

In order to understand the emergence of a global regime of compartmentalized conservation territories, and as a conceptual framework for the chapters that follow, we will outline the expediency of national parks to *civilize, territorialize* and *categorize* nature. Arguably, these were the main principles and forces that facilitated their worldwide proliferation. National parks emerged in an era in which the properties of territory were instrumental for national, imperial and international policies, and in which distinct demarcations and boundaries became the hallmark of the modern nation-state. The discourse of civilization rested upon the assumption of a temporal and spatial divide between Western development and allegedly more primitive states, and it took social relationships with nature as a yardstick of progress: parks to shield nature from the encroachments of industrialization, agricultural modernization and capitalist land grabbing became a benchmark of a society's civility, and they were impressed upon the world with missionary zeal as expression of a peculiarly modern valuation of nature. Understanding parks as both agents and instruments of *civilizing* nature draws attention to their ambivalent role in conservation as a civilizing mission and alternative project of modernity. It also highlights the role of parks to exert an educative, 'civilizing' function through the recourse to nature they provided for modern societies. Both of these functions were predicated upon the fundamental separation of nature, usually understood as wilderness, from society and culture that in turn endorsed the specific *territoriality* of parks and facilitated their implementation in national and imperial regimes of statehood. Finally, the national park provided an appealing conceptual blueprint to *categorize* nature and mobilize conservation efforts, which facilitated its transfer and implementation into diverse polities and ecologies.

Explaining the Globalization of the National Park

The protection of nature in national parks and related protected areas has developed into a significant form of land use worldwide. The polar regions, the seas and virtually every state around the globe feature protected areas in one form or another. Renowned 'environmental states' like Tanzania or Costa Rica have even set aside around a third of their territory for nature conservation and figure as globally influential laboratories of wildlife and tropical conservation.[8] These developments have not escaped the attention of the scholarly community and innumerable case studies analyze the conflicting establishment of parks throughout the continents, adopting the perspectives of park management, indigenous residents, conservation biology, geography, political (and apolitical) ecology as well as environmental history.[9] While an authoritative global history of protected areas is still missing,[10] conservationists as well as scholars from various disciplinary backgrounds have explained the globalization of national parks with varying refinement and complexity. At the risk of gross simplification, four types of explanations can be distinguished.

First, explanations operating within a declensionist paradigm postulate a direct and inevitable causal link between the spread of nature reserves and environmental degradation caused by industrialization, the rationalization of forests, population growth, plantation monocultures and the application of technology and chemistry to agricultural production. Such explanations have been widespread among nature lovers and conservationists, whose rhetoric has been rife with scathing indictments of the rampant destruction of nature on the one hand, and demands for the last-minute preservation of the remaining patches of 'virgin nature' and 'last wildernesses' on the other. In that logic, national parks flourished in direct response to the destruction and spoliation of nature on a historically unprecedented scale over the twentieth century.[11]

A second type of explanation looks for answers on the level of world polity and could be characterized as institutionalist. Sociologist John W. Meyer and his research group, for example, have argued that the global diffusion of national parks can be explained neither by degradation, nor the concomitant rise of environmentalism, nor by an approach that analyzes the establishment of parks merely within the framework of compartmentalized nation-states. Rather, the mechanics of world polity have been responsible for the worldwide proliferation of national parks. Institutions and regimes of 'world society' – international governmental and nongovernmental organizations, treaties or associations of scientific experts – create and promote standardized blueprints of institutions and practices that become implemented into national policies through scientific advocacy, the activities of interested pressure groups and intergovernmental exchange. In this logic, the spread of parks has been tied to various emanations of late nineteenth- and early twentieth-century internationalism. Parks owe their existence to the actors and institutions that produced and framed 'global environmentalism' and advocated national parks as a science-based instrument of environmental policy.[12]

A third strand of interpretations could be termed progressive, respectively modernist and has understood the spread of national parks as the worldwide diffusion of environmental sensibilities and practices that first emerged in the United States.[13] According to environmental historian Roderick Nash, the United States was the first society to combine a democratic culture, unique experience with wilderness, the availability of allegedly empty, undeveloped land and the material affluence to afford the nonutilization of territory. This resulted in the setting aside of public land in the first national park in Yellowstone in 1872. Other advanced, industrialized and urbanized societies also developed a heightened valuation and love for unspoilt nature as an increasingly scarce commodity so that the marginal value of nature increased. A cosmopolitan 'social and economic class of nature lovers' in advanced countries, so the argument runs, either pressed for the establishment of national parks in their own countries, or tried to 'import' unspoilt nature from undeveloped areas where it was still abundant. Therefore, not always the most industrialized or urbanized societies were the first to establish national parks, for their demand could also be satisfied, for example, by wilderness tourism abroad. For Nash, parks essentially functioned as the 'institutional "containers"' provided by developed nations to underdeveloped ones for the purpose of "packaging" a fragile resource'.[14] National parks were the epitome of a preservationist modernization, in which unused, wild nature came to be commodified by states and societies of the global South to satisfy the developed world's desire for wilderness.

Finally, scholars have drawn attention to the astonishing compatibility of conservation and neoliberal capitalism in order to explain why the number of protected areas doubled since 1980. Such an interpretation may appear counterintuitive, for the vast majority of conservation advocates since the late nineteenth century has regarded capitalist-driven economic development as the foremost opponent of nature preservation as an idealist, moral campaign. However, as Dan Brockington, Rosaleen Duffy and Jim Igoe show, several processes and developments combined to make this opposition collapse since the 1980s. Among these was a general proclivity of international funding agencies, but also of transnational conservation NGOs, for market-based solutions in conservation, for example by privatizing the management of protected areas or implementing them in carbon offset schemes. Sustainable development as the overarching paradigm to integrate economic development and conservation replaced 'no touch' and 'fences and fines' approaches to park management and promoted a less rigid and more managerial approach to conservation that encouraged the establishment of protected areas and their utilization for ecotourism. Additionally, the new paradigm of biodiversity conservation reframed wild nature as a massive treasure of hitherto unknown and unused genetic resources that attracted new stakeholders, such as transnational business corporations, to the field. As a consequence, wild nature and its conservation became more valuable and expedient for capitalist enterprise, which provided an enormous boost to the extension of protected areas.[15]

Undeniably, the inventions of biodiversity, sustainable development and green capitalism go a considerable way to explain recent developments in international conservation. Arguably, the compatibility of parks and capitalism has an even longer prehistory in the intertwined histories of parks and nature consumption through tourism that already started with the designation of Yellowstone as a 'pleasuring ground' for the American people. Still, the mechanics of capitalism alone hardly do justice to the multiplicity of actors, motivations and cultural orientations that were involved in park making over the past one and a half centuries. For the majority of these years the relationship between capitalism and conservation was marked by conflict and accommodation rather than cooperation. The declensionist interpretation is right to emphasize the unprecedented and measurable processes of environmental degradation and species loss during the twentieth century,[16] as well as the degree to which industrialization and urbanization have been accompanied by changes in environmental attitudes, above all in Western societies. While these developments cannot be overestimated as a motivation for nature protection, a sole focus on degradation falls short of explaining how and where conservation enclosures were established. Moreover, 'degradation' must be critically examined since in many instances, it was less a verifiable ecological reality than a rhetorical construct that served as a powerful tool to excise previous forms of land utilization and the presence of indigenous residents.[17]

The institutional approach is to be credited for the importance assigned to the actors, institutions and regimes of global environmental governance as the motors of park making worldwide. Pressure exerted by well-connected elite lobbyists such as the British Society for the Preservation of the (Wild) Fauna of the Empire (SPFE) were instrumental in framing 'global environmental problems' and instigating conservationist policies across empires and nation-states since 1900. So were 'conservation entrepreneurs' and the epistemic communities they formed, from the hunter-naturalists of the late nineteenth and early twentieth century to the ecologists and conservation biologists who followed them and whose activism and expertise formed part of the science-based approach of the United Nations Educational, Scientific and Cultural Organization (UNESCO) and the IUCN after 1945.[18] The epistemic community of preservation (often also referred to as the 'parks movement') helped to bring parks on the agenda of international environmental diplomacy and trigger a series of regional and continental conventions that promoted parks as the foremost tool of preservation.[19] However, the institutional approach, particularly in the guise of world polity, has shown little interest in analyzing the actual practice and performance of parks and suffers from too homogenizing an assumption of their global diffusion. Parks are treated as part and parcel of an emerging world environmental regime that is largely Western in its origin, and there is little sensitivity for the political asymmetries, conflicting interactions and the contestations surrounding the adaptation of the park concept to diverse political and cultural settings.

This criticism equally pertains to the progressive reading championed by Roderick Nash. His interpretation overstates American exceptionalism and environmental leadership and operates firmly within a teleological paradigm of modernization:[20] parks and the concomitant sensibilities towards the preservation of nature are wedded to the uniform march of Western civilization. His idea of an exchange of 'wild nature' between equals neglects the unequal power relations and responsibilities between 'importers' in the West and 'exporters' in the developing world.[21] It denies the value of non-Western sensibilities towards nature and obscures significant differences in the way parks were incorporated into non-Western societies. In Africa, Asia and Latin America the top-down imposition of parks made nature conservation for tourism an important instrument in policies of modernization and development, whereas the social disruptions evoked by the establishment of parks often inhibited the very attitude of detached care that Nash postulated as a prerequisite of parks. Nonetheless, the notion of national parks as explicitly modern containers for packaging nature as a resource provides a thought-provoking basis for further reflections on the peculiar territorial regimes of parks.

The global historical perspective proposed in this volume goes beyond the vague and agency-denying metaphors of diffusion or circulation of a seemingly uniform concept. While acknowledging the dynamics of 'virtualism' and the world-making capacity of conceptual visions and virtual blueprints, it is sensitive to the adaptations, modifications and translations that accompanied the transfer of the concept from one cultural context to another, and to the political asymmetries in which these transfers were embedded.[22] It is aware of the insights of recent globalization research that emphasizes the imbrication and mutual production of the 'global' and the 'local' and the interplay of deterritorialization and reterritorialization. A global historical perspective as we understand it is also sensitive to the fact that globalizing processes do not necessarily erase the national but remain essentially shaped, enacted and enabled on the scale of the nation-state.[23] Emphasizing the local diversity and uniqueness of individual national parks cannot release global historians from identifying general principles, common forces and shared properties that made parks such an expedient tool of conservation around the world. What commended the national park as an almost universally applicable format for framing wild nature?

Civilizing Nature

Separating nature from everyday human use has been a long-established cultural practice in human societies across the globe. In African societies, sacred groves not only were sites of spiritual and social importance to communities but also fulfilled ecological functions such as the preservation of plants and wildlife. Forests set aside for the conservation of elephants (especially to use them in warfare) were known in India from the fourth and third centuries BC.[24] Also the enclosure of nature for individual or social delectation has a long tradition in societies worldwide, the ancient game reserves of the Middle East and the feudal game parks or royal forests of the European tradition representing only two examples out of many. Often these enclosures were undertaken by the highest authority of the respective political entity, and there were undeniable continuities, for example, between the designation of 'Crown Land' in medieval and early modern Britain and the establishment of game reserves and national parks within the British Empire.[25] When the Congress of the United States officially 'set apart a certain Tract of Land near the headwaters of the Yellowstone River as a public Park' in March 1872, it was in many respects but a 'novel twist on an old idea'.[26]

Still, the creation of national parks in the decades before and after 1900 was effected by a sea-change in both the predominant attitudes towards nature and the related social practices. It is no coincidence that the first national parks were established when national and imperial projects of colonization and exploration erased the remaining blanks on the physical and mental maps of Europeans and North Americans: the 'unending frontier' (John F. Richards) of wild nature as the opposite of human expansion and conquest drew to a close. Thereafter, wild nature could no longer be conceptualized as an unlimited mental and practical resource *beyond,* but became a finite resource *within* the boundaries drawn by civilization. No matter for what purpose wild nature came to be protected, its enclosure was employed not to exclude nature from civilization but rather to incorporate certain forms of valued nature into schemes of national or imperial development.

'Civilizing nature' is a fitting metaphor to describe this function of parks, both in its suggestive transitive and intransitive meanings. The *Oxford English Dictionary,* for example, lists under 'to civilize' the entries 'To bring (a person, place, group of people, etc.) to a stage of social development considered to be more advanced, esp. by bringing to conformity with the social norms of a developed society'; 'to tame or domesticate'; 'to conduct oneself in a manner appropriate to the norms of civilized society' and 'to subject to civil order, to subdue, pacify'.[27] All of these semantic aspects appear in one form or another in the terminology of conservationists who demanded and justified the establishment of parks in the language of civilization. A commentator of the *New York Times,* for example, hailed the Yellowstone National Park in 1872 as a 'place which we can proudly show to the benighted European as a proof of what nature – under a republican form of government – can accomplish in the great West'.[28] Three decades later, the American wilderness sage John Muir opened his book on *Our National Parks* with the famous line, 'Thousands of tired, nerve-shaken, over-civilized people are beginning to find out that going to the mountains is going home; that wildness is a necessity; and that mountain parks and reservations are useful not only as fountains of timber and irrigating rivers, but as fountains of life.'[29] When in 1962, U.S. President John F. Kennedy hailed national parks as 'places where we can find release from the tensions of an increasingly industrialized civilization', he not only proved a late disciple of Muir but rehearsed a by-then classic trope of the Western park movement.[30]

Another dimension of parks' civilizing nature is addressed by Canadian entomologist Charles Gordon Hewitt, who claimed in 1921 that the mission of conservationists was 'to prove that the advance of civilization into the more remote sections of Canada does not imply the total destruction of the wild life, but that civilization in its true sense signifies the elimination of the spirit of barbarism and the introduction of an enlightened attitude'.[31] Advocates of national parks in Europe as well as within Europe's colonial empires routinely couched their appeals in a language of national or imperial duty and an obligation arising out of one's own civilized status. International conservationists like the founding director of UNESCO, Julian Huxley, used it as a moral yardstick to remind the colonies recently released into independence that 'in the modern world, a country without a national park can hardly be recognized as civilized'. Postcolonial leaders reciprocated this obligation, most famously perhaps in the Arusha Manifesto of Tanzania's Prime Minister Julius Nyerere in 1961.[32] And as late as 2002, geographers Paul Jepson and Roger Whittaker, with a view to the impending degazetting of national parks in Indonesia, framed the preservation of nature in parks as a moral responsibility and part of the 'international values to which civilised nations and societies aspire'.[33]

These assessments from various decades illustrate that parks and civilization were closely entwined, yet stood in a paradoxical and thoroughly ambivalent relationship. Although often inseparable in concrete historical situations, it is useful to distinguish at least four dimensions of civilizing nature. First, the notion of civilizing nature draws attention to the fact that nature protection (and parks as its foremost instrument) became elements of an alternative vision of the future course of (Western) civilization. In the eyes of early nature conservationists, it had been exactly the 'advance of civilization' that necessitated the establishment of parks to preserve the last pieces of intact nature from economic spoliation. This established notion of civilization as human progress through growth-oriented development at the cost of nature was countered by a conservationist vision of civilization as an idealist endeavour that respected the aesthetic, ecological and social value of wild nature. Protecting and valuing nature in its raw, untransformed state became a property of being civilized.

Second, understanding parks as a form of civilizing nature highlights the degree to which conservation became an integral part of 'civilizing missions' within nation-states and empires, but also through international or nongovernmental organizations and postcolonial elites. In its propensity to export and universalize an essentially Western organization of social relationships with nature, the rhetoric of conservationists and park advocates shared many characteristics with other forms of civilizing missions that emanated from Western societies.[34] Conservationist discourse operated through the asymmetrical counterconcepts of civilization vs. savagery that had organized Europe's relationship with the colonial world. These dichotomies helped to legitimize the conservationist agenda and territorial claims of imperial states, but they also justified nongovernmental organizations' participation in park making and global environmental governance. While nature protection was never uncontested or high on the imperial agenda, central governments used parks to excise land-use practices deemed as backward or wasteful, particularly in colonial settings. Nomadic pastoralists were often victims of such policies, and parks complemented policies geared at rendering rural populations controllable or at forcing them onto the labour market. Park management also became a field of scientific governance in which understandings of nature in terms of ecosystems, keystone species or biodiversity marginalized alternative readings of the same landscape. Conservation as a civilizing project assured the ongoing political influence of the former imperial powers in the decolonizing world: the apparatus of conservation and park management remained often dominated by expatriate scientific experts and advisors, while financing conservation was taken over by Western donor agencies and NGOs. However, it needs emphasis that conservation as a civilizing mission was never just a one-way imposition. Several essays in this volume show that conservation was also a self-civilizing mission that reflected back upon environmentally detrimental practices in colony and metropole. And even more significantly, local actors as well as state authorities in non-Western societies adopted and appropriated conservation's language and practices to criticize conservationist policies, to get access to political and financial resources, but also because they came to share its mission and values.

Third, civilizing nature includes the expectation of conservationists that the encounter with wild nature itself exerted a civilizing influence. National parks became the sites where urbanized and industrialized societies should relax and find recourse to wild nature as an antidote to 'overcivilization' and taxing modern lifestyles. The aesthetic qualities of the nature preserved in national parks, as well as the embodied or visual practices of consuming nature in a park, fulfilled a recreational function that only attained importance with the advent of wage labour and leisure as a mass phenomenon in modern, capitalist societies. But parks should do more than cater for recreation. They were sites of learning and education that provided visitors not only with knowledge about the nature in the park through signs and visitor centres. Even more important was the education of sentiment through respect and awe in the presence of wonders that have existed before and independent from human ingenuity – a benign purpose that could gain an exclusive, elitist and often racist edge in colonial settings. Civilizing nature in this third sense thus throws up the fundamental question of what role parks played in the shaping of social attitudes towards nature and conservation, or the making of what has been termed 'environmentality' – 'the knowledges, politics, institutions, and subjectivities that come to be linked together with the emergence of the environment as a domain that requires regulation and protection'.[35]

Finally, as much as nature should civilize, parks must also be regarded as the institutionalized form of civilizing nature in the sense of 'disciplining' nature and assigning it its controllable and consumable place in modern societies. This last aspect of civilizing nature draws attention to the technologies of statehood and science employed in the making of parks: the map, the expedition, the fieldwork, the research station, but also law making, bureaucracy and armed surveillance. Furthermore, park establishment necessarily involved the designation, classification and allocation of space, in other words, the territorialization of nature.

Territorializing Nature

The worldwide spread of the national park makes a powerful case for the globalization of territorialized and nationalized space. As historians have pointed out, globalizing processes in the past did by no means result in the erosion of space, territoriality and the 'national', but often produced new regimes and constellations of territorially bounded space that went hand in hand with nationalist ambitions.[36] The historian Charles S. Maier even proposed to acknowledge territoriality as the defining principle of the century between roughly 1860 and 1970, which he consequently classified as the 'Age of Territoriality'.[37] Following Maier, territoriality, understood as the first and foremost political resource derived from the control of bounded space, is not a timeless property of space but a principle of spatial organization that itself has a history: territoriality experienced a worldwide rise in the second half of the nineteenth century when multiple powers (political as well as economic) scrambled for the remaining uncharted regions on a finite globe. Territoriality involved the enclosure, mapping, survey and control of space 'not just as an acquisition or as a security buffer but as a decisive means of power and rule'.[38]

Although Maier catalogues the principles of territoriality with little recourse to natural spaces, the geopolitical strategies and rewards of territorial control, the practices of mapping and ordering, the importance of the idea of finite space and the territorial merging of power and knowledge make plausible why national parks were so attractive and often so contested.[39] Territoriality was the mindset of the era of foreseeably limited space on earth, in which formerly 'boundless nature' was perceived as a finite resource and contained in defined spaces. Understanding national parks as the key instrument of territorializing nature draws attention to the political, social and cultural prerequisites essential to their spread. They are unthinkable without the existence of a centralized state with the capacity or at least the determination to rationalize, order and control its territory. They were a product of the rational procedures that characterized modern governmental bureaucracies and administrative infrastructures. Although the nationalization of nature was by no means characteristic of every national park, the rise of the nation as the prime social entity to command allegiance and legitimize political and social action proved a great spur for park making. Infusing physical terrain with national meaning helped to 'naturalize' the nation and promote notions of a peculiar rootedness of nations in their landscape.

Maier has identified the 1960s as the period in which the demise of territoriality began. However, the meteoric rise of protected areas over the last few decades casts doubt on this claim and suggests a differentiated interpretation. Networks did not displace territoriality, as Maier proposes. Rather, they were instrumental in its reconfiguration. The 1960s appear not as a decade of disintegrating territoriality but as the beginning of a transformative period in which territorial structures were rearranged and rescaled in a variety of ways. After decolonization, national elites and conservationists appropriated a global blueprint to strengthen authority on a national scale, while trans- and supranational conservationist institutions also worked through the instruments and mechanisms of the nation-state. This transformation of imperial structures and networks into inter- and transnational ones did not result in a weakening of territoriality on a national level. Postcolonial states in the global South appropriated the economic and coercive potential of national parks, while international organizations and transnational NGOs continued to promote 'civility' as a property to be realized from parks. More importantly, they strengthened their maintenance through external funding and expertise.

However, both the legitimacy and adequacy of territorialized 'fortress conservation' through central state agencies have been challenged by at least three developments, each of which involved different sets of actors and forms of governance in the emerging politics of sustainable development. First, in a variety of cases, rigidly bounded parks proved incapable of providing adequate protection, which contributed to the displacement of natural equilibrium theories by more dynamic conceptualizations of ecosystems and impressed the need for more flexible management practices upon park managers. Second, conservationists' frustration with the often poor performance of states in adequately managing and funding protected areas has fuelled hopes that corporate capitalism and market mechanisms could serve as a panacea against the failure, unwillingness or incapacity of states in matters of nature conservation. This neoliberal turn in conservation resulted in the strengthening of the private sector in protected area management. Third, the forced removal and economic displacement of original residents – the regular accompaniment and dark underside of park making in the global South[40] – uprooted established human relations with the land, evoked tensions over access and use, and significantly diminished the local acceptance and thus the performance of parks. Grassroots initiatives emerged to protest against their exclusion from parks and demanded local autonomy, or at least benefit sharing and participation in decision-making processes concerning the park.[41] Starting with the

Arctic Peoples Conference in Copenhagen in 1973 indigenous groups affected by park making themselves forged transnational coalitions and contested the territoriality of parks from below.[42] All these developments did not erase but transform territoriality. Similarly, they weakened the role of the state and increased the number of actors participating in the multilevel yet still territorially based global conservation regime we presently witness.[43]

Categorizing Nature

It has been one of the core insights of recent analyses of cultural transfers that translation, transformation and reinterpretation are keys for the success of travelling concepts. The national park is a prime example for a globally mobilized environmental concept that originated in Western ideological and institutional contexts to be transferred to other places, experiencing a variety of transformations, adaptations and contestations in the process.[44] Nothing testifies more to its successful mobilization than countless frustrated efforts at its standardization, including the desperate attempt of Swiss conservationist Jean Baer in 1949 to introduce a systematic Latin nomenclature in which the enigmatic national park would feature, for example, as *territorium reservatum conservandi aut delectandi causa*.[45] From the 1960s onwards, the IUCN developed an ever-more-refined and totalizing system of categories for protected areas (see Table 0.1 for the latest version of the IUCN classification system from 2008). Within this system national parks became relegated to Category II, consisting by definition of 'large natural or near natural areas set aside to protect large-scale ecological processes, along with the complement of species and ecosystems characteristic of the area, which also provide a foundation for environmentally and culturally compatible spiritual, scientific, educational, recreational and visitor opportunities.'[46] Designed to overcome national peculiarities, the IUCN scheme actually created further confusion, as areas with the national denomination of a 'national park' became distributed over all IUCN categories (see Table 0.2), whereas areas that met the criteria were included in Category II although they do not bear the name 'national park' (see Table 0.3). As the organization has few instruments to enforce its categories, the reform still stands to prove if it can enhance the concept's worldwide coherence and further a universally shared meaning of the national park, or if it will ultimately reduce its transnational purchase and just add to conceptual confusion.[47]

When the term 'national park' was first used in the United States in the 1870s, its meaning was fuzzy and therefore open to change and appropriation. Although broadly used to denote Yellowstone, the term did not appear in federal legislation in 1872, but only three years later when Mackinac Island was set aside 'as a national park'. Later on, this designation was regarded hardly

Table 0.1. IUCN Protected Area Management Categories (2008).[48]

Category Ia	Strict nature reserve
Category Ib	Wilderness area
Category II	National park
Category III	Natural monument or feature
Category IV	Habitat/species management area
Category V	Protected landscape/seascape
Category VI	Protected area with sustainable use of natural resources

Table 0.2. Examples of 'national parks' in the various IUCN categories. [49]

IUCN Category	Name	Location	Size (ha)	Date
Ia	Swiss National Park	Switzerland	16,887	1914
Ib	Nanda Devi National Park	India	62,460	1982
II	Guanecaste National Park	Costa Rica	32,512	1991
III	Yozgat Camligi National Park	Turkey	264	1988
IV	Pallas Ounastunturi National Park	Finland	49,600	1938
V	Snowdonia National Park	Wales, UK	214,200	1954
VI	Expedition National Park	Australia	2,930	1994

Table 0.3. Examples of IUCN Category II 'national parks' with different national designations.[50]

National Designation	Name	Location	Size (ha)	Date
Provincial nature reserve	De Hoop	South Africa	32,160	1956
State park	Denali	United States	130,845	1970
National wildlife special protected area	Utonaiko	Japan	510	1982
Heritage river	Genoa River	Australia	1,300	1992

suitable for the small island in Lake Huron, and the title was removed in 1895. The first American protected area that was named a 'national park' in legislation and kept this designation to the present was Mount Rainier in 1899. In the twentieth century, extensive discussions about the proper use of the term accompanied the approval or rejection of new parks and thereby continuously shifted the common meaning of the U.S. national park.[51]

The globalization of the term further complicated its meaning.[52] While 'national park' became a kind of global brand long before Coca-Cola or McDonald's, there was no international institution or legal framework regulating its use. A bewildering variety of nature protection schemes adopted the label within a few decades, so that a need for an international definition of the national park was increasingly felt. In 1933, the third conference held by the European colonial powers on the preservation of the flora and fauna on the African continent in London agreed upon a definition that emphasized control by the highest legislative authority and the area's double purpose. Parks were to be set aside for 'the propagation, protection and preservation of wild animal life and wild vegetation and for the preservation of objects of aesthetic, geological, prehistoric, historical, archaeological, or other scientific interest for the benefit, advantage, and enjoyment of the general public'. If a concern with wildlife was pivotal in the case of Africa, an American 'Convention on Nature Protection and Wild Life Preservation in the Western Hemisphere' signed by twelve states from Latin and North America in Washington, DC, in 1940 echoed the monumentalism of Yellowstone and Yosemite. It assigned to national parks the 'protection and preservation of superlative scenery' and of 'flora and fauna of national significance'.

The cofounder of the Swiss National Park, Carl Schröter, presumed in 1924 that the term was so widely used because of its rhetorical suggestiveness. Three elements associated with the concept were particularly appealing to proponents of national parks worldwide. First, in an age of rampant nationalism and nation building in full swing, the 'national' was an attractive tag to bestow relevance upon any cause. Framing a landscape as meaningful to the nation was a means to approach governments for funding and protection, mobilize shame and fears of national backwardness, bid for public appreciation and raise patriotic sentiments. Second, the 'park' label associated the respective landscapes with public accessibility and recreation. Finally, the association of the term with the United States gave the conservationist agenda a peculiarly modern image.

But all these elements served as reasons to reject the term as well. The prefix 'national' was hardly applicable to all political settings. In subnational contexts as well as within the framework of empires, the national denomination could be a contested issue.[53] Then there were many instances where the reference to the United States turned out to be double edged: While for some, the United States served as a model of how an advanced industrial society managed to domesticate the dynamic of capitalist exploitation and integrate the preservation of nature into its idea of progress, others rejected the national park label as an alien import and signifier of American materialism, capitalism or imperialism. Finally, the term 'park' was criticized for not appropriately describing what were held to be essentially 'wild spaces'. The governor of Tanganyika, for example, regretted in the late 1930s that the term 'has become accepted currency' for he deemed it not 'particularly suitable to describe the area to be protected on account of its suggestion of artificiality'. And discussing the applicability of the park concept to conservation in Britain after the Second World War, one conservationist associated with the word 'park' 'an artificially laid out and maintained piece of land or a site for assembling vehicles, for example, artillery or automobiles'. However, he regarded it 'useless at this late date to think of changing it, especially as an alternative, short of coining a new word, would be difficult, if not impossible, to suggest'.[54]

Defining and categorizing to render the world legible and governable has been a standard feature of institutions operating through bureaucratic rationality.[55] Such categories not only represented the world in a specific way but also constructed it by generating universal standards. The clarity and comparability provided by such instruments came at a price. On the one hand, categorizations created their own incentive structures, inviting superficial compliance rather than effective preservation. On the other hand, categorizations hardly captured the complexity of the phenomenon at hand and created their own blind spots. For decades, this was the case with the social aspects of parks and their impact on local livelihoods.[56]

This brief problematization of the national park category has pertained only to the definitions and meanings ascribed to it by 'parks people' and official documents. Tourists, scientists, wardens, displaced residents, shopkeepers or hoteliers inscribed a multiplicity of further meanings into parks. The oscillating character of the category as well as the politics of categorization has important ramifications for an analysis of the global proliferation of national parks. Any past or present definition of the national park would be inappropriate for guiding research. On the contrary, attempts to internationally classify and standardize national parks must be part of a global history analysis. If national parks have been fluid in their meanings and subject to intercultural translation and adaptation, then historians must follow the label through time and space and include all kinds of areas that have, for various reasons, been dubbed 'national park', regardless of their present categorization by IUCN. This does not mean to neglect that some concepts were of higher importance for the development of the national park idea than others. However, a global history of the national park must not lose sight of alternative developments, routes not taken and transfers denied or modified to a degree that the original blueprint is hardly discernible anymore. Therefore, also places where the term national park was rejected or dropped have been included in this volume.

National Parks between Imperialism, Internationalism and Nationalism

Imperialism, internationalism and nationalism all provided frameworks and opportunity structures for the global transfer and local appropriation of the national park idea. Empire, internationalism and nation are, therefore, the categories that structure our investigations into the global history of national parks, and this volume is accordingly organized into three sections entitled

Parks and Empires, Organizations and Networks, and Nations and Natures. The case studies in the first part, *Parks and Empires,* examine how national parks were established in 'frontier' settings and resulted from imperial encounters with wild nature. They analyze the varying ways nature was made meaningful in the form of national parks to white European settler communities not only in the United States but all over the globe. Imperialism, the case studies show, enabled hunters, conservationists, naturalists and nature lovers – often in transimperial dialogue and exchange – to frame the setting aside of wild nature as part of Europe's civilizing mission.

Karen Jones deals with Yosemite and Yellowstone as the first protected areas established as national parks in the United States in the 1860s and 1870s. Her contribution decentres the received interpretation of national parks as a genuinely American 'invention' by situating them in a larger history of Euro-American colonial expansionism and transatlantic debates on nature, nation and identity. This partial revision of American exceptionalism notwithstanding, Jones rejects allegations that "the United States provided no model for global diffusion of the idea"[57] by emphasizing both the eminent exportability of the general principles enshrined in US-American national parks, as well as the powerful allure 'Yellowstone' exerted as a mythical point of reference in conservationist discourse abroad.

The second chapter of the section by *Melissa Harper* and *Richard White* continues the theme of Yellowstone's impact upon conservationist discourse and practice abroad. However, the authors question and qualify its 'model' character by emphasizing both the varied experiences with nature and wilderness in the 'Greater Britain' of the English-speaking settler societies as well as the importance of alternative concepts and examples provided by the international concern over nature protection in the decades around 1900. While at first glance there seems to be a common thread in the ways 'nature' was implemented into the national understandings of the English-speaking settler societies, a careful comparison of the siting of parks in Canada, New Zealand and Australia unveils the enormous differences with respect to the purposes of 'national parks', the treatment of indigenous populations and the traditions of spatial conservation and land use that proved influential in the designation of national parks.

Caroline Ford's contribution challenges diffusionist assumptions of a Yellowstone model from another vantage point as she charts the establishment of protected areas in France and her overseas possessions. Ford's analysis reveals a remarkable fluidity of conservation concepts, oscillating broadly between conservation and preservation. She shows how name, nature and purpose of protected areas in the French colonies were negotiated in a complex constellation of factors, including the presence or absence of a French settler population, local resistance and the degree to which state authorities and scientific, conservationist and tourist institutions and advocacy groups managed to bring their ideas about landscape protection to bear. The only 'national parks' in the French colonial empire were established in Algeria, where the preservation of the colony's depleted forests was of 'national' significance because they served as imperial mnemotopes that harked back to a golden past of natural plenty in North Africa during Roman times. In other parts of the empire national parks were rejected as concerned with the spectacular and tourism. Instead, so-called *réserves naturelles intégrales,* or strict nature reserves, were established, which served scientific and biological interests to the exclusion of human access and became the French contribution to international conservation legislation.

Existing analyses of game preservation in Africa and forest conservation in India have established the role of the British Empire as a key promoter of globalized environmental governance. *Jeyamalar Kathiritamby-Wells's* essay on the history of Malaysia's Taman Negara Park shows that British imperial environmentalism was not only more pervasive still but was itself part of trans-imperial processes of exchange and competition in colonial Asia. Established as King George V National Park in 1939 after years of effective lobbying by big game hunters and conservationist organizations, the park was renamed Taman Negara after independence and transformed from an imperial imposition into an emblem of postcolonial Malaysia. In a society marked by discriminatory land rights and nuanced curbs on political expression, the management of Taman Negara as a public space theoretically accessible to all citizens became an important vehicle for the country's growing middle class's claims on government accountability, environmental stewardship and political participation. The fate of the Batek hunter-gatherers is, however, a case in point for the structural legacies of imperial conservation. The fact that the Batek were allowed to remain in the park only as long as their lifestyle remained low impact, 'primitive' and 'authentic' shows that the dichotomies about 'civilized' and 'natural' produced in colonial times continued to motivate park management after independence.

Bernhard Gissibl's concluding chapter of the first section focuses on the entanglements of game conservation between East Africa and Germany. German colonial rule not only was instrumental in laying the foundation of Tanzania's environmental conservation complex before the First World War but also left a deep imprint on German conservationist thinking by conflating space, species and identity in a political geography of the characteristic animal. The ideology of a wilderness essentially animated by the presence of large, 'primeval' game not only motivated the top-down imposition of game reserves in the East African colony, but also resulted in a quest to render the German landscape primeval through the reintroduction of its 'original' big game. The projection of a racialized, masculine national identity onto the bodies of 'characteristic' species linked the spatialities of conservation in Germany's African colonies with conservation at Germany's Eastern frontier in both World Wars and the reestablishment of a primeval fauna that inspired the creation of the country's first national park in the Bavarian Forest in 1970.

The contributions gathered in the section *Organizations and Networks* investigate how trans- and international movements, networks and organizations adopted and adapted the concept of the national park for multiple social and political motifs. Throughout the twentieth century Western conservationists worked hard to turn the national park into a universal conservation tool, and the forging of transnational structures for nature conservation had ramifications far beyond the stated goal of organized nature protection. INGOs as well as NGOs at times assumed parastatal functions in the governance of national parks, which became a laboratory for ecological and social experiments on various scales. The universalism of conservation provided a lever not only to shift, but also to affirm, and often to replace, existing global power relations, while the transfer and application of Western science and technology to park management in colonial and postcolonial settings reshaped the meanings of nature. Networking across borders remained, however, no privilege of conservationists and scientists. Also indigenous communities affected by the establishment of parks formed transnational alliances and adopted the language of human rights to resist and modify the structures of supranational environmental governance.

The section is opened by *Patrick Kupper* who investigates how the national park idea was decisively transformed by its transfer into the cultural landscapes of Europe at the beginning of the twentieth century. His chapter highlights the establishment of the Swiss National Park, the most prominent case of early European park building. Promoting the park as a laboratory for ecological sciences, the Swiss park deviated significantly from the American model with its emphasis on tourist recreation. Kupper also questions the importance of Yellowstone as an international model by tracing the significant role of the Swiss park as the bedrock of early attempts to establish a global network of protected areas. Arguably, conservationists in many countries were first familiarized with the national park concept through the relentless propaganda for *Weltnaturschutz* by the Swiss conservation entrepreneur Paul Sarasin before the First World War.

Anna-Katharina Wöbse takes up from where Sarasin left to delineate the importance of international organizations like the League of Nations and the United Nations as norm- and agenda-setting institutions for the preservation of nature worldwide. As early as the 1920s, the League of Nations embraced the concept of national parks as an appropriate 'container' and institution for the preservation of nature threatened with destruction. Wöbse demonstrates how a small network of white male Western scientists and lobbyists adopted the universalist language of a 'common world heritage' to enforce the claim to the global spread and institutionalization of national parks. These efforts culminated in the UNESCO World Heritage Convention in 1972, which promoted an approach that clearly separated nature from culture and postulated collective human ownership of the nature protected in individual national parks.

Brad Martin investigates the contested power relations behind the benign label of global nature conservation. His essay attends to the clash of globally endorsed ideas of wilderness preservation and local traditions. The ongoing struggles between American and Canadian park planners and indigenous populations in arctic and subarctic regions unfolded in the Yukon-Alaska borderlands in the 1960s and 1970s when large areas were set aside for national parks without adequate participation of affected communities. As indigenous populations contested the boundaries of the planned parks and the ensuing restrictions imposed on their livelihoods, they formed networks that gained increasing strength and influence on determining the design and the use of the prospective parks. Thus, Martin's contribution reveals how the formation of a transnational indigenous movement was able to discredit the original approach of the national park as empty space devoid of humans in favour of more participatory concepts of national park management sensitive to local traditions and cultures.

Etienne Benson concludes the section, showing that the global spread of the national park not only consisted of the transfer of ideas and concepts but of conservationist practices, too. His chapter uses the science and technology of wildlife management in national parks to explore how changes in conservationists' scientific practices fundamentally shaped the management, territory and control of wild nature since the 1960s and 1970s. Benson investigates the appropriation of remote-sensing technologies developed at the peak of the Cold War in the 1960s by conservation biologists and follows a small academic network of wildlife scientists who applied radio tracking technology to grizzly bears in Yellowstone and later to tigers in the Nepalese Chitwan National Park. While it can be argued that the devices for disciplining nature were exported successfully from the United States to other regions of the world, Benson reveals that scientific and technological management strategies neither went uncontested, nor did they entail the straightforward 'modernization' of wildlife management. Park managers in Yellowstone objected to radio-collaring in the late 1960s as a visible violation of wilderness aesthetics. They also feared that the new systematic data on animal territoriality might jeopardize the independent management of the park. In Chitwan, the radio tracking of tigers proved instrumental in the significant extension of the park while incorporating key elements of local aristocratic traditions of tiger hunting. The chapter thus illustrates how a Western practice of park management was culturally adapted and localized. It also introduces animals as influential agents in the transition of national parks from spatially bounded wilderness towards an ecosystem whose boundaries were determined scientifically through examining the functional relations of its parts.

The third part of the book, *Nations and Natures,* explores the close association of national parks with notions of territoriality and processes of nation building throughout the twentieth century. The contributions highlight the expediency of the national park idea for different political and socioeconomic regimes. They show, from an environmental history perspective, that globalized environmentalism and international environmental regimes did anything but weaken the governing capacities of the nation-state. Tracing the transfer of national parks to the latest wave of nation-building processes in Europe after 1990, the volume also questions some received assumptions of current globalization studies and reveals the ongoing importance of territoriality and the enduring allure of nationalized nature well into the twenty-first century.

Emily Wakild focuses on revolutionary Mexico under the presidency of Lázaro Cárdenas in the second half of the 1930s to show how national parks became a core expression of the governments' agenda of social reform, national integration and regeneration of natural resources. Altogether forty national parks were created on Mexican territory trying to serve the aims of making nature accessible to the people and conserving forests for rational exploitation. The chapter highlights the role of scientific foresters as a driving force behind the national park agenda, which proved astonishingly successful in reconciling multiple use and encouraging local support, although conflicts arising from the competing claims of urban regeneration, scientific forest management and land use by local communities were by no means missing. Stressing the degree to which an internationally recognized model of conservation served to foster local participation at the same time it federalised natural resources, Wakild makes a powerful case for the political versatility of an internationally recognized blueprint for conservation. The Mexicanized version of the national park, she argues, "etched a radical and inclusive meaning into the international concept".

The essay by *Henny van der Windt* pursues the transfer of the national park concept into one of the most densely populated countries in the world, the Netherlands. From the outset the small state territory disallowed the usual notions of wilderness as a value for preserving nature in parks. Instead, van der Windt contends, programmes of preserving cultural landscapes reigned supreme, introducing a completely different idea of nature and nature management compared to the park idea as it evolved in the United States. Many conservation projects were privately initiated, resisted the emphasis on the nation, and discarded any notion of pristine nature. Balancing the interests of humans and nature was an essential feature of the Netherlands' parks and shows how institutions that allowed for political participation spawned an understanding of 'nature' markedly different to the politics of conservation exposed by European colonial powers – including the Netherlands – in their overseas empires.

The contribution by *Michael Lewis* focuses on the creation of national parks, tiger reserves and biosphere reserves in postcolonial India in the 1970s. He confronts the official Indian rhetoric of a Third World, anticolonial conservationism sensitive to issues of social justice with the actual performance of the protected areas that were established as a response to the promotion of national parks and biosphere reserves by a series of international environmental conferences since the early 1960s. This science-based assortment of protected areas as offered by the IUCN extended earlier Indian and British imperial traditions of conservation. As Lewis shows, it was impressive in numbers, but comparatively poor in performance. The Indian reception of the Man and Biosphere programme of the UNESCO resulted in the creation of fourteen biosphere reserves, which remained, however, merely a further title without concrete management consequences. They were marked by insufficient implementation and often exerted a detrimental impact upon local livelihoods. A similar ambivalence characterized India's Project Tiger, initiated in 1973. The programme was met with international acclaim and elevated the tiger into the rank of an emotionally integrating symbol of the Indian nation, but privileged tigers over the livelihoods of the poor. Therefore, Lewis qualifies the conservationist policies of India as those of an uncertain state honestly committed to both conservation and relief of rural poverty, yet unable to translate this commitment into viable politics.

Finally, *Carolin Firouzeh Roeder* takes the example of the Julian Alps to demonstrate how nature conservation has continuously been reinterpreted and symbolically harnessed to different political systems throughout the twentieth century. From the times of the Habsburg Empire the idea of a national park developed both a surprising persistence and adaptive ability to survive imperial dissolution, two world wars, and multiple political upheavals and border changes. Imperial and national politics of conservation became repeatedly enmeshed with transnational transfers of concepts and ideas, which became encapsulated in today's Slovenian Triglav National Park. Today, the Triglav mountain provides not only a mental habitat for a new nationalist identity but also a powerful ethnoscape by which Slovenia, like other postsocialist societies, claims its belonging to Europe as a community of shared values that include nature conservation.

In her epilogue *Jane Carruthers* addresses the challenges and the potentials that a global history perspective poses to the environmental historiography of the nineteenth and twentieth centuries. The history of the national park, she argues, by its very 'nature' transgresses the traditional focal point of the nation-state, demanding emphasis on international networks and transnational nature protection schemes. A global history approach also questions long-standing concepts and values of a 'universal', timeless and ubiquitous nature dear to environmentalists and environmental historians alike. Finally, a global historical perspective points to the diverse scales of 'global' environmentalist structures as they intersect with local networks and form the 'web of globalization'. Thus Carruthers corroborates the central idea of this volume, that the history of national parks and their agency in 'civilizing nature' offers a distinguished approach to scrutinize the structures of global environmental governance as they have emerged in the twentieth century, particularly since the 1970s.

Notes

1. World Database on Protected Areas, http://www.wdpa.org (accessed 16 October 2012). Designations below nation-state level, private reserves and international protected areas are not even included in these numbers.
2. William M. Adams, *Against Extinction. The Story of Conservation* (London, 2004), 231.
3. http://www.cmsdata.iucn.org/downloads/powpa_pp_sbstta14_final.pdf (accessed 16 October 2012).
4. http://www.iucn.org/what/tpas/biodiversity/ (accessed 3 April 2011).
5. Consequently, the 2008 World Conservation Congress in Barcelona explicitly encouraged states to step up their efforts in establishing 'national ecological networks and connectivity conservation areas to strengthen the protection of biodiversity'. See also Graeme L. Worboys, Wendy L. Francis and Michael Lockwood, eds., *Connectivity Conservation Management. A Global Guide* (London, 2010).
6. Kenneth Pomeranz, 'Introduction: World History and Environmental History', in *The Environment and World History*, ed. Edmund Burke III and Kenneth Pomeranz (Berkeley, 2009), 3.
7. The debate on how far world and global history in fact constitute different approaches remains as yet unresolved and has resulted in significant terminological overlap in practice; see Bruce Mazlish, 'Global History and World History', in *The Global History Reader*, ed. Bruce Mazlish and Akira Iriye (New York, 2005), 16–20; Marnie Hughes-Warrington, 'World and Global History', *Historical Journal* 51 (2008): 753–61.
8. Sterling Evans, *The Green Republic: A Conservation History of Costa Rica* (Austin, 1999); Elizabeth Garland, 'State of Nature: Colonial Power, Neoliberal Capital, and Wildlife Management in Tanzania'. PhD dissertation, University of Chicago, 2006.
9. Important studies include David Anderson and Richard Grove, eds., *Conservation in Africa: People, Policies and Practice* (Cambridge, 1987); John M. MacKenzie, *The Empire of Nature: Hunting, Conservation and British Imperialism* (Manchester, 1988); Patrick C. West and Steven R. Brechin, *Resident Peoples and National Parks: Social Dilemmas and Strategies in International Conservation* (Tucson, 1991); Jane Carruthers, *The Kruger National Park: A Social and Political History* (Pietermaritzburg, 1995); Krishna B. Ghimire and Michel P. Pimbert, eds., *Social Change and Conservation: Environmental Politics and Impacts of National Parks and Protected Areas* (Lon-

don, 1997); Roderick P. Neumann, *Imposing Wilderness: Struggles over Livelihood and Nature Preservation in Africa* (Berkeley, 1998); Dawn Chatty and Marcus Colchester, eds., *Conservation and Mobile Indigenous Peoples: Displacement, Forced Settlement and Sustainable Development* (New York, 2002); Dan Brockington, *Fortress Conservation: The Preservation of the Mkomazi Game Reserve in Tanzania* (Oxford, 2002); William M. Adams and Martin Mulligan, eds., *Decolonizing Nature: Strategies for Conservation in a Post-colonial Era* (London, 2003); Jim Igoe, *Conservation and Globalization: A Study of National Parks and Indigenous Communities from East Africa to South Dakota* (Belmont, 2004).

10. For the early decades, see John Sheail, *Nature's spectacle. The World's First National Parks and Protected Areas* (London, 2010).

11. See e.g. Bernhard Grzimek, *Serengeti Shall Not Die* (London, 1960); Robert M. Poole, ed., *Nature's Wonderlands: National Parks of the World* (Washington, DC, 1989); Laura and William Riley, *Nature's Strongholds: The World's Great Wildlife Reserves* (Princeton, 2005).

12. David John Frank, Ann Hironaka and Evan Schofer, 'The Nation-State and the Natural Environment over the Twentieth Century', *American Sociological Review* 65 (2000): 99; John W. Meyer et al., 'The Structuring of a World Environmental Regime 1870–1990', *International Organization* 51 (1997): 623–51. This research is, however, not interested in explaining the globalization of parks as such. Rather, it takes the proliferation of parks as an indicator for the making and functioning of a world environmental regime.

13. Roderick Nash, *Wilderness and the American Mind* (New Haven, 2001; 1st ed. 1967); Roderick Nash, 'The American Invention of National Parks', *American Quarterly* 22 (1970): 734.

14. Nash, *Wilderness,* 344. On tourism as a motor for park establishment see Warwick Frost and C. Michael Hall, eds., *Tourism and National Parks. International Perspectives on Development, Histories and Change* (London, 2009).

15. Dan Brockington, Rosaleen Duffy and Jim Igoe, *Nature Unbound. Conservation, Capitalism and the Future of Protected Areas* (London, 2008). See also Karl S. Zimmerer, ed., *Globalization and New Geographies of Conservation* (Chicago, 2006).

16. For a survey, see John R. McNeill, *Something New under the Sun. An Environmental History of the Twentieth Century* (London, 2000), esp. ch. 8.

17. See the contribution of Ford in this volume; Melissa Leach and Robin Mearns, *The Lie of the Land. Challenging Received Wisdom on the African Environment* (Oxford, 1996); Paul Robbins, *Political Ecology. A Critical Introduction* (Malden, 2004); Roderick P. Neumann, *Making Political Ecology* (London, 2005).

18. Martin W. Holdgate, *The Green Web: A Union for World Conservation* (London, 1999); Barbara J. Lausche, *Weaving a Web of Environmental Law: Contributions of the IUCN Environmental Law Programme* (Bonn, 2008).

19. Particularly the 1900 and 1933 London Conventions relating to wildlife preservation in colonial Africa were critical in promoting and defining conservation enclosures, which served as a blueprint for park making well beyond the African continent. Mark Cioc, *The Game of Conservation: International Treaties to Protect the World's Migratory Animals* (Athens, OH, 2009).

20. For a recent critique, see Ian Tyrrell, 'America's National Parks: The Transnational Creation of National Space in the Progressive Era,' *Journal of American Studies* 46, no. 1 (2012): 1–21.

21. See the critique of Ramachandra Guha, 'Radical American Environmentalism and Wilderness Preservation. A Third World Critique', *Environmental Ethics,* 11 (1989): 71–83.

22. James G. Carrier and Paige West, eds., *Virtualism, Governance and Practice: Vision and Execution in Environmental Conservation* (New York, 2009); Anna Lowenhaupt Tsing, *Friction: An Ethnography of Global Connection* (Princeton, 2004).

23. Saskia Sassen, *Territory, Authority, Rights. From Medieval to Global Assemblages* (Princeton, 2006); Roland Robertson, 'Glocalization: Time-Space and Homogeneity-Heterogeneity', in *Global Modernities,* eds. Mike Featherstone, Scott Lash and Roland Robertson (London, 1994), 23–44; Antony G. Hopkins, ed., *Global History: Interactions between the Universal and the Local* (New York, 2006).

24. Michael J. Sheridan and Celia Nyamweru, eds., *African Sacred Groves: Ecological Dynamics and Social Change* (Athens, OH, 2007); Mahesh Rangarajan, *India's Wildlife History, An Introduction* (Delhi, 2006); Thomas T. Allsen, *The Royal Hunt in Eurasian History* (Philadelphia, 2006).

25. Roderick P. Neumann, 'Dukes, Earls and Ersatz Edens. Aristocratic Nature Preservationists in Colonial Africa', *Environment and Planning D. Society and Space* 14 (1996): 79–98.

26. Harriet Ritvo, *The Animal Estate. The English and Other Creatures in the Victorian Age* (London, 1990), 209.

27. Civilize, v., in: Oxford English Dictionary, 3rd ed., November 2010, online version March 2011 (http://www.oed.com/view/Entry/33587; accessed 16 October 2012).

28. 'The Impending Doom of Yosemite', *New York Times,* 13 February 1872, 4.

29. John Muir, *Our National Parks* (Boston, 1903), 1.

30. 'Letter by John F. Kennedy. June 23 1962', as printed in *First World Conference on National Parks,* ed. Alexander B. Adams (Washington, DC, 1964).

31. Charles Gordon Hewitt, *The Conservation of Wild Life in Canada* (New York, 1921), 1f.

32. Julian Huxley, *The conservation of wild life and natural habitats in Central and East Africa. Report on a mission accomplished for UNESCO in July-September 1960* (Paris, 1961), 94; Raymond Bonner, *At the Hands of Man. Peril and Hope for Africa's Wildlife* (New York, 1993), 64–67.

33. Paul Jepson and Robert J. Whittaker, 'Histories of Protected Areas: Internationalisation of Conservationist Values and Their Adoption in the Netherlands Indies (Indonesia)', *Environment and History* 8 (2002): 130.

34. See Jürgen Osterhammel, *Europe, the 'West' and the Civilizing Mission. The 2005 Annual Lecture* (London, German Historical Institute, 2006); Immanuel Wallerstein, *European Universalism. The Rhetoric of Power* (New York, 2006); Boris Barth and Jürgen Osterhammel, eds., *Zivilisierungsmissionen. Imperiale Weltverbesserung seit dem 18. Jahrhundert* (Konstanz, 2005).

35. Arun Agrawal, *Environmentality: Technologies of Government and the Making of Subjects* (Oxford, 2005), 226.

36. See Frederick Cooper, *Colonialism in Question* (Berkeley, 2005), 91–112; Sebastian Conrad, 'Globalization Effects. Mobility and Nation in Imperial Germany 1880–1914', *Journal of Global History* 3 (2008): 43–66.

37. Charles S. Maier, 'Consigning the Twentieth Century to History: Alternative Narratives for the Modern Era', *American Historical Review* 105 (2000): 807–31.

38. Ibid., 818.

39. Questions on the evidence of space and place have long been domains of poststructuralist social sciences, cultural studies, postcolonial studies and critical geography; see, for example, Arjun Appadurai, *Modernity at Large: Cultural Dimensions of Globalization* (Minneapolis, 1996); David Harvey, *Justice, Nature, and the Geography of Difference* (Oxford, 1996); Doreen Massey, *For Space* (London, 2005); Edward W. Soja, *Postmodern Geographies. The Reassertion of Space in Critical Social Theory* (London, 1999); David Turnbull, *Masons, Tricksters and Cartographers: Comparative Studies in the Sociology of Scientific and Indigenous Knowledge* (Amsterdam, 2000).

40. See Mark Dowie, *Conservation Refugees: The One Hundred Year Conflict between Global Conservation and Native Peoples* (Cambridge, MA, 2009); Daniel Brockington, James Igoe, 'Eviction for Conservation: A Global Overview', *Conservation and Society* 4, no. 3 (2006): 424–70.

41. Examples of a comparatively early involvement of local communities into park management are provided by Reuben M. Matheka, 'Decolonisation and Wildlife Conservation in Kenya, 1958–68', *Journal of Imperial and Commonwealth History* 36 (2008): 615–39; Reuben Matheka, 'Antecedents to the Community Wildlife Conservation Programme in Kenya, 1946–1964', *Environment and History* 11 (2005): 239–67.

42. See Martin in this volume, Jim Igoe, 'Global Indigenism and Spaceship Earth. Convergence, Space and Re-entry Fiction', *Globalizations* 2 (2005): 377–90; Alison Brysk, *From Tribal Village to Global Village: Indian Rights and International Relations in Latin America* (Stanford, 2000).

43. The politics of transfrontier parks are a recent example of how efforts of nature conservation as well as network and capacity building have been intricately intertwined with the leverage of transnationally mobile capital and exclusive global political, financial and business networks.

44. Michael R. Dove et al., 'The Global Mobilization of Environmental Concepts: Re-Thinking the Western/Non-Western Divide', in *Nature across Cultures: Views of Nature and the Environment in Non-Western Cultures,* ed. Helaine Selin and Arne Kalland (Dordrecht, 2003), 19–46; Anna Tsing, 'The Global Situation', *Cultural Anthropology* 15 (2000): 327–60.

45. Jean G. Baer, 'A Contribution to Securing a Unified Nomenclature in the Field of the Protection of Nature', Paris, 12 January 1949, UNESCO Archives Paris NS/UIPN/8, Annex IVA.

46. Nigel Dudley, ed., *Guidelines for Applying Protected Areas Management Categories* (Gland, 2008), 16. For the history of the IUCN categories system see ibid, 3–5; Adrian Phillips, 'The History of the International System of Protected Area Management Categories', *Parks* 14 (3/2004): 4–14.

47. The IUCN categories apply to nationally designated protected areas. In addition to and often overlapping with these national designations, there are sites recognized on the international level. Since the 1970s, several thousand World Heritage Sites, Bio-

sphere Reserves and Ramsar Reserves have been created. For the politics and consequences of international categorization see the contributions of Woebse and Lewis in
this volume.

48. For the definition of the categories see Dudley, *Guidelines.*

49. World Database on Protected Areas (WDPA), http://www.wdpa.org (accessed 16 Oc-
    tober 2012), Kevin Bishop et al., *Speaking a Common Language: The Uses and Per-
    formance of the IUCN System of Management Categories for Protected Areas* (Cardiff,
    2004), 16.

50. WDPA (accessed 16 October 2012). It seems that mainly developed countries with a
    long conservation tradition stick to their own national categories.

51. See Roderick Nash, 'The Confusing Birth of National Parks', *Michigan Quarterly Review*
    19 (1980): 216–26; Alfred Runte, *National Parks: The American Experience* (Lincoln,
    1987); Harpers Ferry Center, ed., *The National Parks: Shaping the System* (Washington,
    DC, 2005).

52. See the contributions of Harper/White, Gissibl and Kupper in this volume.

53. Cf. the contribution of van der Windt in this volume.

54. Public Record Office London CO 323/1516/16, Harold MacMichael to Colonial Of-
    fice, 22 November 1937; G.F. Herbert Smith in *Nature,* 4 October 1947.

55. James C. Scott, *Seeing Like a State: How Certain Schemes to Improve the Human Condi-
    tion Have Failed* (New Haven, 1998).

56. These problems are now acknowledged by the World Conservation Monitoring Cen-
    tre. See UNEP-WCMC, ed., *Annual Report on Protected Areas: A Review of Global
    Conservation Progress in 2007* (Cambridge, 2008), 29ff. On the impacts on livelihoods
    see especially the contributions of Kathirithamby-Wells, Martin and Wakild in this
    volume.

57. This is the argument forwarded by Tyrrell, 'America's National Parks', 4.

 PART I

Parks and Empires

 CHAPTER 1

Unpacking Yellowstone

The American National Park in Global Perspective

Karen Jones

On 19 September 1870, the Washburn-Langford-Doane Expedition struck camp on the Yellowstone Plateau. Over the campfire, the group ruminated on a three-week-long Rocky Mountain adventure that had taken in towering peaks, crashing waterfalls, spouting geysers and otherworldly mineral deposits. In keeping with the modish ethos of westward expansionism, discussion swiftly focused on territorial claims, profit and tourist potential. Judge Cornelius Hedges turned to his compatriots and instead proposed that the area be 'set apart as a great National Park'. Fellow explorer Nathaniel Langford later remarked, 'His suggestion met with an instantaneous and favorable response … I lay awake half of last night thinking about it.' Two years on, following political lobbying from the likes of Langford and Hedges (among others), 3,300 square miles of monumental scenery in present-day northwest Wyoming was preserved for posterity as Yellowstone National Park.[1]

The inception of the national park idea by a group of altruistic Americans around the campfire remains a compelling image to this day. From Hiram Chittenden's *The Yellowstone National Park: Historical and Descriptive* (1895) through countless pamphlets and pageants, the Madison Junction campfire became associated with the crafting of an illustrious concept. Even doubts over the authenticity of the story failed to dampen its lustre. In a speech commemorating Yellowstone's 125-year anniversary, then vice-president Al Gore paid heed to Madison Junction as the 'holy ground' of American wilderness. The central themes of the story – environmental philanthropy, frontier exploration, wilderness tourism and monumental landscapes – highlighted the symbolic power of conjoining nature and nation. As historian Richard West Sellars mused, 'Surely the national park concept deserved a "virgin birth" – under a night sky in the pristine American West, on a riverbank, and around a flaming campfire, as if an evergreen cone had fallen near the fire, then heated and expanded and dropped its seeds to spread around the planet.'[2]

In the years since its establishment, Yellowstone has become an American icon. Writer Wallace Stegner issued an effusive celebration of the national park as 'the best idea we ever had. Absolutely American, absolutely democratic.' Yellowstone symbolized the special connections between Americans and their land as well as the egalitarian mores of a new republic. It attracted devotees across the social spectrum. In the late 1950s, Hanna Barbera offered an animated homage in the form of 'Jellystone Park' and the antics of Yogi Bear while Disneyland in California featured a runaway mine train ride (1956–79) that transported theme park visitors to a facsimile 'nature's wonderland' of geysers and mud pots.[3]

Beyond the United States, Yellowstone achieved global resonance in the realms of environmental diplomacy and popular culture. For environmental historian Donald Worster, the national park denoted 'one of America's major contributions to world reform movements'. Just four years after its establishment, the British Earl of Dunraven applauded U.S. authorities for 'having bequeathed as a free gift to man the beauties and curiosities of "wonderland"'. The preserve in northwestern Wyoming swiftly emerged as the 'model': an original national park template that set down critical precepts of protecting wild nature from commercialism, federal/national responsibility for natural resource management and rights of public access and recreation. This formula became a transnational staple for modern states inspired by the remit of civilizing nature, namely, managing relatively unspoiled environments for the purposes of conservation, tourism and identity politics. As historian Aubrey Haines noted, '[Yellowstone] has become synonymous, both here and abroad, with much that is basic to the national park ideal.' By the end of the twentieth century, that ideal had facilitated the creation of 3,881 parks from Arthur's Pass, New Zealand (1929) to Zakouma, Chad (1963).[4]

This chapter explores the formation, evolution and dissemination of the Yellowstone 'model' with a view to understanding its power as a cultural and environmental signifier and globalized conservation product. The first section looks at the birth of the national park movement, situating Yellowstone as a product of American exceptionalism *and* as part of a transnational park-making tradition influenced by ideas about aesthetics, spirituality and 'the wild'; the mechanics of colonial encounter; and Western modes of territorializing nature. The second section explores early management practices in the national park, looking at how foundational (and now iconic) principles of land protection, public access and nature preservation operated on the ground. Here the idea of a Yellowstone 'original' is challenged to reveal the national park as an experimental landscape governed by shifting cultural values. Hence, the civilizing of nature was far from categorical, with practices determined by changing scientific ideas and envirosocial codes. Finally, the third section considers the power of Yellowstone as an export. Despite its overwhelmingly

'American' patina, Yellowstone was an ideal type of the national park brand and a standard for imitation worldwide, with diverse cultures reformulating its basic tenets of resource conservation to fit specific localities.[5]

The National Park Movement in the United States

The national park movement in the United States was irrevocably connected with processes of westward expansion. As Euro-Americans moved westwards across the frontier, taking the modern state, rubrics of 'civilization' and capitalist democracy with them, they engaged with ideas of discovery, progress and environmental transformation. It was precisely this interaction with the 'untamed' West that prompted artist George Catlin to consider the concept of a national park: the first recorded instance of such an idea. Travelling across the Dakotas in the early 1830s, Catlin was mesmerized first by the expanse of the prairie landscape and second, by its residents. Predicting the demise of the Sioux and the bison at the hands of what he termed 'the deadly axe and desolating hand of civilized man', Catlin argued that the government should create a *'nation's Park,* containing man and beast, in all the wild and freshness of their nature's beauty!' In calling for the protection of grasslands, animals and Native American communities as integral aspects of the prairie environment, Catlin's vision proved truly revolutionary.[6]

The establishment of America's inaugural national parks came with the discovery of the soaring peaks and rugged vistas of the far West, a monumental landscape very different to the East. First witnessed by Euro-Americans in the 1850s, the Yosemite Valley of California prompted grandiose commentary from explorers for its redwoods and glacial features. Desires to protect Yosemite from private despoliation led to state park status in 1864, with forty square miles of the Sierra Nevada preserved 'for public resort and recreation'. Moves to protect Yellowstone reflected similar fascination with fantasy worlds of rock and ice. Officially designated as a 'public park' in 1872, Yellowstone stood apart from Yosemite by virtue of its size and federal jurisdiction. Right from the start, Superintendent Nathaniel Langford favoured the appellation 'national park', as did the *Helena Herald,* who proudly referred to Yellowstone as 'our National Park'.[7]

Governed by an emergent cult of wilderness, a reevaluation of nature underpinned the American conservation movement. According to Wallace Stegner, the national park seemed inevitable 'as soon as Americans learned to confront the wild continent not with fear and cupidity but with delight, wonder, and awe'. Whereas the traditional pioneer mentality cast wild nature as a place of temptation, waste and threat, a new generation of Americans (comfortably installed in more urban, and urbane, environments) ventured fresh assessments. No longer viewed as a moral maze requiring subjugation by plough and biblical zeal, untamed spaces earned value for their divine, aesthetic and intellectual qualities. The industrial state came to see wild nature as a place for its citizens to go for spiritual renewal and socioeconomic repose. Modernity demanded pristine nature as its foil. Hence, where pastor William Bradford spoke disparaging of the 'hideous and desolate wilderness' in 1650, Henry David Thoreau proclaimed 'in Wildness is the preservation of the world' by 1851. Significantly, this idolization of wilderness coalesced around the illusion of a pristine American landscape untouched by humanity, a geography without indigenous peoples and hence very different to George Catlin's 'nation's park'.[8]

According to the dominant epistemology, the wilderness cult was a specifically American phenomenon, a signal of the unique connections between the residents of the New World and their soil. As historian Roderick Nash noted, 'The special American relationship to wilderness – having it, being shaped by it and then almost eliminating it – soon provided the strongest reasons for appreciating Yellowstone and subsequent national parks.' The appreciation of wilderness grew from a frontier condition and pivoted on the idealization of landscapes apparently unmodified by agriculture (and thus distinguished from the Old World). To Nash and others, it exemplified American exceptionalism, expressed in natural bounty and assertive nationhood. However, European as well as American factors exerted an influence. In particular, the philosophy of Romanticism, with its veneration of rugged nature as a repository of spiritual inspiration, advanced the worship of the wild. Thus, when explorer David Folsom described the Grand Canyon of the Yellowstone River in 1869 as 'beautiful, picturesque, magnificent, grand, sublime, awful, terrible', he referenced the archetypal superlatives of the European Romantic vernacular. From Gainsborough and Wordsworth to Goethe and Rousseau, a legion of Old World artists, poets and writers had betrayed a hankering for gnarled trees, precipices and waterfalls. Meanwhile, in British landscape parks such as Prior Park, Bath, (1754) and Hampton Court (1515), untended chunks of woodland, filled with winding paths and grottoes promised their own playgrounds of thrill, disorder, and transcendence. Europe too boasted a fetish for 'wildernesses', albeit crafted by gardening conceit rather than primordial design.[9]

Along with Romanticism, patriotism contributed a great deal to the U.S. national park project. In place of the castles and cathedrals of Europe, America boasted equally grand *natural* monuments in the form of ancient trees, soaring peaks and rugged chasms. The West thus emerged as a heroic geography, a territory of profound destiny in which Americans planted claims to national greatness, New World identity and moral turpitude. In 1864, Clarence King offered a litany in nature-jingoism in hailing the Sierra redwoods 'living monuments of antiquity' vastly superior to any 'fragment of human work, broken pillar or sand-worn image'. Beautiful nature signalled a solid and pure basis on which to craft an equally illustrious American empire. Geographic features became figurative ammunition to hurl across the Atlantic in repose to accusations of crass materialism and cultural infancy. Nature was nationalized and nation naturalized. In 1872, the U.S. government paid artist Thomas Moran $10,000 for a seven-by-twelve-foot canvas entitled *The Grand Canyon of the Yellowstone*. Resplendent in the lobby of the U.S. Senate, Moran's homage to Rocky Mountain geo-histrionics offered clear evidence of 'nature's nation' as a foundational myth of the American republic.[10]

Joining affections for wilderness and nation in the story of the American national park was a democratic impulse. According to Nash, the formation of reserves remained 'inconceivable' without a democratic mandate. The creation of national parks predicated on a desire to protect landscapes from rampant commercialism on behalf of the public good. In that sense, the modern industrial state secured its own claims to 'civilization' via altruistic acts of emparkment. Geologist Ferdinand Hayden conveyed such sentiments in a report to the U.S. House Committee (1871) recommending the preservation of Yellowstone from selfish interests. Hayden highlighted profiteering and materialistic practices at Niagara Falls in his argument. As historian Alfred Runte pointed out, if Niagara's British detractors had seized the imperative, 'England, and not the United States, would now be credited as the inventor of the national park ideal.' Instead, the tenets of Republican virtue, access to commons and the rights of the everyman lent the park movement a New World countenance. This democratic rationale distinguished the national park from the preserves of Old Europe, whose ornamental lakes and corralled environmental resources were tied to aristocratic purse strings.[11]

Contrary to the rhetoric of American exceptionalism, Yellowstone and Yosemite did not represent inaugural experiments in 'people's parks'. Setting aside land for civic purpose and public leisure dated back to the classical world. Likewise, the movement to create *rus in urbe*, to open up green spaces in the industrializing cities of Europe, was similarly democratic. Designed by industrial philanthropist and social reformer Joseph Strutt, Derby Arboretum opened to the public in 1840, while Halifax, Yorkshire, boasted a 'People's Park' as of 1857. Stewards of the royal parks of London, Berlin, Prague and Paris tore down park gates and revised selective entrance rules by the early 1800s. In the nineteenth-century city, the public park symbolized civic uplift, urban identity, science, imperial display and healthy recreation for the working class. Frederick Law Olmsted, famous architect of New York's Central Park (1857–61) and Commissioner of Yosemite (1865), visited Birkenhead Park, Merseyside, in 1850. Mesmerized by architect Joseph Paxton's grand experiment in green populism, Olmsted related, 'I was ready to admit that in democratic American there was nothing to be thought of as comparable with this People's garden.' National parks may have illuminated a particularly American blend of natural iconography and democratic zeal, but such associations were already part of the global park phenomenon.[12]

Romanticism, cultural nationalism and notions of popular democracy provided aesthetic and theoretical foundations for the American national park movement. For appreciation to become preservation – and civilizing nature a national prerogative – a sense of imperilment and activist zeal appeared necessary. Both were ignited thanks to processes of territorial expansion that saw the United States become a transcontinental and industrial nation in less than a century. The mechanics of acquisition and discovery along with rapid environmental change explained why national parks emerged first in the United States. As historian Francis Parkman noted in his 1892 edition of *The Oregon Trail*, 'The Wild West is tamed, and its savage charms have withered.' Critical voices castigated the redemptive arrogance of the pioneer ethos, the myth of superabundance and the relentless worship of the almighty dollar. For George Perkins Marsh, author of *Man and Nature* (1864), the capacity of humans to transform their environment demanded a change of mentality and attention to posterity. Likewise, John Muir, co-founder of the Sierra Club (1892), the oldest grassroots environmental group in the United States, lofted wild nature as in need of protection from industrialism. As he proselytized in *Our National Parks* (1901), 'Mountain parks and reservations are useful not only as fountains of timber and irrigating rivers, but as fountains of life.' Appreciation turned to preservation, crucially, at a time when sizeable chunks of grandiloquent Western scenery remained relatively undisturbed. In this regard, Yellowstone represented a prime cut.[13]

Management in Yellowstone: Taming the Wild for Tourists

The bill to establish Yellowstone National Park was introduced into Congress in December 1871, with the park formally established on 1 March 1872. Such swift passage through the bureaucratic machinery suggested little opposition to the national park idea as well as a broad understanding of its purpose. Yellowstone was set aside 'from settlement, occupancy and sale', designated as a 'public park or pleasuring-ground for the benefit and enjoyment of the people', with stipulation 'for the preservation … of all timber, mineral deposits, natural curiosities, or wonders within said park, and their retention in their natural condition'. Such aspects – government protection of a large piece of land, public access and the conservation of nature – became foundational tenets of the national park ideal and were readily exported to other nations keen to civilize nature. However, a closer look at Yellowstone in its formative years reveals a reality more provisional, fluid and, at times, contradictory. As Nash noted, 'We had a national park, in other words, before we realized its full significance.' The

U.S. government did not provide any funds for Yellowstone's management in its first five years. The only guidance that Superintendent Langford had was the enabling act itself. Hence, the Yellowstone 'model' did not represent a finished product in 1872. Instead, the park represented an experimental landscape in which ideas about the West, natural aesthetics, tourist dollars, capital and scientific authority played out. Particularly problematic was Yellowstone's dictate to preserve pristine wilderness while at the same time crafting an accessible and popular tourist resort: an inherent conflict within national park purpose that had significant environmental consequences in later years.[14]

Yellowstone's iconic status in global conservation owed much to the terms of the 1872 Act. The ceding of 3,300 miles of terrain (the size of Rhode Island and Delaware combined) as a national park was a milestone in environmental protection, especially in an age when nature was read in dollar bills, wheat acreage and timber square feet. That said, park establishment did not signal a wholesale governmental commitment to wilderness preservation or a disavowal of materialist readings of nature. Yellowstone's act may have set aside land from spoliation by private interests, but the protection of an ecological system scarcely represented a governing mandate. Instead, the size of the reserve reflected excitement over undiscovered geothermal curiosities. Organic freakery rather than biotic integrity carried the day. For all its altruistic intentions, the creation of Yellowstone did not venture an assault on dominant socioeconomic and commercial valuations of nature. As Alfred Runte contended, the easy passage of the park bill reflected surprisingly little congressional interest in the economic utility of the plateau. Debates focused on marginal agricultural productivity, minerals and timber stands, rendering Yellowstone as 'worthless land' according to the currency of the time. Outside of Congress, people quickly recognized the potential to make Yellowstone into a cash cow. Saluting the park as 'our American wonderland – nay, the world's wonderland', the booster publication *Resources of Montana Territory* (1879) anticipated Yellowstone as 'a great central resort for the lovers of the grand, the beautiful and the sublime in nature from all parts of the inhabited universe'. Nature and capital appeared symbiotic.[15]

Designated as a 'public park or pleasuring-ground for the benefit and enjoyment of the people', tourism and commercialization proved early priorities in Yellowstone. In his inaugural report, Langford insisted on the importance of making the park accessible, while the Bozeman *Avant Courier* enquired, 'What has the government done to render this national elephant approachable and attractive since its adoption as one of the nation's pets?' Early visitors came from the well-to-do classes, often in the guise of aristocratic adventurers, regional dignitaries or soldier-cum-sportsmen. Three hundred tourists braved Yellowstone in the 1872–3 season. Harry Norton published *Wonderland Illustrated,* the first of many Yellowstone guidebooks, the same year. 'Must see' sites

Illustration 1.1. Nature's Cooker. Cooking with only the heat from Hot Springs in Yellowstone Park is a novel experience, c. 1924 (National Park Service Historic Photograph Collection)

swiftly emerged, with the park revealed, in the words of one tourist manual, as 'a succession of pictures, each more striking than the other'. Mammoth Hot Springs, Tower Falls, Old Faithful, the Grand Canyon of the Yellowstone River, the Lower and Upper Falls and Yellowstone Lake all featured on the drive-by 'tour' of nature's carnivalesque. Visitors cooked beans in the mud-pots, filled Old Faithful with laundry and trash to provoke a more colourful eruption, and chiselled out mineral souvenirs. Yellowstone appeared a circus of delights, a Rocky Mountain theme park that encouraged frivolity not unlike later Disney playgrounds. As the editor of a Bozeman newspaper remarked of one party: '"Fun" was their only thought from morn 'til night.' With the arrival of the Yellowstone Park Line from the Northern Pacific Railroad in 1883, Yellowstone combined its reputation for monumentally freakish nature with lavish accommodations. Sojourners travelled west in the decadent elegance of the Palace Pullman railcar before resting at the Yellowstone Lake Hotel (1889–90) and the Old Faithful Inn (1904–5). Resplendent in its pioneer aesthetic, with pine logs and rocky pillars, a fireside seat and a shop selling lantern slides, the ambience of the Old Faithful Inn summed up the 'roughing it deluxe' ethos of the nascent wilderness tourism industry in the American West and across the globe.[16]

In *A Ride Through Wonderland* (1892), British tourist Georgina Synge commended Congress for its wise creation of 'a National Reservation, devoted to the enjoyment of all people'. Synge marvelled at Yellowstone's 'entrancing delights ... untouched by man!' Herein was another conundrum of the national park project: the assumption within the landscape democracy of America's natural wonderland of an unpeopled space where 'man is a visitor and does not remain'. The national preserves conceived by George Catlin had allowed for the perpetuation of Native American subsistence activities. Not so in the Yellowstone version. Early park managers in the Rockies cast indigenous groups as 'pests', with traditional hunting activities an affront to the purpose of protecting game species for visitors to feast their eyes (and, in the early years, their stomachs) on. An indication of the colonial mentality embedded in national park creation in the United States and in other European settler societies, the civilization of nature mandated the removal of so-called primitive peoples. The deer parks of medieval Europe represented obvious landscapes of power in which an aristocratic elite controlled access to land and environmental resources for the purposes of political utility, aesthetic sensibility, economic production and social capital. National parks were not entirely dissimilar. Beneath Yellowstone's egalitarian rhetoric of public space for all existed a less altruistic story of imperialism, territoriality and ethnocentrism.[17]

Yellowstone was roamed seasonally by the Crow, Blackfeet, Shoshone, Bannock, Nez Perce and Snake, and inhabited year round by the Sheepeater. The area provided subsistence in the form of bighorn sheep, elk, berries and roots, room for spiritual quests and a route across the Rockies. Campsites, obsidian quarries, trails and meadows created by fire regimes (later beloved by tourists) all bespoke indigenous presence in the newly formed park. However, once Yellowstone earned its designation as a national playground for industrial America, moves to curtail local native uses proceeded apace. Justification centred on making the park secure for tourists, preserving game and preventing Yellowstone's wild reaches from becoming a safe haven for recalcitrant tribes during the Indian Wars. Having already forfeited most of their land on the Yellowstone Plateau during the renegotiation of the Fort Laramie Treaty (1868), the Crow and Blackfeet lost title to a slither of land in the north of the park courtesy of the lobbying efforts of Superintendent Philetus Norris (1880). The Sheepeater were dispatched to the Wind River Reservation and army patrols mopped up stray hunting parties. In 1877–8, cavalry units pursued the Nez Perce and the Bannock – dubbed by historian Norman Denzin as 'Yellowstone's most reluctant tourists' – through the park as part of their military subjugation of the West. Discourses of nation building and nature protection conjoined, a process starkly illuminated by the management of Yellowstone by the U.S. Cavalry (1886–1918). Meanwhile, as the remnants of indigenous presence were being excoriated from the plateau, officials and boosters traded a line that presented Yellowstone's Indians as 'vanished' (hence the park was safe) and vestigial frontier curiosities (for public titillation). Chittenden's in-augural park history described the Sheepeater as 'formerly dwelling' in the region, while rail passengers apprehended Native Americans as ornaments of a passing frontier, museum pieces to be seen from the secure confines of the Palace Pullman as it made its journey from civilization to Yellowstone's vir-ginal nature park.[18]

If Yellowstone's public access issues related a more complicated dialogue between democracy and sovereignty, then so too did its imperative to preserve the park 'in a natural condition'. Just as the sanctification of Yellowstone as a tourist playground for the 'benefit and enjoyment of the people' precluded indigenous subsistence, so too did resource management policy organize the park according to a specific landscape aesthetic. Hence, preserving wilderness in a 'natural condition' actually meant creating a vision of nature that satisfied Euro-American visual, moral, philosophical, economic and nationalist pa-rameters. Certainly, official discourse consistently promulgated the park as an unspoiled Eden, American terrain in all its untamed, exceptional and iconic glory. Acting Secretary of the Interior B. R. Cowen advised Langford, 'It is not the desire of the Department that any attempt shall be made to beautify or adorn the reservation.' However, for Yellowstone's managers, tinkering with bi-otic systems did not strike as counterproductive to their conservationist remit. Instead, guided by the dictates of tourist access, landscape design, socioeco-nomic utility and hard science, officials saw it well within their purview to im-prove and enhance nature's complement. Like modern-day Capability Browns, park stewards worked with the flora on display to accentuate the picturesque and the pastoral, to please the eye. Tree stands were cut to allow for panoramic views, exotics planted and natural fire regimes stifled. In aesthetic terms, the national park 'look' compared with the English landscape parks of the Ro-mantic period and their lawns, lakes and grottoes. Even John Muir, the patron saint of American wilderness, celebrated his beloved Yosemite as a 'landscape garden with charming groves and meadows'.[19]

In wildlife management too, the maintaining of 'natural conditions' was marshalled by ideas of 'good' and 'bad' animals as dictated by contemporary social mores. Entertainment potential proved a critical factor in the treatment of fauna. Bison were corralled in Hayden Valley and stampeded on demand. Bears, Yellowstone's 'quasi pets' according to *Wonderland Museum* (1901), earned a special place in visitor hearts for their comic anthropomorphism. Crowds gathered to see the bumbling antics of Yellowstone's bruins at feed-ing stations, where the most fearless tourists even queued up to have honey licked from their hands. As Lord Pethick-Lawrence commented, Yellowstone offered a well-choreographed nature show: 'The bears come down at 5:30 and the geyser plays at 6.'[20]

Illustration 1.2. Bear hold-up, c. 1958 (National Park Service Historic Photograph Collection)

Also implicit in park wildlife management was a species hierarchy that graded animals according to a biologically informed morality. Animals perceived as docile, elegant and nonthreatening (herbivores) earned top billing whereas those seen as a threat either to people or other animals (predators) found no place in the park. Superintendent Philetus Norris tendered a distinction between the 'beautiful, interesting, and valuable' elk under his charge and the 'ferocious' and 'sneaking' coyote. Under the umbrella of 'natural conditions', park managers encouraged the multiplication of bison, elk and deer and aggressively prosecuted the extermination of carnivores. Wardens pursued resident wolf packs with guns, dogs and poison, viewing them as criminal interlopers in an ungulate paradise. In this sense, national park rangers appeared analogous to the gamekeepers of Old Europe, with practices in Yellowstone harking back to the original definition of a park in old English as 'an enclosed piece of ground stocked with beasts of the chase'. This was wilderness by design.[21]

From American Icon to Global Export

By 1900, the United States boasted four additional national parks – Sequoia, Yosemite, General Grant and Mount Rainier – all in the West and all marked by their dramatic vistas of rock and ice. Scenic monumentalism presided over the creation of Grand Canyon (1908) and Glacier (1910), and dominated the park-making canon. Newly installed officials looked to Yellowstone as the 'original', the 'crown jewel' and exemplar of park practice. Glacier's superintendent Henry Hutchings regularly wrote to his colleague in Wyoming for advice on predator control. Meanwhile, the creation of the National Park Service (NPS) in 1916 facilitated a broader notion of American primacy in national park matters. With a bureaucratic apparatus, financial backing and scientific infrastructure, the NPS pointed to the emergence of the United States as a global leader in environmental diplomacy.

From its inception, Yellowstone stood Rocky Mountain high as a sacred marker of Americanism. In terms of landscape typology and cultural purchase it intimated a powerful (and perhaps particular) alliance of nature and nation in the New World. And yet, for all its national(ist) qualities, the ideal type of Yellowstone National Park proved eminently transferable. In the years after its establishment, the Yellowstone model influenced park making not only in the domestic sphere but also across the globe. Despite the peculiarly American aspects of its establishment, the global renown and lineage of the broader 'park' label, together with Yellowstone's translatable mantras of government oversight, popular ownership and nature conservation ensured its sizeable international purchase. With many societies keen to work out their own relationships with recently acquired territory, processes of nation building, public belonging and land management, the Yellowstone example provided useful direction: a set of worthy general principles that could be readily grafted onto local conditions and modified at will. The core themes at play in Yellowstone – government protection of unspoiled territory, the overlapping of Romantic readings of nature with commercial intentions, the clearing of space and removal of indigenous humans and symbiotic processes of naturalizing nation and nationalizing nature – proved of global significance and were eminently exportable. The Yellowstone 'model' seemed especially applicable to other settler societies, where 'empty' spaces and exotic scenery conjoined with processes of land assimilation, cultural legitimization and identity formation to create fertile ground for national parks to flourish. The project of civilizing nature via national park creation had broad transnational appeal.

With a similar Western topography and socioeconomic values, Canada was likely to mirror American park making. Both countries established national parks courtesy of grand Western scenery, frontier expansion, Romantic valuations of nature and the lure of tourist dollars. In common with the Northern Pacific in Yellowstone, the Canadian Pacific Railroad played a critical role in the formation of Banff National Park (1885–87), Alberta, from the discovery of hot springs by three of its workers in November 1883 to the advertising of the reserve as a paradise playground in the years that followed. Designated as a 'public park and pleasure ground for the benefit, advantage, and enjoyment of the people of Canada', Banff's enabling legislation paid clear homage to the nomenclature of the Yellowstone Act, albeit with an added addendum and a $141,254 stipend for making the park into a veritable resort that would 'recuperate the patients and recoup the treasury'. As in Yellowstone, Canadian park planners saw their remit as one of conserving scenic splendour, creating a reserve dedicated to the democratic nation and establishing a lucrative tourist destination.[22]

Significantly, Canadian glances across the border were not all about emulation and common experiences. Roderick Nash may have listed national parks along with Coca-Cola and basketball as 'American contributions to world civilization' but local circumstances and the discrete needs of nature and nation ensured the national park was effectively patriated. In the example of Canada, preservationist discourse stressed the nonpareil qualities of scenery north of the 49th Parallel. MP Donald Smith argued that 'anyone who has not gone to Banff ... and not found himself elevated and proud that all of this is part of the Dominion, cannot be a true Canadian.' Moreover, as a Canadian park system developed, officials appeared keen to assert the conservation values and leadership provided by domestic institutions. The establishment of the Canadian Parks Branch (1911) proved a notable point of patriotic reference. Commissioner James Harkin proudly stated how 'Canada was the first country thus to acknowledge its responsibility with regard to the conservation of its places of outstanding beauty or other interest by creating a special government office to protect, administer, and develop them.' Later, in a 1957 policy document, a copy editor replaced the line 'the founders of our Parks system were guided by National park purposes and policies of other countries, especially the United States' with a reference to the establishment of the Canadian Parks Branch five years before the United States. Yellowstone may have offered direction, but the dictates of nationalizing nature took precedence.[23]

Outside North America, Yellowstone's unique reputation, tours by foreign dignitaries and an international dialogue among scientists and politicians collectively fostered the export of the national park idea. Created in 1879, Australia's 'national park' (renamed Royal) became the second national park in the world (although patriotic Antipodeans claim first by virtue of its 'national' designation). Its establishment came about by a blend of national, imperial and American influences. The Yellowstone example provided inspiration for park boosters who came up with the idea of an Aussie reserve in direct response to a U.S. visit. That said, impetus for emparkment also drew inspiration from the European ideology of *rus in urbe,* with Australia's inaugural preserve, just 32 kilometres from Sydney, conceived as a bucolic refuge for urbanites.

Its natural composition, while far removed from the rock and ice freakery of Yellowstone, nonetheless reflected similar processes of frontier assimilation, cultural uplift and identity formation at work. The Australian preserve celebrated connections between settlers and their adopted homelands and also enacted an epistemology of colonial takeover and transplant. As in Yellowstone, park creation reflected a desire to cement a sense of belonging with the landscape - of naturalizing processes of nation building – with a preference for Romantic-Arcadian aesthetics. Hence, amidst the iconic 'bush' landscape were markers of pastoral beauty in the form of 3,700 ornamental English trees, deer and rabbits.

In New Zealand, the Yellowstone precedent also loomed large. In his campaign to create a park at Lake Rotomahana, artist and politician William Fox paid direct homage to the Rocky Mountain preserve. Fox had toured the American West in 1874, painting landscapes of monumental nature, and returned to New Zealand keen to protect the volcanic features and distinctive pink and white terraces of North Island. The establishment of New Zealand's first national park, Tongariro (1887) referenced the language of the Yellowstone Act and depicted familiar themes of scenic preservation, Romantic nationalism and tourist lustre. However, the particularities of the designation – gifted by Maori chief Te Heu Heu Tukino IV to protect the sacred mountain from white settlement – offered a very different indigenous message and one more akin to Catlin's vision.

Impetus to create national parks in Africa largely reflected an imperial exchange between metropole and periphery and focused on the preservation of game animals. However, the Yellowstone template still proved significant. The first national park on the continent, the Parc National Albert (later Virunga) in the Democratic Republic of Congo (1925), reflected the importance of the Yellowstone 'tour' and the involvement of a (largely American) scientific community engaged in a process of 'nature importing'. King Albert of Belgium visited Yellowstone, Grand Canyon and Yosemite in 1919, camping with prominent conservationists John C. Merriam and Henry Fairfield Osborn, Sr. Albert returned to Belgium inspired by the park ideal, believing the colonial landscape of the Congo, marked by its primitive exoticism and 'empty' spaces, to be an ideal place for a similar experiment. Assumptions of wilderness as a place devoid of human modifications operated in the African as well as the American colonial conservation mindset. In South Africa, the glorification of the veldt and the cult of the Voortrekker (both instrumental in the founding of Kruger National Park [1926]) bore distinct similarities with the appropriation of America's Western wilderness as a national(ist) landscape, albeit with animals rather than rugged scenery invested with a range of aesthetic, historical and Romantic signifiers. Direct references were also made here to Yellowstone as a global marker of environmental leadership. Aubrey Woolls-Sampson assured his colleagues in the legislative assembly of the Transvaal (1907) that the reserves in their state could, in time, become like Yellowstone National Park. Yellowstone had become a global signifier representing 'blue-chip' nature and far-sighted governmental legislation.[24]

With its lionization of uninhabited wilderness, exotic scenery and giganticism, the Yellowstone model readily transplanted to other European imperial settler cultures. However, its influence did not stop there. Discussions over the creation of national parks in Britain consistently invoked the spirit of the Wyoming preserve. The symbolic import of Yellowstone, its status as a conservation milestone and signifier for altruistic government action and recreational democracy, lent it currency even in a small, overpopulated island bereft of opportunities for large-scale preservation according to the essentialist wilderness model.

William Wordsworth had called for 'a sort of national property, in which every man has a right and interest who has an eye to perceive and a heart to enjoy' back in 1810, but it took another century for substantive debates about British national parks to take place. James Bryce, MP, mountain climber and advocate of national parks as America's 'best idea', sponsored the Access to Mountains (Scotland) Bill in 1890, while Viscount Bledisloe campaigned for preserves in Britain after visiting Yellowstone, Yosemite and Grand Canyon in 1925–6. Bledisloe roamed the familiar ideological terrain of the Yellowstone brand in his elevation of national parks as 'beautiful sanctuaries for wild animals and birds' as well as yielding 'a most perfect holiday resort for persons of all classes'. Notably, Bledisloe wrote to the prime minister offering his own estate in the Forest of Dean for such purpose, but the Office of Works and the Forestry Commission ruled that the activities of free miners and an unremarkable avian complement (dominated by magpies) did not pass muster as national park material. Three years later, the government-appointed Addison Committee deemed the Cairngorm Mountains grand enough to qualify as national park terrain along 'broadly American lines'. Further documents continued to reference the Yellowstone 'original', including the Standing Committee on National Parks (1938) and the Dover Report (1940). When British national parks were finally created under the auspices of the National Parks and Access to the Countryside Act (1949), the echoes of the Yellowstone cessation could be heard in clauses dedicating space for the 'preservation and enhancement of natural beauty' and 'the enjoyment of the opportunities for open-air recreation'. Nationalism, nature protection and tourist democracy once again facilitated the transplant of the American national park idea, with added refinements dictated by local circumstance. As Lord Pethick-Lawrence noted, 'Unfortunately, we have not the great wonders in this country that they have in the United States … but I do think we have great beauties characteristic of our country which are worthy of being classed as national parks. After all, size is not everything.'[25]

Conclusion

In 1962, the First World Conference on National Parks took place in Seattle. The meeting drew representatives from 63 countries: attesting to the global reach of the national park idea and to the internationalization of conservation discourse. In a series of lectures and workshops, natural resource managers debated salient issues facing the world's preserves based on a governing remit of gaining a 'more effective international understanding and to encourage the national park movement on a worldwide basis'. And yet, for all its lofting of the park as a transnational product, the Yellowstone 'model' still loomed large. Over half of the conference delegates heralded from the United States while conference proceedings affirmed Yellowstone as 'the first such park in the world', which 'created widespread response throughout the world'. Ten years later, the Second World Conference on National Parks took place at Yellowstone itself. At Madison Junction, President Richard Nixon braved a hailstorm for a dedication ceremony in which he symbolically relit the campfire with an Olympic-style torch. Yellowstone stood at the centre of the national park pantheon, its scenery as statuesque, histrionic and American as ever. However, as this chapter has indicated, the Yellowstone 'original' sat in an eco-genealogy of park making dating back to classical civilization. Its creation reflected distinctly American developments, Old World cultural forms and the broader translatable mechanics of colonial expansion. Moreover, the Yellowstone national park 'model' was far from definitive in 1872. Instead, the preserve represented a place of experiment, a wilderness by design and one under constant reinvention. Under the broad dictates of nature protection and tourism, policy on the ground reflected the oscillations of socioeconomics and environmental attitudes. And yet, through all this, Yellowstone held sway as a conservationist signifier and 'model' for worldwide emulation. Despite being grounded in American geology and nationhood, it proved ripe for global export. Yellowstone carried purchase as 'the first', lending it currency and prestige beyond the domestic sphere and also making it a place of pilgrimage and reportage. Scientists, citizens and politicians visited the park, assimilated the essentials of the typology and took 'the Yellowstone image' back as a conceptual cutting to their homelands. That Yellowstone boasted the esteemed (and widely recognizable) 'park' label aided the exchange: parks were already known as places of retreat, play, leisure and romance. Moreover, the founding tenets of America's first national park sported a fertile combination of clarity and flexibility. Yellowstone's principles of protecting pristine nature bereft of human influence, commercial and tourist goals, and the ideologies of Romanticism, democracy and patriotism were plainly articulated, epigrammatic and suitably grandiose in design. And yet, the malleability of such terms as 'natural conditions' and 'for the benefit and enjoyment of the people' allowed other nations to take the template and adapt it to their own proclivities. This ability to evolve, refine and sometimes even reverse the details of park policy ensured the continued relevance and sustainability of the Yellowstone prototype. Both in the United States and beyond, the national park project of civilizing nature allowed for many translations in detail and design. As Jean-Paul Harroy, chairman of the International Commission on National Parks, related at the 1972 conference, 'Although [Yellowstone] has produced followers for a century now, the imitation has often been extremely free.'[26]

Notes

1. Aubrey Haines, *The Yellowstone Story* (Boulder, 1977), 1:130; Nathaniel Langford, *The Discovery of Yellowstone Park* (Lincoln, 1905), 117–18.

2. Richard West Sellars, *Preserving Nature in the National Parks: A History* (New Haven, 1997), 8; Hiram Chittenden, *The Yellowstone National Park: Historical and Descriptive* (Cincinnati, 1915 [1895]), 74; Haines, *Yellowstone Story*, 1:129–130; C. J. Magoc, *Yellowstone: The Creation and Selling of an American Landscape* (Albuquerque, 1999), 13.

3. Wallace Stegner, 'The Best Idea We Ever Had', in *Marking the Sparrow's Fall: The Making of the American West*, ed. Page Stegner (New York, 1998), 135–42. See Alfred Runte, *National Parks: The American Experience* (Lincoln, 1979) for the 'national' story of park creation in the United States.

4. Donald Worster, *Nature's Economy: A History of Ecological Ideas* (New York, 1994), 261; Dunraven quoted in Katherine Early, *"For the Benefit and Enjoyment of the People": Cultural Attitudes and the Establishment of Yellowstone National Park* (Washington, DC, 1984), 42; Haines, *Yellowstone Story*, 3.

5. Discussion of national parks, American leadership, and the transnational context has only recently emerged in scholarly treatments. See Thomas Dunlap, *Nature and the English Diaspora: Environment and History in the United States, Canada, Australia, and New Zealand* (New York: 1999); Ian Tyrrell, 'America's National Parks: The Transnational Creation of National Space in the Progressive Era,' *Journal of American Studies* 46, no. 1 (2012): 1–21. Tyrrell argues that Yellowstone did not represent a 'model' or 'uniform rationale' for national parks in other countries, yet admits the presence of 'transnational connections or influences' (4).

6. George Catlin, *North American Indians* (Philadelphia, 1913), 1:2–3, 1: 294–95. Protection of the plains finally came with Tallgrass Prairie Reserve (1996), while the National Park Service included indigenous subsistence rights under the Alaska National Interest Lands Conservation Act (1980).

7. *Helena Herald*, 28 February 1872.

8. Stegner, 'The Best Idea We Ever Had', 135–42; William Bradford, *Of Plimouth Planta-tion* (Boston, 1901), 94–97; Henry David Thoreau, 'Walking', in *Nature Writing: The Tradition in English,* eds. Robert Finch and John Elder (New York, 2002), 192.

9. Roderick Nash, 'The American Invention of National Parks', *American Quarterly* 22/23 (Autumn 1970): 731; Haines, *Yellowstone Story,* 98.

10. Runte, *National Parks,* 20–21.

11. Nash, 'American Invention', 726; Runte, *National Parks,* 7.

12. See Charles Beveridge and Carolyn Hoffman, eds, *The Papers of Frederick Law Olm-sted, Supplementary Series* (Baltimore, 1997). Tyrrell further argues that international conservation organizations including the American Scenic and Historic Preservation Society (1895) were engaged in international discussions with likeminded organs in Europe as part of a 'transnational circulation of information' that facilitated a range of conservation measures including wildlife treaties and national parks. See Tyrrell, 'America's National Parks', 6–13.

13. Francis Parkman, *The Oregon Trail* (Boston, 1892), ix; John Muir, *Our National Parks* (Madison, 1981 [1912]), 97.

14. Nash, 'American Invention', 731.

15. Runte, *National Parks,* 50–54; Robert Strahorn, *Resources of Montana Territory* (Helena, MT, 1879), 68.

16. Bozeman *Avant Courier,* 31 July 1874; Henry Winser, *The Yellowstone National Park: A Manual for Tourists* (New York, 1883), 7; Bozeman *Avant Courier,* 12 September 1873.

17. Georgina Synge, *A Ride Through Wonderland* (London, 1892), 3.

18. Norman Denzin, *Searching for Yellowstone: Race, Gender, Family and Memory in the Postmodern West* (Walnut Creek, CA, 2008), 51; Chittenden, *Yellowstone National Park,* 9.

19. Nathaniel Langford, 'Annual Report of the Superintendent of the Yellowstone National Park for the Year 1872' (Washington, DC, 1872), 1; John Muir, *The Yosemite* (New York, 1912), 3.

20. Quoted in Chris Magoc, *Yellowstone: The Creation and Selling of an American Landscape, 1870–1903* (Albuquerque, 1999), 153; Hansard HL vol 164 col 989 (19 October 1949).

21. P. W. Norris, 'Annual Report of the Superintendent of Yellowstone National Park to the Secretary of Interior for the Year 1880' (Washington, DC, 1880), 38–42.

22. Robert Brown, 'The Doctrine of Usefulness: Natural Resource and National Parks Policy in Canada, 1887–1914', in *The Canadian National Parks Today and Tomorrow,* ed. J. G. Nelson and R. C. Scace (Calgary, 1968), 1:98.

23. Janet Foster, *Working for Wildlife* (Toronto, 1998), 22; Roderick Nash, 'International Concepts of Wilderness Preservation', in J. Hendee, G. Stankey and R. Lucas, *Wilderness Management* (Washington, DC, 1978), 43; Mabel Williams, ed., *The Origin and Meaning of the National Parks of Canada: Extracts from the Papers of the Late Jas. B. Harkin* (Saskatoon, 1957), 5–6; 'A Policy Statement Respecting Wildlife in the National Parks of Canada', January 1957. RG84, vol. 2140, U300:1, Public Archives Canada, Ottawa. To further complicate Canadian claims, Sweden established a national organization for the oversight of national park areas in 1909.

24. Jane Carruthers, 'Creating a National Park, 1910 to 1926', *Journal of Southern African Studies* 15/2 (1989): 203.

25. William Wordsworth, *A Guide Through the District of the Lakes* (Bloomington, 1952 [1810]), 127; John Sheail, 'The Concept of National Parks in Britain, 1900-1950', *Transactions of the Institute of British Geographers* 66 (Nov 1975): 42; John Mair and John Delafons, 'The Policy Origins of Britain's National Parks: The Addison Committee, 1929-31', *Planning Perspectives* 16 (2001): 294; Hansard, HL vol 164 col 989 (19 October 1949).

26. National Park Service, *First World Conference on National Parks Proceedings, Seattle, Washington, June 30-July 7, 1962* (Washington, DC, 1964), 386; Hugh Elliott, ed., *Second World Conference on National Parks, Yellowstone and Grand Teton National Parks, USA, Sept 18-27, 1972* (Morges, 1974), 24.

CHAPTER 2

How National Were
the First National Parks?
Comparative Perspectives from the British Settler Societies

Melissa Harper and Richard White

The original concept of the national park – a large tract of land left in what was regarded as its 'natural' state, protected and managed for both conservation and recreation – was invented in the late nineteenth century, a gift of the 'new world' to the old.[1] The first wave of national parks appeared in British settler societies: in the United States (Yellowstone, 1872), Australia (Sydney, 1879), Canada (Banff, 1885) and New Zealand (Tongariro, 1887). Although South Africa, the other major British settler society, also began conserving large game reserves in the late nineteenth century (with direct reference to Yellowstone), they were not called 'national' until the Kruger National Park was created in 1926, partly because of white South Africans' ambivalence about their national status.[2] In each of the other four countries, additional national parks were proclaimed before the concept was adopted elsewhere – next in Sweden in 1909, not in Britain until 1951.

Unsurprisingly, scholars seeking to explain the phenomenal spread of the national park have been tempted to look for the answer in what these particular communities had in common.[3] Without diminishing these similarities, the overlaps or the extent to which they were independently reinventing the wheel, this chapter focuses on differences in the origins of these four parks, the national meanings they represented and the relative importance of transnational exchanges of ideas and personnel. While the Canadians and New Zealanders consciously adopted some features of Yellowstone, there were significant variations, and Yellowstone had no significance in the Australian case. However, as the Australian parks evolved into a system and required an articulate rationale, which a group of more professional, progressivist conservationists developed from the mid-twentieth century, there was a greater degree of borrowing from the United States.[4] In other words these parks were not simply reproductions of Yellowstone – least of all in Australia. That is not to say Yellowstone was not actively recruited, even in Australia, as a means by which the advocates of a conservationist philosophy of park management came to dominate by the 1960s.

Following the American Precedent

At first glance there seems to be a common thread in the national understandings promoted by the English-speaking settler societies in Canada, Australia and New Zealand. They regarded themselves as self-consciously modern, advanced and wealthy, and they defined themselves as nations in similar ways, against a common relationship to Europe as the 'Old World'. Their nation making looked to nature rather than culture or history, the vastness of geographical space rather than an immensity of historical time. Their control of abundant natural resources – all awkwardly and often violently appropriated from indigenous populations – gave them a confidence about their place in the world. While they were conscious of a relative 'lack' of history compared to Europe (they were careful to forget the original inhabitants), they brought to their nation making a boundless enthusiasm for the future. Moreover, these communities often self-consciously modelled themselves on the United States. The Australian colonies, for example, were seen as 'another America' throughout the nineteenth century.[5] There were racial, gender and ecological dimensions to this transnational bond at the moment national parks were being established.[6] They shared a sense of 'whiteness' and of masculine endeavour, and assumed the obligation to settle and develop 'white men's countries' in the interests of civilization and modern global race politics. The establishment of national parks assumed a dichotomy between civilization and nature.

Indeed, there were striking similarities in the way nature was reserved for nations imagined as white and masculine. Each of these parks involved government action, and government at a 'national' rather than local level; each covered a large area; each was dedicated for use by the 'people', defined in national terms; and each involved some notion of 'wilderness' or untrammelled nature. All governments recognized the economic value of an emerging tourism industry, but also the way uncontrolled entrepreneurial tourism could destroy the aesthetic values it was based on. These governments were used to setting aside tracts of land for future use, as initially precarious settlement spread into a potentially threatening wilderness. The parks were created at the point where the balance swung, when wilderness was more threatened by settlement than settlement was by wilderness. Each had a racial dimension as indigenous lands were made over to the use of the 'nation', largely defined by its whiteness. Tracey Banivanua-Mar has gone further to suggest that the designation of national parks was a logical end-point to the dispossession of indigenous owners and the triumph of private property: a final insistence that even 'waste' land, which they could see no prospect of 'improving', had some meaning for the invaders, and hence justified their ownership.[7] These British settler national parks were marked by a particular, if contradictory, 'blending of romanticism and utilitarianism', as Michael Hall and John Shultis put it. They also argue economic similarities, particularly the extent to which tourism and railway expansion stimulated park making, were more important than conservation values or environmental concern.[8]

Perhaps the most important point of similarity lies simply in the fact that they were all named 'national', and these similarities suggested to many commentators that the parks established in the wake of Yellowstone were necessarily imitations 'following the American precedent'.[9] But this, as Thomas Dunlap puts it, is 'hindsight and bad history'[10] and elsewhere he makes the point that only the 'culturally tone-deaf would mistake an Australian discussion of wilderness for one in the United States, or believe that New Zealanders meant the same as Americans by the term "national park"'.[11] On closer examination, there were significant differences in the national parks themselves and the 'national' meanings that underpinned them. How were the separate proclamations of these original national parks conceived as 'national' events?

Departing from the American Precedent

It is possible to align the different 'nationalisms' inherent in these four national parks with glib characterizations of distinct national myths. Yellowstone conforms to an American myth of transcendent nature as proof of God's providence and manifest destiny; Australia's with an egalitarian democratic tradition; Canada's with Canadian developmentalism and a harking back to a European aristocratic spa tradition; New Zealand's with an image of nation as the mutually beneficial melding of Maori and *pakeha* (white settler) communities. This is not to advocate essentialist national characters, but rather to note that different nation-states make their national myths in distinct ways. Even so, such a characterization is too neat. It ignores not only the transnational connections and similarities mentioned above but also the accidental elements in the labelling of these parks as 'national'. The term could simply refer to the government entity responsible; it could have more pragmatic or localized meanings; and finally the significant differences between the parks were not necessarily, if at all, national ones.

The first important distinction to be made is the varying relationship of these parks to cities. Most of the parks were 'peripheral', but not all. Whereas Yellowstone and Banff were on the very frontiers of white settlement, and Tongariro was a significant distance from New Zealand's two main cities, Sydney's first and second national parks (and South Australia's first and Victoria's second) derived their very rationale from their proximity to the city. One result was that although all the early parks were dedicated to 'the people', their imagined users were significantly different: Yellowstone and Banff were accessible for a wealthy, urban elite only, whereas the Australian parks enabled far more democratic use. This vital difference was recognized by an American journalist in Sydney with the Great White Fleet in 1908:

> We, by whom I mean the Americans now in Sydney, are delighted to learn that you have vast national parks within Australia close to your principal cities ... Our national parks are too far away from our great centres of population. The Yellowstone is almost inaccessible to the man of moderate means unless he lives near; Yosemite has been inaccessible until recently to all who have not the means to enable them to travel on mere sight-seeing errands.[12]

Second and closely associated with this first point, parks had different gender implications. Whereas America's more remote parks were imagined as spaces for masculine adventure, at least until more luxurious accommodation was provided, the early Australian parks were always understood as heterosexual spaces for gentler activities such as picnicking, boating and walking. The absence of large carnivorous animals in the Australian (and New Zealand) parks also helped. Third, all four parks occupied land that had economic and spiritual value to local indigenous populations. But whereas the original owners were physically removed from Yellowstone, and assumed to have disappeared from the Sydney parks, Maori ownership of Tongariro was effectively incorporated into the process of establishment.[13] As will be shown later, the indigenous connections to the parks would have significant implications for their national meaning. Finally, the landscapes differed: Yellowstone, Banff and Tongariro contained hot springs, dramatic scenery and natural 'wonders' and curiosities. They fitted the hackneyed notion of the sublime, which, despite its clichéd quality by the late nineteenth century, still carried something of Edmund Burke's sense of awe and the infinite. Such grandeur suited their national aspirations. Sydney-siders on the other hand admired their first national parks for their less celebrated, more intimate beauty. They had already found the sublime close by in the Blue Mountains, but they did not call it national.

When we come to the question of how their 'nationalness' was imagined, it is important to recognize the different national jurisdictions. That Yellowstone happened to be a 'national' park was, significantly, largely an accident of lines on maps and timing: it straddled three territories, not yet full-fledged states.[14] Yosemite was already recognized as nationally significant for its sublime beauty, but because it was within and under the jurisdiction of the state of

California, it was not initially described as a national park. At least the United States' post–Civil War national sovereignty was unambiguous. The other three 'nations' were in or approaching that strange twilight zone of 'dominion status' that distinguished British settler societies from the rest of the British Empire. They still had residual ties to British imperial authority but were effectively self-governing: crucially for the establishment of national parks, they had constitutional power over land management. Yet another jurisdictional confusion was that, while Washington, Ottawa and Wellington were the seats of national governments, it was only in 1901 that the Australian 'nation' came into being and a national parliament was established. The jurisdictions that created Australia's first national parks were the self-governing colonies of New South Wales (NSW), South Australia and Victoria, which nevertheless often imagined themselves as 'nations'. Post-federation, the states of Queensland, Tasmania and Western Australia would follow suit.

But nationality was never simply a matter of political jurisdiction. In each case the word 'national' carried more meanings, meanings that were being further elaborated internationally in the late nineteenth century. The variation in those meanings is instructive in understanding the extent to which these national parks were part of a coordinated, transnational development.

Yellowstone

Yellowstone's national status has to be understood within the reshaping of the American national myth following the Civil War, characterised by Judith Meyer as 'a combination of religion, patriotism, and the idea of nature as sublime'.[15] Americans were conscious of their limitations in the 'cultural stakes' compared to the Old World, but God-given nature could produce grand spectacles to match anything Europe had to offer.[16] Cornelius Hedges's much-quoted 1870 article, putting the first case for Yellowstone to be protected, made this plain: 'This great wilderness does not belong to us. It belongs to the nation. Let us make a public park of it and set it aside ... never to be changed but to be kept sacred always.'[17] The park was inserted into the national ethos through the myth woven around its moment of creation, appropriately beside a campfire.[18] The readiness to see these 'curiosities, or wonders' as 'sacred', in trust to the nation, drew on that peculiarly American Transcendentalist tradition. It also drew on a rhetoric of democracy, one that defined democracy as prioritizing public access over the interests of industry or scientific elites. While it is important not to discount other less idealistic motives, especially the role of railway promotion, it was the Transcendental rhetoric that gave the park its national meaning. An emerging group of white, bourgeois conservationists, usually professional men, effectively presented the natural spectacles in the park as embodying something quintessentially American. On that basis they could argue that they deserved the protection of the nation – and the label 'national'.

Banff

No other case quite managed that mix of an awe-inspiring, sacred nature embodying national ideals. Canada's national ideal was more pragmatically concerned with development. Even in the foundation myth woven around the Banff Hot Springs, which continues to be told in video reenactment at the Cave and Basin National Historic Site, profit rather than idealism was the guiding principle. It suggests that an ethos of development loomed larger in the Canadian national myth than the American one. The three railway workers who stumbled across the cave containing hot springs on Sulphur Mountain in 1883 only saw profit in them, and disputes over their control were also about money. When the government annexed the springs to develop a national park with its 1885 Order-in-Council, it was still to be 'a source of general profit': that profit would be 'vested in the Crown'.[19] In Sid Marty's words, 'There is a kind of typically Canadian embarrassment exemplified here, the inability to admire great landscapes without somehow attaching a dollar value' – according to William Cornelius Van Horne, general manager of the Canadian Pacific Railway (CPR), a 'million dollar' value.[20] Even the proposal to exterminate predatory animals in the park, it was suggested, 'could be utilized in a satisfactory manner' with the natural history museum built in Banff in 1903.[21]

The 1887 act itself – for a 'national park and sanitorium' – borrowed from the Yellowstone legislation almost verbatim, dedicating 'a public park and pleasure ground for the benefit, advantage, and enjoyment of the people of Canada'.[22] But while clearly conscious of the Yellowstone example, it was also clear that a different notion of development was at work. The national benefit rested on, in Prime Minister John MacDonald's words, the 'importance that all this section of country should be brought at once into usefulness' – that is, through the development of tourism.[23] The government and the CPR moved quickly (much quicker than Yellowstone) to initiate 'improvements' to 'make of the reserve a credible National Park'.[24] They envisaged an imitation of Switzerland to attract the wealthy from the United States and Europe, and even imported Swiss tour guides to lead visitors up the mountains: 'the doubtful class of people' were discouraged, but villa lots were 'leased out to people of wealth, who will erect handsome buildings upon them'.[25] The CPR built large, luxurious hotels at Banff and Lake Louise, with elaborate spas, fine restaurants and golf courses. There was no waffle about sacred values and little about preservation: the MacDonald government was determined to develop natural resources for the benefit of the national economy, and the reservation, 'admirably adapted for a National Park', promised profit.[26]

However while the nationalness of Banff was caught up in its role in furthering national development and making the Rockies useful, this is not to say it did not also embody a protoconservationist ethic. The recognition of the sublime grandeur of the scenery was of course what made it potentially useful through tourism, and the government's determination to control its development was to ensure the greatest possible profit, by maintaining it as 'high-class' scenery and excluding tacky commercial development. Canadians more generally were developing an appreciation of first the moral value and then the beauty of their landscapes and, as a cult of Canadianism emerged, the Rockies joined the frozen north and the prairies as the quintessential Canada.[27]

Tongariro

Tongariro had yet another claim to being 'national': it was a 'gift' from the Maori people to the nation. Yellowstone and Banff both had sacred meaning for their indigenous populations, but their spiritual claims were ignored in the nonindigenous claims to national significance. The remarkable thing about Tongariro was the way the indigenous sacred was incorporated into the nation that the park supposedly exemplified. As sheep farmers pressed further into Maori lands, a sitting of the Native Land Court in 1886 sought to determine disputed rights to the three spectacular volcanoes (Tongariro, Ngauruhoe and Ruapehu). They held particular spiritual meaning for Tuwharetoa paramount chief Te Heuheu Tukino, who had authority over the land. The Tongariro National Park Board's account in 1927 gives the initiative to Lawrence Grace, a member of parliament and Te Heuheu's adviser and son-in-law, who acted as a go-between. He suggested the chief offer the volcanoes to the nation: 'Make them a tapu place of the Crown, a sacred place under the mana of the Queen. The only possible way in which to preserve them for ever as places out of which no person shall make money ... to be the property of all the people of New Zealand, in memory of the Heuheu and his tribe.'[28] Te Heuheu's letter to the minister the following year confirmed 'the gift of that land as a National Park ... for the use of both Maoris and the Europeans'.[29] Undeniably, this was a gift made under duress, and in 2005 the question of Maori ownership was taken to the Waitangi Tribunal. Yet in 1887 it demonstrated a sense of indigenous participation in the political process not apparent elsewhere: the Maori population was effectively incorporated into the New Zealand state, and the 1840 Treaty of Waitangi served as the founding document of the nation.

The possibility of national parks in New Zealand had been raised earlier, with direct reference to the Yellowstone precedent. One-time premier William

Fox was concerned about the burgeoning tourism around the famous Pink and White Terraces of Lake Rotomahana in 1874. While he saw the profitable possibilities of the 'sanitary' use of the thermal springs around Rotorua, he thought their commercial exploitation bordered on profanity:

> The idea that these majestic scenes may one day be desecrated by all the constituents of a common watering-place ... that they should be surrounded with pretentious hotels and scarcely less offensive tea-gardens; that they should be strewed with orange-peel, with walnut shells, and the capsules of bitter beer bottles ... is a consummation from the very idea of which the soul of every lover of nature must recoil.[30]

Fox commended the Americans for protecting Yellowstone from 'men to whom a few dollars may present more charms than all the finest works of creation', and he commended the Maori for protecting the Terraces from the 'sacrilegious' acts of 'European barbarians' by making strategic gifts of lands as reserves 'for the benefit of the people of the world'.[31] However, less than two decades into their history as New Zealand's premier tourist attraction, it was natural rather than human agency that wrecked them: the terraces were destroyed by the volcanic eruption of 1886. At the same time attention was shifting to Tongariro, with Dr Alfred Newman arguing in parliament that 'it should be preserved from the hands of the spoiler in the same way as Yellowstone and other "lions" of American scenery'.[32] In those earlier discussions, New Zealanders demonstrated not just an interest in protecting generic 'wonders', but added a sense of the distinctiveness of their nation's nature, and a 'hope to preserve its character and its intrinsic value'.[33] Taken together, it suggests New Zealand's national parks – Mount Egmont was declared in 1900 – readily incorporated traditional Maori custodianship into an understanding of their 'nationalness'.

However, over time, the incorporation of Maori into the creation myth of 'the gift' operated to marginalise practical Maori involvement by encapsulating it in a historical moment. Maoris were represented on the park's management board but had little influence. The understanding of Tongariro as a Maori cultural landscape was erased. Once the Department of Tourism and Health Resorts, the world's first national tourism authority, took over the parks in 1914, a tourism perspective prevailed, with proposals to transform the park into a game-hunting ground, introducing grouse, deer, heath and even Scotch thistle.[34] In 1929 a 'Château' was built on a spur below Mount Ruapehu, a luxurious hotel modelled on Banff, with 90 rooms and 45 bathrooms (an extravagance for the day), a cinema, a gym, a dance-floor, a nine-hole golf course and a lounge framing the spectacular scenery. The Château struggled, but the aim of park development was clearly to attract wealthy tourists from the northern hemisphere. Other park users – 'trampers' – felt alienated, albeit conscious of their own superior moral and aesthetic sensibilities.[35]

Sydney

Banff and Tongariro differed from the American model, but both consciously referred to Yellowstone, and in both cases their 'national' significance depended on their natural features. The more distinct origin was the earlier Australian one.

Australia's first park has no creation story to match Yellowstone's campfire, Banff's cave or Tongariro's gift. Whereas Americans understood a spectacular natural feature to have national significance, and therefore deserved preservation for 'the people', in Australia the need of 'the people' provided both the initial impetus and the national meaning. As early as 1866, the New South Wales government had given protected status to a spectacular natural feature, the Jenolan Caves. Waterfalls were also protected, but these were isolated scenic wonders, not national parks.[36] The specific origins of Australia's first national park are murky, but they have been further muddied by later readings that seek to demonstrate how inadequately they measured up against the Yellowstone precedent or later standards of national park management. J. M. Powell has emphasized the context of forestry preservation in providing a precedent; Hutton and Connors the lobbying of the acclimatization movement; Mulligan and Hill the influence of British models of green urban spaces.[37] None provide a lot of direct evidence for their particular interpretation, and all miss the extent to which a recreational impetus shaped the National Park and the way recreation led to a conservation ideal.

The *Official Guide to the National Park of New South Wales* published by the National Park Trust in 1902 gave the most detailed contemporary account of the park's rationale: 'Several public men argued for the government to provide public parks, pleasure grounds and places of recreation adjacent to all thickly populated centres in NSW ... to ensure sound health and vigour of the community.' The wealthy radical, Sir John Robertson, as acting premier, conceived the idea of bequeathing to the people 'a national domain for rest and recreation'. One of the colony's elder statesmen, Robertson had made his name in 1860 with his land acts opening up the land to small farmers (selectors) rather than large pastoralists (squatters). His exact motivation cannot be established, but in 1879, the 'immense people's reserve' (18,000 acres, doubled the following year to 36,300 acres) was dedicated to 'the use of the public forever' in the hope that the 'air of these uplands is pure and invigorating to the jaded citizen of Sydney or her suburbs.'[38]

Interestingly, the 'public men' – mostly politicians – behind the park emphasized not what the park contained, but what, in their view, the people needed in the way of healthy recreation. In some sense, any large undeveloped tract of land would have done. In that regard, Yellowstone was *not* the model, but parks on the outskirts of London – Hampstead Heath, Epping Forest – and even New York's Central Park. However, while the National Park's 147 square kilometres was no match for Yellowstone's 8,987 square kilometres, it was quite a different order from Hampstead Heath's 220 acres (less than one square kilometre) protected in 1871, and the 22 square kilometres protected under the Epping Forest Act of 1878. South Australia's 'National Park', established in 1891 was more like the English examples with a mere 2,000 acres (8 square kilometres). But neither this 'national park' nor Ku-ring-gai Chase, Sydney's second park gazetted in 1894, can be seen as simply copies of either American or English models. Perhaps the closest comparison were those established to cater for the urban populations of Stockholm in 1909 and Mexico City in the 1930s.[39]

While recreation provided the impulse for Sydney's national parks, it should not be assumed that conservation found no place. However, it was conservation based upon the aesthetic appreciation of nature. The natural bushland was a fundamental premise of the parks' existence, and drew on a growing appreciation of the natural landscape and a desire to preserve its 'primitive' character. Of course, the national parks were also 'improved', usually around a central base for visitors.[40] But whereas in the more formal parks of Sydney (Hyde Park, the Domain and Centennial) decorous tree plantings, ornamental flower gardens and elegant statuary attracted visitors, the drawcard for recreation in the national parks was and remained the bush setting. Sydney's national parks did not feature any 'spectacular' scenery or natural formations. The language used to describe them was not the sublime but the picturesque: 'The scenery, though not on a scale of grandeur, charms with its quiet but varied beauty.'[41] Rather than a landscape of tall poppies, this was one of Sydney angophoras, Christmas bush, Gymea lilies, tree ferns, bush orchids, 'a wealth of picturesque and quiet beauty' not to be admired as a set piece from a distance, but one to enter and surround oneself with.[42]

Far from being neglected by an alienated English aesthetic that could not appreciate the beauty of the Australian bush, this sort of landscape had to be protected from its admirers. The threat came from walkers, flower pickers, hunters and fern stealers, and also from the spread of the villa. By 1901 Sydney was a rapidly spreading city of almost half a million, and picturesque landscapes, particularly those with water views and 'natural' bush settings, were being favoured as housing sites.[43] Determined to preserve the flora and fauna committed to their care, the trustees of the National Park declared it a penal offence to discharge firearms; interfere with birds and animals; remove, cut or deface any trees, shrubs, plants, rocks, fences and gates. They had two pet aversions: 'the guns and dogs of so-called sportsmen' and commercial activity. They were determined to 'prevent the modern abomination of advertising ... so prevalent almost everywhere else; so that here at least Nature's beauties can be enjoyed without notifications concerning So-and-so's soap, or Somebody's Embrocation, or Otherman's Pills vulgarising everything.' By-laws explicitly prohibited advertising to keep the parks 'safe from the machinations of ambitious schemers, and secured to the people of this country'.[44] This was even more pronounced in Ku-ring-gai Chase, where the trustees sent out raiding parties to ambush flower gatherers and inserted what must be one of the earliest regulations concerning cultural heritage:

> The defacing or removing of any aboriginal drawings or chippings on rocks is especially prohibited under this Regulation, as also the digging up or removal of any banks of shells and refuse, presumedly Aboriginal Kitchen-middens, in search of skulls, bones or other Aboriginal remains.[45]

Unlike their international colleagues, the Ku-ring-gai trustees could assume there were no indigenous occupants left to worry about, so the regulations and indeed the naming of the park served as a convenient elegy to a dying race.

Certainly, the appreciation of the aesthetic value of the park does not add up to a conservationist rationale based upon the scientific knowledge of the day. A flurry of recent scholarship on conservation movements has agreed that Australian national parks failed to show much concern about protecting environmental values, and they only receive passing mentions in histories of environmentalism.[46] Indeed, the Australian scientific community showed little interest in the parks initially and was more intent on zoos and botanic gardens and in investigating the economic value of Australian flora and fauna. There was nothing in Australia that compared to the articulate conservation movement in the United States, as represented by George Perkins Marsh and John Muir. Despite the variety of organisations springing up – scientific and amateur naturalists, bird-watchers and acclimatizers – their progressivism was ineffectual compared to activists in other areas of public life and other parts of the world.

However, the desire of recent scholars to identify the origins of environmental consciousness leads to something of a Whig interpretation that seeks to find the pioneers of present-day perspectives in the past. Such an approach misses the point that the Australian recreational tradition behind the early national parks was not antagonistic to philosophies of conservation. It is exactly in this recreational tradition that the *national* significance of Australia's original national parks can be found. Other national parks embraced recreation, and other governments established parks primarily for recreational purposes.

But it was in Australia that recreation was a sufficient justification for calling them 'national', and this rationale emerged independently from the Yellowstone precedent. Australians knew about Yellowstone, but the first reference that directly related Yellowstone to Australian national parks appears to have been a 1900 newspaper article comparing Ku-ring-gai's potential for saving threatened species.[47]

Recreation and Nation in Australia's National Parks

Recreation produced no more coherent a philosophy than conservation in Australia. However, the recreational impulse justified calling the early parks 'national' in three ways. First, they were national in the sense of benefiting 'the people'. The colony of Victoria established a 'National Museum' in 1854 and a 'National' Gallery in 1863. Sydney followed suit with a 'National Art Gallery' in 1876, just three years before the 'National Park'. These institutions were national not for the art they contained but 'for the people' they served. Similarly the national parks were national not because nature embodied the nation (as it did in North America and New Zealand) but because the people who would use them did. Park makers believed people to have a deficiency not in material but in spiritual life, a lack that nature as well as art could fill. They were 'destitute' of the 'breathing spaces favoured by Nature'.[48] Whereas recreation in Yellowstone, Banff and later Tongariro tended to be structured around elite tourism, the proximity of the Australian national park to the urban metropole provided nature as a mass experience.[49]

Second, many believed that the enjoyment of leisure was a national characteristic. Among the first to win the eight-hour day, Australians were a holidaying people with more access to leisure and a climate conducive to outdoor pursuits. In this they could be contrasted not only to Britons, but Americans. In 1891, the English visitor, Edward Kinglake, was mildly disapproving: 'There is no nation in the world which treats itself to so many holidays.'[50] Mark Twain, on his 1895 lecture tour, was pleased to be 'in restful Australia, where nobody wants to work and it is always holiday'.[51] Even the conservative *Sydney Morning Herald* could wax lyrical:

> We are the children of the sunny south, and we borrow from the clear skies above us, and from the general clime, much of that lightness of heart and of that vivacity, which so eminently distinguish us as holiday making people ... The free winds of heaven kissing the face of man, the mysterious and many voiced murmurs of the ocean, the hum of insect life, the rustling of the lofty trees, the flight of birds, the invigorating atmosphere, all and each of these touch the heart, inform the mind and educate the soul.[52]

Empty leisure was dangerous, leading to gambling and drinking, but 'innocent' pleasure in uplifting natural settings could be looked on with a benign eye.

Third, directing people's leisure to nature instead of the bar was closely associated with a growing racial consciousness. National parks could beget national fitness. Social Darwinism was only just beginning to demand that a nation's citizens be physically fit for the 'struggle for life', but the dangers of the city were already conceived in social Darwinist and eugenicist terms. This social engineering should not be overstated, however: a national park was still a gift to the people rather than an outdoor gymnasium.

Still, there is an element here of what has been called 'colonial socialism'. In the late nineteenth and early twentieth centuries, the Australian colonies were seen as social laboratories where the state played a major role in the economy, running railways, regulating industrial conditions and establishing banks and butcher shops. The aim in part was to protect working people from the more brutal aspects of capitalism. It attracted notice around the world, the French social theorist Albert Métin labelling it 'socialisme sans doctrines'.[53] These policies derived from accumulated pragmatic interventions rather than a coherent philosophical position. Similarly, when it came to establishing national parks, there was no underlying philosophy. One result was that when a rationale was needed, the vacuum was filled by the more coherent, protoenvironmentalist philosophy being articulated in the United States.

The Twentieth Century

In the twentieth century national parks spread throughout the world under the umbrella of international scientific, environmental and political organisations. New national parks were also established throughout Australia, but their creation had little to do with international debate until the middle of the century. In Queensland the wealthy pastoralist and parliamentarian Robert Collins led the argument for preservation of the Macpherson Ranges as health resorts: although he knew of Yellowstone and had visited Yosemite, the suggestion that they were a significant influence on his thinking was probably a later gloss.[54] Victoria developed a national park system with more support from scientists, amateur and professional.[55] Tasmania's boosters succeeded in having scenic and increasingly iconic landscapes declared as national parks to promote tourism.[56] Bushwalkers lobbied for new national parks in New South Wales;[57] among the most prominent was Myles Dunphy, an architect who promoted himself as the founder of bushwalking in New South Wales and developed a coherent philosophy of conservation in the style of John Muir. Though he never left Australia, he was keenly aware of international developments in conservation and admired the size of the American parks and their categorization into 'primitive' and 'tourist' areas. He also publicized the resolutions of the 1933 London conference in his manifesto for a great national park for the Blue Mountains (it eventually came to fruition with a national park in 1959 and World Heritage Listing in 2000). Yet his philosophy drew more on his own experience as a bushwalker, campaigning most vigorously for places he most enjoyed walking and camping in. Thus he remained within the recreational tradition of NSW national parks: it was just that the form of recreation he preferred demanded rugged country, bush skills and isolation.[58]

Unlike in other countries, scientists played a minor role in park establishment until the mid-twentieth century. Part of the reason is that while science was increasingly organized on a national and international level, Australia's 1901 federal constitution left the states dominant – and they jealously guarded their control of land. This is often seen as anomalous given the 1969 IUCN expectation that national parks be administered by 'the highest competent authority of the country'. But Australia's first national parks were formed when no Australian nation-state existed and individual colonies aspired to 'national' status. Even after federation the states were theoretically the higher authority when it came to disposing land. Thus it is too simplistic to regard the proliferation of national parks in Australia as merely misnamed 'state parks'.[59] The exception that proves the rule is the case of the Kosciusko State Park, proclaimed in 1944 (becoming Kosciusko National Park in 1967). While Dunphy and others had been lobbying for its protection earlier, the stimulus was the development of the massive Snowy Mountains Hydro-Electric Scheme, which was a major *federal* government initiative. In the competing and ongoing negotiations between the claims of grazing, hydroelectricity, skiing, tourism, bushwalking and conservation, and between state and federal authorities, scientists formed an active lobby group. The Royal Zoological Society and others argued for a Strict Natural Reserve as defined by the 1933 London conference. Dunphy opposed them on the grounds that responsible recreational bushwalkers should always have access to such areas.[60] Bushwalkers split over recreation versus scientific conservation, signalling a serious challenge to the recreational tradition. The victory of the conservationists would be sealed in 1967, when all the individual national parks in New South Wales, each managed by a separate trust, were brought under the authority of a National Parks and Wildlife Service modelled directly on the American system.[61] While both bushwalkers and scientists had argued for this, stereotyping the old regime as bumbling amateurs, the next twenty years represented the high point of a strict conservationist ethos guiding national park management.

When the Australian federal government moved somewhat belatedly to establish national parks on land it did control – the Northern Territory – it proved far more responsive to international developments. Kakadu was developed from 1979 with explicit reference to and help from the IUCN. Indeed in negotiating indigenous majority management in Uluru-Kata Tjuta and Ka-kadu national parks and the hand-over of Uluru to indigenous owners in 1985, Australia was in the forefront of the international shift to recognize indigenous rights in national parks. When the states followed suit – for example, the Mu-tawintji National Park in New South Wales was handed back in 1998, follow-ing an Aboriginal blockade in 1983 – they rarely went as far in providing for traditional cultural uses of the land.[62]

Conclusion

When Australians belatedly acknowledged both U.S. and international devel-opments in the concept of a national park, they tended to regard their early parks as an imperfect application of the Yellowstone precedent. We have ar-gued that Yellowstone's influence has been exaggerated. While it was signifi-cant for Banff and Tongariro, neither can be understood as simply following its precedent. Yellowstone had little or no influence on Sydney's 'National Park', where recreation took precedence. Recreation nevertheless required a large area of natural bushland to flourish and, ironically, more stringent protection – in regard to hunting, hotels and commercial activity, for example – than ex-isted in other parks at the same time. The result was a park that conformed to later IUCN definitions, was justified in being called 'national' and established an understanding of national parks largely independent of a transnational discourse.

Notes

1. We would like to thank Jane Taylor for her research assistance on this chapter.
2. Jane Carruthers, *The Kruger National Park: A Social and Political History* (Pieter-maritzburg, 1995), 47–48.
3. The best example of this approach is C. Michael Hall and John Shultis, 'Railways, Tour-ism and Worthless Lands: The Establishment of National Parks in Australia, Canada, New Zealand and the United States', *Australian-Canadian Studies* 8, no. 2 (1991): 57–74. Jane Carruthers argues for an imperial tradition in British colonies (includ-ing South Africa) distinct from the Yellowstone model: 'Nationhood and National Parks: Comparative Examples from Post-imperial Experience' in *Ecology and Empire: Environmental History of Settler Societies,* ed. Tom Griffiths and Libby Robin (Mel-bourne, 1997), 125. Thomas R. Dunlap notes significant differences, but the thrust of his comparative work is to emphasize similarities in settler societies' approaches to nature: *Nature and the English Diaspora: Environment and History in the United States, Canada, Australia, and New Zealand* (Cambridge, 1999). See also Warwick Frost and C. Michael Hall, eds, *National Parks and Tourism: International Perspectives on De-velopment, Histories and Change* (London, 2009); John Sheail, *Nature's Spectacle: The World's First National Parks and Protected Places,* (London, 2010).

4. Between the two world wars particular academic disciplines in Australia – e.g., education, political science – looked to the United States (prompted by funding opportunities) while others continued to look to British intellectual traditions. Conservationists arguably drew on American progressivist sources. Cf. Tim Rowse, *Australian Liberalism and National Character* (Melbourne, 1978), ch. 4.

5. Richard White, *Inventing Australia: Images and Identity* (Sydney, 1981), ch. 4.

6. Marilyn Lake and Henry Reynolds, *Drawing the Global Colour Line: White Men's Countries and the Question of Racial Equality* (Melbourne, 2008); Griffiths and Robin, *Ecology and Empire*.

7. Tracey Banivanua-Mar, 'Carving Wilderness: Queensland's National Parks and the Unsettling of Emptied Lands, 1890–1910', in *Making Settler Colonial Space: Perspectives on Race, Place and Identity*, ed. Penny Edmonds and Tracey Banivanua-Mar (London, 2009), 73–94.

8. Hall and Shultis, 'Railways', 57, 61.

9. Ibid., 57, 65.

10. Dunlap, *Nature and the English Diaspora*, p. 118.

11. Thomas R. Dunlap, 'Ecology and Environmentalism in the Anglo Settler Colonies', in Griffiths and Robin, *Ecology and Empire*, 85.

12. Franklin Matthews, 'An American View, Australia as Seen by Brother Jonathan', unsourced newspaper clipping, Vernon Family Papers MLMSS 6571, Mitchell Library. Thanks to Justine Greenwood for this reference.

13. Karl Jacoby, *Crimes against Nature: Squatters, Poachers, Thieves, and the Hidden History of American Conservation* (Berkeley, 2001), 87; cf. Mark Spence, 'Dispossessing the Wilderness: Yosemite Indians and the National Park Ideal, 1864–1930', *Pacific Historical Review* 65, no. 1 (1996): 27f.; for Tongariro, see below.

14. Montana, Idaho and Wyoming; populations around 20,000, 15,000 and 10,000 respectively. Richard A. Bartlett, *Yellowstone: A Wilderness Besieged* (Tucson, 1985), 2.

15. Judith L. Meyer, *The Spirit of Yellowstone* (Lanham, 2003 [1996]), 16. On Yellowstone and its origins, see Roderick Nash, *Wilderness and the American Mind* (New Haven, 2001); Alfred Runte, *National Parks: The American Experience* (Lincoln, 1979).

16. Bartlett, *Yellowstone*, 3f.; John F. Sears, *Sacred Places: American Tourist Attractions in the Nineteenth Century* (New York, 1989).

17. Cited in Sid Marty, *A Grand and Fabulous Notion: The First Century of Canada's Parks* (Toronto, 1984), 64; cf. Esther Anderson, *Victoria's National Parks: A Centenary History* (Melbourne, 2000), 2.

18. Paul Schullery and Lee Whittlesey, *Myth and History in the Creation of Yellowstone National Park* (Lincoln, 2003).

19. Marty, *Grand and Fabulous Notion*, 32 (citing Sir Sandford Fleming, engineer-in-chief of CPR).

20. Ibid., 44, 42, 48.

21. Ibid., 58.

22. Ibid., 62.

23. Joanna Kafarowski, 'How Attitudes and Values Shape Access to National Parks', *George Wright Forum* 20, no. 4 (2003): 57.

24. Marty, *Grand and Fabulous Notion*, 48.

25. Ibid., 61.

26. Kevin McNamee, 'From Wild Places to Endangered Spaces: A History of Canada's National Parks', in *Parks and Protected Areas in Canada: Planning and Management*, ed. Philip Dearden and Rick Rollins (Toronto, 1993), 20.

27. Dunlap, *Nature*, 103f.

28. James Cowan, *The Tongariro National Park, New Zealand: Its Topography, Geology, Alpine and Volcanic Features, History and Maori Folk-lore* (Wellington, 1927), 30f; also David Thom, *Heritage: The Parks of the People* (Auckland, 1987), 97.

29. Thom, *Heritage*, xxii; Cowan, *Tongariro*, 31.

30. Thom, *Heritage*, 1–4, 80f.

31. Ibid., 81–86.

32. Jillian Louise Walliss, 'The Nature of Design: Influences of Landscape and Environmental Discourse on the Formation on the Australian and New Zealand National Park and Museum', PhD dissertation, Australian National University, 2009, 69.

33. Julius Vogel, speaking on the New Zealand Forests Bill 1874, cited in Thom, *Heritage*, 79; see also 31, 105.

34. Walliss, 'Nature of Design', 71f., 79f.

35. Kirstie Ross, *Going Bush: New Zealanders and Nature in the Twentieth Century* (Auckland, 2008), 67.

36. Julia Horne, *The Pursuit of Wonder: How Australia's Landscape Was Explored, Nature Discovered and Tourism Unleashed* (Melbourne, 2005).

37. J. M. Powell, *Environmental Management in Australia, 1788–1914, Guardians, Improvers and Profit: An Introductory Survey* (Melbourne, 1976); Drew Hutton and Libby Connors, *A History of the Australian Environment Movement* (Melbourne, 1999); Martin Mulligan and Stuart Hill, *Ecological Pioneers: A Social History of Australian Ecological Thought and Action* (New York, 2001).

38. New South Wales National Park Trust, *Official Guide to the National Park of New South Wales* (Sydney, 1902), 7–10. Sir John Robertson (1816–91) was a pastoralist and four-time premier of NSW (1860–61; 1875–77; 1877; 1885–86): for more on his role see Kim Allen Scott, 'Robertson's Echo: The Conservation Ethic in the Establishment of Yellowstone and Royal National Parks', *Yellowstone Science* 19, no. 3 (2011): 6–11.

39. See the contribution of Emily Wakild to this volume.

40. *Official Guide* (1902), 94f.

41. 'In Kuring-gai Chase', *Sydney Morning Herald*, 22 Sept 1902, 5.

42. *Official Guide* (1902), 10.

43. See Caroline Ford, 'The First Wave: The Making of a Beach Culture in Sydney, 1810–1920', PhD dissertation, Department of History, University of Sydney, 2008; Jane Taylor '"An Incubus upon the District": Progress, Private Property and the Field of Mars Common', *History Australia* 7, no. 1 (2010).

44. *Official Guide* (1902), 20, 95, 97.

45. Joan Webb, *Eccleston du Faur: Man of Vision* (Sydney, 2004), 41.

46. Beginning with Powell, *Environmental Management*; more recently Hutton and Connors, *History*; Mulligan and Hill, *Ecological Pioneers*; William J. Lines, *Patriots: Defending Australia's Natural Heritage* (St Lucia, 2006); see also Wendy Goldstein, *Australia's 100 Years of National Parks* (Sydney, 1979); Derek Whitelock, *Conquest to Conservation: History of Human Impact on the South Australian Environment* (Adelaide, 1985).

47. E. D. Hoben, 'A National Pleasure Ground: The Kuring-gai Chase', *Sydney Morning Herald* 14 April 1900, 12.
48. *Official Guide* (1902), 7.
49. Grand government accommodation was built elsewhere in Australia: Mount Buffalo (1910), Mount Kosciuszko (1930), Jenolan Caves (1898) and Yallingup (1905).
50. Edward Kinglake [Edward R. Garnsey], *The Australian at Home: Notes and Anecdotes of Life at the Antipodes* (London, 1891), 69.
51. Lecture in Glenelg, Adelaide *Advertiser,* cited in Thomas Harry and V. L. Solomon, *Australia at Play: Suggested by 'America at Work'* (Adelaide, 1908), 51.
52. *Sydney Morning Herald,* 27 December 1859, cited in Richard White, *On Holidays: A History of Getting Away in Australia* (Melbourne, 2005), 56, 59.
53. Albert Métin, *Le socialisme sans doctrines: Australie et Nouvelle Zélande* (Paris, 1910).
54. Warwick Frost, 'Tourism, Rainforests and Worthless Lands: The Origins of National Parks in Queensland', *Tourism Geographies* 6, no. 4 (2004): 497f.
55. Sarah Mirams, '"For Their Moral Health": James Barrett, Urban Progressive Ideas and National Park Reservation in Victoria', *Australian Historical Studies* 33 (2002): 249–66; Tom Griffiths, *Hunters and Collectors: The Antiquarian Imagination in Australia* (Melbourne, 1996).
56. Greg Buckman, *Tasmania's Wilderness Battles: A History* (Sydney, 2008), 180–84; Melissa Harper, 'Saving the Franklin River: The Environment Takes Centre Stage' in *Turning Points in Australian History,* ed. Martin Crotty and David Roberts (Sydney, 2009), 211–23.
57. Melissa Harper, *The Ways of the Bushwalker: On Foot in Australia* (Sydney, 2007).
58. Melissa Harper, 'Nature by Design: Myles Dunphy and the National Park Ideal in Australia', unpublished paper, Australian Historical Association Conference, University of Melbourne, July 2008.
59. Frost, *Tourism,* 504f.
60. Geoff Mosley, *Battle for the Bush* (Sydney, 1999), 48ff.
61. Including American razzmatazz and an American director: Peter Prineas and Henry Gold, *Wild Places: Wilderness in Eastern New South Wales* (Sydney, 1997), 250; see also Goldstein, *100 Years,* 72–95.
62. Terry De Lacy and Bruce Lawson, 'The Uluru-Kakadu Model: Joint Management of Aboriginal-Owned National Parks in Australia', in *Conservation through Cultural Survival: Indigenous People and Protected Areas,* ed. Stan Stevens (Washington, DC, 1997), 155–88; Penelope Figgis, *Australia's National Parks and Protected Areas: Future Directions, A Discussion Paper* (Sydney, 1999); Jenny Savigny, Peter Thompson and Daniel Bourke, 'Land Rights, National Parks and Plans of Management', *Aboriginal Law Bulletin* 42, no. 2 (1990): 7–9.

 CHAPTER 3

Imperial Preservation and Landscape Reclamation

National Parks and Natural Reserves in French Colonial Africa

Caroline Ford

Much of the historical literature on the creation of national parks in the British Empire and in British settler societies (Canada, Australia, New Zealand) has emphasized how the American model, as embodied in Yellowstone National Park, with its emphasis on civilizing, naturalizing and nationalizing nature; on scenic preservation and on tourism, was imitated, 'translated' or transformed. As a result, many historians have assumed that Yellowstone became a kind of global template or prototype for the national park. In addition, most historians of the British Empire have argued that the first initiatives to create parks emerged primarily from the campaign to promote wildlife conservation, which was spearheaded by white elite hunters. In contrast, Britain's principal imperial rival and Europe's second-most important colonial power, France, consciously rejected the Yellowstone model when it created its own national parks and reserves in Africa, Southeast Asia and the Indian Ocean. The parks and reserves that the French established in Africa were conceived in terms that departed from British, American or German models. These parks and reserves were not primarily created for the preservation of animal life, and the French targeted particular kinds of landscapes that were, more often than not, forested. With the exception of Algeria, tourism was not an important component of the park or reserve, and many of them were created to exclude the presence of man. Parks and reserves were not then associated with the game hunter or with aristocratic pastimes that evoked the royal game park. French parks and reserves were primarily the brainchild of the French scientific community, which had been exploring the world on scientific missions since at least the seventeenth century.[1] Closely associated with the Museum of Natural History in Paris, whose forerunner was the Jardin du Roi, these scientists built on the concept of the botanical garden or the *jardin d'acclimatation,* which was predicated on a view of nature as a laboratory for experimentation, reclamation and regeneration. While France certainly participated in a number of international environmental conferences, signed treaties and shared many of the environmental concerns of the international community, it nonetheless charted its own path, which did not involve the simple (or not-so-simple) translation of the Yellowstone template. The story of the French in Africa clearly illustrates that 'Yellowstone's influence has been exaggerated.'[2] How and why the French embarked on a different course is the subject of this essay.

On 20 January 1933, Paul Lemoine told the audience at a meeting of the French Society of Biogeography that on several occasions international and national congresses had called for the protection of nature and ultimately convinced governments and public opinion that measures had to be taken to prevent the destruction of animal life and existing natural landscapes. The most effective of these measures, in his view, was the creation of natural reserves or national parks, which existed 'in most of the countries of the world and in their colonies'. However, he noted that their 'constitution and organization' had been improvised at best and reflected differing goals. Some, *réserves de conservation,* kept any form of human intervention at a minimum and were left 'in a state of nature'.[3] Others, *réserves de réintroduction,* were those where biologists were permitted to reintroduce plant or animal life that had once flourished and had since disappeared. Still others, *réserves d'acclimatement,* had a value in terms of tourism, and their organization allowed for the introduction of fauna and flora that would be of interest to the general public. These reserves, according to Lemoine, were those that had been created in French colonial Algeria or as forest reserves, zoological parks, botanical gardens and arboreta in metropolitan France.[4]

It is no accident that the diversity of these forms of landscape protection was discussed at length at the International Conference for the Protection of the Fauna and Flora of Africa, which was held in London ten months later (November 1933), following a number of international conferences that were held from 1900 onwards on the problem of the protection of nature more generally.[5] Moreover, the majority of colonial parks and reserves established on the African continent by the British, French and Belgians were created during the same period. These included thirteen national parks in French Algeria, ten natural reserves in Madagascar, the National Albert Park in the Belgian Congo and the Kruger National Park in South Africa. Some of these initiatives came out of a desire to protect vanishing wildlife on the continent and satisfied sportsmen and tourists alike. However, the parks that were established by the European colonial powers differed greatly in form, intent and organization, even as they shared common concerns and interests, as the calling of the 1933 international conference clearly demonstrated.

The French delegation made it clear that they considered the national park, a vast territory accessed by roads and favouring tourism, to be an 'American conception', as evidenced in the first national park created in the world – Yellowstone – in 1872. The definition of 'national park' adopted by the conference was the following:

> The expression 'national park' designates an area a) placed under public control, whose limits will not be altered and in which no part can be transferred except by a competent legislative authority; b) set aside for the propagation, protection and conservation of wild animal and vegetal life, and for the conservation of objects of aesthetic, geological, prehistorical, historical, archeological and other scientific interest for the service of public recreation; c) in which hunting, animal slaughter or the capture of fauna and the destruction or collection of flora are forbidden except…under the direction or the control of park authorities.[6]

The French delegation charged Georges Petit, a laboratory vice-director at the National Museum of Natural History in Paris, to present an alternative 'French notion' regarding the protection of nature, which was embodied in the *réserve naturelle intégrale,* which was to be found in its purest form on the island of Madagascar off the coast of Africa in the Indian Ocean.[7] The French established the models of the national park and the *réserve naturelle intégrale* in both metropolitan France and its overseas colonies from 1913 to the Second World War, but there was a particularly sharp debate regarding the question of form and purpose in these protected sites in France's African colonies, where France's first extended network of national parks and natural reserves was established. This debate raises the following questions: Why were the parks or reserves that were created in North Africa, West Africa and Madagascar organized differently from one another and from metropolitan France? To what extent did they differ from British and other colonial counterparts in Africa? Finally, what were historical antecedents that informed the French debate regarding landscape protection in metropolitan France and in the colonial context of Africa in the interwar period?

Landscape Protection in Metropolitan France

The first governmental initiative to protect a natural landscape in metropolitan France in legal terms was undertaken in 1861. Sixteen hundred hectares in the historic royal forest of Fontainebleau were set aside as a *réserve artistique* for the purposes of aesthetic enjoyment after considerable lobbying on the part of the guidebook writer Claude François Denecourt and the Barbizan School of landscape painters.[8] Indeed, Fontainebleau was conceived of as a 'national museum' intended for contemplation. It is not surprising that a forest should be the first designated site for landscape preservation, as the first glimmer in France of an environmental consciousness regarding the possible limits of natural resources was associated with those in charge of forest administration in both the metropole and in France's colonial possessions in the seventeenth century.[9] This consciousness guided Colbert's 1669 forest ordinance, which established a structure for the French forest service, the Eaux et Forêts. Pierre Poivre decried the widespread deforestation on his tropical island Eden of Mauritius in the same period and called for measures to halt it. In the nineteenth century landscape protection in France was associated with the forest service, which was reorganized in 1827 and called for the protection of France's forests. The voices of painters and a new middle class added to its chorus, even though this diverse constituency frequently conflicted with one another.[10] It was from these beginnings that the first generalized legislation concerning the protection of natural sites and monuments was enacted (21 April 1906). This law reflected the spirit of the decree governing Fontainebleau in that it pertained only to natural sites and monuments 'de caractère artistique' – intended for human contemplation and associated with France's historical past.[11]

By the early twentieth century calls for landscape protection came from a variety of organizations. These included the National Museum of Natural History (1793) and the Society of Geography (1821) as well as newer organizations, such as the Touring Club of France (1890), the Alpine Club (1872), the Société Nationale d'Acclimatation (1854) and the Society for the Protection of the Landscapes of France (1901). Although each of these organizations was devoted to the protection of natural landscapes, their goals were often in conflict with one another as the various constituencies suggest. While some stressed the importance of the protected landscape's 'scientific' value, others emphasized its touristic, aesthetic or 'national' appeal.

Like the decree governing the forest of Fontainebleau, the 1906 law was justified in aesthetic and 'national' terms, and the sites protected were conceived of as *patrimoine*.[12] One of the chief supporters of the law, Maurice Faure, declared in the National Assembly during the course of the law's discussion that landscape was in some sense an expression of the nation, which was not 'solely an abstract conception, a geographical and historical expression. It is in some way a material and visible representation of the country itself.'[13] The 1906 law, often named the 'Beauquier law' after its most vigorous advocate Charles Beauquier, was applicable to all of metropolitan France as well as Algeria and consisted of six articles. The first article provided for the establishment of a commission in every administrative department of France, which was to be presided over by the prefect, engineers, locally elected officials, representatives from the local artistic, scientific and literary community as well as delegates from the Touring Club and the Society for the Protection of Landscapes.[14] The task of the departmental commissions was to draw up a list of sites that should be protected, according to the law's second article. As the composition of the commissions suggest, the Touring Club of France and the Society for the Protection of Landscapes played a pivotal role in this endeavour and had, in fact, spearheaded the 1906 law, which was devoted to the protection of landscapes and sites that had an aesthetic, historical, scientific or legendary interest.[15] But time and again it was the aesthetic or picturesque aspect of a landscape and its historical associations that trumped other considerations in determining which sites were selected. Among the first sites to be protected under the new law, for example, were the unique pink granite rock formations of Ploumanac'h off the coast of Brittany in the *département* of Côtes-Du-Nord.

In metropolitan France in general, there was a clear divide between those who conceived of landscape protection in terms of conservation (for the purpose of managing natural resources) and those who conceived of it as preservation of a landscape in and of itself for historical or aesthetic reasons. Those who followed in the tradition of the foresters conceived of landscape protection in the form of parks as a means of effecting reforestation, conserving natural resources and preventing natural disasters, such as floods.[16] Those who followed in the footsteps of the Barbizan school painters were associated with the myriad of nature associations, the most influential of which were the Touring Club and the Society for the Protection of the Landscapes of France, who embraced a more preservationist, aesthetic vision of landscape protection. It was the latter that was embodied in the Beauquier law. A second law passed on 2 May 1930 strengthened the protectionist approach and added landscapes of zoological, botanical and geological interest to a potential list of protected sites.

Preservationist and conservationist efforts in metropolitan France culminated in the foundation of France's first national park, the Parc de la Bérarde, which became the Parc National du Pelvoux in 1923. The park had multiple, in the words of Charles Valois, 'contradictory' aims.[17] The Ministry of Agriculture's decree of 31 December 1913, which established the park, was designed to restore land that had been devastated by the overgrazing of sheep and goats. It was formed through the French state's acquisition of 4,248 hectares from the commune of Saint-Christophe-en-Oisans in the *département* of the Isère, in addition to 5,798 hectares from Pelvoux and 3,368 hectares from Guillaume-Peyrouse and Clémence-d'Ambel in 1914.[18] In creating the park the French state attempted to satisfy the scientific community as well as touristic and artistic organizations, whose interests were frequently in conflict with each other. While called a national park, it was not modelled on Yellowstone, but rather on the Swiss National Park, which privileged scientific interests and de-emphasized recreational functions of a park.[19] However, as most of Pelvoux's land was inaccessible as a result of being above an altitude at which most trees and other forms of vegetation could grow, it ultimately satisfied neither the scientific community nor the Touring Club of France.

Scientists, naturalists and foresters increasingly came to favour scientific 'reserves' in metropolitan France, which could be distinguished from national parks for their scientific purpose. It was the preference for the 'biological' natural reserve that came to hold the greatest sway in the interwar period among those naturalists and scientists who championed landscape protection. Representatives from the Museum of Natural History in Paris and the Société d'Acclimatation in particular put their weight behind the establishment of biological reserves in metropolitan France. These included the Réserve Zoologique et Botanique de Camargue, a vast tract of marshy wetlands in southern France; the Réserve des Sept-Iles on the Breton archipelago around Perros-Guirec in the department of Côtes-du-Nord; the Réserve Naturelle du Néouvieille in the central Pyrenees mountains and Le Lauzanier in the lower Alps, bordering Italy.[20]

Landscape Protection and Reclamation in the French Colonial Empire

Initiatives launched to protect landscapes in France's colonial possessions in Africa originated in the years before 1914 but materialized only in the interwar period. They made Africa the main focus of French conservation efforts overseas. In the colonies, the tension between conservationism and preservationism was also evident. Indeed, a participant at the Second International Congress for the Protection of Nature, held in Paris in 1931, stated that it was 'in the colonial domain that our country has shown itself to be particularly active' in creating parks and reserves.[21] The series of parks and reserves that were set up in each of its colonies differed in terms of whether the colony was a settler colony, as in the case of Algeria, with real or imagined long-standing historical ties to the metropole, when a territory was acquired and in terms of the ecological specificity of each colony. These differing colonial dispositions determined how the French were tied to the land and governed both the use of land and the extent to which they articulated a policy of conservation.

The issues raised by the colonial context were emphasized, for example, by André Joubert, an official for the department of Eaux et Forêts in Montpellier. He contended that in countries with 'young civilizations', such as the United States, it was a relatively simple enterprise to isolate vast areas of 'primitive nature' that had not been touched by man. The task became more difficult in countries that had long been inhabited and that had been subject to man's destructive influences. The landscape of metropolitan France and North Africa, which were regions of 'old civilizations', as Joubert defined them, presented the French, in particular, with a challenge.[22] Indeed, one official in the Algerian forest service argued that nowhere in Algeria or in any other part of North Africa could one find a region whose 'integral conservation' would inspire enthusiasm, even though it had a collection of interesting sites: 'Nothing comparable here to a Yellowstone Park'.[23] He further noted that Algeria, for example, was so overpopulated that there was no area where virgin natural territory remained untouched. Animal life, including bears and the stags of the Barbary Coast, had largely disappeared, and the last Algerian lion was killed in 1893 close to the town of Batna. Only wild boar and gazelles appeared to be unaffected. The establishment of protected landscapes therefore had to take into account two aspects of a common problem: First, should one seek to establish a system through which to protect landscapes in such a way as to ban the destructive actions of man while encouraging existing forms of animal life? Second, how could one find means of encouraging forms of nature that had been profoundly altered and return them to their original state? For Joubert, the national park, according to its original 'Anglo Saxon formula', was above all a 'tourist conception', sometimes with the aim of protecting wild game, whereas the 'biological' natural reserve necessarily restricted access and was smaller in size.[24] Their common aim, in his view, should be to assure the maintenance and often the reintroduction of a landscape's original fauna and flora to as great an extent as possible.

It was the model of the national park as a tourist destination, as opposed to the natural reserve, that won out in the jewel in France's colonial crown, Algeria, but only after considerable debate. In a meeting of the Société d'Histoire Naturelle de l'Afrique du Nord on 3 February 1912, René Maire, professor of botany at the University of Algiers, proposed that the society adopt a resolution regarding land in certain forested regions of Algeria to be turned into reserves and natural parks. The resolution was justified in terms of the existence of regions that had a particular scientific, artistic and tourist interest, as in metropolitan France, but he called for the creation of protected areas in order to restore fauna and flora to their original 'integral natural condition'.[25] In its resolution, the society noted that landscape protection was 'particularly desirable' in forested regions where the zoological and botanical vestiges of earlier climates were still so numerous.[26] They therefore concluded that reserves be established in these areas and that all forms of grazing and agricultural and commercial activity be banned, including the removal of dead wood. Maire transmitted a letter on behalf of the society in this regard to Charles Lutaud, the governor general of Algeria, and proposed the creation of twenty reserves that would cover 45,000 hectares. Soon afterwards the president of the Société d'Horticulture d'Alger, Louis Trabut, made a proposal similar to that of Maire, arguing for the creation of a national park analogous to those established in other countries. The propositions of the Société d'Histoire Naturelle de L'Afrique du Nord were seconded by a number of scientific, sylvicultural and tourist organizations in metropolitan France. Lutaud responded sympathetically to the idea and instructed the director of the Algerian forest service to formulate a proposal.

In early 1913 the Station de Recherches Forestières du Nord de l'Afrique (North African Station for Forest Research) also subscribed to the proposed creation of twenty reserves, comprising a surface area of approximately 45,000 hectares in the three *départements* of Algeria – Alger, Constantine and Oran. It declared that in eight of them the government would have to ban further cultivation and provide monetary indemnities for indigenous Algerians who cultivated it.[27] The station, however, proposed the creation of only one national park, the state-owned forest of Téniet-el-Haâd in the *département* of Alger, which it considered to be best suited for this designation because of its easy access, high altitude and cool and dry climate. In addition, it noted that the forest presented no problems in terms of the displacement of an indigenous population because no rights of cultivation or grazing existed in these areas. The forest was filled with very old cypress groves as well as cork trees that already attracted numerous visitors.

This proposal languished as a result of the First World War and was officially adopted five years later by a tourist commission instituted by the Algerian colonial administration, which included the head of the Station de Recherches Forestières du Nord de l'Afrique. In the meantime the administration had come to see the 'scientific' basis of the proposal to be subordinate to tourism. This preference shaped the decree signed by the governor general on 17 February 1921, which laid the groundwork for the creation of not one, but thirteen national parks in Algeria. Acknowledging the necessity of 'assuring the protection of the natural beauty of the colony, developing tourism and encouraging the creation of vacation centres', the first article of the decree stipulated that forests or parts of forests that could become centres of scientific/botanical study, tourism or recreation could be designated 'national parks'.[28] According to Article 4, all plant and animal life within the confines of the park would be protected. All cultivation and livestock grazing were banned, and concessions of ninety-nine years would be granted to encourage the building of hotels.

France's first national parks on the African continent were thus created in Algeria and covered an area of 27,600 hectares. They included Les Cèdres (Téniet-el-Haâd) (1923), which had originally been proposed as a park by the Station de Recherches forestières de l'Afrique du Nord; Dar-el-Oued Taza (1923 and 1927); L'Ouarsenis (1924); Djebel Gouraya (1924); L'Akfadou (1925); Chrea (1925); Le Djurdjura (1925); Les Planteurs (1925); Saint-Ferdinand (1928); Aïn-N'sour (1929); Le Babor (1931); La Mahouna (1931) and Bugeaud-L'Edough (1931). However, the colonial administration established only six of the twenty reserves proposed by the station in 1913. These six reserves were established within the boundaries of these parks, a hybrid model that might be seen as a kind of harbinger of the zoning that is common in national parks today. The Société d'Histoire Naturelle de L'Afrique du Nord, however, which was at the origin of the initiative, was sorely disappointed. For one official in the department of Eaux et Forêts this outcome demonstrated the 'fundamental antinomy between the conception of the *réserve scientifique* and the national park. While a national park was an area with an aesthetic interest to be preserved and exhibited because 'a beauty that belongs to all must be accessible to all', in his view a *réserve scientifique* did not necessarily have an aesthetic character and should be kept as much as possible in a 'state of nature' and subject to scientific observation.[29] It was for this reason that the French delegation, which was largely composed of scientists associated with the Museum of Natural History, demanded that the distinction be made in the final text of the London Convention for the Protection of the Fauna and Flora of Africa in 1933.

The colonial administration's apparent preference for the model of the national park as opposed to the natural reserve in Algeria can in part be explained by Algeria's large settler population. This population had a greater potential investment in tourism, particularly in the years preceding France's centenary of Algeria in 1930 and the International Colonial Exhibition, which was held in Paris in 1931. In short, this population created a constituency and a demand for parks that could be accessed by the public and that did not exist elsewhere in France's colonial empire. In addition, one of the striking aspects of the governmental decree regarding the establishment of national parks and natural reserves in Algeria – in contrast to other parts of colonial Africa, where the preservation of big game was often at the centre of proposals to create reserves – was that it exclusively targeted forested landscapes.[30] Article 1 of the Algerian governor general's decree stipulated that only 'forests or parts of forests' would be considered in determining the areas to be considered for the designation of 'national park' or natural reserve. Once designated, the removal of dead wood, setting fires and the grazing of animals would be prohibited. Policing of the parks and the establishment of roads would be undertaken by the Algerian department of Eaux et Forêts, which would determine fines for park violations. Indeed, many of the most ardent defenders of landscape protection in the form of parks or reserves in North Africa were officials in the forest service.

The creation of national parks in Algeria was linked to larger anxieties that characterized this unique European settler society. The French settlers who relocated to Algeria were deeply concerned about environmental degradation and deforestation, to which the problems of rainfall and climate were directly linked. The forested and coastal locations selected for all of France's national parks in Algeria are significant in this regard. Algeria was part of 'la plus grande

France' and viewed as an extension of metropolitan France – significantly, it was the only colony to be administratively divided into three *départements,* like France itself. For this reason the principle of preservation as much as conservation tended to guide measures to protect the natural landscape. The French constructed the forests of North Africa as sites of memory, reminders of North Africa's golden Roman past— which had allegedly been destroyed by the Arab invasions of the seventh and eleventh centuries, when the Maghreb ceased to be the 'granary of Rome'.[31] The myth of the granary of Rome was also invoked in ways that turned landscape protection in the form of reforestation, national parks and reserves into landscape reclamation projects with a particular historical resonance.

This distinction between national park and *réserve naturelle intégrale* governed policies and practices regarding the protection of natural landscapes in French colonies throughout Africa. Tunisia, which was a protectorate without a large settler population, had one forest 'park', Aïn-Draham, which was created just after the First World War, and no *réserves naturelles.* Louis Lavauden, professor at the Institut National Agronomique, attributed this in part to Muslim resistance to the protective measures and to the indifference of French authorities in Tunisia.[32] Lavauden posited that Tunisia was not without areas that could be designated as natural reserves, including the island of Djebel Ischkeul or the forest of Gommiers, which had been one of the last refuges of the North African elephant, disappeared long since it had been mentioned by Pliny. He lamented, as did a number of other commentators, that the 'destruction' was largely the work of the Arab population, even if they were not the only agents of environmental degradation.[33] A similar tension between national park and natural reserves can be found in Morocco, where a decree promulgated on 11 September 1934 provided for the creation of reserves and parks. Here, reserves were given preference. Most of them were dedicated to the preservation of game, and hunting was completely banned.[34]

In French West Africa (Afrique Occidentale Française, AOF), the favoured type of landscape conservation was the forest reserve, and the initiative came from the forest service and representatives from the Museum of Natural History. Louis Mangin, director of the Museum of Natural History in Paris from 1919 to 1931, lamented the situation in AOF: 'It is above all in French West Africa'—in Senegal, Dahomey, Sudan—that 'a magnificent fauna is in danger of extermination', due to the disappearance of its natural habitat and hunting.[35] Protecting forests was thus closely associated with the preservation of animal habitat, and thirty-four of such forests, some of which tolerated tourism, were created in the Ivory Coast between 1926 and 1932 and seven in Senegal between 1932 and 1934.[36]

The model of the *réserve naturelle intégrale* was most successful in Madagascar where the governor general created ten reserves by decree in 1927 and placed them under the stewardship of the Museum of Natural History in Paris. All rights of cultivation and grazing were strictly forbidden, and they were out of bounds for the general public. Georges Petit, who headed the French delegation at the International Conference for the Protection of the Fauna and Flora of Africa, described the aim of the reserves as one that worked toward 'the conservation in their natural state of the last vestiges of the flora and the last representatives of the indigenous fauna of the great island'. He argued, moreover, that it was the only pure enterprise 'of this genre conceived in a French possession'. [37] The idea to create such reserves was launched in 1925 when the Commission for the Protection of Colonial Fauna, set up by the Minister of Colonies, charged Petit, who was then about to go to Madagascar on a scientific mission for the Museum of Natural History, to study the merits of national parks or natural reserves while he was there. After speaking with the governor general about the urgency of creating such reserves, he made a presentation to the Malagasy Academy, which in turn named a commission to study how this might be achieved. The report was published in the colony's *Bulletin économique* in 1927, which recommended, in contrast to France's other African colonies, that the reserves be administered by the Museum of Natural History and the Société d'Acclimatation, rather than the forest service. A decree of 1927 provided for the creation of the reserves.[38]

Conclusion

With the exception of Algeria, the favoured model of landscape protection in all of France's colonies – Madagascar, Tunisia, Morocco, French West Africa and also Indochina – was the *réserve naturelle intégrale* or the forest reserve whose purpose was one of restoration.[39] It was one that was concerned with the protection of fauna and flora and with restoring landscapes to their original natural state. The Algiers-based French entomologist Paul de Peyrimhoff stressed the 'fundamental antinomy' that separated the 'scientific reserve' from the 'national park'. A national park in his view focused on the spectacular and the aesthetic and implied a human presence that would consume and appreciate it. A scientific reserve was, for him, 'a region where natural productions, independent of any aesthetic character, are still intact or almost preserved and permit, in this state, diverse disciplines to study them in privileged conditions'.[40] It therefore precluded the intervention of man or any domesticated plants or animals, remaining in a state of nature. Debates over the creation of protected landscapes and sites from the nineteenth century to the interwar period in both the metropole and the colonies illustrate just how fluid differing conceptions of landscape protection were, even if a fundamental distinction was made early on between conservation and preservation.[41] Competing impulses guided efforts to conserve, protect and restore natural landscapes. The guiding forces behind French initiatives came from many directions: scientists, many of whom were associated with the Museum of Natural History in Paris as well as with colonial administrators, and forest officials who advocated the creation of natural and forest reserves; diverse informal groups dedicated to the protection of nature, which included the Alpine Club or the Society for the Protection of the Landscapes of France in metropolitan France; the tourist industry; the government and the public at large. The irony surrounding French initiatives behind creating 'national' parks from 1913 to the 1930s is that the majority of these parks were created outside of France in French colonial Africa.[42] Much of the reason for this is that in a colonial context the indigenous population could be displaced far more easily. Throughout the nineteenth century forest officials in particular blamed the peasantry for environmental degradation and deforestation. This pattern was repeated in France's colonies, but the racial denigration of the 'indigène' or 'native' became very pronounced in France's colonies. When a series of forest fires swept colonial Algeria during the early Third Republic (1871–1914), it was the native Arab who was accused of environmental mismanagement or even deliberate arson, while the French saw themselves as responsible stewards of the land.[43] At the 1923 international congress on the protection of nature, for example, Louis Mangin noted that 'in Corsica, in North Africa, in the colonies the damage [to the environment] is more serious,' and he attributed this to the indigenous population, adding that 'colonial flora is still less well managed [there] than that of Europe.'[44] In cases in which the French acknowledged their contribution to environmental degradation, it was less in terms of their own actions than in terms of their insufficient policing of the indigenous population. At the second international conference on the protection of nature in 1931 Paul Reynaud noted in a discussion of France's colonial possessions that 'you are going to hear about the destruction of forests, the extermination of wild animals and the depredations of the natives. But, gentlemen, is it not necessary to consider that we have our own responsibility, if we haven't been able to discipline the native and to combat his destructive activity with scientific methods?'[45]

In a broad sense landscape protection in the form of national parks or reserves was conceived of more in terms of preservation than in terms of conservation in metropolitan France until the second half of the twentieth century. This had much to do with the early history of landscape protection in France and the aesthetic and nationalist impulse that underpinned it. With the exception of Algeria, France's colonized landscapes, lacking in those associations, were conceived of more in terms of conservation. There were, moreover, significant differences in initiatives governing landscape conservation in the British and French colonial contexts. The colonial power that followed most closely in France's footsteps was Belgium. The Belgians clearly agreed that their African reserves should be protected from visitors, though they would allow a few in restricted parts of Albert National Park, where they were far from encouraged. This might in part be explained by the fact that Belgium, like France with the exception of Algeria, did not have a large settler population that would pressure the government into providing access to parks and reserves.[46] While the aesthetic impulse behind landscape protection was never absent among the French and forested landscapes were always privileged, as in metropolitan France, 'scientific' and 'biological' interests always held greater sway in French colonial Africa. This might be attributed to the fact that it was governmental administrators, associated with the forest service, and scientists, associated with the Museum of Natural History in Paris, who led the charge and not big game hunters, who were insignificant as a constituency in most of France's colonies. The initiatives of scientists and forest administrators who spearheaded the creation of parks and reserves in French colonial Africa were tempered by one nature association that did cross the Mediterranean from metropolitan France and that was encouraged by the French colonial government in Algeria: the Touring Club of France. The French ultimately eschewed the American model of Yellowstone Park, preferring the integral natural reserves almost everywhere. They targeted forested landscapes, which provided a link between conservation in Africa and France's longer history of forest conservation and management in France. The French also made distinctions between old landscapes and new landscapes, which shaped their approach to conservation. There was nonetheless an ever-present tension among the French that was less pronounced in British settler societies: the tension between the goal of conservation, embodied in the reserve, and tourism, embodied in the national park However, despite the diversity of conceptions among European empires about how nature should be preserved or conserved in national parks or reserves, the process by which they were established on the African continent resulted in the gradual and systematic expropriation of land and natural resources from indigenous populations, which was one of the lasting legacies of empire in Africa.[47]

Notes

1. See, for example, Emma C. Spary, *Utopia's Garden: French Natural History from the Old Regime to the French Revolution* (Chicago, 2000).
2. Harper and White in this volume.
3. Quoted in Paul Vayssière, 'Réserves naturelles et parcs nationaux', in *Contribution à l'étude des réserves naturelles et parcs nationaux,* ed. André Aubreville et al. (Paris, 1937), 1.
4. Ibid., 2.
5. Several important congresses were held between 1900 and 1933. See Mark Cioc, *The Game of Conservation: International Treaties to Protect the World's Migratory Animals*

(Athens, OH, 2009): 34–40; *Le premier congrès international pour la protection des paysages* (Paris, 17–20 octobre 1909), ed. Raoul de Clermont, Fernand Cros-Mayrevieille and Louis de Nussac (Paris, 1910*); Congrès international pour la protection de la nature: Faune, flore, sites, monuments naturels. Paris—mai–juin 1923: Rapports, voeux, réalisations* (Paris, 1925); and *Deuxième congrès international pour la protection de la nature (Paris 20 juin–4 juillet 1931), procès verbaux, rapports et voeux,* ed. Charles Valois and Georges Petit (Paris, 1932).

6. Quoted in Georges Petit, 'Protection de la nature et questions de definition', in Aubreville et al., *Contribution,* 8.

7. Arnold Pictet, 'Les équilibres naturels de vie et la protection de la nature: contribution à l'étude scientifique des parcs nationaux et des réserves naturelles', *Mémoires de l'académie royale de Belgique,* 2eme série, vol 17 (Bruxelles, 1938).

8. Anon.,'La série artistique de la forêt de Fontainebleau: discussion à la Chambre des Députés (séance du 16 décembre 1876)', *Revue des eaux et forêts* 16 (1877): 5–10 and Simon Schama, *Landscape and Memory* (New York, 1995): 547–60. See also Greg. M. Thomas, *Art and Ecology in Nineteenth-Century France: The Landscapes of Théodore Rousseau* (Princeton, 2000) and Nicholas Green, *The Spectacle of Nature: Landscape and Bourgeois Culture in Nineteenth-Century France* (Manchester, 1990).

9. Richard Grove, *Green Imperialism: Colonial Expansion, Tropical Island Edens and the Origins of Environmentalism, 1600–1860* (Cambridge, 1995).

10. Caroline Ford, 'Nature, Culture, and Conservation in France and her Colonies 1840–1940', *Past & Present* 183 (2004): 184. For the forest service's conception of the relationship between forest management and the rural economy see Bernard Kalaora and Antoine Savoye, *La forêt pacifiée: sylviculture et sociologie au XIXe siècle* (Paris, 1986)

11. Pierre Leroux de la Roche, *La protection des paysages* (Paris, 1932), 31.

12. André Chastel, 'La notion de patrimoine', in *Les lieux de mémoire,* ed. Pierre Nora, vol. 2, part 1 (Paris, 1984–86). Also see Françoise Dubost, *Vert patrimoine: la constitution d'un nouveau domaine patrimonial* (Paris, 1994).

13. *Bulletin de la société des paysages de France* (1906), 17.

14. Leroux de la Roche, *La protection des paysages,* 32.

15. Patrick Young, 'A Tasteful Patrimony? Landscape, Preservation and Tourism in the Sites and Monuments Campaign, 1900–1935', *French Historical Studies* 32, no. 3 (Summer 2009): 447–77.

16. It was this impulse that guided measures taken to reforest vast tracts of land in France from the 1860s to the 1880s, see Tamara L. Whited, *Forests and Peasant Politics in Modern France* (New Haven, 2000).

17. Charles Valois, 'Le parc national de Pelvoux', in Aubreville et al., *Contribution,* 85.

18. Ibid.

19. Patick Kupper in this volume.

20. Gabriel Tallon, 'La réserve zoologique et botanique de Camargue', in Aubreville, *Contribution,* 39–57; A. Feuillée-Billot, 'La réserve des Sept-Iles', in ibid., 59–64; Pierre Chouard, 'La réserve naturelle de Neouvieille dans les Pyrenées centrales', in ibid., 65–74; P. Marié, 'Les réserves naturelles des Basses-Alpes', in ibid., 75–83; and Adek Selmi, 'L'émergence de l'idée du parc national en France: De la protection des paysages à l'experimentation colonial', in *Histoire des parcs nationaux: Comment prendre soin*

de la nature?, ed. Raphaël Larrère, Bernadette Lizet and Martine Berlan-Darqué (Versailles, 2009), 43–58.

21. Charles Valois and Georges Petit, eds., *Deuxième congrès international pour la protection de la nature (Paris 20 juin-4 juillet 1931), procès verbaux, rapports et voeux* (Paris, 1932), 3–4.

22. A. Joubert, 'Constitution et choix de réserves naturelles: réserves biologique forestières', in Aubreville et al., *Contribution,* 29

23. Paul de Peyerimhoff, 'Les "Parcs nationaux" d'Algérie', in Aubreville et al., *Contribution,* 127.

24. Joubert, 'Constitution et choix de réserves naturelles', in Aubreville et al., *Contribution,* 30.

25. Quoted in de Peyerimhoff, 'Les "parcs nationaux" d'Algérie', 128.

26. Ibid.

27. Ibid., 129–31. The 7,225 hectares included about a thousand hectares in the southern territories bordering the Sahara at the summit of Djebel Mzi and Djebel Aïssa.

28. Ibid., 132.

29. Ibid., 138.

30. See, by contrast, Jane Carruthers, *The Kruger National Park: A Social and Political History* (Pietermaritzburg, 1995).

31. See Diana Davis's extended and thorough discussion of how this narrative came to be constructed in Algeria from its conquest to the twentieth century in *Resurrecting the Granary of Rome: Environmental History and French Colonial Expansion in North Africa,* (Athens, Ohio, 2007), esp. chapters 3 and 4. Also see Caroline Ford, 'Reforestation, Landscape Conservation and Anxieties of Empire in French Colonial Algeria', *American Historical Review* 113, no. 2 (April 2008): 341–62. For the place of this Roman heritage in the French imagination see Patricia M. E. Lorcin, 'Rome and France in Africa: Recovering Colonial Algeria's Latin Past', *French Historical Studies* 25, no. 2 (Spring 2002): 295–327. Nabila Oulebsir explores the French initiatives to save the archeological vestiges of North Africa's Roman past as French 'patrimoine' in *Les usages du patrimoine: monuments, musées et politique coloniale en Algérie (1830-1930)* (Paris, 2004).

32. Louis Lavauden, 'Tunisie et les réserves naturelles', in Aubreville et al., *Contribution,* 139.

33. 'La destruction, dont les Arabes sont coutumiers, mais dont ils n'ont pas, hélas! le monopole, s'est exercée depuis les siècles sur toute cette région', Ibid., 147.

34. Léonce Joleaud, 'Réserves naturelles du Maroc', in Aubreville et al., *Contribution,* 151–57.

35. *Congrès international pour la protection de la nature: Faune, flore, sites, monuments naturels. Paris—mai–juin 1923,* 318.

36. André Aubreville, 'La protection de la flore en Afrique Occidentale Française', in Aubreville et al., *Contribution,* 223–25.

37. Georges Petit, 'Les réserves naturelles de Madagascar', in Aubreville et al., *Contribution,* 229.

38. Henri Perrier de la Bathie, 'Les reserves naturelles de Madagascar', *La terre et la vie,* no. 7 (August 1931): 427–42.

39. For Indochina, see Frédéric Thomas, *Histoire du régime et des services forestiers français en Indochine de 1862 à 1945* (Hanoi, 1999).
40. De Peyerimhoff, 'Les "parcs nationaux" d'Algérie', 138
41. Ford, 'Nature', 173–98.
42. De Peyerimhoff seems to recognize this irony in placing national parks in quotation in the title of his essay, 'Les "parcs nationaux" d'Algérie', 127.
43. Ford, 'Reforestation', 347, 358–60.
44. *Congrès international pour la protection de la nature: Faune, flore, sites, monuments naturels. Paris—mai–juin 1923*, 318–19.
45. Valois and Petit, *Deuxième congrès international*, 45.
46. Nicholas Luard, *The Wildlife Parks of Africa* (London, 1985), 55. He suggests that while the Belgian model potentially provided a bigger safeguard when it came to protecting the natural environment, this could be undercut by lack of funding because there would not be a public willing to vote and pay for sites from which they were excluded. Luard, however, does not acknowledge the significant number of reserves and parks that the French created in Africa in saying that 'the French, not a nation historically noted for vision or altruism, had surprisingly and to their credit proclaimed several important reserves in their African colonies during the 1940s' (60).
47. Daniel Brockington and James Igoe, "Eviction for Conservation: A Global Overview," *Conservation and Society* 4, no. 3 (2006): 424–70.

 CHAPTER 4

From Colonial Imposition
to National Icon
Malaysia's Taman Negara National Park

Jeyamalar Kathirithamby-Wells

The national park concept is perceived by some as incongruous and problematic with reference to the developing world associated with poverty, land
shortage and subsistence economies. Such critics see community-based forests, akin to traditionally protected areas, such as sacred groves, as more appropriate and viable alternatives.[1] Malaysia's Taman Negara, on the contrary,
makes a case for protected areas where circumstances favorable to rapid economic change have conditioned a different development trajectory. Helped by
the easy transition of a relatively small peasant population from a forest- to a
cash-crop rubber and oil palm economy,[2] the national park concept has served
as an easy fit for Malaysian development and nation building. Evolving from
the concept of sanctuaries for fauna preservation by the white hunting elite,
national parks in the tropics sought to reposition human-nature relations after
the example set by the Yellowstone National Park. As in the West, national
parks have privileged the aesthetic, scientific, educational and recreation interests of Southeast Asia's post-colonial urban middle class, in step with the
processes of democratization and modern nation building. Unprecedented
environmental degradation stemming from post-Second World War development has further emphasized the biological value of national parks as reposi-
tories for biodiversity, enhancing their importance as national heritage.[3]

Wildlife Preservation as a Colonial Project

Biological explorations during the age of European expansion transcended the
borders of empire and state, emphasizing the importance of co-opting nature
for national good, as amplified in the ideologies of the influential naturalists
Carl Linnaeus and Joseph Banks. The subsequent conquest of territory and the

associated 'taming' of the wilderness translated into environmentally embed-ded prejudices of place, race and individual rights.[4] The dismantling of these structures in the process of nation building in the developing world has inevi-tably interfaced with problems of nature conservation. The introduction of co-lonial forest reserves and protected areas as part of colonial 'territorialization' criminalized preexisting indigenous rights and practices and escalated prob-lems generated by population expansion and landlessness. Yet, the intrinsic value of nature has meant that protected areas have continued to remain firmly within the agenda of post-colonial development. Earlier debates surrounding their desirability have given way to present concerns over their management.[5] Furthermore, as Donald Worster has argued, despite popular perceptions of the elitist origins of 'protected areas', emerging concepts of democracy and values of social equality in Europe and North America have played no small part in shaping ideas of nature preservation.

> [A] huge paradox lay at the heart of democracy's relationship with nature. While proving terribly destructive to the environment, democracy at the same time encouraged people to seek in nature, rather than in traditions of church authority, a source of order, virtue, spirituality and value.[6]

Early European protected areas largely supported the recreational needs and national ethos of a fast-growing, urbanized middle class. Apart from helping to re-engage with the natural world, national parks as national monuments, in the sense of the *Naturdenkmal* promoted by the German forester Hugo Con-wentz, inspired feelings of shared cultural heritage.[7] But in the colonies pro-tected areas originated in the less lofty concern over big-game preservation by and for the hunting fraternity, promoted by the New York-based Boone & Crockett Club and the London-based Society for the Preservation of the (Wild) Fauna of the Empire (SPFE). Such reserves, created specifically for the preservation of selected big game principally in Africa, downgraded resident and dependent populations engaged in a symbiotic relation with their envi-ronment, such as the below-mentioned Batek of Taman Negara.

Though the initiatives of the Euro-American fauna preservationists focused primarily on the spectacular big game of the African continent, they deeply in-fluenced wildlife enthusiasts in colonial Asia. An outstanding example was the hunter-turned-conservationist Theodore Hubback, progenitor of peninsular Malaysia's Taman Negara (National Park). Born in Liverpool in 1872, Hub-back arrived in colonial Malaya (the present West Malaysia) in 1895, just two decades after Britain had extended its imperial arm into the barely explored and sparsely settled peninsular hinterland.[8] Hubback's encounter during his Malayan career with the rich and spectacular fauna included elephant, gaur (*serow*), rhinoceros, tapir, deer and wild pig. Familiar to planters as 'vermin',

they were attracted both to scrub surrounding the plantations and the suc-
culent rubber saplings within.[9] These herbivores, in turn, attracted tigers that,
not infrequently, preyed on humans, creating the perfect scenario that bred the
European planter-*shikari* (hunter).[10]

Bearing a deep affinity with the natural world, Hubback's interests clearly
extended beyond the profit motives of fellow plantation owners. Shortly after
the First World War, he left to study the rare sheep *Ovis dalli* in Alaska. The
North American sojourn familiarized Hubback with the wildlife preservation
movement and, inspired by Theodore Roosevelt (1859–1919), he turned from
hunting to game preservation. Upon his return to Malaya, Hubback settled
permanently in a remote village in the headwaters of the Jelai, a tributary of
the Pahang River. It proved an ideal location for his wildlife pursuits and near
enough to the state capital, Kuala Lipis, to steer a precocious conservation
campaign that soon alienated him from the European plantation community
and a government that backed plantation interests.

At the time Hubback arrived in Malaya, access to wild animals in the colony
was regulated by game laws based on the issue of revenue-generating hunting
licenses through the institution of 'closed' and 'open seasons'. Exempted was
subsistence hunting among the Malay peasantry and the relic forest dwellers
who used traps and snares and had little access to guns. The licensed shooting
of wild animals in defence of person and property under the new laws was
used liberally by gun-happy planters. Their activities, combined with those of
licensed trophy hunters, took a heavy toll on the rarer mammal species, push-
ing numbers to the brink of extinction. By the 1930s, rarely sighted were the
one- and the two-horned rhinos (*Rhinoceros sondaicus* and *Dicerorhinus su-
matrensis* respectively), hunted for their horns prized by the Chinese for their
averred pharmaceutical properties. Likewise, the shy gaur, which had followed
the trail of prehistoric swidden cultivators from mainland Asia, was reduced
to small relic populations.[11]

Official institutions in the colony, like the government museums service,
were well aware of the potential extinction of rare species but had insufficient
power to influence policy on wildlife protection. Instead, museums concentrated their resources on preparing for such an outcome by collecting and
inventorying faunal specimens for scientific study and display in local and metropolitan museums.[12] In 1921, Herbert Christopher Robinson, curator of the
Federated Malay States Museums Service, made a case for the preservation of
ten representative habitats, in line with current advances in tropical ecology, but
failed to win official support.[13] The lack of official action lent, however, a spur to
private initiative for fauna protection, with Theodore Hubback in the lead.

Hubback took the bold step of initiating separate wildlife administration
in the Malay Peninsula, challenging the established colonial practice of placing wildlife protection under forest management, such as in India and Burma.

He forged a new direction for fauna protection by forming, in 1921, an ad hoc Game Department with other European hunter-turned-preservationists serving as honorary game wardens. Existing game laws were upgraded and wildlife reserves created where virtually none had existed previously – with the exception of the Cior Reserve established in Pelus Valley, Perak (1903) for the protection of the gaur, which served exclusively the hunting pleasure of the Malay royalty and British officials. Locating herds within viable areas in terms of size and habitat, Hubback established a total of seven game reserves over the period 1921–37, including the Gunung Tahan reserve that formed the core of the later Taman Negara National Park. Envisaged as sanctuaries, the reserves provided refuge and breeding ground for threatened species, just like those established since the late 1890s in Britain's African colonies.

Though Hubback's bold and abrasive personality alienated him from officialdom in the peninsula, his enthusiasm for conservation and unrivalled knowledge of Malayan fauna gained support from metropolitan game conservation circles. Travelling to London in November 1925, he used his connections as a member of the SPFE to make a case for Malayan fauna protection with the Parliamentary Under-Secretary, W. G. A. Ormsby-Gore. However, the intermeshing lines of official and unofficial influence worked equally for the peninsula's planting community, overwhelmingly opposed to game protection and powerfully represented by the London-based Rubber Growers' Association. In the long-protracted controversy that followed, the fate of Hubback's vision was influenced by an evolving philosophy in the West of nature protection for the long-term interests of humanity.

Asia and the Internationalization of the National Park Concept

The dawn of the twentieth century saw the emergence – with the partial convergence by way of semiofficial social channels – of three streams of cross-Atlantic preservationist movements. These were, namely, the Boone & Crockett Club in the United States, founded in 1887 by President Theodore Roosevelt; the SPFE, founded in London in 1903 by Edward North Buxton, Member of Parliament; and the Amsterdam-based Society for the Protection of Nature Monuments (Vereeniging tot Behoud van Natuurmonumenten) founded in 1904 by Pieter Gerbrand van Tienhoven.[14] In addition to the Dutch effort, nature monument initiatives in Brussels, Paris and Geneva (1904–10) culminated in the International Commission for the Protection of Nature (1913). Transimperial attempts at coordinating wildlife protection resulted in the landmark Conference on African Wildlife convened in London in 1900, with a shift in emphasis from the sole protection of game to all forms of wildlife.[15] In the British colonies it implied abandoning confidence in the sufficiency of game laws in favour of the German concept of wildlife reserve, akin to the American campaign for 'fenced range'. It was symptomatic of an inter-European consensus on nature preservation.[16]

Fully in line with international developments in nature protection, Theodore Hubback proposed the creation of a national park in April 1926 by extending the existing Gunung Tahan Game Reserve in Pahang into the headwaters of the Kelantan and Terengganu rivers. Just a few months before in 1925, the King Albert National Park in the Congo (later renamed Virunga) had been established as a gorilla sanctuary of just 20,270 hectares, evincing the growing appreciation of single species as part and parcel of a more complex natural environment. Resonating Hubback's ambition in the peninsula was the consolidation, in 1926, of several game reserves in South Africa to form the Kruger National Park.[17] Hubback's scheme to preserve the ecologically important yet sparsely populated lands around the headwaters was far sighted, pragmatic and well timed.

In Britain, the Earl of Onslow succeeded Buxton as President of the SPFE, continuing the direct line of communication between wildlife preservation and the politics of empire. When two years later the above-mentioned Under-Secretary of Parliament Ormsby-Gore visited Malaya, he envisaged Hubback's national park proposal as a tangible solution to the wildlife controversy, since it drew a clear boundary between the zones of wildlife protection and agriculture. Hubback's national park proposal anticipated Onslow's plea to the House of Commons in 1929 that the government make 'every proper and reasonable effort' to preserve game through the creation of reserves and national parks. The motion was tacitly supported by the Fourth Pacific Science Congress held in Bandung in the same year, where the London-based anatomist and anthropologist Elliot Smith highlighted the scientific dimensions of protection and the importance of extending its remit beyond colonial Africa.[18] Faced with the conflicting claims of conservation and the plantation economy, the Colonial Office resolved that agricultural protection should be matched by adequate provision for wildlife through the creation of one large reserve.[19] By the end of 1929, the Sultans of Kelantan and Terengganu, approached by their respective British Advisors, indicated their willingness to add 98,797 hectares and 68,420 hectares respectively for extending the existing 142,000-hectare Gunung Tahan Reserve in Pahang to create a national park.[20] In anticipation of its realization, all other reserves were abolished with the single exception of the Kerau Game Reserve in Pahang. The reserve was saved through the intervention of Governor Sir Hugh Clifford who, during his early carrier as a pioneer administrator in the state, had nurtured a deep affection for its people and environment.[21]

In conjunction with the policy for wildlife protection, the Colonial Office also set up a commission to investigate the current status of wildlife in the country.[22] This Wild Life Commission was headed by Hubback. Its insightful report, published in 1932, was based on the comments of over 500 stake-holders, representing a cross-section of the peasant and plantation sectors and related government officials. In marked contrast to the lack of consulta-tion on the similarly controversial on-going decentralization issue,[23] the Wild Life Commission Report represented, arguably, the first public referendum in Malaya. Compared to the materialistic bias of the European plantation sec-tor, the views of the Asian populace, especially the Malay peasantry, reflected philosophical tolerance and practical accommodation to the ambiguities of nature. Indeed, they shared a concern over the fast pace of development and cognizance that indiscriminate hunting would have a ripple effect through the food chain. The reduction of tigers would arrest their check on the wild pig population destructive to agriculture. Similarly, the sambar (*Cervus unicolor*), if more intensively hunted for food, 'may upset the balance of nature to such an extent that tiger may take to cattle killing'. One witness feared that the sam-bar, unless protected, might never be seen by his grandchildren. Generally, the anxiety expressed by the largely Malay rural witnesses over wildlife depletion was rooted in mixed religious, utilitarian, ethical and aesthetic concerns, not widely different from informed attitudes in the West.[24]

Traditional Malay perceptions of nature were defined by spatial division between the wild and the tame. The former, represented by the forest, was the habitation of beasts and the aboriginal people (Orang Asli); the latter, the cultivated landscape of the peasantry. Less well defined were their respective claims on forest resources, resolved, ideally, through ethical values of fair play. As one Malay interrogated by the Wild Life Commission pointed out:

> The Lord God created man and beast; the beast like us, has to look for food, and so long as the beast keeps to his proper haunts and limits, no action should be taken against him … I like seladang, elephant and tiger who all do good to the jungle as men do good outside.[25]

The ambiguous relation between people and the forest was complicated by colonial interventions. Government forest reserves impinged on local live-lihoods by restricting customary access to land and the extraction of forest products. In British Malaya, resolution of this problem dovetailed with the policy of peasantization through the colonial government's promotion of settled agriculture. But it left unresolved the fate of the forest-resident com-munities that, as elsewhere in the developing world, continued to dominate the wildlife park narrative. The Malayan national park project represented Hubback's bold and imaginative contextualization of a Euro-American con-cept within the constraints of colonial development. As such, it was character-ized by similar problems that plagued the designation of wildlife parks and reserves in other colonial settings. If forest-dwelling people represented one issue, agricultural development posed another, and earned a higher priority on the imperial agenda in British Malaya. The 434,340 hectares earmarked for the Malayan national park comprised largely steep land above an altitude of 150 meters, rising to an average of 1,600 meters. Though fulfilling the aim of preserving the spectacular, in this case big mammals, the park incorporated barely 10 percent of the species-rich lowlands.[26]

Pride of Empire and Nation

Plans for the national park were arrested by the Great Depression. Governor Sir Cecil Clementi revived the controversial plans for decentralization as an economy measure but within the context of a wider vision for Malayan Union involving the integration of the Straits Settlements, the Federated Malay States and the Unfederated Malay States. The proposal involved administrative re-trenchment and decentralization that ran contrary to Hubback's plan for fully integrated wildlife management. Nevertheless, he skilfully used the notion of a union to promote the national park as a symbol of unity and national pride.

The conservation lobby, though European led, appreciated the importance of engaging Malayans in the national park project. Turning adversity to advantage, it co-opted the English language press to launch a protracted campaign to extend public understanding of the national park concept, novel in Asia, and to contextualize it within the Malayan socio-political landscape. The SPFE representative, Sir Thomas Comyn-Platt, who visited Malaya in 1935 under the auspices of the Colonial Office, placed his confidence in the sovereign influence of the Sultans to create greater environmental awareness among the Malays as part of a wider effort to win public cooperation. National sentiments, which within the Malayan federal system of separate sovereign states had had little scope for foment, was evoked for the first time by the English-language press, which included within its readership a small but important Malayan middle class.

The issue of nature conservation was ardently supported by the Malayan press. It reminded the economically focused Malayan government about the pledge to protect nature made by the Labour Prime Minister, Ramsay Macdonald, at the 1931 Paris International Congress for the Protection of Nature. A keen conservationist and subsequently honorary member of the Society for the Prevention of Cruelty to Animals (SPCA), he had declared the British government 'a trustee for the protection of nature' for future generations and the world at large. The Malayan press hit upon the compelling notion that if the proposed national park were implemented without delay, it would be 'the first of its kind in Asia' and a national pride.[27]

A strong rival was the neighbouring Netherlands Indies, which did not experience the same three-way tension between conservationists, estate owners and the official body of administrators and scientists. In fact, in the Netherlands Indies, Dutch scientists had secured the 1916 Nature Monuments Ordinance, based on which several nature reserves were established in Java.[28] Dutch initiatives culminated in a unanimous vote cast in 1930 by the Volksraad (People's Council, with local and European representatives) for the creation of wildlife sanctuaries. Between 1932 and 1940 some seventeen sanctuaries were established shortly after Malaya had abolished all, except the Tahan Reserve set aside for the national park.[29] The headway being made in the Netherlands Indies spurred SPFE support for Hubback's ambitions.[30]

The irrefutable merit of the political ideology at the heart of the campaign compromised the government. The national park as a symbol of a pan-Malayan identity could help mend the ethnic fissures bred by economic hardship and the awakening of self-identity associated with the rise of nationalism across Asia. The pro-Malay British policy had done little to alter the status of the Chinese and Indians as sojourners and contributed to ethnic nationalism inspired by political transformations in India and China, in parallel with the rise of pan-Malay nationalism.[31] The concept of a national park as a shared heritage made sense in a society divided by race and religion. The argument, vigorously campaigned by the influential English-language press, was reminiscent of the role played by newspapers, like the *Springfield* [Massachusetts] and the *Republican,* during the 1880s national parks campaign in the United States.[32] The Malayan scientific civil service, unsympathetic to separate wildlife management, remained out of the press debate. But its publications on salient issues of tropical conservation, namely, erosion and biodiversity loss as by-products of deforestation, were strong endorsements for the press campaign.[33] A leading daily candidly observed: 'It is absolutely imperative that large sections of the country should be allowed to remain in the primeval condition … and so long as this is recognized it is surely also no great step to keep not only the forest but also the fauna in that forest in a state of conservation.'[34]

The Malayan press campaign was further boosted by the success of the 1933 International Convention for the Protection of Fauna and Flora held at the House of Lords, with Onslow at the head of the British delegation. This meeting was significant in two respects. First, it represented an important shift in British policy from reliance on game laws to the provision of game parks for wildlife protection. Second, the declaration by Crown Prince Leopold of Belgium at a post-conference lecture that nature conservation was an 'ethical and economic necessity of civilized nations' gave public expression to a new imperial philosophy.[35]

Despite wide support within the empire, translation of the policy for wildlife protection proved problematic for the Malayan administration under the strain of economic depression. The conservation lobby was quick to respond by advertising tourism as a potential source of profit from the national park. Hubback questioned:

[W]hy ignore that Wild Life is one of the resources of the country? It is so recognized in North America, in South Africa and many other countries. It is probably not recognized as such in China, Tibet or Siberia. Whom shall we follow?[36]

Given the resounding success of nature tourism in the United States, he was widely supported by press editorial leads promoting the national park as a worthy investment for recreation and tourism. During his 1935 visit to Malaya, Sir Thomas Comyn-Platt explicitly vouched for the national park's potential for sightseeing and recreation, probably under the spell of the Tembeling River, which subsequently marked the southern border of Taman Negara. The same year the three Malayan rulers involved in the park concession acceded to naming it the King George V National Park, in commemoration of the twenty-fifth jubilee celebrations of the British monarch. The generous gesture symbolically incorporated the colony within the conservationist ideals of empire. Due to legal and administrative delays, formal declaration of the national park was postponed until 1939.

In comparison, the Netherlands East Indies, which had steered a smoother course towards colonial conservation, designated large protected areas during 1934–36 ranging between 200,000–400,000 hectares each, but declared national parks only long after independence. Malaya, nevertherless, lost out in the race to India where Jim Corbett, Hubback's counterpart, had in a parallel campaign backed by the SPFE created the Hailey (the later Corbett) National Park located in the Himalayan terai.

In contrast to colonial conservation in Asia, nature conservation in the United States had originated in the preservation of monumental and scenic features and landscapes, such as the Yosemite Park (1864), as cultural artifices. Concerns over species and ecological preservation developed only gradually, as attested in the creation of the less visually spectacular Everglades National Park (1934). Conversely, nature preservation, first mooted in colonial Asia for the preservation of rare fauna sans the cultural trappings, soon became part of the British mandate for fostering progress and civilization. In both instances nature protection evolved into the provision of multiple services, with tourism standing in for capitalist development.

A National Icon: From George V to the 'National Park'

On Malaya's independence in 1957, King George V National Park was renamed 'Taman Negara', literally meaning 'National Park'. The new denomination thus severed the park from its colonial moorings and heralded its status as the peninsula's only 'national park'. Once seen by nationalists as created for

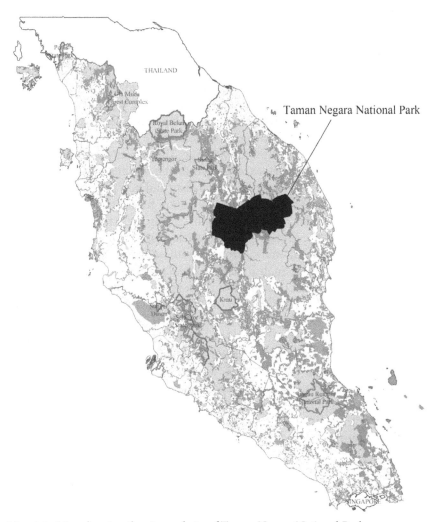

Map 4.1. Map showing the size and site of Taman Negara National Park.

the recreational needs of the colonizers, it soon gained an iconic status among citizens of the new nation, following neglect during the Second World War and postwar reconstruction. As of the 1970s, rising environmental conscious- ness among a rapidly expanding middle class – a by-product of development – brought Taman Negara back into the nation's consciousness.

The steep and difficult terrain of Taman Negara, which shelters the au- tochthonous hunter-gatherer people of the Negrito Batek, was little known to the majority Malayan populace. Even among the rural Malays only a small number were settled in the upper Tembeling. The majority lived in the coastal areas and lower river valleys, except when driven into the interior by conflict and economic distress.[37] However, nationalism and new perceptions of sover- eignty, territoriality and heritage drew attention to the 2,000-meter Gunung Tahan – the peninsula's highest mountain – rising majestically over the park landscape. Within the climate of nascent Malay nationalism in the 1930s, Gu- nung Tahan (meaning literally: 'strong', 'steadfast', 'firm') inspired the 'inven- tion of tradition' by the English-educated Malay nationalist and intellectual, Ishak Haji Muhammad. Drawing from past Hindu traditions associated with the holy Mount Meru,[38] he imbued the little-known Gunung Tahan (Mount Tahan) with national significance in his satirical Malay novel *The Prince of Gunung Tahan* (1937). In the narrative, the prince presides over the exclu- sive mental and physical space of the Malay world in harmonious interac- tion with nature and the aboriginal people, traditionally perceived as wild (*liar*). The park's creation under colonial initiative, incorporating the sacred Mount Tahan, is portrayed as a transgression of indigenous sovereign space. In retrospect, the novel serves as an insightful political comment on the er- ror of Western development and the desecration of nature by park-related tourism.[39]

Reprinted at independence in 1957, *The Prince of Gunung Tahan* symbol- ized the reappropriation of nature by its legitimate custodians. At the time, there was little in the way of recreational and educational tourism among Malayans to repudiate Ishak's perception of Taman Negara as serving strictly colonial interests. With the fast pace of development, attitudes soon changed. Improved education and rising standards of living triggered the growth of a middle class seeking a better quality of life. As well as serving new recreational needs, Taman Negara in its pristine quality and permanence became a meta- phor for nature among a people witnessing the disappearance of their natural environment.

Symptomatic of a new national consciousness was the first major scientific survey undertaken in 1971 by the Malayan Nature Society, the nation's long- established and articulate conservation NGO. In the face of escalating logging in the peninsula (and indeed in the region) the society sought to secure the integrity of Taman Negara by creating a wider awareness and interest in its importance as a natural heritage. Apart from providing basic information on the park's natural history, the report stressed its recreational value. Suggested were river trips, wildlife observation and hiking.[40] These efforts helped instil in the young a sense of the intrinsic value of Taman Negara. The concurrent development of the tourist industry and the related boost to international tourism played no small part in shaping public perception of Taman Negara as a flagship of the nation. The facilities the park offered for recreational tourism and outdoor adventure resonated with the improved quality of life sought by the rising middle class. Increasing urbanization among Malayans and a sharp rise in population dispelled perceptions of national parks as elitist projects and exacerbated the lack of recreational and green spaces.[41] However, state reluctance to relinquish land to the central government for protected areas has led to the creation of 'State Parks'. These, such as the Endau-Rompin Park (1987) straddling the Johor-Pahang border and the Wang Mu State Park in Perlis (1997), remain outside the purview of the 1980 National Parks Act. Despite their recreational and scientific value, their insecurity serves to emphasize Taman Negara's unique status.

Compared to Indonesia and Thailand where peasant encroachment and illegal and extra-legal logging constitute the single-most threat to protected areas,[42] challenges to Taman Negara's sanctity have been largely state sponsored. These include development projects during the 1970s and 1980s for logging, mega-dam building on the upper Tembeling, and jeep track construction to link the park headquarters to the foot of the mountain. NGOs, including the Malayan Nature Society and the Malaysian branch of the World Wide Fund for Nature (WWF), were involved in educating the public about the implications of proposed development in the national park in violation of the original 1939 National Park Act. The campaigns progressively raised the level of public outrage, which even the allegedly authoritarian government under Prime Minister Mahathir Muhammad during the 1980s and 1990s was unable to ignore. Only a conciliatory discourse between government and scientists within the environmental NGOs averted political foment.[43]

In a society where public expression is often muted by political sensitivities, the stewardship of Taman Negara, as an articulation of democratic rights and the rule of law, has given citizens a sense of empowerment. Moreover, Taman Negara's profile within the development of international environmentalism has contributed hugely to the emergence of an articulate civil society able to engage with the democratic concerns of public rights, accountability and the enforcement of law.[44] Within this context, stewardship of the national park has lent a new dimension to national identity. Transcending federal-state rivalries, preferential land rights and racial and religious divisions that continue to run deep, the national park as a shared heritage for common good serves as a symbol of unity.

Illustration 4.1. View of Gunung Tahan, the highest peak in Taman Negara (T. Whitmore)

Illustration 4.2. A Tapir (*Tapirus indicus*), one of the keystone species protected in the national park (T. Whitmore)

Illustration 4.4. Visitors canoeing (K. Rubeli)

Illustration 4.3. Batik foraging (K. Rubeli)

One Size Fits All?

A 'park' (Malay *taman*: garden, park) serves, fundamentally, as a vehicle for social interaction with nature at the aesthetic, educational and recreational level. However, at another level parks are perceived as 'wilderness', or nature in its pristine state, the living space of forest-dependent people and all life forms. In Malaysia, this ambiguous aspect of park making is encapsulated in the controversial status of Taman Negara's hunter-gatherer Batek population, a subdivision of the Negrito or Semang.[45]

Approximately 600 Batek are currently resident within the boundaries of Taman Negara, including some who sought refuge from development pressures outside. Like the Pygmies of the Parc National Albert, the Batek were classified under colonial rule as part of the fauna.[46] Regarded as the wild 'other' by the succeeding post-colonial government as well, the Batek 'problem' highlights the ambiguous status of national parks as both managed areas and wilderness. The Batek's traditional use of blowpipes and a strict ban on guns inform the park's management policy of sustainable foraging and protection of the eco-system, which condemns them to an externally imposed imagined 'tradition' that denies change. Such pursuance of a low-impact Batek hunter-gatherer lifestyle disregards the impinging cash economy and the changes in the Batek's demographic structure arising from population increase, falling infant mortality and the influx of refugees displaced by government land development schemes. Especially contentious are the ban on guns and the restriction on the historic trade in forest products, mainly bamboo and *gaharu* (eaglewood from *Aquilaria malaccensis*), which encourages poaching and smuggling across the porous Thai-Malaysian border.[47] All this said, even critics who voice the lack of a clear official policy for the Batek concede that the national park offers the best option for their survival.[48] Protected from the pressures of development, the Batek are able to bring their skills to the tourist sector thereby gaining the opportunity to adapt to the forces of socio-economic change, as they had had before the fast pace of development since independence.[49]

Taman Negara has experienced neither the large displacement of humans by reservations in Africa and India nor the scale of peasant and logging encroachments witnessed in Thailand's 'model' Khao Yai National Park and Indonesia's national parks of Kutai in Kalimantan (1982) and Gunung Leuser (1993) in Sumatra.[50] Yet, Taman Negara is no exception to the human-nature tensions inherent in the concept of nature protection. Discernable are the pressures of tourism, agricultural expansion, settlement in the adjacent Tembiling area and illegal logging and poaching.[51] The infringement of development on buffer areas and biological corridors foreshadows the imminent 'island status' of Taman Negara in biological terms.[52] With the peninsula's forests reduced, the national park has become more critical than ever before for providing a refuge for endangered species.

Since the 1970s Malaysia's forests have been substantially reduced through accelerated plantation development and logging. Only 5.2 percent, or 7,000 hectares, of permanent forest was left by the end of the last millennium, with more than half lying within Taman Negara.[53] Its value as the largest single protected biological unit, constituting a representative sample of virgin tropical forest, further enhances its value in biodiversity terms.[54] With reference to trees alone, it carries 746 out of the peninsula's 2,830 endemic tree species.[55] In the post-Rio 1992 era of renewed emphasis on biodiversity and indigenous knowledge, the implied importance of the national park as a biological resource pool enhances its economic value far beyond the gains from tourism.

As the example of Taman Negara demonstrates, national parks have followed the trajectory of human advancement for more than a century, taking on a multiplicity of functions beyond those originally envisaged by their early proponents. An indispensable prescription for negotiating nature-human relations within the framework of economic development and nation building,[56] the national park concept remains, perforce, a 'one size that fits all'.

Notes

1. Madhav Gadgil and V. D. Vartak, 'The Sacred Uses of Nature', in *Social Ecology*, ed. Ramachandra Guha (Oxford 1994), 82–85; Madhav Gadgil and Ramachandra Guha, *Ecology and Equity: The Use and Abuse of Nature in Contemporary India* (London 1996), 159–62.

2. The success of smallholder rubber stands in stark contrast to the disastrous East African Groundnut Scheme. See Roderick P. Neumann, 'Ways of Seeing Africa: Colonial Recasting of African Society and Landscape in Serengeti National Park', *Ecumene* 2, no. 2 (1995): 157; and Jeyamalar Kathirithamby-Wells, 'The Implications of Plantation Agriculture for Biodiversity in Peninsular Malaysia: An Historical Perspective', in *Beyond the Sacred Forest: Complicating Conservation in Southeast Asia*, ed. Michael Dove, Percy E. Sajise and Amity A. Doolittle (Durham, 2011), 62–90.

3. These objectives were explicitly stated in the Third Malaysia Plan, see Government of Malaysia, *Third Malaysia Plan 1976–1980* (Kuala Lumpur, 1976), 219–20.

4. David Arnold, *The Problem of Nature: Environment, Culture and European Expansion* (Oxford, 1987), 189.

5. Navjot S. Sodhi et al., eds., *Biodiversity and Human Livelihoods in Protected Areas: Case Studies from the Malay Archipelago* (Cambridge, 2008); Lena Topp and Christina Eghenter, eds., *Kayan Mentarang National Park in the Heart of Borneo* (Jakarta, 2005); Tuck-Po Lye, 'The Wild and the Tame in Protected Areas Management, Peninsular Malaysia', in Dove, Sajise and Doolittle, *Beyond the Sacred Forest*, 46–49 and 52–58.

6. Donald Worster, 'John Muir and the Modern Passion for Nature', *Environmental History* 10, no. 1 (2005): 12.

7. Hugo Conwentz, *The Care of Natural Monuments* (Cambridge, 1909), 185; Paul Jepson and Roger Whittaker, 'Histories of Protected Areas: Internationalisation of Conserva-

tion Values and Their Adoption in the Netherlands Indies (Indonesia)', *Environment and History* 8 (2002): 135–36.

8. The British settled Penang (1786) and Singapore (1819), which together with Melaka, acquired from the Dutch in 1824, formed the Straits Settlements under the Governor in Singapore. Intervention into the Malay states, beginning in 1874, led to the formation in 1900 of the Federated Malay States (FMS), comprising the states of Perak, Selangor, Negeri Sembilan and Pahang under the indirect rule of Residents, headed by the governor in Singapore acting as High Commissioner. The remaining states of Kedah, Perlis, Terengganu and Kelantan, which received British Advisors, constituted the 'Unfederated Malay States'.

9. Jeyamalar Kathirithamby-Wells, 'Human Impact of Large Mammal Populations in Peninsular Malaysia from the Nineteenth- to the Mid-twentieth Century', in *Paper Landscapes: Explorations in the Environmental History of Indonesia*, ed. Peter Boomgaard, Freek Colombijn and David Henley (Leiden, 1997), 215–24.

10. Big-game hunting was largely the prerogative of the ruling class. The average peasant, who hunted deer for consumption by trapping and shooting, was generally more tolerant of vermin, regarded as part and parcel of the natural order.

11. Kathirithamby-Wells, 'Human Impact', 221–22.

12. Jeyamalar Kathirithamby-Wells, 'Peninsular Malaysia in the Context of Natural History and Colonial Science', *New Zealand Journal of Asian Studies* 11, no. 1 (2009): 361–63.

13. Jeyamalar Kathirithamby-Wells, *Nature and Nation: Forests and Development in Peninsular Malaysia* (Copenhagen, 2005), 168–72.

14. Jepson and Whittaker, 'Histories of Protected Areas', 133–36.

15. For a background to the 1900 Convention see Bernhard Gissibl, 'German Colonialism and the Beginnings on International Wildlife Preservation in Africa', *German Historical Institute Bulletin Supplement* 3 (2006): 121–43.

16. John M. MacKenzie, *The Empire of Nature: Hunting, Conservation and British Imperialism* (Manchester, 1988), 202; Jepson and Whittaker, 'Histories of Protected Areas', 137–38.

17. Jane Carruthers, *The Kruger National Park: A Social and Political History* (Pietermaritzburg, 1995); MacKenzie, *Empire of Nature*, 266–67.

18. Smith was appointed the first chairman of a Standing Committee for the Protection of Nature in and around the Pacific, formed during the congress.

19. For species that could not effectively be protected in the proposed national park, a second was proposed in Johor under the patronage of Sultan Abu Bakar, a keen hunter and naturalist, which never materialized.

20. By the subsequent Enactment 14 of 1938 for the constitution of the 434,300 hectare-National Park Terengganu contributed 101,300 hectares, Kelantan 85,300 hectares and Pahang 247,700 hectares.

21. See Hugh Charles Clifford, *At the Court of Pelesu and Other Malayan Stories* (Kuala Lumpur, 1993).

22. See Kathirithamby-Wells, *Nature and Nation*, 204–8.

23. Rupert Emerson, *Malaysia: A Study in Direct and Indirect Rule* (Kuala Lumpur, 1964), 321.

24. Keith Thomas, *Man and the Natural World: Changing Attitudes in England 1500–1800* (Harmondsworth, 1984): 23–24.

25. Government of Malaya, *Report of the Wild Life Commission: Recommendations* (Singapore, 1932), 135.
26. David R. Wells, 'Taman Negara and Ornithology', *Journal of Wild Life and Parks* 10 (1990): 143.
27. *The Straits Times*, 27 August 1931, Editorial; *The Straits Times*, 5 August 1931; see Kathirithamby-Wells, *Nature and Nation*, 210–11.
28. Karel Willem Dammerman, *Preservation of Wildlife and Nature Reserves in the Netherlands* (Bandung, 1929), 67–68; Pieter Honig and Frans Verdoor, *Science and Scientists in the Netherlands Indies* (New York, 1945), 420.
29. Peter Boomgaard, 'Oriental Nature, Its Friends and Its Enemies: Conservation of Nature in Late Colonial Indonesia, 1889–1949', *Environmental History* 5 (1999): 269; Jepson and Whittaker, 'Histories of Protected Areas', 151.
30. The National Archives/Public Record Office London, CO 717/62/4, SPFE to Lord Passfield, 5 September 1929.
31. Emerson, *Malaysia:* 322–23, 505–6; William R. Roff, *The Origins of Malay Nationalism* (Kuala Lumpur, 1967), 148–49.
32. See Alfred Runte, *National Parks: The American Experience* (London, 1987), 12–13.
33. See Kathirithamby-Wells, *Nature and Nation*, 169–76.
34. *The Straits Times*, 4 October 1929.
35. Jepson and Whittaker, 'Histories of Protected Areas', 142–43; Kathirithamby-Wells, *Nature and Nation*, 214–15.
36. *The Times of Malaya*, 8 December 1930.
37. Ronald G. Cant, *An Historical Geography of Pahang* (Singapore, 1973), 71.
38. Jeya Kathirithamby-Wells, 'Socio-political Structures and the Southeast Asian Ecosystem: An Historical Perspective up to the Early Nineteenth Century', in *Asian Perceptions of Nature: A Critical Appraisal,* ed. Ole Bruun and Arne Kalland (London, 1995), 27.
39. See Kathirithamby-Wells, *Nature and Nation*, 246–47.
40. *Malayan Nature Journal* 24 (1971): 112–17.
41. Kathirithamby-Wells, *Nature and Nation*, 418–19, 422–23.
42. Peter Dauvergne, *Loggers and Degradation in Pacific Asia: Corporations and Environmental Management* (Cambridge, 2001), 132–33, 158; Kim H. Tan, *Soils in the Humid Tropics and Monsoon Region of Indonesia* (Boca Raton, 2008), 356.
43. Kathirithamby-Wells, *Nature and Nation*, 325–28.
44. Habibul Haque Khondker, 'Environment and Global Civil Society', *Asian Journal of Social Sciences* 29, no. 1 (2001): 58–59.
45. Kirk Endicott, 'Batek History, Interethnic Relations and Sub-group Dynamics', in *Indigenous Peoples and State: Politics, Land and Ethnicity in the Malay Peninsula and Borneo,* ed. Robert L. Winzeler (New Haven, 1997), 31–32.
46. For a discussion of British colonial policy on the human element in protected areas see Neumann, 'Ways of Seeing Africa', 164–65.
47. See 'Smuggling of Tiger from Malaysia', 15 July 2009 and 'Fighting Back: Working with the Local Community to Protect Taman Negara Tiger Corridor', 25 September 2009, Malaysian Conservation Alliance for the Tiger; S. M. Moh. Idris, President of Sahabat Alam Malaysia (SAM), 'Wildlife Protection: Snuffing Out the Smugglers', *Malay Mail,* 26 January 2011.

48. See e.g., Lye, 'The Wild and the Tame', 55–56.
49. Endicott, 'Batek History', 37–42.
50. On these parks, see Jin Sato, 'Public Land for the People: The Institutional Basis of Community Forestry in Thailand', *Journal of Southeast Asian Studies* 34, no. 2 (2003): 335; John F. McCarthy, 'Power and Interest in Sumatra's Rainforest Frontier: Clientelist Coalition, Illegal Logging and Conservation in the Alas Valley', *Journal of Southeast Asian Studies* 33, no. 1 (2003): 82–83; Moira Moeliono, 'Hands off, Hands on: Communities and the Management of National Parks in Indonesia', in *Biodiversity and Human Livelihoods in Protected Areas: Case Studies from the Malay Archipelago,* ed. Navjot S. Sodhi et al. (Cambridge, 2008), 167.
51. Mohd Khan b. Monin Khan, 'Large Animals of Taman Negara', *Journal of Wild Life and Parks* 10 (1990): 166; W. E. M. van der Schot, 'Aborigines in Taman Negara: The Impact of a [hunter-gatherer] Community on a Lowland Forest Eco-system', *Journal of Wild Life and Parks* 10 (1990): 172–83.
52. Wells, 'Taman Negara and Ornithology', 143, 145; David J. Chivers, 'The Primates of Taman Negara', *Journal of Wild Life and Parks* 10 (1990): 157.
53. Forest Department, *Annual Report 2000,* Table 1: 77.
54. Timothy C. Whitmore, *Tropical Rain Forests of the Far East* (Oxford, 1984): 21–22.
55. Francis S. P. Ng, 'Taman Negara as a Centre for Endemicity for Trees', *Journal of Wild Life and Parks* 10 (1990): 52.
56. Both Indonesia and Thailand created national parks as part of their development agendas. See Robert Cribb, *The Politics of Environmental Protection in Indonesia* (Clayton, Vic., 1988), 13–25; Pinkaew Laungaramsri, 'On the Politics of Nature Conservation in Thailand', *Kyoto Review of Southeast Asia* 2 (October 2002): 2, http://kyotoreview .cseas.kyoto-u.ac.jp/issue/issue1/article_168.html (accessed 29 October 2011).

CHAPTER 5

A Bavarian Serengeti

Space, Race and Time in the Entangled History
of Nature Conservation in East Africa and Germany

Bernhard Gissibl

In 1964, the Frankfurt Zoo director and conservation celebrity Bernhard Grzimek approached the government of the German federal state of Hesse with the plan to establish a 'new kind of landscape zoo' in the forested mountain range of the Taunus. As an outpost of the Frankfurt Zoo, the proposed *Tierfreiheit* should translate the wildlife experience of East Africa's national parks into Germany's cultural landscape. European and exotic game were to be kept together in herds in one single, vast estate, and zebras and antelopes as well as European bison, beavers, lynxes and wild horses should be allowed to roam unimpeded by cages. A miniature train was supposed to shuttle visitors through the park and allow for visual recourse to Europe's and Africa's charismatic wildlife. In Grzimek's vision, the animals would soon habituate to the presence of human spectators. Western Germans would thus have an opportunity to see Africa's magnificent game as well as their own native fauna free in a natural habitat, while the abandonment of all forest management should allow the landscape of the *Tierfreiheit* to gradually reverse into the presumed original state of the German forest centuries ago. Germany would gain at least one place where the country's almost extinct, original fauna could be observed.[1]

Several Frankfurt-based natural scientists supported the project as suited to 'inculcate due respect for living nature' into people, while the Hessian government sympathized with its potential to draw tourists to a rural backwater.[2] Professional organizations of German foresters and hunters as well as homeland (*Heimat*) preservation societies, however, were appalled by the prospect of 'lions under oak trees'.[3] They feared the devastation of well-managed forests through the detrimental impact of gregarious ungulates and decried Grzimek's 'miniature translation of the African Serengeti' as an alienation of the German landscape through non-native species. 'Exotic game parks', the Schutzgemeinschaft Deutscher Wald (Society for the Protection of the German Forest) stated apodictically, 'do not fit into the German landscape.'[4]

Fierce opposition, insecure funding and a lack of political will nipped the project in the bud. Grzimek's undetermined attempt to collapse safari park, zoological garden and national park into one hybrid landscape could thus be relegated to an odd footnote in the history of German conservation if the project didn't reveal the awkward relationship between animals, landscape and German environmental identities that have hitherto been overlooked in the historiography of German conservation. The *Tierfreiheit* highlights entanglements between nature conservation in Germany and Africa and the instrumental role of individual conservation entrepreneurs like Bernhard Grzimek in transferring ideas and concepts of conservation across continents. Inspired as it was by the example of East African national parks, the *Tierfreiheit* was an important precursor to the establishment of Germany's first national park in the Bavarian Forest in 1970. At the same time, the controversies over animals and German nature in the 1960s stood in a longer tradition of efforts to reclaim an 'original' German nature by restoring the presence of the country's large fauna. These concerns over German environmental identities date back to the late nineteenth century, when German conservationism originated in anxieties over environmental degradation and species extinction on a global scale. Already then, ideas about German nature were negotiated in a global context, and the conflation of space, species and identity was forged at the frontiers of Germany's colonial encounter with the charismatic big game of East Africa.

This chapter seeks to integrate the colonial experience into German environmental historiography by reflecting the entanglements between conservationist thinking and practice in Germany and East Africa from the late nineteenth century up to the establishment of Germany's first national park in 1970. Adopting a transnational and postcolonial perspective on German conservation, this essay pursues three separate yet intertwined objectives. First, it establishes the importance of the colonial encounter for nature conservation and environmental identities in Germany. The obsession with 'characteristic' animals and their geopolitical and racialized interpretation as products and signifiers of their *Lebensraum* was essentially shaped in the colonial encounter and had far-reaching ramifications for German ideas about nature. Second, an analysis of the conservationist entanglements between Germany and East Africa extends the focus of existing interpretations of Tanzania's conservation history, which usually concentrate on the British period and after.[5] This essay situates the origins of Tanzania's 'environmental-conservation complex'[6] in the decades of German colonial rule previous to the First World War. Finally, by introducing East Africa as a triangulation point for the transfer of the national park idea between the United States and Germany, this essay restores a hitherto overlooked dimension of the reception and implementation of the national park idea in Germany.[7] It complicates narratives of global diffusion of a 'Yellowstone model' of conservation. In the making of West Germany's first national park in 1970, the media-transmitted, virtual ecology of the Tanzanian Serengeti was more influential than any other place in shaping German assumptions of what a national park ought to be.

In what follows, I shall first outline the significance of German colonial rule for the localization and implementation of 'Western' ideas, sensibilities and practices of nature conservation in East Africa. The chapter will then explore the consequences of the colonial encounter with Africa's wildlife for conservation in Germany. The confrontation with an allegedly primeval wilderness in Africa resulted in a quest for restoring a lost originality to the German landscape that will be traced until the establishment of Germany's first national park in the Bavarian Forest in 1970.

'A Kind of National Park': Reserving Space for Wildlife in Colonial Tanzania

The foundations of Tanzania's system of wildlife conservation were laid by the German colonial administration prior to the First World War.[8] In 1896, Hermann von Wissmann, an avid hunter and then governor of German East Africa, proposed to the German Foreign Office in Berlin to turn some of the game-rich areas of the colony into 'a kind of national park'. These 'partially very scenic landscapes' should, 'when unpopulated and teeming with game', be reserved as government property. All hunting was to be forbidden unless special permission was obtained from the governor.[9] Consequently, two areas were set aside for the conservation of wildlife in May 1896, one in the area west of Mount Kilimanjaro towards Mount Meru, another in the south along the Rufiji River.

Regimes and practices of conservation in East Africa were by no means a colonial invention. African societies had developed a broad range of political as well as social, religious and economic institutions that had allowed for the coevolution of humans and large animals in the savannahs of East Africa. Low population density minimized pressure on wildlife habitats, and the appropriation of wild animals was circumscribed by gender, social and religious restrictions, chiefly authority and complex sets of rituals. However, these institutions came under extreme strain and largely collapsed when growing consumption of ivory in India as well as in Europe and North America resulted in an unprecedented surge in the commercialized human predation on elephants. The imposition of colonial rule from the middle of the 1880s did little to curb the regime of unbridled trade and exploitation until authorities registered a marked decline both in the number and size of exported tusks by the middle of the 1890s. This impression combined with the perception of a rapid depletion of wildlife in general, effected by an increasing number of European hunters and by the Rinderpest pandemic that swept through East Africa in the early 1890s. Game reserves were, therefore, introduced as sanctuaries supposed to guarantee the reproduction of 'game' species valued as a resource for hunting. Initially, they stood clearly in the tradition of the managed game estate and conservation enclosures in Europe and Asia. The feudal practice to enclose common land as a hunting reserve fused the sustainable management of game with restricted social access, royal or aristocratic pageant and the symbolic assertion of authority over nature.[10] Such feudal aspirations were not missing from Wissmann's initial conceptualisation of game reserves also as possible hunting venues for visiting German dignitaries.

Reserving space for the reproduction of wildlife was a highly controversial form of landscape utilisation. There was no automatic translation of game 'degradation' into legislation, and much depended on the respective governor's commitment to hunting. Wildlife preservation rivalled with other schemes to render the land productive, such as husbandry or the cultivation of cash crops, and its practicability was seriously challenged during the tsetse controversy after 1900, when settlers and veterinary scientists questioned the coexistence of game and livestock for the role of wildlife in the transmission of animal sleeping sickness.[11]

The fact that, all controversies notwithstanding, the number and extent of reserves in German East Africa increased considerably until 1914 suggests that reserves were a politically expedient form of landscape utilisation. This expedience enabled the counterhegemonic discourse of conservation in industrializing Europe to become implemented in colonial structures of domination and oppression. Game, conservationists argued, was an asset that could earn millions from tourist hunters if it was treated as the 'goose that laid golden eggs'.[12] During the tsetse controversy, the functionalism of game production was supplemented by framing reserves as landscapes of consumption. This shift from utilitarian game conservation to science- and tourism-oriented nature preservation was expressed in increasing demands to replace the reserves by *Naturschutzparke* – the contemporary German translation of the American national park – that could not be decreed and abolished at will by the governor. Plans to turn the caldera of Ngorongoro into a *Naturschutzpark* did, however, not materialize before the outbreak of the First World War.

Declaring areas as reserved for game was a powerful form of asserting the authority of the colonial state over the land and the natural resources of the colony. The high-handed reservation of allegedly wild and uninhabited stretches of land was preceded by a Crown Land Declaration in November 1895, which proclaimed the state's entitlement to all land that was not 'effectively' occupied or cultivated.[13] Often, sparse population or nonutilization of land was misunderstood as a 'natural' and timeless condition although it was often the exceptional state of a peculiar historical situation. The imperative of 'rational' land utilisation also excluded many forms of African land use, such as the nomadic pastoralism of the Maasai. Societal responses to the establishment of reserves are hard to assess, but archival evidence suggests that the new purposes of the land were often poorly communicated, leaving local residents under the assumption that hunting was banned in areas declared as game reserves as well as in Crown land or forest reserves.[14] Surely, reserves were far too extensive to be effectively surveyed, but the hunting ban imposed by their establishment must be seen alongside other measures that circumscribed indigenous resource use, like the ban of bush fires and game drives or the gazetting of forest reserves.[15] In Tanzania's Southern Highlands, the establishment of several game reserves upset local human ecologies, curbed access to ivory as a resource that commanded social, economic and political alignments, and thus played a pivotal role in the outbreak of the Maji Maji War.[16] The ravages of scorched-earth warfare and war-related famine depopulated vast stretches of land. This allowed the government to double the size of the Upper Rufiji Game Reserve in 1907 and set the stage for the wilderness that was to become the Selous Game Reserve in the 1920s.[17]

German colonial conservationism was an integral part of the global geopolitics of conservation. The establishment of reserves was motivated by a 'global conservationist view'[18] that projected a variety of cultural concerns and anxieties onto African nature and wildlife. The proponents of this view were game lovers of various backgrounds – hunters, colonial officials, naturalists and aristocrats – who monitored game legislation in the European colonies and commanded exclusive social networks. Their outlook was equally global when it came to institutional learning from abroad, or at least the external recruiting of argumentative support for species preservation.[19] The reserves introduced by von Wissmann in the German colony triggered the designation of protected areas for wildlife in all British colonies bordering German East Africa in the 1890s. German and British conservationists were instrumental in convening representatives of the European powers holding territory in sub-Saharan Africa for a conference on African wildlife conservation in London in 1900. This meeting instigated the establishment of further game reserves in colonial Africa.[20] Moreover, German conservationists admired and strove to imitate the railway line skirting the Southern Reserve in Kenya as the perfect example of how 'colony' and 'zoological garden', Pleistocene originality and technical modernity, could be reconciled to create tourist revenue.

Yet, the most important example that influenced the discourse and practice of conservation in German East Africa was the U.S. Yellowstone National Park. This said, German conservationists were not fascinated by an alleged 'Yellowstone model'. Rather, they modelled Yellowstone according to their needs. The U.S. national park served as a projection screen for all the perceived shortcomings of conservation in the German colony. For example, the hunter-conservationists inside and outside of the German colonial administration understood America's first national park less as a site where a sublime scenery was preserved 'for the people' but as a huge game reserve for the American bison. This was by no means a misperception. Yellowstone's status and purpose was undefined and experimental still decades after its establishment, and American conservation celebrities like Theodore Roosevelt, whose voluminous hunting accounts were immediately translated into German, created the impression that Yellowstone was essentially established as a sanctuary for the characteristic fauna of the American West.[21] Seen through the eye of the hunter, the national park appeared less as an institution that democratized people's access to unspoilt nature than as a reinvention of the European game estate. When the rationalities behind reserve establishment in German East Africa shifted from game production towards nature preservation, the perception of Yellowstone shifted, too. Then, conservationists praised the U.S. national parks for their permanence, and also the scientific justification of reserves was anchored in Yellowstone's alleged function as an ecological laboratory that allowed for the study of the interrelations between flora and fauna. In a climate of nationalist zeal and imperialist competition, the constant reference to presumed achievements abroad served to motivate political action by portraying conservation as a cause to which 'civilized' nations aspired. 'No measure requested on behalf of the preservation of nature can be dismissed as utopian', Germany's foremost conservationist Carl Georg Schillings reproached the German Colonial Office in 1912, 'if it has already been put into practice by another nation under similar circumstances.'[22]

At the heart of the global conservationist view was a genuine apprehension about species extinction derived from the earlier experience of the destructive potential of European expansion and free trade in Southern Africa and the North American West.[23] This apprehension was combined with a temporalization of space that rendered African nature as a heterotopian wilderness equalling the prehistoric landscape of Europe thousands of years ago. For the imperial eye accustomed to the European cultural landscape, the presence of 'antediluvian' megafauna was usually enough to create the impression of wilderness and noncultivation. The reserves established upon such representations cast the 'denial of coevalness' into space,[24] and their localization was no neutral undertaking of demarcating a wilderness that was somehow already out there. Reserves enshrined landscapes as perennial, timeless and backward and were, therefore, inseparable from the mental geographies of 'wilderness' that Europeans projected onto African landscapes.[25]

The colonial discourse of conservation was further underwritten by a frontier mythology that recognized nothing but primitivism at the margins of 'civilization'. This primitivism was double edged. It justified colonial intervention in the name of progress, but it was equally invoked by a discourse of 'anti-civilization' that viewed 'Africa' as an antidote to the syndrome of an alleged European 'overcivilization' and its emasculating complexities of urban and industrial modernity. The best-selling book publications, wildlife photographs and lantern slide lectures of Germany's foremost hunter-conservationist Carl Georg Schillings, for example, spread the image of East Africa as a threatened paradise of wildlife. They established African conservation as a detached and virtual European concern characterized by the severance of Western desires and projections from the realities of coexisting with wildlife on the ground. The wilderness that hunter-conservationists wanted to preserve in East Africa was also a heterotopian repository of a simple and primal virility where man was hunter and in touch with the elemental realities of life.[26] For decades, the preservation of an original, authentic and individual *Urnatur* was the concern of hunters and naturalists for whom Africa's large and potentially dangerous game encapsulated the essence of a masculinity they regarded as sapped and jeopardized by social and economic modernization in Europe. The global conservationist view that motivated the preservation of wildlife in East Africa was, therefore, not only informed by idealist motivations. It was detached, temporalized, gendered and racialized, too.

The designation of reserves under German colonial rule was a defining moment in the history of wildlife conservation in Tanzania. For the first time, the conservation of wild animals in the 'public interest' was enshrined in codified law. The assertion of stewardship over 'nature' by a centralized colonial state in protected areas marked the beginning of a standard practice in the field of wildlife preservation in colonial and independent Tanzania throughout the twentieth century. When the British took over Tanganyika as a mandated territory under the League of Nations, they retained the majority of reserves since the 'Germans appear to have been actuated by very sound reasons in the choice of many of their reserves.'[27] 'Fortress conservation' was still a few decades away, but undeniably its foundations had been laid by German wildlife policies. In a global perspective, imperialism promoted the globalization of environmental responsibility and the assumption of European stewardship for Africa's wildlife. The introduction of game reserves established a constellation of transcontinental environmental governance that was of equal long-term significance. The politics of place in East Africa was governed by structures and developments that extended beyond the respective locality. The areas reserved for wildlife had become globalized localities governed by the authorities of a centralized state in Dar es Salaam, imperial decision makers in Berlin and the interests and sensibilities of conservationist elites located in the global North.

A Quest for Rootedness: The Political Geography of Big Game in Germany

The colonial encounter with the big game of East Africa not only spawned a spatial regime of conservation in colonial and postcolonial Tanzania but also shaped the perception and ideas of nature in Germany. The debates about the conservation of East Africa's wildlife were characterised by an epistemic configuration that conflated space and species, habitat and time, in what could be termed the political geography of the characteristic animal. The assumption that certain animals had been shaped in their evolution by their habitat and vice versa and therefore embodied its characteristics in more or less pure form had its scientific origins in the zoogeographic ordering of the world's fauna especially by Alfred Russel Wallace.[28] Originally a relational category that was to be established by careful comparison, hunters and popular scientists tagged the label 'characteristic' to the more spectacular species associated with certain regions. Conspicuous large vertebrates, like elephants, rhinoceroses or the varieties of bison on both sides of the Atlantic, figured as signifiers of their *Lebensraum* (living space), as remnants of deep time and a bygone world, and as living natural monuments. The survival of Africa's Pleistocene fauna into the present was taken to underwrite the colonial ideology that Africans were seemingly unable to master the nature of their continent. Large game thus embodied the powerful originality of a nature that Europeans had already domesticated in the process of settling and colonizing their own continent and that was just being conquered in the colonisation of frontier territories in Africa.

For German conservationists, who not only perceived the last giants of the animal kingdom as remnants of an earlier age but, by implication, African landscapes as the past landscapes of Europe,[29] the confrontation with the 'antediluvian fauna' of East Africa was as much a source of melancholic regret as of negative pride. On the one hand, the dearth of wild animals in Europe and the transformation of once threatening into threatened nature was a marker of a society in an advanced state of civilisation. On the other, the confrontation with big game not only mediated a sense of place and progress but also caused a sense of lost rootedness, originality and connectedness to nature as the flipside of industrialization, urbanization and agricultural transformation. Germany's well-managed and ordered landscape contrasted unfavourably with the East African savannah, and conservationists interpreted the global vanishing of the giant fauna in Africa, the Arctic and North America as a continuation of the disappearance of bears, wolves, elk and the European bison from the German landscape in previous decades and centuries.[30]

The debates about wildlife conservation in the German colonies and the global vanishing of the giant fauna thus exposed an emotional blank in German environmental identities that found its expression in the mammalian displays of German museums of natural history, geographers' quest for the morphology of the German *Urlandschaft* and in German conservationist discourse. It was, therefore, more than mere coincidence that German hunting and conservationist periodicals dedicated increasing attention to the fate of the last remaining herds of the European bison (*Bison bonasus*) as a corollary to the fate of the so-called transatlantic bison in Yellowstone. The European bison, extinguished from German forests since about the middle of the eighteenth century, became increasingly understood as the one animal characteristic of a true and original 'Germanic' nature. Popular wildlife painters of the day, like Wilhelm Kuhnert or Richard Friese, preferred elk and bison as their favourite objects next to the big game of Africa. For Kuhnert, these species bore the 'stamp of original power and untameable vitality', strength and the 'wildest vigour', while Friese was hailed as the 'painter of the free and fighting beast'.[31] These animals embodied the very values of masculinity and a precivilized, 'natural' simplicity that the hunters claimed to have experienced in Africa and sought to reclaim in 'overcivilized' Europe.

The deeply felt lack of the wild in German environmental identities resulted in attempts to restore some of the former species diversity and primeval originality back to the German landscape. Motivating these efforts was the impression gleaned from protected areas in Africa and North America that it only needed the characteristic animals to restore the wildness in landscapes and render them 'Germanic'.

Reversing the global division of 'civilized' nature here and 'wild' nature there by restoring the wild' to the German landscape constituted a hitherto overlooked strand in German conservationist thinking. The advocates of *Naturschutzparke* in Germany not only strove for the preservation of the country's characteristic landscapes. Particularly the hunters among them translated the preservation of the characteristic animal life in protected areas in North America and East Africa into an ecology of restoration.[32] This quest for the primeval German landscape began in the *Kaiserreich*, when efforts were made in 1912 to reintroduce the original denizens of the German forests into a *Heimatpark* in the forested Harz mountains in northern Germany.[33] The project failed, yet the restoration of the German *Urnatur* was continued in and after the First World War, and it was conducted within as well as beyond the country's changing borders in the Age of the two world wars. The conflation of space and species can, for example, be traced in the mental and practical reclamation of the East as the 'actual frontier' and *Lebensraum* of the German people.[34] Anchored in a mythology of German eastward settlement since the Middle Ages and predicated upon the basic opposition between the cultural landscape of Germany and a Slavic 'wilderness', the projection of wilderness onto the East supplemented the geopolitical ideology of the 'people without space' (*Volk ohne Raum*) with a space seemingly without people. Once more, the bodily presence of large animals such as elk and bison was taken to 'naturalise' the fiction of a wild, undeveloped and underused emptiness.

Indeed, the conservation of the supposedly 'Germanic' big game was accompanied by the very ideology of dispossession espoused earlier in colonial Africa. One of the main concerns of the higher ranks of the German military in the campaigns of both world wars was the protection of the surviving stock of bison in the 'primeval forest' of Białowieża (or Bialowies, as the Germans used to call it). As virtually the sole remaining habitat of bison in Europe, the forests of Białowieża were subject to competing Russian and German imperial aspirations as well as Polish national agendas. Białowieża occupied an almost mythical place in the mental world of German hunters, who monitored the development of bison stocks in the forest very closely.[35] Białowieża owed its originality to the fact that it had for centuries served as a hunting estate first of the Lithuanian and Polish rulers, and in the nineteenth century for the Russian tsar. Occupied by the Germans during the First World War, the forest was subjected partially to ravenous exploitation,[36] partially to serve as an *Urwaldheiligtum* (primeval forest sanctuary) for the preservation of big game. However, when war conditions deteriorated, most of the bison provided meat for the troops, and the last specimen died in 1921.[37] The forest was reclaimed by the Polish nation after the war and declared first a reserve, then a Polish national park in 1932, and the administration of Białowieża was busy tracing surviving specimens in zoos and private estates to reintroduce them to the forest. In Germany, an International Society for the Preservation of the European Bison (Internationale Gesellschaft zur Erhaltung des Wisents) formed with the explicit aim of systematically breeding bison for reintroduction. Although international in denomination, the core membership was German, including several of the proponents of colonial conservation previous to the war. The key figure among the bison conservationists was, however, Lutz Heck.[38] Born the son of Ludwig Heck, the Berlin Zoo director and another champion of game conservation in the colonies, Lutz Heck not only inherited his father's office but also the fascination with big game, as expressed in a series of expeditions dedicated to hunting, capturing and filming wildlife in Africa during the 1920s.[39] Being an intimate friend of Nazi Germany's supreme conservationist Hermann Göring, Heck was employed to advance the systematic breeding of the bison that Göring admired as a symbol of 'Teutonic bullishness'.[40] For that purpose, the hunting estate of the erstwhile Emperor Wilhelm II in the Schorfheide was declared as *Urwildpark* (primeval game park) in 1934. The whole venture was shaped by a 'restorative' approach to conservation, a racialized hunting ideology and the conviction about the native 'Germanness' of certain species of game.

This ideology found its clearest expression in the monument marking the entrance to the park. It showed an attacking bison modelled by the sculptor

Max Esser. An inscription on the backside eternalized the origins of the German national character in the spirit of the chase:

> Once, primeval big game roamed through Germany's forests. Its hunting was a trial of courage for our Germanic ancestors. In 1934, this wildlife park was erected where bison and aurochs, elk, deer, wild horse, beaver and other animals of our home should find a refuge to testify to future generations the diversity of wildlife at a time when Germany was not yet conquered by man.[41]

Another inscription on the pedestal quoted a line from the medieval *Nibelungenlied* (Song of the Nibelungs) that celebrated Siegfried's bravery as a hunter of big game.

The monument visualized the ideology of Germanic/German man hardened in the contest with a wild nature that Nazi conservationists regarded as a root of the superiority of the German 'race'. Like the German 'race', also animals were products of the soil so that the bison became an embodiment of racialized Nazi geopolitics.[42] The Schorfheide was poised to form part of an extensive system of *Reichsnaturschutzgebiete* (imperial nature reserves) and national parks with the explicit aim to give the German people recourse with the ideologically charged nature of home. Bears, elk, bison and wolves were to convey originality and serve as 'mediators between man and nature'.[43]

Illustration 5.1. The bison monument at Eichhorst, northeast of Berlin

While the Second World War deferred and ultimately thwarted these plans, the violent reclamation of the East as Germanic landscape in the campaign against the Soviet Union resulted in Białowieża once more being declared a sanctuary for the Germanic flagship species. Only weeks after German troops had crossed the Soviet border, systematic burning of villages, the extermination of thousands of Jews and soldiers measuring their 'bags' of killed 'partisans' set the stage for the forest as a combined reserve and hunting estate that was to form the core of a completely transformed landscape for German settlement. With its human residents erased, the *Urwildpark* of Bialowies should be turned into 'a great, living laboratory of purely Teutonic species'.[44] The reclamation of the forest was only brief, and in the nostalgic literature that memorized German eviction and the loss of the East after 1945, elk and bison loom large as embodiments of the East's melancholic and original landscape.[45] Curt Strohmeyer, for example, a blood-and-soil writer during the Third Reich, invoked large game as a metaphor of the 'lost paradise' of Schorfheide and Białowieża that had become inaccessible behind the Cold War borders:

> In the very moment we Germans had to leave the elk forests of Eastern Prussia, I realized what an enormous treasure had been locked up in these woods. For the first time in my life, I encountered this majestic animal, indeed a whole herd of bison roaming freely in the wild, as if to symbolize the beauty of the fatherland we once possessed.[46]

Domesticating the Wild in the 'Bavarian Serengeti'

The identification of the nation and its alleged characteristics with certain charismatic animals and the associated attempts to restore a particularly 'German' landscape through the reintroduction of these species was not confined to the age of racialized geopolitics. The deeper anxieties about 'civilization', progress and national identity that were enshrined in the fascination with large game all but vanished in the second half of the twentieth century. In July 1966, Bernhard Grzimek proposed to the government of the Bavarian state to establish a national park in the Bavarian Forest. Pointing at the need of a predominantly urbanized society to reconnect with nature, Grzimek argued that the citizens of (West) Germany should at least have one place where they could watch 'our native animals undisturbed and free in our landscape'. Only the forests along the Czech border would still come close to the country's original forests, and they could become a national attraction if only the species that were once native to the German forest could be reintroduced. Unsurprisingly, the list contained, amongst others, the European bison, elk, wild boar, bear and lynx.[47]

Grzimek's proposal reiterated many points already raised in the debates about the *Tierfreiheit,* without, however, the introduction of African mammals proposed earlier. His renewed motion to set aside nature of allegedly national significance was put forward at a time when the nation was divided and more people crowded on less space than ever before. Although it clearly rehearsed the very conflation of space and species that had inspired Nazi conservation three decades earlier, the project of reintroducing bear, elk and bison in the Bavarian Forest was hardly reflected as a continuation of these policies. Grzimek's ecology was that of a zoo director rather than a hunter, and his vision of European bison peacefully grazing next to herds of elk upon artificially created meadows in an otherwise unmanaged forest was patterned on the model of the East African savannah that he had encountered during his campaigns for the preservation of national parks in Tanganyika since the middle of the 1950s. Drawn to Africa to restock the depleted Frankfurt Zoo after the Second World War, Grzimek intervened as a seemingly 'honest broker'[48] into the late colonial debates over wildlife conservation in Tanganyika. His books and the Oscar-winning documentary film *Serengeti Shall Not Die,* both published in 1959, came too late to achieve the demarcation of the national park's boundaries according to the seasonal migration patterns of the wildebeest that Grzimek had established by aerial survey.[49] Yet, the film made the Frankfurt Zoo director one of the most renowned conservationists worldwide, and his celebrity status, together with well-orchestrated publicity campaigns and a weekly TV series, gave Grzimek access to considerable funds and donations.

The money thus raised allowed Grzimek and his Frankfurt Zoological Society (ZGF) to play a key role not only in the future management of the Serengeti National Park, but in Tanzanian and African conservation in general.[50] He became an informal counsellor of Tanzanian Prime Minister Julius Nyerere in matters of wildlife conservation, promoted wildlife tourism as a form of external development aid and was instrumental in tapping and coordinating funds from various Western NGOs to enable the rapid growth of protected areas in Tanzania during the 1960s. Moreover, Grzimek orchestrated the substantial German engagement in wildlife conservation in its former colony especially during the 1960s. German development aid helped to put the College of African Wildlife Management in Mweka on track in 1963 and continued to support the education of future game wardens by grants and stipends. The ZGF furnished game wardens with technical equipment in what was commonly framed as a 'war against poaching' and helped create the modern Tanzanian citizen by running education campaigns that enlightened Tanzanians about the economic value of – at least rhetorically – their national parks. ZGF funds and money solicited from the Fritz Thyssen foundation contributed significantly to the establishment of the Serengeti Research Institute in 1970 and bolstered the Serengeti conservation fortress by turning it into an ecological and ethological laboratory of international significance.[51]

Several of Grzimek's East African experiences were transferred to the *Tierfreiheit* and to the forests of Eastern Bavaria in the middle of the 1960s. Among these were the use of charismatic megafauna as a magnet to satisfy the urbanized masses' desire to see wild animals and thereby draw revenue to an 'underdeveloped' area; the 'civilizing' functions of a national park and an ecology of paradise predicated upon the 'national park effect' of animals habituating to the presence of humans. African nature provided the peculiar lens through which Grzimek portrayed the nature of home as a potential national park. By means of the 'Grzimek effect' of regular exposure to the Frankfurt Zoo director's TV documentaries on the threatened wildlife of the world,[52] conservationists and politicians in Bavaria as well as a majority of the German public associated a 'national park' essentially with viewing large, charismatic fauna in its natural habitat.

When Grzimek lured Western Germans with the prospect of a national park full of charismatic wildlife in the late 1960s, he did so in the context of a rapid growth in worldwide park making, particularly in former colonial territories. Grzimek was untiring in mobilizing shame by pointing out how the backward 'coloured' nations would embarrass 'civilized' Europe in protecting their nature. A flurry of letters from conservationists abroad, whom Grzimek had organized to petition the government of the Bavarian State, played the same tune. 'So many countries, even the underdeveloped countries of Africa nowadays boast reserves and national parks', one English conservationist complained. 'I am really surprised that a progressive country like Germany does not feature any.'[53] While international developments may have favoured Grzimek's plans, critics in Germany clearly discerned the African blueprint behind what they disparaged as 'Bavarian Serengeti'.[54] Particularly staunch opposition formed among foresters, the forestry administration and wildlife biologists, but also conservationist organizations like the Verein Naturschutzpark (VNP) opposed the project. Since the VNP advocated the preservation of aesthetically pleasing landscapes in a comprehensive system of nature parks, it rejected both the imposition of wilderness upon a historical landscape and the internationally attractive label of a national park, which they feared would outshine the less glamorous *Naturpark*. The arbitrariness of Grzimek's restoration ecology was exposed from different vantage points. The Austrian wildlife biologist Peter Krott, for example, attacked the assumption that a characteristically German fauna could be found exactly a millennium ago. Equally, he opined, one could argue that a horse-drawn carriage was the characteristic means of transport between Hamburg and Munich.[55] Others objected to the introduction of large game without fences to protect fields and people, but the main point of criticism concerned the ecological incompatibility of Grzimek's

Germanic game reserve with the dense forests of Eastern Bavaria: A dense stock of large mammals may be compatible with the steppes of East Africa, but not with the carefully managed, near-natural and serene high forest eternalized in the works of the nineteenth-century poet Adalbert Stifter.

Three years of discussions and negotiations followed about what nature was 'German' and what nature was to be preserved in a national park. Independent expert commentary by the landscape ecologist Wolfgang Haber finally paved the way for a compromise.[56] While the plan to develop tourism via a natural area designated as national park was acknowledged in principle, the proposed introduction of extinct species to roam freely in the forest was rejected and deemed possible only in fenced enclosures. Predicated upon this assessment, the Bavarian Parliament finally enacted the establishment of a national park in June 1969. In doing so, the Parliament not only approved of the first area designated under the label 'national park' in Germany but of a landscape that mirrored the colonial and transnational entanglements of German conservationist thinking. Translated from an African experience, the park integrated the managed forest and the cultural landscape of the German tradition and the import of the characteristic animals of both the 'German East' and the German past. Confined to fences, the wild was finally domesticated and incorporated into a territory that would more adequately be named as Germany's first transnational park.

Notes

1. Bernhard Grzimek, 'Die Hessische Tierfreiheit – eine neue Art von Landschafts-Zoo', *Natur und Landschaft* 40 (1965): 168–71; 'Mit der Kleinbahn durch Zebraherden', *Frankfurter Allgemeine Zeitung*, 21 May 1965, 37.
2. 'Starkes Echo auf Landschaftszoo', *Frankfurter Allgemeine Zeitung*, 25 September 1965, 69.
3. 'Löwen unter Eichen', *Der Spiegel*, 11 August 1965, 44.
4. Deutscher Jagdschutz-Verband, 'Zum Plan der Tierfreiheit Taunus des Herrn Prof. Dr. Grzimek', *Natur und Landschaft* 40 (1965): 171f.; Schutzgemeinschaft Deutscher Wald, 'Kein Platz für wilde Tiere', *Natur und Landschaft* 40 (1965): 172; Karl Korn, 'Rettet das Land jetzt!', *Frankfurter Allgemeine Zeitung*, 20 October 1965, 20.
5. Roderick P. Neumann, *Imposing Wilderness: Struggles over Livelihood and Nature Preservation in Africa* (Berkeley, 1998); John M. MacKenzie, *The Empire of Nature. Hunting, Conservation and British Imperialism* (Manchester, 1988); Dan Brockington, *Fortress Conservation. The Preservation of the Mkomazi Game Reserve, Tanzania* (Oxford, 2002).
6. Dan Brockington, 'The Politics and Ethnographies of Environmentalism in Tanzania', *African Affairs* 105 (2006): 102–4.
7. See Kupper, this volume.
8. The issues raised in the following paragraph are comprehensively discussed in my PhD dissertation, forthcoming under the title *The Nature of German Imperialism. Conservation and the Politics of Wildlife in Colonial East Africa* (Oxford, in press).

9. Bundesarchiv Berlin-Lichterfelde (henceforth BAL) R 1001/237-1, fol. 55: AA KA to Gov DOA, 23 April 1896; BAL R 1001/7776, fol. 56: Memorandum on Game Preservation by Hermann von Wissmann, 20 March 1898.

10. Thomas T. Allsen, *The Royal Hunt in Eurasian History* (Philadelphia, 2006); Roderick P. Neumann, 'Dukes, Earls and Ersatz Edens: Aristocratic Nature Preservationists in Colonial Africa', *Environment and Planning D: Society and Space* 14 (1996): 79–98.

11. On the ecology and colonial policies of sleeping sickness see John Ford, *The Role of the Trypanosomiases in African Ecology* (Oxford, 1971); William Beinart and Lotte Hughes, *Environment and Empire* (Oxford, 2007), 184–99; Helen Tilley, 'Ecologies of Complexity. Tropical Environments, African Trypanosomiasis, and the Science of Disease Control in British Colonial Africa, 1900–1940', *Osiris* 19 (2004): 21–38.

12. BAL R 8923/2236, fol. 23: Bericht über die Hauptversammlung der Deutschen Kolonialgesellschaft im Oberen Museum zu Stuttgart am 9. und 10. Juni 1911, 76.

13. Achim von Oppen, 'Matuta. Landkonflikte, Ökologie und Entwicklung in der Geschichte Tanzanias', in *Tanzania. Koloniale Vergangenheit und neuer Aufbruch*, ed. Ulrich van der Heyden and Achim von Oppen (Münster, 1996), 47–84.

14. BAL R 1001/726, fol. 91: Bericht der zur Untersuchung der Ursachen des Aufstandes eingesetzten Kommission, Daressalam, 4 December 1905; TNA G 58/40, unfol.: BA Morogoro to Gov DOA, 5 August 1912.

15. Thaddeus Sunseri, 'Reinterpreting a Colonial Rebellion: Forestry and Social Control in German East Africa, 1874–1915', *Environmental History* 8 (2003): 430–51.

16. Thaddeus Sunseri, 'The War of the Hunters: Maji Maji and the Decline of the Ivory Trade', in *Maji Maji: Lifting the Fog of War*, ed. Jamie Monson and James Giblin (Leiden, 2010), 117–47.

17. Gordon Matzke, *Wildlife in Tanzanian Settlement Policy: The Case of the Selous* (Syracuse, 1977), 228–31.

18. Jan Bender Shetler, *Imagining Serengeti: A History of Landscape Memory in Tanzania from Earliest Times to the Present* (Athens, OH, 2007), 201–12.

19. Ulrike Kirchberger, 'Wie entsteht eine imperiale Infrastruktur? Zum Aufbau der Naturschutzbürokratie in Deutsch-Ostafrika', *Historische Zeitschrift* 291 (2010): 41–69.

20. Mark Cioc, *The Game of Conservation: International Treaties to Protect the World's Migratory Animals* (Athens, OH, 2009).

21. Theodore Roosevelt, *Outdoor Pastimes of an American Hunter* (New York, 1906), 320, 327; see also Arnold Hague, 'The Yellowstone Park as a Game Reservation', in *American Big Game Hunting. The Book of the Boone & Crockett Club*, ed. Theodore Roosevelt and George Bird Grinnell (New York, 1893), 240–70.

22. BAL R 1001/7772, fol. 69: Schillings to Solf, 18 November 1912.

23. Andrew C. Isenberg, *The Destruction of the Bison. An Environmental History, 1750–1920* (Cambridge, 2000); John F. Richards, *The Unending Frontier: An Environmental History of the Early Modern World* (Berkeley, 2003).

24. Johannes Fabian, *Time and the Other: How Anthropology Makes Its Object* (New York, 2002 [1983]), 31.

25. Neumann, *Imposing Wilderness*; William M. Adams, 'Nature and the Colonial Mind', in *Decolonizing Nature. Strategies for Conservation in a Post-colonial Era*, ed. William M. Adams and Martin Mulligan (London, 2003), 16–50.

26. John M. MacKenzie, 'The Imperial Pioneer and Hunter and the British Masculine Stereotype in Late Victorian and Edwardian Times', in *Manliness and Morality: Middle-*

Class Masculinity in Britain and America, 1800–1940, ed. J. A. Mangan and James Walvin (New York, 1987), 176–98.

27. TNA TT AB 145, fol. 26: Circular A. C. Hollis, 4 August 1921, attachment: Memorandum on Game Preservation and Tsetse Control by C. F. M Swynnerton [undated].

28. Alfred Russel Wallace, *The Geographical Distribution of Animals. With a Study of the Relations of Living and Extinct Faunas as Elucidating the Past Changes of the Earth's Surface*, 2 vols. (London, 1876).

29. See e.g., Ernst v. Stromer, 'Die einstige Verbreitung afrikanischer Säugetiere', *Naturwissenschaftliche Wochenschrift* 10 (1911): 814–16; Wilhelm Bölsche, *Die deutsche Landschaft in Vergangenheit und Gegenwart* (Berlin, 1915).

30. See e.g., Paul Matschie, 'Deutschlands Säugetierwelt einst und jetzt', *Natur und Haus* 5 (1897): 261–67; Ludwig Klages, 'Mensch und Erde', in *Freideutsche Jugend. Zur Jahrhundertfeier auf dem Hohen Meißner*, ed. Arthur Kracke (Jena, 1913), 89–106.

31. Wilhelm Kuhnert, *Im Lande meiner Modelle* (Leipzig, 1918), 3; Emil Friese, *Richard Friese. Ein deutsches Künstlerleben* (Berlin, 1930), 20, 46.

32. For the broader framework see Marcus Hall, *Earth Repair: A Transatlantic History of Environmental Restoration* (Charlottesville, 2005).

33. 'Ein großer Naturschutzpark im Harz', *Blätter für Naturschutz* 3, no. 18 (1912): 23; Susanne Ude-Koeller, *Auf gebahnten Wegen. Zum Naturdiskurs am Beispiel des Harzklubs e.V.* (Münster, 2004), 227–29.

34. On Eastern Europe as continental German frontier see Robert L. Nelson, ed., *Germans, Poland, and Colonial Expansion to the East, 1850 through the Present* (New York, 2009); David Blackbourn, *The Conquest of Nature. Water, Landscape, and the Making of Modern Germany* (London, 2006), ch. 5; Jeffrey K. Wilson, 'Environmental Chauvinism in the Prussian East: Forestry as a Civilizing Mission on the Ethnic Frontier, 1871–1914', *Central European History* 41 (2008): 27–70.

35. See e.g., H. E., 'Das Schicksal des transatlantischen "Wisent"', *Deutsche Jägerzeitung* 24 (1894/95): 408f.; Franz Genthe, 'Der Wisent in der Kulturgeschichte', *Wild und Hund* 26 (1920): 203–6, 227–30, 245f.; Kurt Floericke, *Wisent und Elch. Zwei urige Recken.* (Stuttgart, 1930).

36. Significantly, the management of the Białowieża forest was entrusted to Georg Escherich, a forester partially trained in the management of 'primeval forests' in the German colony of Cameroon; see Thaddeus Sunseri, "Exploiting the *Urwald*. German Post-Colonial Forestry in Poland and Central Africa, 1900-1960", *Past & Present* 214 (2012), 305–42.

37. Kurt Escherich, 'Forstentomologische Streifzüge im Urwald von Bialowies. Eine waldhygienische Betrachtung', in *Bialowies in deutscher Verwaltung*, ed. Militärforstverwaltung Bialowies (Berlin, 1917), 99. On the forest's prehistory see Tomasz Samojlik, *Conservation and Hunting. Białowieża Forest in the Time of Kings* (Białowieża, 2005).

38. *Erster Jahresbericht der Internationalen Gesellschaft zur Erhaltung des Wisents*, August 1923–31 December 1924. [s.l.] 1924.

39. Lutz Heck, *Auf Tiersuche in weiter Welt* (Berlin, 1941).

40. Simon Schama, *Landscape and Memory* (London, 2004 [1995]), 68.

41. Inscription on the back of the monument. See also Frank Uekötter, *The Green and the Brown. A History of Conservation in Nazi Germany* (Cambridge, 2006), 99–109.

42. Heck, *Auf Tiersuche*, 265–85; see also Walter Schoenichen, *Urwaldwildnis in deutschen Landen. Bilder vom Kampf des deutschen Menschen mit der Urlandschaft* (Neudamm, 1934), 51; Walter Schoenichen, *Urdeutschland. Deutschlands Naturschutzgebiete in Wort und Bild*, vol. 2 (Neudamm, 1937), 308–11. Mark Bassin, 'Blood or Soil? The *Völkisch* Movement, the Nazis, and the Legacy of Geopolitik' in *How Green Were the Nazis? Nature, Environment, and Nation in the Third Reich*, ed. Franz-Josef Brügge-meier, Mark Cioc and Thomas Zeller (Athens, OH, 2005), 204–42.

43. Heck, *Auf Tiersuche*, 290f. On the planned park in the Schorfheide see the correspond-ence and press coverage in German Federal Archives Koblenz B 245/233.

44. Schama, *Landscape and Memory*, 71; Andreas Gautschi, *Walter Frevert. Eines Weid-manns Wechsel und Wege*. (Melsungen, 2005).

45. Georg Thum, 'Mythische Landschaften. Das Bild vom "deutschen Osten" und die Zä-suren des 20. Jahrhunderts', in *Traumland Osten. Deutsche Bilder vom östlichen Europa im 20. Jahrhundert*, ed. Georg Thum (Göttingen, 2006), 205.

46. Curt Strohmeyer, *Der letzte Garten Eden. Durch die Naturreservate der Welt* (Berlin, 1958), 13.

47. Bernhard Grzimek, 'Primitiv-Zoo oder Nationalpark im Bayerischen Wald?', *Das Bay-erland* 69 (1967): 40; Bernhard Grzimek, 'Ein Nationalpark im Bayerischen Wald', *Das Bayerland* 69 (1967): 43–47. For a differently focussed interpretation of Germany's first national park see Sandra Chaney, *Nature of the Miracle Years. Conservation in West Germany, 1945–1975* (Oxford, 2008), 213–42.

48. Thomas Lekan, '*Serengeti Shall Not Die*: Bernhard Grzimek, Wildlife Film, and the Making of a Tourist Landscape in East Africa', *German History* 29 (2011): 230.

49. Surveys of the Serengeti debate are provided by Shetler, *Imagining Serengeti*, 201–37; Neumann, *Imposing Wilderness*, 122–56 and Lekan, '*Serengeti Shall Not Die*'.

50. The Frankfurt Zoological Society currently counts among the ten largest NGOs en-gaged in African conservation; see Katherine Scholfield and Dan Brockington, *Non-Governmental Organizations and African Conservation. A Preliminary Analysis*, BWPI Working Paper (Manchester, 2009), 20.

51. See the correspondence in e.g., Institut für Stadtgeschichte Frankfurt/M., Zoologischer Garten Korr 195; Arbeitsgemeinschaft deutscher Stiftungen, ed., *Die Fritz Thyssen Stif-tung 1960–1970* (Tübingen, 1970), 127–32; on Mweka see Elizabeth Garland, 'State of Nature: Colonial Power, Neoliberal Capital, and Wildlife Management in Tanzania' (PhD dissertation, University of Chicago, 2006).

52. See Franziska Torma, *Eine Naturschutzkampagne in der Ära Adenauer. Bernhard Grzimeks Afrikafilme in den Medien der 50er Jahre* (Munich, 2004).

53. Bayerisches Hauptstaatsarchiv Munich StK 17033, Michael Fryer to Ministerpräsident Alfons Goppel, 21 July 1968.

54. Erich Menzing, 'Ein bayerisches Serengeti', *Bayern-Kurier*, 16 July 1966.

55. Peter Krott, 'Ein "Nationalpark" im Bayerischen Wald?', *Deutsche Jäger-Zeitung* no. 20, 25 December 1966, 790–92.

56. Wolfgang Haber, 'Gutachten zum Plan eines Nationalparkes im Bayerischen Wald', *Landschaft und Erholung. Schriftenreihe des Deutschen Rates für Landespflege* 11 (1969): 8–23.

 PART II

Organizations and Networks

 CHAPTER 6

Translating Yellowstone

Early European National Parks,
Weltnaturschutz *and the Swiss Model*

Patrick Kupper

Europe is not a primary place for national parks. In 2003, the continent's share was only 7 percent of the global number of national park sites and a mere 2 percent of the global area.[1] These figures seem to suggest that one is better off investigating national parks and their history in other places and, indeed, the European continent has received comparatively little attention. Furthermore, methodological nationalism, which prevailed in the field of history until recently, hindered a transnational approach to the topic. For the most part historical accounts have been limited to the national level, which has resulted in a state of research where the existing literature on European national parks is scattered within national historiographies.[2]

The aim of the present text is to explore the conditions in which the national park idea was translated to Europe at the turn to the twentieth century as well as the consequences of this process. A main challenge to contemporary European conservationists was to conceptualize a preservation policy for cultural landscapes at a time when the national park was predominantly associated with the United States, in particular Yellowstone, and the preservation of extensive stretches of uninhabited wilderness. Europe, however, featured an intensively cultivated and densely populated landscape in which private property rights were entrenched. Barely were there any territories left that met the criteria of space and unmodified wilderness. Whoever wanted to make use of the national park idea in Europe had to translate Yellowstone such that it met the European condition, or (taking into account the diversity of conditions) European places and discourses.

In what follows, the European approach to national parks is explored by comparing various ways of adoption and transformation of the idea as well as by tracing the mutual transfer of concepts within Europe and beyond. The first section investigates the early discourses of national parks in Europe at the beginning of the twentieth century and asks how the national park idea was transformed by them. The second section focuses on Switzerland, which was among the first European nations to establish a national park. Most importantly, by advancing scientific research as its main rationale, the Swiss gave the concept a new twist. As highlighted in the third section, this had global implications. The Swiss national park became an appealing model for international conservation and served as an alternative ideal to the recreational concept of the U.S. precedent.

The European Experience of National Parks

When the U.S. Congress established Yellowstone National Park in 1872 European newspapers covered the topic. 'A new region of thermal sources attracts the attention of the world of geography', the *Journal de Genève* reported in 1872. In the following year, the *Neue Zürcher Zeitung* predicted that 'in a few years' time this national park is likely to become a place where sick people from all over the world will gather; in a region completely uninhabited so far, seldom accessed by an American Indian and, until recently, by no civilized man.' Indeed, Yellowstone appeared to have all the prerequisites for a popular spa, and the forecast of the respected Swiss newspaper turned out to be surprisingly appropriate. Yellowstone National Park was developed as a health resort in the early years, and bathing in the hot springs was permitted well into the twentieth century.

In general, the European perception of Yellowstone followed the American one, albeit without the nationalistic rhetoric. Yellowstone was the 'wonderland' of the American West, a land of outstanding natural curiosities, above all of hot springs and geysers, uninhabited and virtually untouched by man. The establishment of a national park was seen as a means to preserve these curiosities and to make them accessible to the people as 'a public park or pleasuring ground'. The wonderlands of the American West were regarded as the equivalents of Europe's man-made monuments and came to stand for a nationalized natural history. In order to preserve them for public enjoyment and to impede private speculation, they had to be safeguarded and controlled by the state.[3]

In the European context nation building by preserving untamed nature did not seem meaningful. European states strived to foster national identity by subsidizing cultural institutions and national events: monuments and museums commemorating national history; national festivals and exhibitions; promotion of art, craft and tradition. Some of these policies, however, involved spatial conservation measures, especially in the realm of the preservation of historical monuments. For example, in 1836, Prussia placed the *Drachenfels*, an impressive rock formation overlooking the Rhine River near Königswinter enclosing a picturesque castle ruin, under state control and protection.[4] Quite a similar kind of rationales as those informing the creation of Yellowstone led to the preservation of the *Rütli* in Switzerland in 1860. After the Swiss Civil War and the subsequent foundation of the Swiss Federal State in 1847 and 1848, the ruling liberals promoted a discourse that linked the emergence of the modern nation-state to the history of the ancient Swiss Confederation. A national myth, rapidly winning popularity, held that the *Rütli,* a meadow on the shores of Lake Lucerne, was the nation's birthplace where, back in the Middle Ages, representatives from the Alpine communities of Uri, Schwyz and Unterwalden had first sworn the eternal oath of the Confederation. When, in the late 1850s, a private investor planned to build a hotel on the *Rütli,* a national campaign to save the place for the public was launched. The meadow was bought and transferred to the federal state as 'inalienable national property'.[5]

In all these preservation campaigns, including Yellowstone, nature preservation was only a more or less important side effect. It was not until the turn of the century that nature preservation became the centre of attention. This was also the time when the representation of Yellowstone started to change. Both in the United States and Europe Yellowstone grew into a symbol of large-scale landscape preservation and species conservation. It was no longer just a place of natural curiosities but also the place where the American buffalo had found its last resort. It was in this function that Yellowstone was grasped by the contemporary colonial discourse on the extinction threat to the African megafauna, in particular the elephant.[6] At the turn to the twentieth century a preservation movement evolved that was global in spread, focus and ambition. It was built on a discourse that constructed 'pristine nature' as a limited good severely endangered by encroaching civilization. The last blanks were rapidly disappearing from the maps of the globe. Not only Americans saw their 'frontier' closing but also Europeans felt they were living at a historical turning point where the world was prized of its last secrets. While the achievements of Western civilization were still hailed, there was a growing body of dissenting voices pointing to associated costs and further consequences of what had been acclaimed as cultural progress. This train of thought not only worried about the disappearance of pristine nature but connected it directly with the fate of civilization. With the loss of pristine nature civilization was believed to be deprived of its own origin as well as of its 'other', its corrective and curative outside. Thus, human civilization, self-evidently equated with Western civilization by contemporary Europeans, was jeopardizing itself.

On both sides of the Atlantic, national parks appeared to be a handy means not only to limit the sprawl of civilization but also to provide escapes from the evils of modern life. Nature was detected as a remedy against the widespread fears of a progressive degeneration of society and loss of virility. 'Thousands of tired, nerve-shaken, over-civilized people are beginning to find out that going to the mountain is going home', as the pioneer of the American preservation movement, John Muir, stated on the first page of his book *Our National Parks,* published in 1901.[7] Furthermore, national parks were seen as advancing idealistic values in a thoroughly materialistic society. Each new park was a sign of hope that a better, more philanthropic world was possible. In this fin-de-siècle crisis of Western civilization the American national park idea, remodelled as a tool for nature preservation, increasingly attracted nature conservationists throughout Europe. Now it was regarded as 'the greatest thing ever undertaken to preserve natural monuments, an idea worthy of the great American republic, of the country of "boundless opportunities"'.[8] However, the question of how this great idea could be adapted to the intensively cultivated and densely populated landscapes of Europe was open to debate.

First governmental action was probably taken in Germany in 1898 when Prussian deputy Wilhelm Wetekamp asked for state facilities and means to preserve 'the monuments of natural history'. In his speech in the Prussian parliament Wetekamp pointed to the American national park. The idealism of the Americans, otherwise reputed as being overly materialistic, could and should serve the Germans as a paradigm.[9] Wetekamp's speech heralded the creation of the Prussian state department for *Naturdenkmalpflege* in 1906. Hugo Conwentz, a biologist and director of a natural history museum, was appointed its director since he had already started to compile an inventory of *Naturdenkmäler* (natural monuments), a term that was to become a key concept of the pre–First World War European nature preservation movement that was surprisingly transnational in scope. The Dutch Vereeniging tot Behoud von Natuurmonumenten (founded 1905) bore the term in its name, and so did the Swiss Kommission für die Erhaltung von Naturdenkmälern und prähistorischen Stätten (1906) and the Italian Lega Nazionale per la Protezione dei monumenti naturali (1913). Laws protecting natural monuments were passed in France in 1906 and in Sweden in 1909, and the term was also introduced into the Russian language as *pamiatniki prirody* around that time.[10]

In many respects, the natural monument was Conwentz's answer to the American national park. In his view, the selective preservation of a variety of singular features of nature, like unique trees, small parts of forests, wetlands and swamps, in a net of monuments was superior to the preservation of large stretches of land in parks. This was held true especially for Central Europe, which Conwentz regarded as entirely penetrated by civilization. Consequently, Conwentz opposed the establishment of parks in Germany as promoted by the German-Austrian Verein Naturschutzpark. Other European societies had fewer difficulties both in connecting the concepts of large nature reserves and small natural monuments and in adopting the term 'national park' from the United States. Sweden and Switzerland took the lead. Both national discourses were well informed by Conwentz's work, but proceeded to single out national parks as a key instrument of nature preservation. The Swedish parliament simultaneously passed two laws in 1909, one regarding natural monuments and the other regarding national parks. The national park law adopted to a large extent the American model. The parliamentary commission spoke of the 'dual character' of national parks, 'being at once a natural curiosity and an outstanding tourist area'. Sweden inherited from the American model not only that parks fell into the domain of the national government but also that they had to serve the paradoxical double purpose of nature preservation and public use. In 1910, the boundaries of nine parks were established encompassing a total of 3,500 square kilometres of public land. While the five southern parks were very small, totalling only six square kilometres, the four parks in the Norrland had American dimensions, a welcome underpinning of Norrland's image as 'Sweden's America'. Sweden was perhaps geopolitically and culturally too peripheral to hallmark the development on the transnational and international level, or its adaptation of the national park may have been too close to the American one to attract a distinct reception, or there may simply have been no promoters willing and able to sell the own concept abroad. In any case, the focus of transnational attention became not the Swedish parks but the national park established in Switzerland in the same years.[11]

Creating Wilderness in the Swiss National Park

The Swiss nature protection movement emerged at the beginning of the twentieth century. In 1906 the above-mentioned Commission for the Conservation of Nature Monuments and Prehistorical Sites (abbreviated as Commission for Nature Protection, CNP) was created within the Swiss Society of Natural Sciences. The commission immediately got frantically active in various fields. It took up Conwentz's term of the 'nature monument' and engaged in the small-scale preservation of natural features, but soon decided the establishment of large nature reserves to be most urgent and valuable. Already three years after its establishment, at the end of 1909, the commission managed to lay the cornerstone to a national park by leasing a mountain valley of 20 square kilometres in the Lower Engadine in the southeast of Switzerland. Additional land was leased in the following years, so that in 1914, when the Swiss federal state took charge of the park, it covered an area of approximately 150 square kilometres, 0.36 percent of Switzerland's territory. The fact that the responsibility was transferred to the national state made 1914 the official year of park establishment.[12]

The selection of the Lower Engadine to host the park was driven by an innovative national park concept but also by contingency. Five factors were of importance: first, the coevolution of nature preservation and ecological sciences; second, the local structure of land ownership and the high degree of communal political autonomy; third, the preservationists' objection to international tourism; fourth, the transnational transfer of ideas; and fifth, the incorporation of nature protection into nationalistic discourse.

The prominence of scientists in the emergence of the Swiss nature preservation movement guaranteed that scientific reasoning had a pivotal role in the conceptualization of the national park in Switzerland. The CNP was an official body of the Swiss scientific community and counted leading Swiss scientists among its ranks. Their interest in large nature reserves was driven by scientific reasoning. From the outset, ecological research and nature preservation merged. Most influential in this respect was Carl Schröter (1855–1939), professor of special botany at the Federal Institute of Technology ETH Zurich from 1884 to 1926, pioneer ecologist, and founding father of the internationally renowned Zurich school of plant sociology. Schröter was the author of an essential book on Alpine plant geography, first published in 1908, and took special interest in the growing field of ecological succession research. He was among the initiators of the International Phytogeographic Excursions, which brought him together with the leading plant ecologists from the British Isles and the United States like Arthur G. Tansley, Henry C. Cowles and Frederick E. Clements.[13]

The park that Schröter and his colleagues in the CNP envisaged would serve as a large outdoor laboratory where natural processes could be observed undisturbed by human interference. They spoke of 'a grandiose experiment to create a wilderness'. In the park they hoped to witness a process of 'retrograde succession' leading gradually to the reestablishment of 'the old primitive biocenose', as it existed before civilized man set foot in the Alps and disrupted the natural equilibrium.[14] For this purpose the CNP strove for an area as remote as possible from civilization where the impact of past and present human settlement and land use would be most minimal. Spectacular sights and exceptional phenomena were of less importance. The words most frequently used to characterize the area of the Lower Engadine were 'typical', 'primitive', 'rugged' and 'wild'.

The Lower Engadine had been suggested by Schröter as a superb location for a Swiss national park at the first meeting of the CNP in 1906. Schröter knew the area first hand as he had explored and described the region in the preceding years. In 1908, the CNP conducted a nationwide inquiry to locate suitable land for nature reserves, but the Lower Engadine was never seriously challenged by other proposals as the place where the first Swiss national park should be realized. For Central European standards the Lower Engadine was remote, indeed. The rural region was part of the Rhaeto-Romanic Alpine valleys of the canton of Grison. Population stagnated at best with many young people traditionally emigrating. Most people made a modest living in agriculture and forestry. The once flourishing cross-border trade of forest products and charcoal had deteriorated in the second half of the nineteenth century with the

Illustration 6.1. Val Cluozza, c. 1920. The Cluozza valley, under protection since January 1910, was the cornerstone of the Swiss National Park in the Lower Engadine.

advent of railway transportation. The poor state of the regional economy was of double advantage to the aims of the nature preservationists. First, it meant that pastures and forests had been used only marginally in recent decades and, thus, were already in the process of becoming a wilderness again. Second, land was of low economic value. This was crucial as land in Switzerland was not only comparably expensive but also generally owned either by private persons, neighbouring cooperatives or local communes, which expected to be granted ample compensation. As it turned out even the acquisition of comparatively worthless parcels of land put the CNP to the test. Purchasing went far beyond its capabilities, which is why the land was only leased. In order to finance both the leases and the costs of park maintenance and surveillance, the CNP created a popular society, the Swiss League for Nature Protection (SLNP). Yet, as fundraising could not keep up with the mounting costs of the park, the project was soon on the verge of financial collapse. This was only averted by the federal state's take-over of most of the lease treaties in 1914.[15]

As most of the park land was owned by the local communes, all treaties had to pass popular votes in the communal assemblies. The accompanying negotiation process proved to be difficult. The preservationist ideas as well as the well-educated, German-speaking scientists from the faraway urban centres were regarded with scepticism by the local people. While the political elites of the region generally appreciated the chance to generate a secure income from communal land, ordinary people seemed to have feared the interference of outside powers and the curtailing of traditional individual rights such as gathering and hunting. To dislocate people was not a political option; thus, only areas with no permanent settlements came into consideration. In exchange for a yearly rent the communes agreed to ban former economic activities such as pasture, forestry, hunting and fishing.

A crucial brokering role in the negotiations was played by a man who had been born and raised in the region, but then moved to urban centres to study biology and become a high school teacher. Steivan Brunies became a student of Schröter under whose supervision he completed a thesis on the flora of the later national park region. In 1908, CNP president Paul Sarasin invited him to join the commission. At that time, Brunies had just moved to Basle, the hometown of the Sarasin family and centre of the emerging Swiss preservation movement. Beside his job as a teacher, Brunies ran the secretariat of the SLNP from 1909 to 1935 and, from 1914 to 1941, served as chief supervisor of the Swiss National Park, a duty he assumed on an honorary basis. Most importantly, however, Brunies moderated the discourse between the urban-based park promoters and the local communes. He translated not only Rhaeto-Romanic into German but also elitist scientific reasoning into rural everyday language, and vice versa. He was familiar with both cultures and accepted by both communities. It is uncertain if the park would have been realized without such a border-crossing figure.

The remoteness of the area was also the result of the absence of grand-scale tourism. Unlike the Upper Engadine with its fast-growing international resorts like St. Moritz, the Lower Engadine had not become a focus of the thriving Belle Époque tourist industry. The preservationists marvelled that its valleys and mountains were 'like having been left out in favour of a large nature reserve'.[16] The advent of modern mass tourism was perceived by preservationists as seriously endangering nature. Many saw tourism as an even stronger threat to nature than industrialization and urbanization, as the tourist industry pushed the frontier of civilization to the very fringe. It did not even halt in front of the mighty peaks of the Alps, which were gradually made accessible to the ordinary tourist by cog railways. The announcement of plans for a tourist railway to the summit of the famous Matterhorn at the end of 1906 provoked a popular outcry. The plans became the target of a national campaign of the newly formed Heimatschutz and were also grist to the park promoters' mill. The 'Matterhorn vandalism' caused CNP member Hermann Christ to ask for instant steps towards the creation of national parks to prevent the vulgarization of the last unspoiled Alpine regions.[17] While the preservation movements in the United States and Canada collaborated with railway companies and tourist agencies at that time, this was no option in Switzerland. It was pure coincidence that the Lower Engadine was connected to the railroad network in the years of the establishment of the national park. And it was not without irony that the Swiss tourism industry set benchmarks for the development of North American national parks in a time it incurred the wrath of conservationists at home.[18]

While it was intended to keep tourist parties away from national parks, so-called friends of nature were welcome in the Engadine park, which was made accessible with a network of hiking trails. Within the park an Alpine hut provided basic board and lodging. As there was no practicable way to formally restrict park visits, the authorities tried to select visitors by making park access strenuous and uncomfortable. This strict policy was (negatively) informed by an analysis of U.S. national park regulations. A CNP report from 1908 qualified them as viable but insufficient for the Swiss situation. Especially all the regulations for the 'enjoyment of the public' had to be ruled out and the regulations regarding nature preservation had to be more exclusive, with large parts of the park completely closed to the public. As a consequence, later park regulations strictly prohibited sidestepping the official trails. Furthermore, the CNP report stated that the American national parks differed widely not only in size but also in intention from their own plans. Whereas in the United States preservation was ruled by the demands of recreation, in Switzerland the focus was entirely on ecological science.[19]

In spite of this conscious differentiation the CNP borrowed the term 'national park' from the United States. Two motivations were decisive for its adoption. First, the term initially used by the CNP, 'reservation', led to confusion in the French part of Switzerland as the French *réservation* differed in meaning from the German *Reservation*. Thus, different terms had to be used in French and German, and misunderstandings were programmed. The term 'national park', in contrast, lent itself easily to a translation into all four national languages, German, French, Italian and Rhaeto-Romanic. Second, it was recognized that the label 'national park' was well suited to win public support and to promote the establishment of large nature reserves as a national endeavour. The labelling was encouraged by the positive image of the United States in Swiss society. In spite of some anti-American resentments cultivated in the German-speaking bourgeoisie, echoing the Wilhelminian animosity, the United States were conceived, first and foremost, the 'land of boundless opportunities' and Switzerland's large 'sister republic'. However, as the Swiss preservationists' ideas widely deviated from the American standard, they had to sustain their meaning of the national park. Therefore, they ceaselessly distinguished their concept from the American one and moreover stressed that the term 'park' should not raise wrong expectations, e.g., that exotic species would be cultivated. A politics of complete preservation (*Totalschutz*) and of nonintervention into natural processes became the hallmark of the Swiss approach.[20]

Responsibility of park management was shared between the Swiss government, the SLNP and the Society of Natural Sciences. From 1914 onwards, the government paid for most of the leases while the SLNP was responsible for providing the financial means for all running expenses of the park, like the salaries of the guardians, the costs of infrastructure as well as of scientific research. The latter was in the responsibility of the Society of Natural Sciences, which appointed a scientific commission to organize and coordinate research in the park. This commission consisted of an interdisciplinary board of scientists headed by Schröter and of four subcommittees for meteorology, geography-geology, botany and zoology. Three meteorological stations recorded the climate, and each season during the summertime twenty to thirty researchers worked in the park. With scarce finances and little manpower in the commission, much rested on the individual researcher. Accordingly, the durability of research agendas, the quality of studies and the transferability of results differed widely.[21]

Finally, not only humans and ideas but also nature crossed national borders. When the Swiss park was created, the region was only sparsely populated by ungulates. Solely the chamois was present in significant number. The red deer had just started to re-immigrate from the east after having been eradicated from the region in the nineteenth century. The Alpine ibex, the heraldic animal of the canton Grison, was extinct since the sixteenth century. It was reintroduced into the park in several releases from 1920 onwards. The animals were delivered by two Swiss zoos that had succeeded in raising ibex in captivity. The zoo animals stemmed from the Italian royal hunting estate of Gran

Paradiso, the last resort of the Alpine ibex, and were, after the refusal of Italian king Victor Emmanuel III to sell some specimen to Switzerland, obtained from poachers.[22] The reintroduction of the ibex was somewhat at odds with the park philosophy of complete preservation. However, the issue had already been raised along with the national park idea and was legitimized by the former existence of the species in the region. Old documents and later on also a skull found in the park substantiated this claim.[23] The reintroduction of the ibex was not only celebrated as an achievement in species conservation but also as a highly popular public event. Bear, wolf and lynx, who had also formerly lived in the area (a last bear was shot near the future park in 1904), could not count on a similar social prestige. While the park advocates rejected the common contemporary partition of useful and harmful animals and, at least in theory, appreciated the free roaming of predators in the park, they were not so bold to repopulate the park with these species.

As plans for further national parks did not materialize, the park in the Engadine gradually became the 'Swiss National Park'. It tied up much of the manpower and financial means of the Swiss preservation movement, which redirected its further efforts to the more feasible establishment of smaller nature reserves. With its exclusive research-oriented approach, the Swiss National Park never became as popular as its overseas counterparts. However, it received a fair amount of international attention as preservationist elites all over the world referred to it as a model.

Weltnaturschutz and the Transfer of the Swiss Model

In 1947, the British journal *Nature* published an article discussing the prospects of creating national parks in Great Britain. The author elucidated that 'there are two distinct and mutually incompatible concepts of the purpose of a national park. The first is the conservation of the scene and the wild life contained in it, which necessarily entails the restriction of human access … The second concept is the use of the area as a public pleasure ground.' The author found the first concept realized in the Swiss National Park where 'no one is allowed to stray from the high road except by permission or under guidance, and no interference with natural processes is tolerated; even fallen trees are allowed to decay in peace.' The American national parks stood for the second concept, though the author remarked that if 'there is ample space for the accommodation and the amusement of tourists' as in the United States, 'the two concepts may easily be harmonized … Even so, warding is necessary to ensure that tourist do obey the regulations and do not harm.'[24]

The Swiss National Park's international reputation can be traced back to the first years of its existence. As early as 1912, only two years after the first preservation measures had been enacted, the park was praised as 'a great achievement'. *Nature* regarded it as 'the most important in Europe', which, in respect to its complete preservation scheme, even excelled the 'celebrated' American parks. This reputation was maintained over the following decades. When, for example, a commission of the League of Nations made a global survey of national parks in 1928, the Swiss park was rated highest.[25] In that same year, an American botanist, Harvey M. Hall, investigated European approaches to national parks and nature reserves. In his report, published in the *Journal of Forestry* in 1929, Hall concluded that the term 'national park' had a different meaning in Europe than in the United States. 'There it usually signifies an area set aside for educational or scientific purposes, rather than for recreation.' Hall's conclusion was strongly influenced by his visit to the Swiss National Park in the company of Carl Schröter. The park's strict preservation policy and the important role played by science and scientists left a deep impression on him. Back home Hall criticized his fellow scientists for their 'absence of enthusiasm and organization' and called for the immediate creation of 'complete reservations' in the United States. 'Our warning as to danger of delay comes from the experience in Europe. The problem there is much more difficult than with us, for they no longer have extensive natural areas to protect. They must first re-create natural conditions through long periods of protection, sometimes accompanied by replanting and by reintroduction of the indigenous fauna ... Our task is to preserve what such people as the Swiss and the Italians strive to re-create.'[26]

Two men were instrumental in the promotion of the Swiss model abroad, Carl Schröter and Paul Sarasin. They untiringly publicized the Swiss National Park in articles, at international conferences and through their wide correspondence networks. While Schröter's efforts were directed to scientific circles and the public sphere, Sarasin became also active in national and international affairs. Paul Sarasin (1856–1929) was a naturalist and explorer in the tradition of Alexander von Humboldt. His boundless scientific interests reached from prehistory and botany to animal psychology and astronomy. Thanks to a wealthy family background he could afford the independent life of a private scholar. His reputation stemmed from voluminous scientific accounts and more popular travel accounts on Ceylon and Celebes, which he published together with his cousin Fritz Sarasin. Repeatedly journeying through Southeast Asia in the heyday of European imperialism, the Sarasins became eye witnesses to the advance of Western civilization and were deeply ambivalent about what they saw. In the journal of their travels to Celebes, published in 1905, the Sarasins expressed their anxiety that Western globalization would lead to cultural uniformity. 'The philanthropist must be pleased to see the civilized Minahassa. The natural scientist and ethnographer, however, are secretly horrified at the thought of the prospect of a future world wearing one and the same livery!'[27]

From his colonial experience Paul Sarasin gained two insights for his later involvement in nature preservation: First, the problem of the encroachment of civilization was global in scope and, second, the protection of indigenous people had to be an integral part of it. In view of the widespread dispossession of indigenous populations accompanying the creation of national parks in North America, Sarasin's attitude was inventive. On the other hand, his approach was entirely Eurocentric and extremely patronizing. He suggested preserving 'primitive people' in the same manner as natural features. As 'anthropological nature monuments' they should be entirely isolated from 'civilization'.[28]

When Sarasin was elected president of the newly founded CNP in 1906, his approach was transnational from the outset, urging his Swiss colleagues to form a national organization of the kind 'that could be connected to the neighbouring states without hiatus like the geographic net of longitudes and latitudes'.[29] The constitution of the CNP with a central national board and cantonal commissions served Sarasin as a blueprint for a worldwide organization of nature protection. He intended to reproduce it on the international stage with an international board and national commissions. Additionally, the Swiss park was his model for what should be achieved in every nation in order to establish a worldwide web of nature reserves. Sarasin exposed his vision of *Weltnaturschutz* for the first time at the International Zoological Congress in Graz in 1910. Subsequently, he convinced the Swiss government to host an international conference on nature preservation in its capital Berne in 1913. The seventeen countries represented agreed on the establishment of an Advisory Commission for the International Protection of Nature situated in Basle and presided over by Sarasin. The invitations for a follow-up conference had already been spread when, in the summer of 1914, the First World War broke out in Europe. The initiative was halted abruptly, and Sarasin's attempts to revive it after the war were altogether frustrated.[30]

In spite of the failure to build an international organization, Sarasin's vision and the Swiss model spurred further park movements, namely, in Germany, Italy and Russia where private fundraising organizations were created to back the establishment of national parks, similar to the Swiss League for Nature Protection. Sarasin's legacy was finally resumed after the Second World War. Encouraged by a meeting of European naturalists in the Swiss National Park in 1946, the SNLP decided to organize an international conference on nature protection. This conference, held in Brunnen in 1947, kicked off postwar international nature conservation and set the stage for the foundation of IUCN in Fontainebleau in the following year. In his 100-year appraisal held on the Second World National Park Conference in 1972, Jean-Paul Harroy celebrated the Swiss park for having brought science to the national park.[31] Its scientific commitment was most closely shared in faraway Russia. The Russian delegates at the Berne conference were impressed by Sarasin and made sure that the entire conference proceedings were translated and published in Russia. It backed the already strong position of scientists in the matters of nature preservation and gave support to a research-based organization of the Russian and later Soviet *zapovedniki*. In other park movements, science did not attain the same pivotal position. While nature preservationists in many parts of the world referred to the Swiss park model, other priorities like the promotion of tourism and the preservation of cultural heritage prevailed.[32]

Conclusion

The Europeanization of the national park had much further-reaching implications than the current modest number of European parks suggest. Embedding national parks in the cultural landscape of Europe not only transformed the overall concept of the national park but also broadened and diversified it. The concept of the national park became popular in Europe when it was remodelled as a nature preservation tool in the context of the fin-de-siècle crisis of European civilization. The different national cultures fostered a rather heterogeneous handling of the concept. While the concept was rejected in Germany, which instead promoted the concept of small nature monuments as the adequate alternative for the civilized European nations, Switzerland became a main reference for a distinctive adaptation of the (American) national park. In the course of events it was of utmost importance that nature conservation achieved prominence in Europe concurrently with the advancement of ecological sciences and thinking. The close involvement of science in the national parks was an innovation enhancing the national park with a new set of actors and rationales.

The prime mover in this respect was Switzerland with the Swiss National Park established mainly as a laboratory for ecological research. A scientific rationale was used to impose strict preservation regulations and, thereby, avoided most contradictions raised by tourism. The fundamental paradox of preservation and use did not entirely disappear from science-oriented parks, however, as research practices tended to be invasive as well, albeit to a smaller extent than recreational activities. Furthermore, as access was restricted and behaviour regulated, scientific parks were less beneficial to the popularization of the park idea and to the generation of financial returns from visitation.

The Swiss concept proved influential in instigating park movements in Europe and beyond. Promoted by internationally well-known scientists like the naturalist Paul Sarasin and the botanist Carl Schröter, the Swiss approach became an important international model for conservation. It was frequently evaluated as an alternative to the hitherto dominant American model. Arguably, conservationists in many countries were familiarized with the concept of the national park through Sarasin's relentless propaganda for the Swiss institution rather than the American 'original'. Both the American and the Swiss national park concept were ideal types with real-world correspondents, but also distinct discursive lives that inspired park promoters worldwide. The concepts were incorporated into the prevailing civilization discourse by making nature conservation an additional field of Europe's historical civilizing mission.

Notes

1. There were 273 national parks encompassing a total of approximately 100,000 square kilometres in Europe (excluding the former Soviet Union except for the Baltic States, using IUCN categories). Stuart Chape et al., eds, *2003 United Nations List of Protected Areas* (Gland, 2003).

2. For a first outline of a European national park history see Patrick Kupper, 'Nationalparks in der europäischen Geschichte', *http://www.europa.clio-online.de/2008/Article =330* (2008).

3. *Journal de Genève*, 28 July 1872 ; *Neue Zürcher Zeitung*, 5 August 1873 (my translations). Cf. *The Times*, 10 April 1873; *The Times*, 23 November 1877; Alfred Runte, *National Parks: The American Experience* (Lincoln, 1987). Cf. Jones, this volume.

4. See Thomas M. Lekan, *Imagining the Nation in Nature: Landscape Preservation and German Identity, 1885–1945* (Cambridge, MA, 2004).

5. See Georg Kreis, *Mythos Rütli: Geschichte eines Erinnerungsortes* (Zürich, 2004). Cf. Daniel Speich, 'Switzerland', in *Nations and Nationalism: A Global Historical Overview*, vol. 1 (1770–1880), ed. Guntram H. Herb and David H. Kaplan (Santa Barbara, 2008), 244–55.

6. See Gissibl, this volume.

7. John Muir, *Our National Parks* (Boston, 1901), 1. For fears of degeneration cf. Donna Haraway, *Primate Visions: Gender, Race, and Nature in the World of Modern Science* (New York, 1989), 26ff.; Joachim Radkau, *Das Zeitalter der Nervosität: Deutschland zwischen Bismarck und Hitler* (Munich, 1998).

8. Robert Glutz-Graff, *Ueber Natur-Denkmäler, ihre Gefährdung u. Erhaltung* (Solothurn, 1905), 18.

9. *Stenogr. Berichte über die Verhandlungen des Preussischen Hauses der Abgeordneten*, 3. Bd. 1898, 1958f.

10. See Hans-Werner Frohn and Friedemann Schmoll, eds, *Natur und Staat: Staatlicher Naturschutz in Deutschland, 1906–2006* (Bonn, 2006). Arguments on Conwentz's lines were also made for the British Isles (*The Times*, 11 April 1910). For France, see Ford, this volume. In the United States, the Antiquities Act of 1906 enabled the president to designate national monuments (see Hal Rothman, *Preserving Different Pasts: The American National Monuments* [Urbana, 1989]). There are, however, no tangible connections between the American and the European nature monument discourses in spite of the temporal simultaneity.

11. Tom Mels, *Wild Landscapes: The Cultural Nature of Swedish National Parks* (Lund, 1999), 68ff. The Swedish development was noticed in Switzerland (Ferdinand Rudio and Carl Schröter, 'Naturschutz in der Schweiz und anderswo', in *Vierteljahrsschrift*

der Naturforschenden Gesellschaft in Zürich, Jg. 54 [1909], 484), but it was not of special relevance to the Swiss preservation discourse. On the German *Naturschutzpark* cf. Gissibl and Woebse, this volume.

12. Patrick Kupper, *Wildnis schaffen: Eine transnationale Geschichte des Schweizerischen Nationalparks* (Bern, 2012).

13. See Arthur G. Tansley, 'Obituary: Carl Schröter, 1855–1939', *Journal of Ecology* 27, no. 2 (1939): 531–34.

14. *Annual report CNP* 1908/09, 52–57. See also Carl Schröter, 'Hooker Lecture: The Swiss National Park', *Journal of the Linnean Society of London, Botany* 47, no. 318 (1927): 637–43.

15. Later on, the SLNP thrived counting over 25,000 members in the late 1910s. 'Worthless land' was also an important factor in national park creation in the U.S. See Runte, *National Parks;* Cf. Warwick Frost and C. Michael Hall, 'National Parks and the "Worthless Lands Hypothesis" Revisited', in *Tourism and National Parks: International Perspectives on Development, Histories, and Change,* ed. Warwick Frost and C. Michael Hall (New York, 2009), 45–62.

16. *Annual Report CNP* 1908/09, 33.

17. *Basler Nachrichten,* 8 May 1908.

18. See Patrick Kupper, 'Science and the National Parks: A Transatlantic Perspective on the Interwar Years', *Environmental History* 14, no. 1 (2009): 58–81. Car traffic was kept away from the park until 1925 by a cantonal ban on automobiles.

19. Hermann Christ, 'Gutachten über die Gesetze der amerikanischen Reservationen', 2 May 1908, 3f., Burgerbibliothek Bern, Archiv SANW, Box 537.

20. Kupper, *Wildnis,* 55ff. When *The Times* wrote about the Swiss park creation in 1910, it was still unsure about the appropriate terminology. The British newspaper headlined 'A Swiss "Yellowstone Park"' and used the term 'reservation'; both expressions were put in quotation marks. *The Times,* 12 March 1910.

21. Kupper, *Wildnis,* 179ff.

22. See Marco Giacometti, ed., *Von Königen und Wilderern: Die Rettung und Wiederansiedlung des Alpensteinbocks* (Wohlen/Bern, 2006).

23. Rudio and Schröter, 'Naturschutz', 505; Schröter, 'Hooker Lecture', 640.

24. *Nature,* 4 October 1947, 457.

25. *Nature,* 24 October 1912, 224. Cf. Wöbse, this volume.

26. Harvey M. Hall, 'European Reservations for the Protection of Natural Conditions', *Journal of Forestry* 27, no. 6 (1929): 683. Beside the Swiss National Park, Hall toured nature reserves and national parks in Holland and Italy. In the 1930s, a network of scientists and preservationists tried hard to establish research reserves in the U.S. national parks, with modest success. See Kupper, 'Science'.

27. Paul Sarasin and Fritz Sarasin, *Reisen in Celebes ausgeführt in den Jahren 1893–1896 und 1902–1903* (Wiesbaden, 1905), 46.

28. Paul Sarasin, *Über die Aufgaben des Weltnaturschutzes* (Basel, 1914), 54 ff. Primitive or uncivilized people were basically non-European by definition. Few exceptions, however, were made regarding the nomadic people in the far north. In Sweden's national parks the vested rights of the Saami were upheld as being part of primitive nature. Mels, *Wild Landscapes,* 93ff. For the handling of indigene rights in Malaysia and North America see Kathirithamby-Wells and Martin, this volume.

29. *Annual Report CNP* 1906/07, 95f.

30. Stefan Bachmann, *Zwischen Patriotismus und Wissenschaft: Die Schweizerischen Naturschutzpioniere (1900–1938)* (Zürich, 1999), 271ff.

31. Jean-Paul Harroy, 'National Parks: A 100-Year Appraisal', in *World National Parks: Progress and Opportunities,* ed. Jean-Paul Harroy (Brussels, 1972), 16.

32. Cf. Ford, Wakild, van der Windt and Wöbse, this volume. For Italy and Russia see James Sievert, *The Origins of Nature Conservation in Italy* (Bern, 2000), 101ff. Douglas R. Weiner, *Models of Nature: Ecology, Conservation, and Cultural Revolution in Soviet Russia* (Bloomington, 1988), 7ff.

 CHAPTER 7

Framing the Heritage of Mankind
National Parks on the International Agenda

Anna-Katharina Wöbse

The homepage of the American National Park Service gives a remarkable account of the genesis of the United Nations' World Heritage Convention. According to its interpretation, the concept of World Heritage represents the globalized climax of a straight success story made in America – that of a mission fulfilled:

> The United States established Yellowstone as a national park in 1872 and initiated the world-wide movement to protect such areas as national treasures. One hundred years later ... the United States proposed the World Heritage Convention to the international community and was the first nation to ratify it. The World Heritage Convention, the most widely accepted international conservation treaty in human history, *is the American national park idea being carried out world-wide.*[1]

With some nonchalance the report blends items that are of rather contradictory character. How could a concept created in a very specific historical situation – Roderick Nash described this situation as that of a young nation manifesting its unique non-European identity by celebrating its natural wonders[2] – turn into a global label and role model for international conservation strategies? Did the conversion of national treasures into global commons really run as the crow flies? Are today's World Heritage sites just an extended version of national parks? When musing about the 'nationalization of nature', Richard White suggested environmental history offered 'a model for avoiding simple binary choices in scale between the national and the global'.[3] In the case of national parks this applies to the cultural and natural, too. Thus, writing the history of the global proliferation of the national park idea means to scrutinize the shifting, sometimes contradictory and yet connected relationships between the natural and the cultural, between the national and the international.

It is worthwhile to take a closer look at the expansion of the park idea and to identify more of its actors and historical determinants. International organizations like the League of Nations, which started its work in 1920, and its successor in 1945, the United Nations, promoted the idea of safeguarding the cultural and the natural 'heritage of humankind' on an international scale. Culture and nature seemed to be two sides of the same coin – heritage. They provided a new arena for transferring and converting existing local and national concepts. The national park idea was essential in developing new strategies for this purpose. International organizations themselves played a crucial role in establishing role models for reserves. They not only globalized localities but also translated heterogeneous ideas into a universalist notion of heritage. Studying the sources in the archives of the League and the UN might help to shed light on the question as to where to situate national parks between nationalism, trans- and internationalism and globalization. Both the League of Nations and the United Nations fostered the discussion and helped to broadcast the ideas around the globe. Nevertheless, the international organizations relied on a social infrastructure for information and expertise. Again, this infrastructure had a history. Many of its protagonists belonged to an international scientific community that exchanged its findings, nomenclature and worldviews. Thus, the international organizations set the agenda, but small networks used them to promote their particular interpretation of how and which nature was to be protected worldwide. The success story of national parks cannot be understood without sketching the growing transnational web of activists and exchange.

This essay explores the growing obsession with the national park idea at the turn of the twentieth century, the diversity of national park concepts and the role they played in the heritage debate. It furthermore takes a look at alternatives put forward and visions lost. The first part gives a short account of how the national park concepts inspired both the European community of conservationists and the embryonic international network. The second part examines the debates on heritage and on 'spots of natural beauty' in the League of Nations, while the final part discusses the postwar initiatives for the global schemes initiated by UNESCO.

A Rising Star: The American Model at the Beginning of the Twentieth Century

National parks undoubtedly played an inspiring role in the building of international networks of experts and activists for nature protection. At the turn of the nineteenth to the twentieth century we find a steadily growing community of nature lovers and conservationists all over the Western and industrializing world. There were not necessarily many of them, but they drew their members from the influential elite of the flourishing natural sciences. In order to institutionalize nature protection the small conservation community sought help and inspiration. The protagonists used existing arenas to broadcast their interests. Especially blossoming networks like the international unions of ornithology, zoology, geography and maritime studies provided effective systems of exchange.[4] These hot spots of data exchange were characterized by both national rivalry and international co-operation. Researchers and scientists were often cosmopolitans or at least used to cultivating transboundary contacts. Characteristic of the cosmopolitan ambitions of science was the founding of the Zoological Station at Naples by Anton Dohrn, 'a pilot center of a worldwide network of research facilities for studies in marine biology'[5] that hosted scientists later involved in international nature protection like Paul Sarasin or Julian Huxley. Leading periodicals like the British journal *Nature* gave accounts of new discoveries, debates and findings; they were disseminated worldwide and received by their respective scientific communities. Tourism was another phenomenon triggering a transnational consciousness for nature protection. The expanding travel industry, itself a threat to fragile habitats, drew attention to the natural beauties and spectacular wildlife abroad. The attempt to turn the yet-unclaimed archipelago of Spitsbergen into the first international nature reserve before the First World War gives an example of the combined interests of tourism and nature protection.[6] The Swiss scientist Paul Sarasin, introducing his avant-garde global nature protection scheme in 1910 at the International Zoological Congress in Graz, asked to protect the icy islands according to the 'shiny ideal of American large reservations' – that is, according to national parks.[7]

The American model turned into the spatial *leitbild* of the community. National parks were typically large areas, mostly undisturbed by human action, that offered spectacular scenery, abundant wildlife and unique geologic features. They allowed and encouraged visitors to come for recreational, cultural and educational purposes. The efforts of the public relations machinery, which heralded the establishment of the reserves, echoed back from abroad. Yosemite and Yellowstone quickly turned into icons of a modern nature protection scheme that supported economic and also national objectives. While the national park concept gained momentum almost right away in Australia, New Zealand and Canada, it took some decades until the Europeans discovered the political potential of the American concept of national parks and promoted it as a desirable model. One of its persuasive aspects was its aura of official legitimacy and power. National parks were both supporting the state and supported by the state. Besides, from a European point of view, the United States were almost synonymous with modernity. Conservationists, often defamed as being sentimental and retrograde, were happy to promote the American model and thus to overcome the status of romantics. In 1898 the Prussian deputy Wilhelm Wetekamp referred to Yellowstone to persuade the government into financing state parks and an agency for coordinating nature protection activities.[8] The

German *Naturpark* movement, which fought for large areas to be protected, was clearly inspired by the American idea. Its first huge success, the creation of a reserve in the Lüneburg heath, a beautiful but barren cultural landscape close to Hamburg, caricatured the American national park idea of preserving wilderness. Nevertheless, it met with the idea of providing the urban population with some kind of natural experience.

Other activists were more successful in using the 'National Park spirit' for their activities.[9] While in 1909 the Swedish adopted the American model mixed with some parts of the German scheme for scientific and administrative standards, the Swiss materialized their own specific interpretation of what a national park should be like in the Lower Engadine in 1914.[10] They emphasized the scientific rather than the touristic aspect of the national park and restricted public access. This venture set European standards. In 1912 *Nature* had already hailed the Swiss National Park initiative as the 'most important in Europe' – it would even 'excel the American Reservations'.[11] Hugo Conwentz told his Russian colleagues in 1913, that 'If a small country like Switzerland manages to establish a reserve of some square miles, it should be possible to establish large protection areas in the Caucasus.'[12] The campaign for an Italian national park in the Abruzzo mountains was directly inspired by the U.S. model but interspersed with Swiss elements as far as the scientific attitude was concerned.[13] The various debates had one thing in common: the difficult process of balancing the aesthetic, the scientific, the economic and the public interests on the European continent where there were hardly any vacant spaces left for preserving wilderness. The landscapes preserved in such reserves were not so much threatened ecological entities but rather symbolic spaces, reserves for something 'original' that was said to represent the soil and the soul of the nation rooted in. Thus, reserves turned into tools in nation-building processes.

The debate on reserves and national parks was equivocal. On the one hand, it had a strong national momentum. Protecting natural monuments, landscapes and species had developed into one of the most impressive universal parameters for measuring the degree of cultivation and civilization of Western states. Taming wilderness and civilizing man had long been seen as reciprocal processes. Having conquered nature, truly civilized and thus superior nations would be noble enough to give some space to the besieged. Rescuing sites of special natural interest or beauty turned into a synonym for elaborated thought and manners.[14] As the nations were in a permanent state of cultural rivalry with one another as to which one represented the most advanced and civilized society, activists could use this competitive atmosphere to plead for governmental support for their own cause. International competition helped to push national ambition.

On the other hand, although the protagonists kept playing the patriotic chord, they were eager to build international networks, set up co-operations, organize international conferences and team up with their colleagues abroad. Such debates on spatial concepts and shared interests influenced international politics and fostered the genesis of environmental diplomacy. Saving not only beautiful scenery but also protecting species essential for certain industries like big game, waterfowl and birds turned into an issue of international conventions. Like the Convention for the Preservation of Wild Animals, Birds and Fish in Africa (1900) and the Convention for the Protection of Migratory Birds between the United States and Canada (1916) most of them focused on establishing reserves for migrating species.[15]

Cooperation and Common Heritage: The Interwar Period

The First World War put a sudden stop to any international co-operation for nature protection. It took a while to restructure the prewar ambition and networks. Nature was only a peripheral item on the list of the statesmen. The Peace Conference in Paris in 1919 had to sketch a new political map. It was a moment when the European nation states were in motion. There were many new ones on the map – others had been dissolved or had shrunk in territory. It was in this very moment of political readjustment that the interest in national parks grew again. Most of the states involved in the war were confronted with their national identity being either shattered or at least severely irritated. To stabilize national self-perception, spatial reassurance seemed worthwhile. States like Yugoslavia, Poland and Romania were among those eager to protect parts of their regained homelands and to underscore their importance for the nation-building process. National parks and the safeguarding of the nation's natural beauties became part of the standard repertoire of artificial national paraphernalia, like flags, anthems and sport teams.

When the League of Nations put 'the protection of natural beauty' on its agenda in 1925 it reacted to an elitist but nevertheless well-established discourse. The League's covenant had promised 'to promote international co-operation and to achieve international peace and security' not only by diplomatic means but also by fostering practical internationalism in the sphere of culture, economics, science and health.[16] The League was eager to identify a common ground for all peoples in the world and to emphasize shared experiences and universal values. The idea of a common heritage had already become an uncontested paradigm of Western culture, capable both of constructing national identity and of inducing international understanding.[17] Originally, the idea of a heritage of mankind derived from the French Revolution when revolutionary forces threatened monuments and art. In the late nineteenth century so-called natural monuments and museums of living nature had been integrated into a more general concept of heritage.[18] 'Merging memory and preservation',[19] the term 'heritage' was wide and flexible enough to cope with anything that seemed to contain the past – spectacular sites, rare species and cultural landscapes. One of the technical organizations of the League, the International Committee on Intellectual Co-operation (ICIC), coordinated the international efforts and set up networks of memory. Without any dispute the commission's Sub-commission on Arts and Letters decided to study the problem of safeguarding natural beauty as part of the common goal of preserving the inheritance of humankind. From the outset national parks were of special interest to the experts involved in the investigations.[20]

It was the Western world that would frame the future idea of a common heritage. In 1928 the first report on the issue on 'the protection of natural beauty' was presented in Geneva.[21] One reason for the report being rather biased was the fact that the executive partner of the ICIC was based in Paris. Apparently, its most important witness for evidence and material was the French activist Raoul de Clermont, who had been involved in organizing two international conferences for landscape and nature protection in Paris in 1909 and 1923. Moreover, the investigation had not been exactly meticulous. One of the staff members admitted shortly after the report had been presented that it 'was prepared with some haste and the material we could get hold of mostly dealt with Europe and America'.[22] To be more precise, it completely ignored the efforts being made for nature protection in the rest of the world, even the ones in the colonies and the British Commonwealth like the accelerating creation of national parks in Canada, Australia, New Zealand, Asia and South America. However, the report summarized the status of nature protection by praising the initiatives of private organizations and institutions. It briefly explained some legal models for protecting nature to elaborate extensively on the most popular type of reserve, the national park.

The report reflected the status quo of the discussion and the almost mythological character of the national park concept.[23] It stated that various organizations recommended the establishment of national parks as the best option for preserving natural beauty and thus provided the common ground for the international debate. However, there were still various interpretations of what national parks were to be created for. Should they be established to preserve picturesque scenery or to protect species of flora and fauna? This controversy implied another basic question: Should people – like tourists, foresters, farmers etc. — be allowed in the parks or not? Should they be biological reserves or 'museums of nature'? The League's experts tried to avoid this controversy by suggesting an integrative interpretation – a jack-of-all-trades version of national parks: '[C]es trois buts [safeguarding flora, fauna and landscape, A.-K. W.] étant poursuivis séparément ou collactivement [*sic*] dans la même parc.'[24]

Eventually, the members of the committee prepared something like a hit list of national parks. Amazingly enough, it was not the American prototype that scored the best results, but the Swiss model with its evident scientific approach, its concept of noninterventionist management and its policy of very restricted public access. Second in the list were the Spanish national parks. The Covadonga National Park had been created in 1918 with the explicit intention to foster tourism and to provide the necessary infrastructure for that purpose. It granted permission to public access and to existing forms of forestry and pastoral agriculture.[25] While the report mentioned the national parks in the United States and the 'parcs d'elevage' in the French colonies in Western Africa only briefly, it focused on a park project in the Tatra Mountains. This project had aroused special attention by the League of Nation experts due to its unique history, which was entangled with the League's own past. The newly (re-)born nations of Poland and Czechoslovakia had struggled over border issues after the First World War. Eventually these disputes were settled with the help of the League. The settlement included the future creation of a shared national park along the joint border – a binational park, really.[26] The community was delighted, and many journals reported on the project.[27] This binational park was supposed to cover some 60,000 hectares – a promising venture. One of the leading Polish environmentalists, Walery Goetel, explained the concept to the international community and called attention to the pacifying character of such a binational reserve: Borders would no longer separate people. Instead nature would bring them together.[28] This was a quite sensational interpretation as it suggested that the nationalism inherent in national parks could be transcended.

However, the top five reserves listed in the final report demonstrated one point clearly: nobody really knew what national parks exactly were, due to the variety of conservation concepts. The only thing reconciling these models was the tag 'national park'. The heterogeneity of concepts proved to be too bewildering to draw a simple road map for future international action. Or, as the report stated, there was an urgent 'nécessité de délimiter le sujet, nécessité de déterminer des méthodes'.[29] This lack of coherence thwarted international cooperation. After having examined the existing concepts and models of nature protection and national parks, the League's experts reckoned that the first step to be made was to systemize the information available on nature protection. In order to encourage states and private organizations to take up the issue, the experts had to provide them with the essential information and to bring together the protagonists. The ICIC combined the forces of its arts, law and science departments in order to manage such an interdisciplinary investigation. But the findings did not really offer any new insight. After years of comparative research it was stated that 'the subject is a very wide one.' Even the minimalistic aim to publish a brochure and a survey of the laws concerning conservation and nature protection 'was found to be impossible owing to lack of funds'. As the institute found itself incapable of coming to terms with the confusing variety of protection schemes, it confined itself to studying nothing but the most popular type of reserve. As the director stated, 'The examination of the problem should be restricted to national parks.'[30]

Even this modest plan was not accomplished. Due to the worsening situation of the ICIC, the interest in nature protection withered although there were frequent signs of good will. Marie Curie, for instance, one of the many famous members of the ICIC, explained in 1931 that this was a question of general interest and that the movement should be encouraged.[31] Nevertheless, just like the League itself, the subject of nature protection and national parks soon started to hibernate. The League had meant to empower nations to save their natural heritage and to promote nature protection as a common endeavour, but in the end its drafts proved too vague and its political standing too weak to make conservation a universal objective of humanity.

Turning the World into a Park?
Global Ambitions after World War II

The work of the ICIC was revived by its successor, the United Nations Educational, Scientific and Cultural Organization (UNESCO). The general political situation was similar to the one after the First World War. Nationalism had been the driving force for the hostilities that had devastated Europe. The diplomatic systems had failed to prevent aggression, ideas of a global citizenry had been belittled and the League of Nations had been ridiculed. But the basic idea of institutionalizing a system of collective security and international understanding prevailed. The United Nations Organization set out to maintain peace, to foster friendly relations among states and to cooperate internationally in solving economic, social, humanitarian and cultural problems. UNESCO was responsible for restructuring the mental, scientific and cultural cooperation. Its first general director, Julian Huxley, had been part of the international or rather imperial conservation community for years. When presenting his ideas about the future work of UNESCO he emphasized the entangled character of nature protection and heritage. UNESCO was to support institutions and organizations 'which are devoted to the twin functions of preserving the world's scientific and cultural heritage and of making it available when preserved'.[32]

Nature reserves and national parks were important means for saving this heritage, implying the separation of the human from the natural sphere: 'The recognition of the fact that the wild life of the world is irreplaceable, but that it is being rapidly destroyed, is necessary if we are to realize in time that areas must be set aside where, in the ultimate interests of mankind as a whole, the spread of man must take second place to the conservation of other species.'[33] Moreover, according to Huxley, UNESCO should care for 'enlarging the emo-

tional capacity of mankind and increasing the possibilities of emotional sat-
isfaction' through drama and painting, architecture and good planning – and
national parks.[34] The famous biologist, ecologist and evolutionary theorist had
actively supported such private organizations like the International Office for
Nature Protection (IOPN) in Brussels. The scientific network of experts engaged in preservation had started in 1928 to collect information worldwide.
Now all of a sudden Huxley was a key player with the political and financial
power to make existing networks actually work. He helped to revive the former IOPN under the new name of International Union for Nature Protection (IUPN; some years later, Protection gave way to Conservation to make
it IUCN) and thus established a small but influential hybrid organization
that was to provide UNESCO with environmental know-how and ecological
expertise.[35]

Many of the people involved in the young IUPN were 'parks persons' with
colonial experience, like the Belgians Victor van Straelen and Jean-Paul Harroy, the American Harold Coolidge or the Swiss Charles Bernard and the Polish Wladyslaw Szafer. All of them had been involved in one way or another in
the creation and management of national parks at home or abroad. UNESCO
– actively backing the new network – helped to design a political platform
for discussing environmental issues. The experience of the infernal Second
World War had changed the tone of environmental debates. The Holocaust,
the atomic bomb, the entanglement of states and commerce, the pace of decolonization and the starving populations literally remodelled the world-view
of the community. Disturbing apocalyptic forecasts like Fairfield Osborn's
Our Plundered Planet and William Vogt's *Road to Survival* (both 1948) struck
a new chord. Nature protection was not only about rare species or thrilling
views anymore but also had to deal with the basic question of how life on a
rapidly changing planet could be guaranteed.

The debate was pushed forward when the Economic and Social Council of
the UN (ECOSOC) planned an international conference 'on the conservation
and utilization of natural resources' and asked UNESCO for administrative
and organizational support. The staff of Huxley's office challenged the biased
approach of ECOSOC as tending towards a purely technical interpretation
of natural resources. Indeed, the ECOSOC conference had been kicked off
by U.S. President Harry Truman who intended to put an end to armed conflicts caused by resource scarcity. That implied open access to and security of
supplies.[36] To UNESCO such a reduction of the resource debate seemed too
short sighted and smelled of a postcolonial extension of the Western control of
natural resources. Instead, the UNESCO staff emphasized the cultural, ethical
and moral aspects of the resource problem and promoted the idea of a global
legacy: 'All natural resources (like all human knowledge) are the common
heritage of mankind and consequently we should always keep in view before

us our responsibility of mutual trusteeship to one another, and to the unborn generations to come.'[37]

UNESCO tried to influence ECOSOC's conference agenda by sending experts lecturing on education and the preservation of wildlife. Besides, it insisted on organizing an embedded 'International Technical Conference on the Protection of Nature' that took place in Lake Success in 1949 and was actually not so much a conference dealing with technical but scientific and cultural issues.[38] Although it is almost forgotten in today's environmental historiography, it was an amazing get-together. In collaboration with IUPN, UNESCO invited nearly 300 institutions and organizations, ranging from the Argentine National Parks Administration, the Chinese Forest Conservation Service, the Rockefeller Foundation, the Bombay Natural History Society and animal protection societies from Nicaragua to the Natural Sciences Museum of Venezuela.[39] Eventually, 130 delegates gathered for ten days in the temporary UN headquarters in Lake Success to discuss the environmental problems of the world. The majority of the participants were from the United States, which was the hosting nation but also dominated international programmes and scientific institutions.[40] In the interwar period American conservationists had actively supported the IOPN by paying many of its bills. Now they framed the agenda of IUPN. They had the expertise and also the money the Europeans lacked. The list of speakers resembled very much a who's who of international environmentalism. The conferences radiated the atmosphere of hope and the will to change. The political and social tabula rasa caused by the war encouraged people to think big.

The scope of the agenda was unparalleled. It contained the worldwide education of the public regarding nature protection, international cooperation to promote ecological research, the balance of nature (threatened by the use of pesticides like DDT), the danger of the uncontrolled introduction of exotic species and the problem of the extinction of large mammals in Asia and Africa. Besides, a World Convention on Nature Conservation was discussed, as was the role of IUPN and the special problems arising from national parks bordering a frontier.[41] The role national parks should play in the cultural and aesthetic education of the general public remained uncontested. On a national level they were supposed to provide the outdoor experience people needed to understand ecological complexities and to accept the necessity to safeguard diversity. But UNESCO sought to transcend the national horizon. When listing topics to be discussed in Lake Success, one of the staff members, J. G. Crowther, had already suggested raising the issue of 'the surface of the globe as a World-Park.'[42] He had studied the U.S. national park system and concluded that 'the land surface of the world will gradually evolve into appropriate sections for agriculture, forestry, wilderness and recreation of the unity of man with nature, and a source of aesthetic inspiration and health. The technique necessary for the satisfactory control of the land as a world-park requires to be developed.' Crowther imagined the whole world being internationalized and divided into spheres – of which national parks would form a vital part. According to Crowther, the 'park' was a spatial concept characterized by control and management. Such ambitions to overcome remoteness were characteristic of the planning euphoria of the postwar years. Crowther's vision implied that international institutions would supervise the entire world. Moreover, it proved that UNESCO had not yet found a way to overcome the model of separate spheres for the exploitation respective to the sacredness of nature. UNESCO was still far from suggesting integrative models for a new relation between humans and the natural world.

The session dealing with the problems of frontier national parks showed that UNESCO and IUPN tried to develop new visions of international intervention. As the areas along the frontiers tended to be rather neglected and often underdeveloped, they were attractive for creating bi- or international parks. The park's administration was then to be supervised by an international commission.[43] Again, the international organization intended to act as a mediating body encouraging nations to create common parks, and as a board of arbitration, whenever bilateral problems would occur in such regions. It seemed a fair deal: IUPN offered help, professional expertise and an international and neutral perspective and would thus gain influence on spatial development along the borders.

Another amazing vision of international collaboration was presented at the conference in Lake Success. It suggested a kind of internationalization of national reserves. One of the most precious and acknowledged habitats in Europe, the Camargue – marshy wetlands in the delta estuary of the river Rhone with a unique variety of flora and fauna – had badly suffered from the Second World War (the German line of defence ran across the Camargue) and from various postwar development plans like draining parts of the wetlands for cultivating rice.[44] The reserve was in a bad state: its status was unclear and frequently menaced by new economic projects, poaching and air traffic. Due to its relevance to migrating birds and to the general biological importance of the Camargue, one of the French protagonists of the IUPN, Roger Heim, asked to introduce a resolution forcing the French government to provide the reserve with a definite legal status (like a national park) and to draft a scheme 'by which institutions of other countries would be associated in the control of the Camargue Reserve'. Moreover, the government should initiate 'a formula by which international cooperation might subsequently be extended to other protected territories'.[45] The resolution acknowledged that no reserve was an island. Did not the Camargue present one of the most important habitats and resting places for the European avifauna? Heim's suggestion was fully endorsed. In a way it represented the attempt to dissolve the national stigma attached to reserves and the first step towards a truly global concept of nature protection. It also asked of the states to share a part of their sovereignty to thoroughly globalize a locality. This idea seemed rather utopian. However, the imaginative atmosphere of the Lake Success conference encouraged visions that understood national parks as being important but only temporary steps on the way to a global scheme.

The 1950s introduced a rather prosaic discussion. From the outset, the experts of the postwar international community had called for a kind of environmental Esperanto, respectively an approved nomenclature to 'facilitate international understanding'.[46] This proved to be a Sisyphean task. In the first general debate of the Nomenclature Committee the experts spent most of the time discussing if the future terminology should be in Latin or French. In 1958 IUCN established a Provisional Committee on National Parks with five members representing Africa, three for Asia, and one each for North America, Latin America and Europe – 'a clear demonstration of the importance of bringing in the South'.[47] At this stage the predominance of the Yellowstone model was already questioned – the IUCN had been confronted with the accusation of 'protecting nature *against* rather than for people'.[48] There were growing doubts that the 'original' concept of national parks would satisfy the increasing requirements.

The 1960s saw the standardization of national parks: the IUCN managed to design an international taxonomy and presented the first global list of national parks in 1961.[49] In 1962 the IUCN sponsored the First World Conference on National Parks in Seattle. As the scope of content bearing the label 'national park' grew constantly, the IUCN insisted that a basic quality should be warranted and should have some protection itself. In a figurative sense the term 'national park' turned into a registered trademark and a currency. The list of UN's national parks and equivalent reserves prepared by IUCN got a loose-leaf format, underscoring its working-tool character. It served two main purposes – as a 'scaling ladder for all those already committed to the National Parks idea, and as a lever on governmental thinking and responses'.[50] After fifty years of investigation the ambitions of the international organizations had not really changed. They still acted as normative agencies with no executive power. All they could do was to collect data, set standards and evaluate progress, and thus foster the international advancement of nature protection by providing facts to be used by activists for encouraging governments to establish or maintain national parks for competitive reasons and prestige motives.

The national park concept eventually globalized when the idea of a World Heritage Trust to safeguard sites in developing countries emerged from a White House Conference on International Co-operation in 1965. The protagonists thought the scheme to protect sites in developing countries would make a topic for the centenary of the first national park, 'because it would seek to establish the "Yellowstone value" worldwide' – apparently unaware 'that the Yellowstone values were coming under sharp attack, for example in Africa,'[51] as Martin Holdgate observed. Although the World Heritage Programme – indeed one of the most successful flagship programmes of the UN – was no unique American invention but derived from Western concepts developed around the turn of the nineteenth to the twentieth century, it contained much of the initial park idea. It united the formerly separated strands of cultural and natural heritage and thus 'culturalized' the environmental issue and vice versa: the cultural issue was 'environmentalized' too. Conservationists' tools like red lists became popular for all sorts of cultural topics, and the terminology of threat and extermination influenced the heritage debates. Moreover, it promoted a conservation strategy that was based on a variety of spatial concepts developed in the United States and Europe and made its way from the League of Nations via IUCN and UNESCO to the Stockholm Conference, where it was launched in 1972. There are some more common features. The term 'national park' – like the globalized World Heritage – provided a convincing and catchy label. Moreover it offered a very comprehensible concept. Like national parks, World Heritage sites were and still are of insular character. They symbolize the separation of spheres into areas to be used and areas to be protected. Another feature they have in common is the role they play in consumer societies. Both have become 'emblematic products' of an industry producing cultural goods to be sold on the global market.[52] The labels indicate quality. Like national parks used to attract the intention of tourists, the World Heritage list has turned into a travel guide offering a global geography of superlatives.[53]

Separate Spheres in a United World – Concluding Remarks

To return to the initial question of where to situate national parks between nationalism, trans- and internationalism and globalization, paradoxically enough, nationalism helped a great deal to kick off the international debate on the protection of nature. This was not due to the uniqueness of the American concept but rather to the brilliant labelling. The linguistic persuasiveness of the label 'national park' had attracted the attention of the League of Nations in the first place. The prefix 'national' ennobled any reserve. Carrying the insignia of governmental protection and institutional/official appreciation, the national underscored patriotic attentiveness. Roderick Nash emphasized the positive connotation of the second part of the label: parks 'were symbols of [...] control over nature.'[54] This was especially true for the wilderness preserved in national parks. The wilderness was stalled by its insular status, the scientists' permanent 'surveillance', by rangers and roaming tourists. The term 'park' signified wilderness's limited character and preciousness. Last but not least, both terms could be found in all Romance languages and many others: *parc national* in French, *parco nazionale* in Italian, *Nationalpark* in German etc.

The role international organizations played in the dissemination of the national park and World Heritage concepts is equivocal. International organizations are normative institutions. They pronounced the creation of reserves as a universal necessity, collected information to prepare the common ground for future conventions and systemized, regulated and in a way also homogenized the standards of the labels. This was not necessarily a democratic process. For decades the Western perspective dominated the discussion about what national parks should not be or had to be. Moreover, a rather small network of Western male, white protagonists pursued the debate. The standardization of the labels was essential for guaranteeing a common terminology and also for building a corporate identity among these 'parks people'. In 1940 Arno B. Cammerer, then director of the U.S. National Park Service, had already predicted that the project of international cooperation would concern semantics: 'If we are far-seeing enough, park benefits can become an international heritage. The nature reservations and historic shrines of all countries can be united, not only by international peace parks, but by the international language of the park idea.'[55]

Eventually a new and fast growing transnational force tremendously accelerated the international collaboration: tourism. Tourism provided the customers ready to buy the product the international organizations offered – outstanding beauty and first-class scenery. And tourism created a market subsidizing the items on the World Heritage List. The invention of the World Heritage Convention reflected the global ambitions of international actors and organizations by declaring that the common heritage would eventually transcend national thinking and overcome national claims of ownership: 'World Heritage sites belong to all the peoples of the world, irrespective of the territory on which they are located.'[56] Ever since the programme for World Heritage was launched, however, it has been criticized for its Western approach and its one-dimensional scope of what should be nominated and what does or does not deserve to be listed. Probably it is this constructive criticism that will ensure the globalization of the concept in the long run.

Notes

1. http://www.nps.gov/oia/topics/worldheritage/worldheritage.htm (accessed 11 April 2011), author's emphasis.
2. Roderick Nash, 'The American Invention of National Parks', *American Quarterly* 22, no. 3 (1970): 726–35.
3. Richard White, 'The Nationalization of Nature', *Journal of American History* 86, no. 3 (1999): 986.
4. Evan Schofer, 'Science Associations in the International Sphere, 1875–1990', in *Constructing World Culture: International Nongovernmental Organizations Since 1875*, ed.

John Boli and George M. Thomas (Stanford, 1999), 249–66; David John Frank et al., 'The Rationalization and Organization of Nature in World Culture', in Boli and Thomas, *Constructing World Culture*, 81–99.

5. On the history of the Statione Zoologica see http://www.szn.it/SZNWeb/showpage /107?_languageId_=2 (accessed 11 April 2011).

6. Anna-Katharina Wöbse, 'Tourismus und Naturschutz – die internationale Dimension einer schwierigen Beziehung', in *"Wenn sich alle in der Natur erholen, wo erholt sich dann die Natur?" Naturschutz, Freizeitnutzung, Erholungsvorsorge und Sport – gestern, heute, morgen*, ed. Hans-Werner Frohn et al. (Bonn Bad Godesberg, 2009), 185–206.

7. Paul Sarasin, *Weltnaturschutz* (Basel, 1910), 12–13.

8. For details on the German and Swiss debate on national parks see the contribution by Patrick Kupper in this volume.

9. William M. Adams, *Against Extinction: The Story of Conservation* (London, 2004), 82.

10. Tom Mels, *Wild Landscapes: The Cultural Nature of Swedish National Parks* (Lund, 1999); Björn-Ola Linnér and Ulrik Lohm, 'Administering Nature Conservation in Sweden during a Century: From Conwentz and Back', *Jahrbuch für Europäische Verwaltungsgeschichte* vol. 11: 'Nature Use and Nature Conservation in European Legal and Administrative History' (Baden-Baden, 1999); Stefan Bachmann, *Zwischen Patriotismus und Wissenschaft: Die schweizerischen Naturschutzpioniere (1900–1938)* (Zürich, 1999).

11. *Nature* 90, no. 2243 (24 October 1912): 224.

12. Hugo Conwentz, 'Bericht über die Naturschutzsitzung beim XIII. Kongreß Russischer Naturforscher und Ärzte in Tiflis am 18. Juni a. St. 1913', *Blätter für Naturdenkmalpflege*, vol. 4 (1913): 448.

13. James Sievert, *The Origins of Nature Conservation in Italy* (Bern, 2000), 165–81.

14. Danny Trom, 'Natur und nationale Identität. Der Streit um den Schutz der "Natur" um die Jahrhundertwende in Deutschland und Frankreich', in: *Nation und Emotion: Deutschland und Frankreich im Vergleich 19. und 20. Jahrhundert*, ed. Etienne Francois, Hannes Siegrist and Jakob Vogel (Göttingen, 1995), 155.

15. Marc Cioc, *The Game of Conservation: International Treaties to Protect the World's Migratory Animals* (Athens, OH, 2009); Kurk Dorsey, *The Dawn of Conservation Diplomacy: U.S.-Canadian Wildlife Protection Treaties in the Progressive Era* (Seattle, 1998); Charles C. Chester, *Conservation across Borders: Biodiversity in an Interdependent World* (Washington, DC, 2006).

16. Preamble of the League of Nations, 19 April 1919; Akira Iriye, *Global Community: The Role of International Organizations in the Making of the Contemporary World* (Berkeley, 2002), 9–36.

17. Sarah Titchen, 'The Construction of Outstanding Universal Value: UNESCO's World Heritage Convention', PhD diss., Australian University, 1995); Astrid Swenson, '"Heritage", "Patrimoine" und "Kulturerbe": Eine vergleichende historische Semantik', in: *Prädikat 'Heritage': Wertschöpfung aus kulturellen Ressourcen*, ed. Dorothee Hemme, Markus Tauschek and Regine Bendix (Münster, 2007), 69f.; Mechtild Rössler, 'Weltkulturerbe und Globalisierung: Vom Weltwunder zum Erbe der Menschheit', in *Welt-Räume: Geschichte, Geographie und Globalisierung seit 1900*, ed. Iris Schröder and Sabine Höhler (Frankfurt/New York, 2005), 235–57.

18. Friedemann Schmoll, *Erinnerung an die Natur: Die Geschichte des Naturschutzes im deutschen Kaiserreich* (Frankfurt/New York, 2004).
19. Rössler, 'Weltkulturerbe und Globalisierung', 239.
20. LoN Archive, Geneva, Sitzungsprotokoll des Internationalen Komitees für geistige Zusammenarbeit, 16. Juli 1927, C.I.C.I./L.A./ 4th session/P.V.1–5(1), p. 18.
21. LoN Archive, Geneva, 5B/5189/5189; Rapport G.16.1928 (point 6).
22. LoN Archive, Geneva; 5B/5189/5189. Letter of the Artistic Relations Section to Georges Opresco, Secretary of the International Committee for Intellectual Cooperation, 13 July 1928.
23. UNESCO Archive, Paris, I.I.C.I. Correspondence, G.XIX.1 'Protection du Paysage et Beautés naturelles'.
24. LoN Archive, Geneva, 5B/5189/5189; Rapport G.16.1928 (point 6), p. 4.
25. Eduardo Hernandez-Pacheco, 'La protection de la Nature en Espagne', in *Premier Congrès International pour la Protection de la Nature,* ed. Raoul de Clermont et al. (Paris, 1925), 286–92.
26. http://www.senat.cz/zajimavosti/tisky/3vo/tisky/T0854_06.htm (accessed 11 April 2011).
27. Waléry Goetel, 'Les Parcs Nationaux en Pologne', in *Deuxième Congrès International pour la Protection de la Nature 1931,* ed. A. Gruvel, Charles Valois and G. Petit (Paris, 1932), 508–511.
28. Ibid., 511.
29. LoN Archive, Geneva, 5B/5189/5189; Rapport G.16.1928 (point 6), p. 5.
30. LoN Archive, Geneva, C.I.C.I./L.A./26, Report, 25.7.1930, p. 5.
31. C.I.C.I./Com/Ex/3eme session/P.V.4; Comité executif, Extrait, 11 April 1931.
32. Julian Huxley, *UNESCO, Its Purpose and Its Philosophy* (Paris, 1946), 55–56.
33. Ibid.
34. Ibid., 44.
35. Martin Holdgate, *The Green Web: A Union for World Conservation* (London, 1999), 18–19.
36. Björn-Ola Linnér, *The Return of Malthus: Environmentalism and Post-war Population-Resource Crises* (Isle of Harris, 2003).
37. UNESCO Archive. 502.7 A 06 /73) "49". Part I up to 30/IV/1948. Memorandum Dr Yeh Chu-Pei, ca. early 1947.
38. Anna-Katharina Wöbse, "'The World after all was one': The International Environmental Network of UNESCO and IUPN, 1945-1950', *Contemporary European History* 20, no. 3 (2011), 331-48.
39. UNESCO Archive, Paris: International Technical Conference on the Protection of Nature 1949, 502.7 A 06 (73) "49" 18.
40. Michael Lewis, *Inventing Global Ecology: Tracking the Biodiversity Ideal in India, 1947–1997* (Athens, OH, 2004); Adams, *Against Extinction.*
41. Holdgate, *Green Web*, 41–43.
42. UNESCO Archive, Paris: U.N. Scientific Conference on the conservation and utilization of resources. Final report by J. G. Crowther, Part II.
43. UNESCO Archive, Paris: Unesco/IUPN/Conf.2/ III Rep. Lake Success, 25 August 1949. Section III: World Convention and Frontier Parks.

44. Jaques de Cafarelli, 'Histoire de la réserve de Camargue', in: *Le Courrier de la Nature* no. 213, special SNPN 150e Anniversaire (Juin 2004): 58–60.

45. UNESCO Archive, Paris: Unesco/IUPN/Conf.2/ III Rep. Lake Success, 25 August 1949. Section III: World Convention and Frontier Parks.

46. IUPN, ed., *Preparatory Documents to the International Technical Conference on the Protection of Nature, August 1949, U.S.A.* (Paris/Brussels, 1949), 44–55.

47. Holdgate, *Green Web*, 69.

48. Ibid., 67, emphasis by Holdgate.

49. http://www.unep-wcmc.org/protected_areas/data/cnppa.html (accessed 11 April 2011); Holdgate, *Green Web*, 70.

50. Hugh Elliot, 'The United Nations List of National Parks and Equivalent Reserves and Its Development as a Tool for Achieving Higher Standards and Wider Coverage in the National Parks of the World', in *World National Parks: Progress and Opportunities*, ed. Richard van Osten (Brussels, 1972), 71.

51. Holdgate, *Green Web*, 106–7.

52. Rössler, 'Weltkulturerbe und Globalisierung', 248.

53. Anna Leask and Alan Fyall, *Managing World Heritage Sites* (Amsterdam et al., 2006).

54. Nash, 'American Invention of National Parks', 727.

55. Arno B. Cammerer as cited by Hillroy A. Tolson, Frontier and international park problems. UNESCO Archive, Paris: Unesco/IUPN/Conf.2/ III Rep. Lake Success, 25 August 1949. Section III: World Convention and Frontier Parks.

56. http://whc.unesco.org/en/about/ (accessed 11 April 2011).

 CHAPTER 8

Global Values, Local Politics

*Inuit Internationalism and the Establishment
of Northern Yukon National Park*

Brad Martin

Since the dawn of the conservation movement, the creation of national parks and other protected areas has often forced the removal of indigenous peoples from their traditional homelands and caused serious harm in their communities. In diverse regions of the globe, imperial, national and international efforts to 'civilize nature' by imposing Western conservation practices have undermined subsistence economies and contributed to the erosion of native institutions and cultural values. Such impositions have left a legacy of bitterness in some quarters and given rise to various forms of opposition rooted in distinctive moral ecologies. Not surprisingly, then, interactions between indigenous peoples and conservationists have often been fraught with tension, conflict and violence.[1]

Yet in recent decades, many indigenous leaders and state environmental managers have begun to collaborate in unprecedented ways. This new willingness to cooperate has resulted in a wide range of innovative conservation measures that make provision for local decision making and permit resource use and the presence of human communities inside protected areas. The most far reaching of these new arrangements recognize aboriginal land claims and have been designed to help ensure the survival of indigenous cultures.[2]

How did this transformation in global environmental protection occur? What explains the emergence in the second half of the twentieth century of new conservation models that incorporate indigenous values and community aspirations? Answers to these questions demand study of indigenous environmental activism, for, in many cases, indigenous peoples themselves brought about these changes through political pressure. In addition, such questions highlight how the global spread of Western conservation norms has been challenged, adapted and translated in local contexts. How successful have indigenous peoples been in opposing dominant national park ideals, and what sort of political strategies have they employed in their efforts?

This essay explores these questions by examining the creation of Northern Yukon National Park (later re-named Ivvavik National Park) in the western Canadian Arctic.[3] During the 1960s and 1970s, indigenous leaders from this region and neighbouring Alaska made determined efforts to influence the management of federal conservation areas on their traditional territories.[4] These efforts were sparked by the rapid expansion of oil and gas exploration in the Beaufort Sea, which threatened to destabilize Inuit communities. Subsequent disputes over land and natural resources were profoundly shaped by the distinctive borderland geography and politics of the region. In their efforts to influence conservation officials, indigenous leaders shared tactical knowledge across a porous international border and adopted legal and moral arguments from native rights struggles in southern Canada, the United States and abroad. As part of a wider effort to control the impacts of outsiders on their communities, they drew on these resources to chart new directions for northern protected areas.

Environmental historians and historians of indigenous peoples have seldom examined the influence of native political activism on state and international conservation efforts. By contrast, this essay shows how the Inuvialuit – the Inuit of the western Arctic – played pivotal roles in transforming national park policy in northern Canada by building transnational political relationships that helped challenge the imposition of universalist conservation practices. In foreshadowing the convergence of human rights, native rights and environmental politics in the final decades of the twentieth century, these efforts provided a model for others to follow in their own struggles with national park planners.

Of course, the Inuvialuit were not the first indigenous peoples to oppose the incursions of interlopers intent on protecting nature. As abundant scholarship has shown, aboriginal groups the world over have been victims of state-sponsored environmental encroachment and have frequently fought back. Pioneering works often drew on subaltern studies to show how colonial conservationists sparked popular defiance in rural Africa and South Asia, where distinctive resource uses and local environmental values prevailed.[5] Following James Scott, much of this literature highlighted how peasant communities challenged foreign forms of nature protection through 'criminal' behaviour and varied kinds of everyday protest.[6] Before long, historians of other parts of the globe, including North America, followed suit. In a path-breaking work, Mark David Spence demonstrated how the creation of the first national parks in the American West resulted in the dispossession of indigenous communities.[7] More attuned to the ideological bases of rural protest, Karl Jacoby and Louis Warren showed how local opposition to protected areas and wildlife laws in the United States during the nineteenth and early twentieth centuries was rooted in the moral ecologies of the countryside.[8] Finally, John Sandlos took research in useful new directions by showing how the efforts of the Canadian government to simultaneously civilize nature and domesticate northern native peoples bred scattered local protests in the same period and later contributed to the emergence of a wider political movement.[9]

This international literature has influenced the broad conceptualization of this essay, especially its attention to the conflicting environmental values of national park planners, other state conservationists and the Inuvialuit. While rich and compelling, however, this work holds limited value because it either focuses explicitly on colonial contexts or embraces colonialism as a key explanatory tool. Framing rural environmental protest as a colonial encounter is problematic for three reasons. First, it necessarily implies deeply unequal power relations between the colonizer and colonized. Second, it focuses scholarly attention on isolated acts of 'resistance', while neglecting more coordinated forms of political protest. Third, it is incapable of explaining how formal political organizations created by marginalized social groups have influenced conservation practices in modern liberal democracies, often through international activism. As scholars such as Ronald Niezen and Alison Brysk have shown, indigenous communities in various parts of the globe organized powerful political movements in the final third of the twentieth century and challenged established authorities by forging transnational political alliances.[10] Not infrequently, they targeted state and international conservation projects. Rather than a conceptual framework that takes colonialism for granted or focuses narrowly on happenings at the local level, events in the northern Yukon demand an approach that highlights regional, national and international developments and charts the complex interaction between them. In keeping with the key insights of the 'new global history', such an approach is essential for understanding how Inuvialuit leaders helped transform national park planning in the western Canadian Arctic and beyond.[11]

The Western Arctic: An International Arena

When outsiders consider the Arctic, they often imagine it as a remote and isolated place. Bookshelves around the world groan with an ever-expanding literature that describes the region as variously harsh, forbidding, distant and lonely – and, therefore, as an ideal location for exploration and adventure.[12] In the second half of the twentieth century, such popular imaginings were powerful resources for national park planners in Canada. Impelled by national and international developments to create new parks in the Yukon and Northwest Territories, they justified their proposals by stressing the need to protect the untouched wilderness of a fragile and frozen hinterland.[13] These proposals drew on a global iconography that situated the Arctic beyond the edge of civilization and depicted it as a symbol of sublime isolation. Rooted in such imagery, conservation in the North seemed like a patriotic duty to many Canadians, for they had come to believe in the century since confederation that their national character and identity were intimately tied to the wild seclusion of the region.[14]

In the 1970s, however, parts of the Canadian Arctic were not as isolated as many people thought. Indeed, as scholars have recently demonstrated, the northern regions of North America have a long history of international engagement and exchange that defies popular conceptions of them.[15] The western Canadian Arctic, in particular, had become an international arena as early as the 1890s, when whalers from the United States and other countries, having depleted their catch in the Pacific Ocean, arrived in the Mackenzie Delta in pursuit of new supplies.[16] Most of the whalers were gone a decade later, but they were soon followed by other outsiders. Missionaries linked with global proselytizing efforts operated in the region at the turn of the twentieth century, ministering and establishing religious schools among the Inuvialuit.[17] After the Second World War, southern social workers, healthcare professionals and educators descended on the region as the Canadian welfare state expanded its reach to include native northerners.[18] But it wasn't until the early 1960s, as the federal government made determined efforts to counter foreign influence in the Arctic, develop northern natural resources and carve out a new role for Canada on the international stage, that the western Arctic began to be characterized by the sort of dense and transformative international connections that Bruce Mazlish and other historians of globalization have associated with the new global epoch.[19]

Fittingly, it was an event that took place across the international border in Alaska that served as a tipping point for the developments examined in this essay. The discovery of massive oil and gas reserves at Prudhoe Bay in 1968 set off a rush by some of the world's largest oil companies to locate further deposits in adjacent Canadian waters – a situation that only intensified when the OPEC oil crisis was declared several years later. The Beaufort Sea and Mackenzie Delta were targeted as particularly promising for exploration, which led to escalating drilling and seismic activities in the area. The Canadian government supported the rush wholeheartedly, granting generous leasing permits through the chief agency responsible for administering Crown lands in the region, the Department of Indian Affairs and Northern Development (DIAND). By contrast, national and international environmental groups were dismayed by what they perceived as an unholy alliance between industry and government. By the middle of the decade, organizations as diverse in size, philosophy and political sophistication as the Sierra Club, the World Wildlife Fund, the National and Provincial Parks Association of Canada, the Canadian Arctic Resources Committee and the Federation of Ontario Naturalists had decried the desecration of northern ecosystems by domestic and foreign oil companies and called for the creation of some form of protected area in the region.[20]

For their part, the Inuvialuit were alarmed by the rapid expansion of oil and gas development in the western Arctic and feared it would undermine their culture and communities. The waters of the Beaufort Sea and Mackenzie Delta, as well as the terrestrial regions of the northern Yukon and Northwest Territories, had long sustained their subsistence lifestyles by serving as habitat for critical wildlife species, including barren ground caribou, bowhead whales and various waterfowl.[21] A relatively small cultural group – about 2,500 people divided among six settlements – the Inuvialuit made a formal land claim against the federal government in 1977 in part to protect their traditional territories from further industrial harm. This move committed community organizers to a framework for negotiations recently designed by federal authorities to facilitate the exchange of land, cash and economic benefits for the extinguishment of aboriginal title.[22] Given the tenor of native politics in North America at the time (symbolized for many by the violent clash between American Indians and the United States government at Wounded Knee, South Dakota, in 1973), some observers expected the Inuvialuit to aggressively oppose oil and gas development in the western Arctic.[23] However, while developed by community organizers familiar with the political radicalism of the Dene Nation and the Red Power movement, the negotiating position they took was not as hostile as many of their critics feared. Instead, as historian Paul Sabin has suggested was typical of many northern indigenous communities in the 1970s, the primary response of Inuvialuit leaders to the expanding operations of multinational companies on their traditional territories was not to oppose them outright, but rather to attempt to control their scope and pace.[24]

Despite this moderate position, the organization charged with negotiating the Inuvialuit land claim, the Committee for Original Peoples' Entitlement (COPE), faced daunting challenges as a result of its lack of money, experience and other resources. In response, it drew on a range of political tools and partnerships in efforts to level the playing field with federal authorities. Most important for this essay, COPE forged strong political connections with the Inupiat Eskimos of northern Alaska in order to learn from their earlier land claim experiences. On several occasions during the 1970s, the organization sent delegations across the international border to discuss the Alaska Native Claims Settlement Act (ANCSA), the sweeping piece of federal legislation that settled land claims in that state based on a model of native corporate development in 1971.[25] Inupiat leaders urged COPE officials to place the highest priority in their political battles on protecting subsistence activities, something many Alaska Natives felt ANCSA did not do.[26] Inuvialuit leaders subsequently used this advice as a guidepost in their land claim negotiations to maintain access to key wildlife areas in their traditional territories, secure legal protection for hunting and trapping lifestyles and gain influence in government wildlife management bodies.

The relationship between Inupiat and Inuvialuit politicians was nurtured by their geographical proximity and built upon strong cultural and familial ties that existed well before an international boundary was charted through their shared homeland at the turn of the twentieth century. These close connections, common in borderland regions, help explain the singular importance of this relationship in Inuvialuit politics. But COPE reached out to other indigenous leaders as well, as a political awakening spread among aboriginal groups throughout the circumpolar North in the 1970s. Early on, COPE sent representatives to two important gatherings where indigenous leaders from across northern Canada shared common concerns and developed strategies to exploit the new federal willingness to address their grievances.[27] Later in the decade, its delegates attended the Arctic Peoples' Conference sponsored by the Inuit Tapirisat of Canada in Copenhagen, Denmark, and the first meeting of the Inuit Circumpolar Conference. These gatherings provided Inuvialuit leaders with strategic insight and an appreciation for the global scope of their struggles that foreshadowed their involvement with many regional, national and international organizations in the years to come. In the more immediate future, the knowledge and experience they gained from this emerging network of indigenous activists proved critical in the conflict over Northern Yukon National Park.

Negotiating a New Cultural Landscape

Given the intense interest of national and international environmental groups in the future of the western Arctic after the Prudhoe Bay oil strike, it was perhaps inevitable that a protected area would be established in the region. In the mid-1970s, however, numerous proposals, ranging from a designation under the International Biosphere Programme to a National Wildlife Area run by the Canadian Wildlife Service, had been made, and it was by no means clear what form the protected area would take, who would manage it or where it would be located.[28] While Parks Canada had studied the possibilities of establishing a national park in the northern Yukon since the early 1970s, the agency was only one of several conservation interests operating in the region.[29] Moreover, reflecting historic tensions in the federal bureaucracy, the efforts of national park planners were typically trumped by officials in more powerful departments when land uses and natural resources were contested. Nor had a consensus been reached among government officials on the roles and rights that indigenous peoples should have in protected areas.[30] This issue became a matter of national debate as the northern land claims movement evolved, mirroring earlier discussions within the International Union for the Conservation of Nature (IUCN) and at international gatherings such as the First World Conference on National Parks held in 1962. At mid-decade, then, the western Arctic remained a tangle of conflicting interests and vexing management dilemmas that left the question of conservation up in the air.

In an effort to address the polarized political climate in the region, the federal government established the Mackenzie Valley Pipeline Inquiry in 1974. Intended as an impartial assessment of the potential social and environmental impacts of an oil and gas pipeline running the length of the Northwest Territories, the exercise profoundly influenced debates over northern protected areas. Conducted over three years, the inquiry visited numerous northern communities, where native residents repeatedly voiced their opposition to the project. Importantly for this essay, Inupiat Eskimos from Alaska testified on behalf of their Inuvialuit neighbours at inquiry hearings in the western Arctic, describing the destructive influence of the construction of the Trans-Alaska Pipeline on their communities and voicing concerns over the impact of industrial development on international wildlife populations. In the end, the inquiry recommended against the construction of a pipeline until native land claims in the area were settled, a conclusion accepted by the federal government. In addition, deeply influenced by the testimony of Inuvialuit and Inupiat witnesses, the inquiry called for the establishment of a 5,000-square-kilometre wilderness park along the Arctic coast of the Yukon.[31]

While the commissioner of the inquiry, Thomas Berger, a provincial Supreme Court justice and renowned native rights lawyer, has sometimes been credited with the idea for the wilderness park, it was in fact an international organization led by Canadian and American academics that initially made the proposal. Typical of the sort of transnational networks of conservationists and scientific experts discussed elsewhere in this collection, the organization, the Arctic International Wildlife Range Society (AIWRS), had been formed in the late 1960s to promote the idea of a vast international reserve incorporating the Alaska National Wildlife Range and adjoining land in the northern Yukon.[32] When the Mackenzie Valley pipeline hearings began, AIWRS leaders viewed them as an ideal venue to lobby Canadian officials and made a lengthy submission that focused on the need to protect caribou populations, migratory waterfowl and the delicate tundra ecosystem. However, in his final recommendations on the pipeline project in 1977, Berger incorporated the arguments of indigenous witnesses into the AIWRS plan and proposed a new kind of protected area that enshrined native access to land and wildlife.[33]

In the months and years that followed, the wilderness park idea became a focal point of discussion in the Inuvialuit land claim negotiations. While COPE initially opposed the creation of any form of protected area in the northern Yukon (preferring the Inuvialuit to own the land themselves), the organization later changed its position. In fact, within the first year of negotiations, Inuvialuit leaders had concluded that any settlement package they received would likely confirm the federal government as the majority land owner in the western Arctic. Therefore, they focused their efforts on securing access to wildlife and gaining a measure of control over natural resources on Crown territory.[34] This strategy was confirmed in the 1978 Agreement-in-Principle (AIP), a mutual commitment by COPE and federal negotiators to finalize the settlement. This agreement documented Inuvialuit support for the creation of a large reserve along the Beaufort Sea coast based on the management principles Berger outlined in his wilderness park recommendation. The proposed reserve allowed for native hunting and trapping, permitted the construction of temporary human settlements and guaranteed economic opportunities for the Inuvialuit. In addition, the AIP established the National Wilderness Park Steering Committee (NWPSC), an advisory group charged with devising management practices for the reserve and a conservation strategy for the vast region of boreal forest bordering it to the south.[35]

While the product of distinctive negotiations, plans for a new kind of protected area in the northern Yukon bore the marks of wider regional, national and international developments. Since the early twentieth century, indigenous peoples throughout the Canadian North had opposed state conservation in small but meaningful ways, insisting it displaced established communities and imposed objectionable wildlife laws.[36] Given their exclusionary character, government efforts to preserve empty 'wilderness' were anathema to hunting and gathering peoples.[37] Such efforts increased in the North after the Second World War as public interest in the region grew, environmental lobby groups began to influence national park politics and the National Parks Branch prioritized the preservation of nature over recreational use.[38] Simultaneously, international efforts to rationalize the designation and management of protected areas began to shape events in North America. This development spurred Canadian park officials to envision a network of vast reserves in the Arctic and sub-Arctic based on systematic planning, technical expertise and scientific practice.[39] By the early 1970s, northern indigenous peoples were using new federal institutions to mount legal and moral challenges to these plans. In particular, spokesmen from the Council for Yukon Indians and the Inuit Tapirisat of Canada convinced House of Commons and Senate committees that a new category of protected area called a 'national park reserve' was required to prevent the denial of aboriginal title when national parks were established.[40] Such efforts were reinforced by ongoing debates in the IUCN and other international forums over the very meaning of 'ecology' and 'environment'. Initially dominated by biologists and anthropologists, but increasingly influenced by indigenous peoples by the early 1980s, these discussions centred on the roles of human communities in natural ecosystems and thus fundamentally challenged conventional conservation practices worldwide.[41]

Parks Canada was profoundly influenced by these entangled developments and was forced to change its management practices. The agency was very active in international conservation debates during the 1970s and responded to the emerging native rights movement by rethinking its relationship with aboriginal Canadians. In 1979, the following statement was added to Parks Canada policy guidelines in an effort to make national parks more attractive to northern indigenous peoples:

> Not all national parks are the same. In remote or northern areas, potential national parks may be identified which are the homeland of people who have traditionally depended on the land and its resources for their survival. Their culture reflects this fundamental relationship. In certain cases, lands which have been traditionally used by native people are the subject of unresolved claims. If such areas are to be protected within the national park system, they must be planned and managed in a way which reflects these special circumstances.[42]

Following the signing of the Agreement-in-Principle, members of the National Wilderness Park Steering Committee began discussions on a conservation regime for the northern Yukon. The discussions involved representatives from Parks Canada, the Canadian Wildlife Service, the federal Department of Environment, the federal Department of Fisheries and Oceans, the Inuvialuit and a neighbouring First Nation, the Vuntut Gwich'in. The participation of the Inuvialuit reflected their keen awareness of the powerful forces of change arrayed against their communities and a pragmatic acceptance of the potential benefits of government conservation, even if they were determined to shape any new protected areas to their own ends. In fact, it was clear right from the start of committee deliberations that all of the participants would be dogged in pursuit of their goals and that agreement among them would be difficult to reach.[43]

Parks Canada felt a vast new park straddling the traditional territories of the Inuvialuit and Gwich'in should be created and managed under the National Parks Act. This proposal expanded Berger's wilderness park recommendation by more than 3,000 square kilometres and sparked tensions between the two indigenous groups, neither of which supported the creation of a traditional national park. Like their native counterparts, representatives from the Canadian Wildlife Service opposed the tourist objectives and recreational focus of Parks Canada. Instead, they felt conservation in the western Arctic should focus on the protection of caribou habitat, a goal that worried proponents of oil and gas development. For their part, the departments of Environment and Fisheries and Oceans objected to demands by the Inuvialuit for preferential harvesting rights in the region on the grounds that they would create conflict with nonindigenous hunters.[44] Meanwhile, the Yukon government, intent on establishing an energy corridor to the Beaufort Sea, initially refused to participate in discussions at all, although it later proposed a planning model for the region that favoured industrial activities.[45]

The resistance Inuvialuit leaders encountered in NWPSC deliberations was compounded by opposition to their wider land claim negotiations. In addition to the Yukon government, oil and gas companies, neighbouring indigenous peoples and the government of the Northwest Territories all denounced the COPE claim for a variety of economic, ethical and jurisdictional reasons in the late 1970s.[46] These objections led federal officials to renege on promises made in the Agreement-in-Principle, prompting a breakdown in negotiations in 1980.[47] While formal talks were suspended, industry executives moved forward with plans to build oil and gas production facilities in the northern Yukon. In particular, Gulf Canada Resources developed a proposal for the construction of a deep-water port within the boundaries of the proposed wilderness park, and a Toronto consulting firm made arrangements to develop a rock quarry nearby. These plans included a network of supporting roads, pipelines and offshore drilling platforms that deeply concerned many northern residents.[48] Due mainly to objections voiced by the Inuvialuit, the federal government did not grant permits for these projects, but the plans themselves suggest how development pressures were increasing in the western Arctic as land claim negotiations languished. As a result, when formal talks resumed in 1983, COPE – already faced with dwindling financial resources and growing frustration among its supporters – felt compelled to reach a quick settlement.

In the end, rather than the protected area Berger had proposed for the region, a conservation regime reflecting the interests of diverse stakeholders and emphasizing multiple use was established in the northern Yukon. A key component in this arrangement, Northern Yukon National Park was created in the northwest corner of the territory, where it abutted the international border and included the critical calving grounds of the Porcupine caribou herd. To the east of the new park, a 'special conservation area' managed by the Canadian Wildlife Service permitted limited industrial development. To the south, the aboriginal title of the Vuntut Gwich'in First Nation remained unresolved, although a second national park was created on their traditional territories years later.[49] In the months preceding this final resolution, COPE negotiators made significant concessions in their land claim negotiations, yet they prioritized the creation of protected areas that took Inuvialuit cultural values into account and safeguarded local subsistence needs. The establishment of a national park as part of the 1984 Inuvialuit Final Agreement (IFA) reflected their commitment to this goal and to the process of making state conservation in the North more responsive to the concerns of indigenous peoples.

The unique circumstances surrounding the origins of Northern Yukon National Park made it fundamentally different from all other protected areas in Canada. The first national park created in conjunction with a modern land claims settlement, it was distinguished by its accommodation of indigenous political demands. To start, the settlement legislation provided for the exclusive right of Inuvialuit hunters to harvest game in the park. This right was circumscribed by conservation regulations designed to ensure the survival of key wildlife species, but it effectively reserved the total allowable harvest for settlement beneficiaries. In addition, the IFA mandated the protection of related subsistence activities. Two provisions COPE worked especially hard to include permitted the use of modern hunting technologies within park boundaries and safeguarded traditional economic activities in the northern Yukon, including the trade, barter and sale of animal products. These novel arrangements were supplemented by employment benefits and the promise of limited self-determination. In particular, the settlement legislation guaranteed equal participation for the Inuvialuit on advisory bodies reporting to the responsible federal minister, which gave them increased influence over park and wildlife management in the Beaufort Sea Region.[50] The combination of these unique features of the IFA ensured that Northern Yukon National Park was far less burdensome for local residents than many other protected areas across the country. Indeed, powerfully shaped by the politics of COPE, it institutionalized a profound criticism of the disruptive and exclusionary practices that had characterized conservation in Canada for more than a century.

Conclusion: Parks as Globalized Localities

In the years and decades following the signing of their land claim agreement, the Inuvialuit increasingly pressed for the protection of their traditional territories and subsistence lifestyles on the international stage. In fact, several residents from the remote communities in the western Arctic that were so transformed by oil and gas development in the 1970s assumed prominent positions in the Inuit Circumpolar Conference (ICC). This pattern of Inuvialuit activism was part of a broader political development involving indigenous groups the world over in the final decades of the twentieth century. No longer content to work solely within domestic channels, native activists in diverse regions of the globe linked their local environmental grievances to transnational institutions and languages and pressured their political adversaries in international arenas. For the ICC, such activism continues to the present day, typified by the signing in May 2011 of *A Circumpolar Inuit Declaration on Resource Development Principles in Inuit Nunaat,* a document developed by Inuit leaders in Russia, Canada, Greenland and Alaska. The Canadian signatory to the declaration was ICC Vice-Chair Duane Smith, an Inuvialuk from the western Arctic whose views on conservation and resource use were shaped in the 1990s by his roles in implementing the IFA and negotiating wildlife management agreements with the Inupiat Eskimos.[51]

This recent international activism is part of the legacy of political ideas and relationships first developed by the Inuvialuit when the creation of Northern Yukon National Park was being debated. Equally determined to preserve their access to critical wildlife species and control the impacts of oil and gas development on their communities, they forged regional and international political connections and demanded new approaches to state conservation on their traditional territories. These demands were made in the context of wider land claim negotiations, a situation that decisively shaped them. Initially opposed to the creation of federal protected areas in the western Arctic, the Inuvialuit later came to accept the principle of state conservation as part of a pragmatic political trade-off. Still, the establishment of Northern Yukon National Park heralded the arrival of a new kind of conservation in northern Canada because the park acknowledged indigenous interests and institutionalized local values. This outcome, in turn, reflected the development by the Inuvialuit of a novel brand of environmental politics shaped in important ways by national and international forces. In the years after the park was created, the Inuvialuit refined their political ideas and partnerships and brought them to bear in other conservation struggles on their traditional territories and beyond.[52]

The story of Northern Yukon National Park demonstrates how powerful international conservation norms can be adapted and appropriated in local settings. Motivated by an emerging global ethic of scientific rationalism and the desire to preserve Arctic wilderness in the 1970s, Canadian national park planners were confronted by indigenous activists determined to protect their communities. Scholars have often shown how the imposition of foreign conservation models can harm local residents. By contrast, this essay highlights how a national park in the Canadian North was established as a tool for indigenous cultural survival and used as a vehicle for making claims on the state. In addition, the story reveals how seemingly discrete conservation struggles are often shaped by global developments. For good reason, scholars of national parks frequently adopt local or national analytical frameworks in their research. But the early history of Northern Yukon National Park shows how future scholarship might benefit from taking a wider view. Even when studying the most remote and isolated national parks, much can be learned by approaching them as globalized localities.

Notes

1. The literature in this area is abundant. Helpful recent overviews include: Dawn Chatty and Marcus Colchester, eds., *Conservation and Mobile Indigenous Peoples: Displacement, Forced Settlement, and Sustainable Development* (Oxford, 2002); Arun Agrawal and Kent Redford, 'Conservation and Displacement: An Overview', *Conservation and Society* 7, no. 1 (2009): 1–10; Daniel Brockington and James Igoe, 'Eviction for Conservation: A Global Overview', *Conservation and Society* 4, no. 3 (2006): 424–70.
2. William M. Adams and Martin Mulligan, eds., *Decolonizing Nature: Strategies for Conservation in a Post-Colonial Era* (London, 2003); Vasant Saberwal, Mahesh Rangarajan and Ashish Kothari, eds., *People, Parks, and Wildlife: Towards Coexistence* (New Delhi, 2001).
3. For a detailed discussion of the negotiations surrounding the creation of Northern Yukon National Park, see Brad Martin, 'Negotiating a Partnership of Interests: Inuvialuit Land Claims and the Establishment of Northern Yukon (Ivvavik) National Park,' in *A Century of Parks Canada, 1911–2011,* ed. Claire Elizabeth Campbell (Calgary, 2011), 272–301.
4. Daniel Nelson, *Northern Landscapes: The Struggle for Wilderness Alaska* (Washington, DC, 2004); Thomas R. Berger, *Northern Frontier, Northern Homeland: The Report of the Mackenzie Valley Pipeline Inquiry,* rev. ed. (Toronto, 1988); Theodore Catton, *Inhabited Wilderness: Indians, Eskimos, and National Parks in Alaska* (Albuquerque, 1997).
5. Nancy Lee Peluso, *Rich Forests, Poor People: Resource Control and Resistance in Java* (Berkeley, 1992); Roderick P. Neumann, *Imposing Wilderness: Struggles Over Livelihood and Nature Preservation in Africa* (Berkeley, 1998). For seminal works in subaltern studies, see the scholarship of Ranajit Guha and Gayatri Chakravorty Spivak.
6. James C. Scott, *Weapons of the Weak: Everyday Forms of Resistance* (New Haven, 1985); James C. Scott, *The Moral Economy of the Peasant* (New Haven, 1976).
7. Mark David Spence, *Dispossessing the Wilderness: Indian Removal and the Making of the National Parks* (New York, 1999).
8. Karl Jacoby, *Crimes Against Nature: Squatters, Poachers, Thieves, and the Hidden History of American Conservation* (Berkeley, 2001); Louis S. Warren, *The Hunter's Game: Poachers and Conservationists in Twentieth-Century America* (New Haven, 1997).
9. John Sandlos, *Hunters at the Margin: Native People and Wildlife Conservation in the Northwest Territories* (Vancouver, 2007).
10. Ronald Niezen, *The Origins of Indigenism: Human Rights and the Politics of Identity* (Berkeley, 2003); Alison Brysk, *From Tribal Village to Global Village: Indian Rights and International Relations in Latin America* (Stanford, 2000).
11. Bruce Mazlish, *The New Global History* (New York, 2006). For a broad sampling of work in the area, see the peer-reviewed online journal, *New Global Studies, http://www.bepress.com/ngs/.*
12. Recent scholarly studies include Russell A. Potter, *Arctic Spectacles: The Frozen North in Visual Culture, 1818–1875* (Montreal, 2007); Jen Hill, *White Horizon: The Arctic in the Nineteenth-Century British Imagination* (Albany, 2008). A key contemporary work is Barry Lopez, *Arctic Dreams: Imagination and Desire in a Northern Landscape* (New York, 1986).

13. On the plans of the National Parks Branch to expand the park system into the North in the 1960s, see Lloyd Brooks and Harold Eidsvik, *National Park Potentials: Northwest Territories and Yukon: Report of Field Operations and Recommendations* (Ottawa, 1963). For a wider perspective on the perception of northern 'wilderness' among government conservationists in Canada, see John Sandlos, 'From the Outside Looking In: Aesthetics, Politics, and Wildlife Conservation in the Canadian North', *Environmental History* 6, no. 1 (2001): 6–31.

14. On the connections between ideas about 'the North' and Canadian identity, see Sherrill E. Grace, *Canada and the Idea of North* (Montreal, 2001).

15. John R. Bockstoce, *Furs and Frontiers in the Far North: The Contest among Native and Foreign Nations for the Bering Strait Fur Trade* (New Haven, 2009); Ernest S. Burch, Jr., *Alliance and Conflict: The World System of the Inupiaq Eskimos* (Lincoln, 2005).

16. John R. Bockstoce, *Whales, Ice, and Men: The History of Whaling in the Western Arctic* (Seattle, 1995); David Morrison, 'The Winds of Change Blow Hard: The Whaling Era, 1890–1910', in *Across Time and Tundra: The Inuvialuit of the Western Arctic*, ed. Ishmael Alunik, Eddie D. Kolausok and David Morrison (Seattle, 2003), 79–111.

17. Morrison, 'Winds of Change', 93–7, 104.

18. Eddie D. Kolausok, 'Boom, Bust, and Balance: Life Since 1950', in Alunik, Kolausok and Morrison, *Across Time and Tundra*, 162–65. On the expansion of the Canadian welfare state into other regions of the Arctic, see Frank James Tester and Peter Kulchyski, *Tammarniit (Mistakes): Inuit Relocation in the Eastern Arctic, 1939–63* (Vancouver, 1994).

19. Mazlish, *New Global History*. On the growing interest of federal authorities in the resource and military potential of the Canadian North during the Cold War, see P. Whitney Lackenbauer and Matthew Farish, 'The Cold War on Canadian Soil: Militarizing a Northern Environment', *Environmental History* 12, no. 4 (2007): 920–50.

20. Kevin A. McNamee, 'The Northern Yukon', *Probe Post* (1984): 13–16; George W. Calef, 'The Urgent Need for a Canadian Arctic Wildlife Range', *Nature Canada* 3, no. 3 (1974): 3–10; Edgar J. Dosman, *The National Interest: The Politics of Northern Development, 1968–1975* (Toronto, 1975).

21. Peter J. Usher, *Eskimo Land Use and Occupancy in the Western Arctic*. A report submitted to the Inuit Land Use and Occupancy Project, 24 September 1974.

22. On the origins of the Inuvialuit land claim, see Peter Usher, *History of COPE* (Ottawa, 1973), 20–23; Robert McPherson, *New Owners in Their Own Land: Minerals and Inuit Land Claims* (Calgary, 2003), 64–66; Barry Scott Zellen, *Breaking the Ice: From Land Claims to Tribal Sovereignty in the Arctic* (Lanham, MD, 2008), 140–43, 156–60; Barry A. Hochstein, 'New Rights or No Rights? COPE and the Federal Government of Canada', MA thesis, University of Calgary, 1987, 49–106.

23. Zellen, *Breaking the Ice*, 166.

24. Paul Sabin, 'Voices from the Hydrocarbon Frontier: Canada's Mackenzie Valley Pipeline Inquiry (1974–1977)', *Environmental History Review* 19, no. 1 (1995): 17–48.

25. On ANCSA, see Donald Craig Mitchell, *Take My Land, Take My Life: The Story of Congress' Historic Settlement of Alaska Native Land Claims, 1960–1971* (Fairbanks, 2001).

26. Zellen, *Breaking the Ice*, 141, 196.

27. The two meetings were the Coppermine Conference of Arctic Native People, held in Coppermine, Northwest Territories, in July 1970, and the Federation of Natives North of Sixty meeting, held in Whitehorse, Yukon Territory, in May–June 1973.

28. Constance Hunt, Rusty Miller and Donna Tingley, *Wilderness Area: Legislative Alternatives for the Establishment of a Wilderness Area in the Northern Yukon* (Ottawa, 1979).

29. Parks Canada, *The Firth River, Yukon Territory: A Wild Rivers Survey Descriptive Report* (Ottawa, 1972).

30. Scholars have recently begun to examine how Parks Canada was wrestling with this issue in the 1970s and afterwards. See David Neufeld, 'Kluane National Park Reserve, 1923–1974', in Campbell, *Century of Parks Canada*, 235–72; I. S. MacLaren, 'Rejuvenating Wilderness: The Challenge of Reintegrating Aboriginal Peoples into the "Playground" of Jasper National Park', in Campbell, *Century of Parks Canada*, 333–70; Paul Kopas, *Taking the Air: Ideas and Change in Canada's National Parks* (Vancouver, 2007), 83–88, 121–29.

31. Berger, *Northern Frontier*; Martin O'Malley, *The Past and Future Land: An Account of the Berger Inquiry into the Mackenzie Valley Pipeline* (Toronto, 1976).

32. On the AIWRS, see 'Proceedings of the Arctic International Wildlife Range Conference, October 20–22, Whitehorse, Yukon Territory', *University of British Columbia Law Review* 6, no. 1 (1971): 1–107.

33. Berger, *Northern Frontier*, 74–77.

34. The Inuvialuit likely adopted this strategy as a result of their prior involvement in the Nunavut land claim negotiations under the direction of the Inuit Tapirisat of Canada (ITC). On this strategic decision, see Terry Fenge, 'National Parks in the Canadian Arctic: The Case of the Nunavut Land Claim Agreement', *Environments* 22, no. 1 (1993), 26.

35. *Inuvialuit Land Rights Settlement Agreement in Principle*, 31 October 1978, 61–66.

36. Peter Kulchyski and Frank James Tester, *Kiumajut (Talking Back): Game Management and Inuit Rights, 1900–1970* (Vancouver, 2007); Sandlos, *Hunters at the Margin*.

37. Tungavik Federation of Nunavut, 'Land Claims, National Parks, Protected Areas, and Renewable Resource Economy', in *Proceedings of the Arctic Heritage Symposium, 24–28 August 1985, Banff, Alberta, Canada*, ed. Gordon Nelson, Roger D. Needham and Linda Norton (Waterloo, ON, 1985), 285–97; Inuit Tapirisat of Canada, *Inuit Tapirisat of Canada Report on Proposals to Establish National Wilderness Parks in Inuit Nunangat* (Ottawa, 1979); Nicholas Lawson, 'Where Whitemen Come to Play', *Cultural Survival* 9 (1985): 54–56.

38. These national developments are key themes in Campbell, *Century of Parks Canada*. In particular, see the introduction: Claire Elizabeth Campbell, 'Governing a Kingdom: Parks Canada, 1911–2011', 1–19.

39. Kopas, *Taking the Air*, 53–58.

40. Ibid., 83–84, 86–88; Fenge, 'National Parks in the Canadian Arctic', 23; *Bill S-4, An Act to Amend the National Parks Act*, 1st Session, 29th Parliament, 1973; Canada, House of Commons, Standing Committee on Indian Affairs and Northern Development, Minutes, no. 29 (Whitehorse, Yukon, 12 December 1973), 31.

41. Kopas, *Taking the Air*, 121–2; Raymond Chipeniuk, 'The Vacant Niche: An Argument for the Re-Creation of a Hunter-Gatherer Component in the Ecosystems of Northern National Parks', *Environments (Canada)* 20, no. 1 (1989): 50–59.

42. Parks Canada, *Parks Canada Policy* (Ottawa, 1979), 40. On the exclusion of aboriginal peoples from national parks in Canada in an earlier period, see John Sandlos, 'Federal Spaces, Local Conflicts: National Parks and the Exclusionary Politics of the Conserva-

tion Movement in Ontario, 1900–1935', *Journal of the Canadian Historical Association* 16 (2005): 293–318; John Sandlos, 'Not Wanted in the Boundary: The Expulsion of the Keeseekowenin Ojibway Band from Riding Mountain National Park', *Canadian Historical Review* 89, no. 2 (2008): 189–221; Theodore Binnema and Melanie Niemi, '"Let the Line Be Drawn Now": Wilderness, Conservation, and the Exclusion of Aboriginal People from Banff National Park in Canada', *Environmental History* 11, no. 4 (2006): 724–50.

43.   Lloyd Brooks, *The Northern Yukon National Wilderness Park Proposal: Report of the Chairman of the National Wilderness Park Steering Committee*, 1 May 1980.

44.   'Minutes of the National Wilderness Park Steering Committee, First Meeting, Whitehorse, Yukon, 12–13 September 1979', Parks Canada Western Service Centre files, Whitehorse, Yukon.

45.   Letter from C. W. Pearson to the Honourable John Fraser, 11 February 1980. Library and Archives Canada (hereafter LAC), RG 108, vol. 47, box 148, file 5600-36/N112, pt. 1; Letter from Dan Lang to the Honourable John Roberts, 19 November 1980, LAC, RG 108, acc. 1989–90/079, box 60, file 9440-34-1, vol. 2; 'YTG Slams Feds for Park Approach', *Whitehorse Star*, 27 April 1978; Government of Yukon, *Northern Yukon Resource Management Model* (Government of Yukon, October 1980).

46.   'NWT Wants Own Parks', *Whitehorse Star*, 17 February 1978; 'Mutual Claim Blame', *Whitehorse Star*, 21 November 1978; 'COPE No Model for Yukon Say Native Leaders', *Whitehorse Star*, 17 July 1978.

47.   Zellen, *Breaking the Ice*, 164–71. On discussions within the Department of Indian Affairs and Northern Development about renegotiating the Agreement-in-Principle, see letter from Maurice LeClair, Treasury Board, to Arthur Kroeger, DIAND, 10 March 1978, LAC, RG 108, vol. 111, file 1165-36/C242; DIAND, 'Native Claims Policy – Comprehensive Claims', 20 July 1979, copy in Committee for Original Peoples Entitlement Archives (hereafter COPE Archives), Inuvik, Northwest Territories, Canada; DIAND, 'Discussion Paper: Native Claims Policy – Comprehensive Claims', 5 November 1980, copy in COPE Archives.

48.   'What Future for Northern Yukon?', *Beaufort Outlook* 1, no. 2 (1982): 2.

49.   Vuntut National Park was created in 1995 following the negotiation of the Vuntut Gwitch'in First Nation Final Agreement.

50.   Indian and Northern Affairs Canada, *The Western Arctic Claim: The Inuvialuit Final Agreement* (Ottawa, 1984), 18–22.

51.   The declaration is available at: http://www.inuit.org/index.php?id=432&contUid=0.

52.   In addition to Northern Yukon (Ivvavik) National Park, two other national parks have been created on Inuvialuit traditional territories: Aulavik National Park in 1992 and Tuktut Nogait National Park in 1996.

 CHAPTER 9

Demarcating Wilderness and Disciplining Wildlife

Radio Tracking Large Carnivores in Yellowstone and Chitwan National Parks

Etienne Benson

In the twentieth century, as national parks became sites for scientific research and objects of scientific management, they began – tentatively and incompletely – to leave behind their roots in nineteenth-century landscape aesthetics. Some new parks were established as scientific preserves where scientists could study apparently pristine ecosystems with minimal interference from competing human activities. Many existing parks, historically oriented toward recreation and nature preservation, found themselves caught between two visions. While they made room for park-based scientific research and attempted to integrate science into their management and interpretation practices, they also sought to prevent research and science-based management from undermining their identity as aesthetic or moral refuges from modern civilization. The clash between scientific and aesthetic visions of the parks should not be exaggerated; scientific insights into the geophysics of Yellowstone's geysers lent gravity to the spectacle of Old Faithful, and scientists were often drawn to study the natural phenomena of the parks because of their aesthetic appeal and cultural significance. Nonetheless, tensions did exist and regularly erupted into full-blown controversies over the proper relation between the scientific and aesthetic values of national parks.[1]

Although scholars have investigated the history of such tensions with regard to parks in the United States, Africa and, to a lesser extent, other regions of the world, the story that emerges has often been simplistic. Scientists have either been lionized as seekers of truth fighting a two-front war against starry-eyed romanticists and obstinate bureaucrats or unveiled as callous rationalists unable to appreciate aesthetic or moral values or the needs and hopes of local people. This essay attempts to avoid such extremes as well as the unsatisfying middle of 'sometimes one, sometimes the other'. Instead it shows how a particular scientific intervention and the criticisms to which it was subjected transformed discourses around wilderness and wildness in two national parks in the 1960s and 1970s, a crucial moment in the development of the national park as a land-use institution with global reach. One of the parks, Yellowstone, was, perhaps needless to say, the inheritor of a long tradition of disputes over park management. The other, Chitwan National Park in Nepal – then known as Royal Chitwan National Park – was established only in 1973, a year after Yellowstone celebrated its hundredth anniversary. The scientific intervention in question was the use of wildlife radio tracking to study large carnivores, which profoundly influenced the way territory was demarcated and wild animals were disciplined at these two very different but intimately connected sites.[2]

It is common to speak of the 'national park idea' or the 'Yellowstone model', but national parks have always been more than a concept or a set of principles; they have also been collections of very concrete practices that travel within what are often surprisingly small circuits. In describing the relationships between parks such as Yellowstone and Chitwan, there are two pitfalls to be avoided. The first is a comparative approach that ignores the contemporary connections and shared heritage linking the sites under consideration. The second is a diffusionist approach that emphasizes connections between sites but understands them only in terms of a one-way transfer from centres to peripheries. The new national parks that emerged around the world after the Second World War in both developed and developing nations were neither autochthonous inventions nor slavish copies of Yellowstone. They were the contingent products of the intersection of a universalizing discourse and highly mobile practices with various local conditions.

Yellowstone: Conflicting Ideas and Practices of Wilderness

The story begins with John and Frank Craighead's research on Yellowstone's grizzly bears (*Ursus arctos horribilis*) from the late 1950s to the early 1970s, which environmental historians have seen as a turning point in the U.S. National Park Service's often awkward relationship to science since its founding in 1916. The twin brothers' involvement in national park science began when the Park Service invited John Craighead to submit a proposal for studying grizzly bears in the northern Rocky Mountains. The invitation was motivated by concern about the increasingly dangerous interactions between the shrinking grizzly population of the Northern Rockies – the last refuge of the species in the United States outside of Alaska – and park visitors, whose numbers had grown explosively since the end of the Second World War. Park Service officials hoped that new techniques of wildlife management would help Yellowstone and Glacier National Parks maintain viable populations of grizzlies while minimizing attacks on tourists. Beginning with their postwar dissertation research at the University of Michigan, which had introduced several new methods for monitoring and censusing raptor populations, the Craighead brothers had rapidly risen to prominence among U.S. wildlife biologists. As a result of the Park Service's invitation, they co-led a study of grizzlies from 1959 to 1971 that pioneered a number of new research techniques, transformed the way the U.S. parks managed their bear populations, and resulted in a bitter and highly public dispute over the proper role of science and scientists in the parks.[3]

Wildlife radio tracking played a central role in this dispute for two reasons. First, more than any other technique deployed by the Craigheads in the course of their multifaceted research programme, radio tracking symbolized the application of innovative science and technology to the problems of conservation. The Craigheads were among the first to conduct field research with the technique, which at the time of their first field season in Yellowstone in 1959 had only just become a possibility. Wildlife radio tracking emerged in the United States from the intersection of wildlife management and Cold War technology in the decade or so after the launch of Sputnik in 1957, with generous funding from the Office of Naval Research and the National Science Foundation. As a way of demonstrating their discipline's maturation into a 'real' science, the Craigheads and other wildlife biologists touted radio tracking's roots in avionics and space research and its similarities to the sophisticated instrumentation of the physical sciences. The Park Service, then in the midst of an initiative to expand and modernize park facilities, also tried to capitalize on the technique's space-age associations. A few years after the Craigheads' study had begun, for example, the Yellowstone administration boasted in a press release that the park was hosting wildlife research involving the latest in 'modern devices'.[4]

At a moment in U.S. history when the physical sciences and engineering were seen as central to national security and economic prosperity, radio tracking's associations with Cold War technoscience helped bolster wildlife biologists' claims to authority. These associations also had a negative side, however, which became evident over the course of the 1960s as scepticism toward narratives of inevitable scientific and technological progress grew. In the case of national parks, this scepticism complemented a longer tradition of anti- or countermodernism. Radio tracking suited the technocratic ethos of many postwar wildlife managers, whose primary goal was the production of sustainable harvests of huntable game, but it sat less easily with the Park Service, which had always prided itself on serving higher goals. Many visitors to and employees of the national parks valued the parks precisely because they provided an escape, however temporary and self-contradictory it might be, from civilization and its gadgets. To these critics, the Park Service's embrace of radio tracking, at least in the Craigheads' first years in the park, represented a betrayal of core national park values. The hiker who spotted a grizzly in Yellowstone's back country would be robbed of a vital encounter with wildness, they suggested, if the grizzly turned out to be one of those the Craigheads had trapped, tattooed, ear-tagged and radio-collared.[5]

Among the most influential of the Craigheads' critics, despite his hesitance to speak on the matter in public, was Adolph Murie, a wildlife biologist and wilderness advocate with a long career in the Park Service. Murie had begun studying wildlife in the national parks in the 1920s and saw the parks as sanctuaries where wildlife could live without human persecution and where modern men and women could find spiritual rejuvenation. In 1963, justifying his opposition to a proposal to use recreational hunters to reduce Yellowstone's growing elk population, he explained to a colleague that there were

> scientific and other values in parks, but in my opinion the most fundamental values are in the realm of the esthetic and the spiritual. Our park ideals are an expression of the best in us. Our better instincts are given free play, and we have an opportunity to show tolerance and kindness toward our fellow creatures. This, I believe is uplifting to the human race.[6]

To Murie, radio tagging seemed neither tolerant nor kind and, most importantly, threatened to undermine the parks' aesthetic and spiritual values. Although he limited his written criticism of radio tracking to private correspondence and internal Park Service memos, by the end of the decade Murie was joined by other critics who were less shy about publicly criticizing the Craigheads and the parks for their reliance on 'invasive' techniques of wildlife research and management.[7]

These critics gained important allies within the Yellowstone administration when a new superintendent, Jack Anderson, took the reins in the summer of 1967. Together with Yellowstone's chief biologist, Glen Cole, Anderson began limiting the Craigheads' ability to conduct research where, when and how they saw fit. The conflict over research methods and park aesthetics was exacerbated by a disagreement between the Craigheads and the park administration over bear management. When the Craigheads found that their recommendations were being ignored, they turned to the popular press, which largely sided with them against the Park Service. The latter retorted that the Craigheads were abusing the privilege of conducting research in the park by trying to dictate park policies through the media rather than working through established channels.[8]

In 1969, as the dispute rose into national visibility, Anderson told John Craighead that the 'conspicuous marking of park wildlife seems to have reached the point where it detracts from the scenic and esthetic values obtained from viewing wildlife' and urged him to bring the tagging studies to an end.[9] Attacking the Craigheads' use of traps, tranquilizers, tags, tassels and tattoos suited the Park Service's turn toward a more 'natural' look for the parks in the 1960s as well as the Yellowstone administration's desire to terminate the Craigheads' research without seeming to be punishing whistleblowers or rejecting science. In 1971, the Craigheads refused to sign a memorandum of agreement that would have allowed them to continue working in the park, but only at the cost of severe restrictions on their research. With the Craigheads on the way out, Anderson instructed rangers to begin removing tags, tassels and collars from grizzlies and other wild animals in preparation for Yellowstone's 1972 centennial anniversary, when the park would host the Second World Congress on National Parks.[10]

As noted earlier, there were two reasons that wildlife radio tracking played a central role in the controversy over science and aesthetics in Yellowstone in the 1960s and 1970s. The first reason was that the technique served as an icon of Cold War technoscience for boosters and critics alike. The second reason was that radio tracking made possible new kinds of field practices and produced new kinds of data. That is, in addition to being an icon or a symbol, radio tracking was a tool whose use as part of a broader social and technical system transformed ways of knowing about and relating to the objects it was used to study. How significant was that transformation? Radio tracking might be seen as merely extending bird banding and other techniques for individually marking and tracking of wild animals that by 1960 had been in wide use by biologists for decades.[11] The extension was so dramatic in scope, however, that it necessitated qualitative shifts in field practices and data analysis methods, which eventually helped produce new understandings of grizzly bear habitat and behaviour. Ultimately, despite the breakdown of the relationship between the Craigheads and the Park Service and the temporary ban on tagging, these shifts profoundly changed Yellowstone's relation to science and to scientific views of ecosystem management.

Radio tracking had not been part of the Craigheads' initial research proposal to the Park Service, but by the time of their first field season in Yellowstone in 1959 it had come to seem like a singularly promising component of the project. The Craigheads' overall goal was to understand the demographics and distribution of the park's bear population, which required developing what they called, in an article published in *National Geographic* in 1960, 'identity cards' for bears.[12] Their initial proposal had focused on conventional marking techniques, such as attaching brightly coloured plastic ear tassels to individual bears so that they could be individually identified from a distance. Radio tracking did not replace such methods, but it did expand the horizon of research possibilities. In their *National Geographic* article, the Craigheads explained that miniaturized transmitters might make it possible to track bears as they prepared for winter, something that had proven nearly impossible with visual tags. It would allow researchers to locate marked bears at will rather than by accident and therefore, as they elaborated in a technical article several years later, 'to place observations on a quantitative level'.[13] As Gregg Mitman has argued, radio tracking was well suited to postwar U.S. biologists' vision of nature as the subject of expert surveillance and control.[14] On the basis of the data acquired through a combination of conventional tagging, radio tracking and field observation, the Craigheads would eventually argue for the necessity of managing the bears as part of a larger ecosystem that extended beyond the park's official borders. In the 1970s and 1980s, that concept would come to serve as a rallying point for conservationists under the rubric of the 'Greater Yellowstone Ecosystem'.[15]

Years before then, however, techniques developed by the Craigheads had already begun to transform the park's bear management practices. In April 1960, after reviewing Craigheads' first published scientific article on grizzlies, the Park Service's regional chief of interpretation told the Yellowstone superintendent that their techniques for trapping, tranquilizing, tagging and translocating bears would be useful for managing 'troublesome' bears.[16] Troublesome or 'problem' bears were those animals, most often black bears but sometimes grizzlies, that begged for food along roadsides or raided campgrounds in search of food. They were bears, in other words, whose behaviour violated an evolving understanding of the importance and nature of 'wildness' in park wildlife. As Alice Wondrak Biel has shown, bear feeding was tolerated and even, under certain conditions, encouraged in Yellowstone in the early twentieth century. By the 1960s, however, there was a widespread consensus, supported by Murie and other wilderness advocates, that feeding and the 'tame' bears that it produced – often disparaged as animal 'beggars' or 'bums' – undermined the value of the parks both as nature preserves and as sites for moral and spiritual rejuvenation.[17] Yellowstone and other parks adopted new policies under which problem bears that failed to respond to aversive conditioning and forced relocation and that continued to exhibit inappropriate behaviours, such as searching for food in campgrounds, were eventually killed. It was in the intermediate stage after identification as a problem animal but before execution as an incorrigible that radio tracking made the key biopolitical difference. By rendering individual animals locatable and identifiable, it enabled park administrators to assert a fine-grained disciplinary power in the name of the preservation of wildness.[18]

Radio tracking also contributed to a redefinition of the relevant territorial scope for wildlife management in the parks. As Michael Lewis has argued, radio tracking studies of large carnivores are particularly well suited to expansive conceptualizations of protected areas. The technique helps scientists map the enormous expanses over which individual animals can range, which often exceed the boundaries of any single park or reserve.[19] Similar information can, of course, be acquired using conventional tags. When a grizzly that had been captured and tagged near Yellowstone's geographical centre was shot by a hunter outside the park boundaries, as happened repeatedly during the Craigheads' twelve-year study, it was clear that the bear's 'home range' or at least its occasional wanderings exceeded the park's territory. But only radio tracking, with its potential for producing nearly continuous tracking data, could quantify the amount of time spent by the bears in various areas within and beyond the park. By the late 1960s, drawing from a vast collection of such data, the Craigheads had begun arguing strenuously that a bear management plan that considered Yellowstone as an island or fortress, insulated against threats and developments in the territories beyond its borders, was bound to fail.[20]

After Anderson and Cole's arrival in 1967, the Yellowstone administration became highly resistant to the Craigheads' attempts to redefine the park's territory as a porous and vulnerable component of a broader landscape. The differences between the two parties came to a head over the issue of the park's open-pit garbage dumps. In line with the Park Service's turn toward a more natural look for the parks in the 1960s, the Yellowstone administration had proposed closing the last remaining dump at Trout Creek, located near the geographical centre of the park. The dump had long served as a gathering place for grizzlies, and much of the Craigheads' research had been based on bears trapped and observed there. The Craigheads argued that most of the park's bears relied on the dump for at least part of their sustenance during the summer months and that a sudden closure would inevitably send hungry bears into campsites in search of food. The result, they argued, would be more bears identified as problem bears and eventually killed, which would threaten the survival of an already dangerously small population.[21]

Cole, Yellowstone's chief biologist, argued in response that only a portion of bears, those most likely to become problem bears in any case, had become reliant on garbage. The impact of closing the Trout Creek dump on the population as a whole would thus be minimal.[22] Behind this immediate conflict lay a deeper divergence in spatial imaginations of the park, which were in turn linked to differing ideas of wilderness. If the fate of the park and its bears were inextricably tied to developments outside the park borders, as the Craigheads suggested, then the only choice was between intentional and unintentional human manipulation. In contrast, if the park could be isolated from surrounding areas, as Cole and Anderson suggested, then it might be allowed to manage itself naturally. Moreover, the question of territory was also one of jurisdiction and interagency relations. If Yellowstone's bear population was, in fact, a regional population whose survival depended in part on decisions made by the state and federal agencies that managed surrounding lands, then the Park Service would be obligated to coordinate its bear policy with those other agencies. Each conception of territory entailed its own philosophy of wilderness and its own political consequences.

As of 1972, the year of Yellowstone's centennial, the park administration's perspective seemed to have won out in regard to both the aesthetics of wildlife tagging and the question of dump closure. Not only had the Craigheads been forced to terminate their research, but tagging even of relocated problem bears had been abandoned. The Trout Creek dump had been closed without the slow weaning-off period or the provision of alternative food sources that the Craigheads had recommended. These conflicts over research methods and management policy served as proxies for deeper questions about the nature of wildness and wilderness in the United States' most iconic national park. By abandoning tagging, Anderson and Cole took a stand against the intensive surveillance and management of the park's wildlife; by closing the dumps, they endorsed natural processes over human manipulation and wagered that the park could survive, with its bear population intact, as a wilderness island in a sea of cultivated or managed land. As I have argued elsewhere, this victory was short-lived but had long-term consequences for national park management in the United States.[23]

Chitwan: Hunting Traditions in the Era of Conservation

Just as the Yellowstone administration seemed to have definitively rejected the Craigheads' vision of an intensively managed, spatially porous national park in favour of hands-off research methods and so-called natural regulation within a sharply bounded territory, several of the Craigheads' students were attempting to transplant their ideas and practices from the Northern Rockies to the forests and grasslands of South Asia.[24] Maurice G. Hornocker, the first of John Craighead's graduate students to work on the grizzly project, had since earned his doctorate under Canadian wildlife biologist Ian McTaggart-Cowan with a study of Idaho's mountain lions (*Puma concolor*) and had, in turn, advised the doctoral research of one of the Craigheads' former undergraduate research assistants, John C. Seidensticker. In 1971 the Smithsonian Institution asked Hornocker to investigate opportunities for research on Bengal tigers (*Panthera tigris tigris*) in India, which was in the process of launching an ambitious new conservation programme called Project Tiger. After visiting India, Hornocker recommended Seidensticker, who had just finished a radio tracking study of mountain lions, as the lead researcher for an intensive tiger study.[25] For reasons described by Michael Lewis, however – including nationalism, Cold War geopolitics and cross-cultural misunderstandings – the chances of the project winning approval from the Indian government were far smaller than the Smithsonian initially believed. By the summer of 1972, when the Second World Congress on National Parks was convening in Yellowstone and Jackson Hole, Seidensticker and the Smithsonian had begun to doubt that approval would be forthcoming.[26]

A serendipitous meeting with the Nepalese delegation to the national parks conference provided an alternative. Although Nepal's tiger population was minuscule in comparison to India's, there were several sites on its southern border where the intensive study of tiger behaviour that Hornocker and Seidensticker had envisaged could be conducted. A key member of the Nepalese delegation was Kirti Man Tamang, a former forest officer who had recently served as the general manager of the Tiger Tops tourist lodge in Chitwan, a royal hunting reserve designated as Nepal's first national park in 1970 but not officially established until 1973. At the time, Tamang was studying for his doctorate in wildlife management at Michigan State University and searching for funding for research in Nepal. In the months after Tamang and Seidensticker's meeting it became clear to the Smithsonian that Indian approval would not be forthcoming and that Nepal, while not ideal in terms of the Smithsonian's long-term goals in South Asia, would be more than adequate in the short term. In December 1972, Tamang and Seidensticker visited Chitwan together and obtained official approval for the study in Kathmandu.[27] It took nearly an additional year for the Smithsonian and the Nepalese government to agree on a contract and for the necessary radio tracking gear and other equipment to make it through Nepal's customs office, but by the end of 1973 Tamang, Seidensticker and their assistants had made their first attempts to capture and collar one of Chitwan's tigers.[28]

Seidensticker's original research proposal had been modelled on his own radio tracking study of mountain lions, which had in turn been modelled on Hornocker's mountain lion work and on the Craigheads' grizzly study. Techniques such as chemical immobilization and radio tracking that had succeeded with large carnivores in the Rocky Mountains, he suggested, would work just as well with their equivalents in South Asia. In practice – as many biologists before and after Seidensticker also discovered – such techniques required significant adaptations to work with the particular animals and environments in question. Though capturing mountain lions had hardly been easy, tigers were comparatively more dangerous and more elusive. Tamang's experience as a forest officer and manager at the Tiger Tops Jungle Lodge, Chitwan's only wildlife tourism concession, proved crucial in the project's beginning stages, when procedures for capturing live tigers were still being developed. Later visitors to the project would note that experienced elephant drivers and *shikaris* (native hunters), such as Prem Bahadur Rai, a hunting guide who had previously tracked tigers for Nepal's royal family, continued to play an essential role in the project's scientific work even after the basic procedures were established.[29]

Those procedures were influenced as much by Nepal's aristocratic hunting traditions as they were by space-age developments in the Northern Rockies. To catch a tiger, the project staff would, after determining the animal's general location, wind two long sheets of white muslin cloth through the trees or tall grasses to form a funnel. Armed with a dart gun, one of the researchers would wait in a tree at the end of the funnel while the other project staff, mounted on elephants, attempted to drive the tiger out of hiding. When the darting was successful, the immobilized tiger would be weighed, measured and fitted with a radio collar and left to recover while researchers kept watch from a safe distance.[30] Except for the fact that the tiger was immobilized rather than killed, the procedure was virtually identical to that used in aristocratic tiger hunts throughout the twentieth century by Nepalese elites and foreign visitors, including the British royalty whose extravagant hunts have been described by John MacKenzie.[31] The connections between scientific research and hunting traditions were evident to visitors to Chitwan. When the president of the U.S. branch of the World Wildlife Fund, Russell Train, participated in a leopard tagging in Chitwan in 1981, he noted that while he was glad that large-scale hunts were a thing of the past, 'a sad aspect of the matter is that the training and keeping of elephants is a rapidly disappearing art. Our tiger project is one of the last – perhaps even the last – examples of their utilization in this fashion.'[32] Scientific research was not just dependent on the hunting tradition; it was also helping to keep key elements of that tradition alive in the era of conservation.

Generally speaking, government officials in Nepal such as Hemanta Mishra, then a young forest officer, strongly supported the Smithsonian project. As Seidensticker noted several months before fieldwork began, the fact that Nepal's government had granted permission to use radio tracking equipment – 'a sensitive issue everywhere on the Indian subcontinent' – was an important sign of support.[33] For some observers, however, the Smithsonian-Nepal Tiger Ecology Project raised concerns about conflicts between hands-on science and the preservation of wildness that resembled those expressed regarding the Craigheads' research. Particularly vocal was the management of Tiger Tops, which claimed that the appearance of collared tigers at the viewing stations that it baited with live goats or buffalo on most evenings would disappoint its visitors and threaten its bottom line. As Tiger Tops's research director Charles McDougal explained to the Nepalese government, 'a tiger with a radio hanging around its neck is no longer an attraction.' If the study had to be conducted in the park, McDougal requested that the government order the researchers to avoid collaring the lodge's 'resident tigers', a male and two females with cubs that regularly appeared at the bait stations.[34] Tiger Tops's position was supported by a number of prominent international conservationists, including the European leadership of the World Wildlife Fund and the International Union for the Conservation of Nature, who argued that the study would compromise the tiger's status as an icon of wildness while siphoning money from more pressing conservation needs.[35]

Nepalese officials were not without their own concerns about the impact of radio tagging in the park, but they also recognized, as the Yellowstone administration had in the early years of the Craigheads' research, that the ability to easily locate and identify individual animals provided them with a powerful management tool. The park did not have to worry about tigers begging at roadsides or raiding campground trash bins, but it did have 'problem' animals of its own. Unlike Yellowstone, which was located in a sparsely populated area, Chitwan was surrounded by an agricultural zone whose population had grown dramatically as a result of postwar economic development and population redistribution efforts by the Nepalese government in partnership with international aid agencies. The result was an increasing number of deadly attacks by tigers on livestock and, less often, on humans, which in turn led to accusations from local villagers that the government valued tigers' lives over their own. The government regularly called on Smithsonian project staff to capture tigers that had killed humans or livestock, particularly when the attacks took place outside park boundaries. In December 1978, one of the study's radio-collared tigers killed a man just beyond the park boundary. Villagers responded with what Mishra, who had replaced Tamang as the Nepalese leader of the project in 1977, later described as a 'small riot'. Within twenty-four hours Mishra and the project staff had tracked down and immobilized the tiger, which was then transported to the National Zoo in Kathmandu.[36] In contrast to the days of Jim Corbett, the famous British tiger hunter-turned-conservationist, 'man eaters' could now be repurposed as zoological ambassadors rather than killed outright.[37]

Radio tracking thus helped the Chitwan administration to police the borders of the park and to reduce, though never eliminate, the friction produced at the meeting-point of wilderness and civilization. The use of the technique also contributed to a reconceptualization of the territory of Chitwan National Park in terms of the territories of the tigers that inhabited it. After a few years of research with radio tracking and other methods, enough data had accumulated to suggest that tigers of both sexes were highly territorial, which was something that wildlife biologist George Schaller had postulated in his influential 1967 work *The Deer and the Tiger* but had been unable to prove definitively.[38] If that was the case, then there was a limit to the number of tigers that could be squeezed into the park. Especially in light of the rapid agricultural development of surrounding areas, any hope of expanding the population beyond the dozen or so tigers then known to inhabit the park would depend on expanding the park's boundaries.

Such arguments played a major role in the Nepalese government's decision to expand the park in the late 1970s to nearly double its original size and later to create an adjacent reserve as a buffer area into which tigers could roam without immediately encountering human settlements.[39] Whereas the Craigheads' evidence of the enormous 'home ranges' of individual grizzlies had been a threat to the autonomy of the Yellowstone administration from the government agencies that managed the land surrounding the park, evidence of tiger territoriality provided an opportunity for the Chitwan administration and the National Parks and Wildlife Conservation Office of which it was a part to expand their own territorial reach.

Soon after the decision to expand the park had been made, the Smithsonian-Nepal Tiger Ecology Project began to wind down. The relationships among the Smithsonian, the Nepalese government, and the WWF–U.S. (which had funded much of the project despite the opposition of WWF's European leadership) had never been without tension, but all three parties had reasons to bring the radio tracking study to a close. As early as 1976, Smithsonian administrators in Washington had begun to feel constrained by the project's focus on tigers. They began urging the project's leaders, both American and Nepalese, to focus on the broader goal of discovering 'parameters for delineating natural reserve areas', even though, for the moment, they would have to continue presenting their work 'under the tiger rubric'. In the long term, however, Smithsonian administrators believed that the only way to truly broaden the work of the project was to shift attention away from the tiger.[40]

The Nepalese government also had reasons for seeking change. Among them was the high-risk nature of radio collaring for both researchers and tigers. In 1979, the park's largest male tiger drowned in a small pool after being struck with an immobilizing dart. Researchers had captured around twenty-six tigers since 1973, some of them repeatedly, and by 1979 nearly half of the park's tigers wore radio collars. Soon after the accident, the National Parks and Wildlife Conservation Office told the Smithsonian that it believed it was time to begin wrapping up the project.[41] Finally, when Russell Train took over the presidency of WWF–U.S. in 1979, he sought to strengthen the organization's own research programmes and deemphasize its role as a grant maker to organizations such as the Smithsonian.[42] Fieldwork ended with the completion of Mishra's radio tracking study of one of the tiger's main prey species in mid-1981. Tiger Tops research director McDougal, who had vociferously opposed the study a few years earlier, agreed to help monitor the tigers whose collars were still operational.[43]

Transnational Networks of Expertise

In 1969, in the middle of one of many rounds of tortuous contract negotiations with the Yellowstone administration, John Craighead tried to convince Superintendent Anderson that the novel wildlife research techniques that he and his brother had developed represented the future of national park wildlife management. 'At the risk of appearing immodest', he wrote, 'I think I can say that the techniques of color marking, immobilizing, handling, radiotracking, and data gathering that we, our colleagues, and our students developed or perfected in the course of ten years of research effort in the Park are now being widely applied in other national parks throughout the world.'[44] Despite the Craigheads' important contributions, they were hardly the only ones to have 'developed or perfected' such techniques, and in 1969 many of those techniques, including radio tracking, were still being used in only a few parks, most of them in the United States. However, as the introduction of radio tracking and other techniques to Chitwan by his former students Hornocker and Seidensticker in the 1970s suggests, there was also an element of truth to his claim. In the 1970s and 1980s, the Craigheads' research methods would influence research and management practices for large carnivores in numerous parks beyond the United States. That influence would most often be exercised as it was in the case of Chitwan: through tightly connected circuits of expertise that made it possible for people with disparate backgrounds and complementary sets of skills, such as Tamang and Seidensticker, to work together.

To return to a point made in the introduction, this was a case neither of simple diffusion nor of independent development, but rather of contingent and mutual adaptation. Though there is not space here to do so, the story could be continued by showing how developments in new parks such as Chitwan subsequently influenced canonical parks such as Yellowstone as well as other recently established parks. Just as researchers such as Tamang and Mishra returned from sojourns in the United States or Europe with new perspectives on conservation in Nepal, so researchers such as Seidensticker or Hornocker returned from research trips to South Asia with new perspectives on conservation in the United States. Network-building events such as the World Congress on National Parks, held every ten years since 1962, were complemented by training and technical assistance programmes and by informal transnational links between scientists and park managers. These piecemeal connections gradually led to the construction of a global network of park professionals with a shared toolkit of ideas and practices that could be imported and adapted to local conditions and then, in many cases, reexported and readapted once again. The radio tracking of large carnivores in Yellowstone and Chitwan is only one example of how techniques circulating within these networks helped to transform practices of wilderness and wildness – of territory and discipline – across national borders.

Notes

1. For the U.S. context, see Alfred Runte, *National Parks: The American Experience*, 3rd ed. (Lincoln, 1997); Richard West Sellars, *Preserving Nature in the National Parks: A History* (New Haven, 1997); James A. Pritchard, *Preserving Yellowstone's Natural Conditions: Science and the Perception of Nature* (Lincoln, 1999); Alice Wondrak Biel, *Do*

(Not) Feed the Bears: The Fitful History of Wildlife and Tourists in Yellowstone (Lawrence, 2006).

2. More details on radio tracking in Yellowstone and Chitwan can be found in Etienne Benson, *Wired Wilderness: Technologies of Tracking and the Making of Modern Wildlife* (Baltimore, 2010).

3. On the Craigheads' grizzly project, see Sellars, *Preserving Nature,* 249–52: Pritchard, *Preserving Yellowstone's Natural Conditions,* 201–50; Biel, *Do (Not) Feed the Bears,* 86–112; Benson, *Wired Wilderness,* 52–93; Gregg Mitman, 'When Nature *Is* the Zoo: Vision and Power in the Art and Science of Natural History', *Osiris* 11 (1996): 117–43; Alston Chase, *Playing God in Yellowstone: The Destruction of America's First National Park* (Boston, 1986).

4. On radio tracking's Cold War connections, see Mitman, 'When Nature *Is* the Zoo'; Benson, *Wired Wilderness,* 5–51. For 'modern devices', see Memo for the Press from Yellowstone National Park, 20 October 1961, Box N-371, Natural and Social Sciences Records, Yellowstone National Park Heritage and Research Center, Gardiner, Montana (hereafter, Yellowstone Archives). On the Park Service's 'Mission 66' initiative to modernize park facilities, see Ethan Carr, *Wilderness by Design: Landscape Architecture and the National Park Service* (Lincoln, 1998), 135.

5. On the Cold War U.S. technological sublime, see David Nye, *American Technological Sublime* (Cambridge, MA, 1996), 225–56; Thomas P. Hughes, *American Genesis: A Century of Invention and Technological Enthusiasm, 1870–1970* (Chicago, 2004), 443–72.

6. Adolph Murie to Anthony Wayne Smith, 27 January 1963, Box 21, Murie Family Papers, Series I: Adolph Murie Files, 1834–1982, American Heritage Center, University of Wyoming, Laramie (hereafter Adolph Murie Papers). On Murie's career, see Timothy Rawson, *Changing Tracks: Predators and Politics in Mt. McKinley National Park* (Fairbanks, 2001).

7. Filmmaker Walter Berlet, for example, began attacking the Craigheads' research methods in public lectures in 1967; see Walter E. Berlet to John J. Craighead, 25 May 1967, Box N-176, Yellowstone Archives.

8. Research Biologist to Superintendent, Yellowstone, Re: 'Comments on Craighead Report on Bear Management in Yellowstone National Park', 21 August 1967, Box 2, Adolph Murie Papers; 'Attacks of Grizzlies Stir Debate', *New York Times,* 2 September 1969, 49.

9. Jack K. Anderson to John J. Craighead, 7 April 1969, Box N-91, Yellowstone Archives.

10. Jack K. Anderson to John J. Craighead, 8 July 1970, Box N-91, Yellowstone Archives; Jack K. Anderson to John J. Craighead, 9 February 1971 and 20 August 1971, Box N-112, Yellowstone Archives.

11. Mark V. Barrow, Jr., *A Passion for Birds: American Ornithology after Audubon* (Princeton, 1998), 154–81; Robert M. Wilson, *Seeking Refuge: Birds and Landscapes of the Pacific Flyway* (Seattle, 2010), 65–98.

12. Frank Craighead and John Craighead, 'Knocking Out Grizzlies for Their Own Good', *National Geographic* 118 (August 1960): 283.

13. Craighead and Craighead, 'Knocking Out Grizzlies', 291; F. C. Craighead, J. J. Craighead and R. S. Davis, 'Radiotracking of Grizzly Bears', in *Bio-Telemetry: The Use of Telemetry in Animal Behavior and Physiology in Relation to Ecological Problems,* ed. Lloyd Slater (Oxford, 1963), 135.

14. Mitman, 'When Nature *Is* the Zoo'.

15. See Pritchard, *Preserving Yellowstone's Natural Conditions*, 251–306.
16. John J. Craighead, Maurice Hornocker, Wesley Woodgerd and Frank C. Craighead, Jr., 'Trapping, Immobilizing and Color-Marking Grizzly Bears', *Transactions of the North American Wildlife Conference* 25 (1960): 347–63; Regional Chief of Interpretation to Superintendent, Yellowstone National Park, 1 April 1960, Box N-371, Yellowstone Archives.
17. Biel, *Do (Not) Feed the Bears*.
18. On biopolitics, see Michel Foucault, *Security, Territory, Population: Lectures at the Collège de France 1977-1978*, ed. Michel Senellart, trans. Graham Burchell (New York, 2007).
19. Michael Lewis, *Inventing Global Ecology: Tracking the Biodiversity Ideal in India, 1945–1997* (Hyderabad, 2003), 274.
20. Frank C. Craighead, Jr., *The Track of the Grizzly* (San Francisco, 1979), 191–230.
21. John J. Craighead and Frank C. Craighead, Jr., 'Grizzly Bear-Man Relationships in Yellowstone National Park', *BioScience* 21 (1971): 845–57.
22. Glen Cole, "Preservation and Management of Grizzly Bears in Yellowstone National Park," *BioScience* 21 (1971): 858–864.
23. Benson, *Wired Wilderness*, 93–138.
24. Lewis, *Inventing Global Ecology*, 167–68; Hemanta Mishra, *Bones of the Tiger: Protecting the Man-Eaters of Nepal* (Guilford, CT, 2010); Fiona Sunquist and Mel Sunquist, *Tiger Moon: Tracking the Great Cats of Nepal* (Chicago, 2002).
25. Maurice G. Hornocker to Kennedy D. Schmertz, 23 July 1971, Box 15, Smithsonian Institution, Office of Environmental Sciences, Ecology Program Records, 1965–73, Record Unit 271, Smithsonian Institution Archives, Washington, D.C. (hereafter Smithsonian RU271).
26. John C. Seidensticker, Report on Tiger Research Development Trip, March 1972; S. Dillon Ripley to Kennedy D. Schmertz, 12 October 1972, Box 15, Smithsonian RU271; Lewis, *Inventing Global Ecology*, 159–98. See also the contribution by Lewis in this volume.
27. John C. Seidensticker to Michael R. Huxley, 30 August 1972; Kirti Man Tamang to Michael R. Huxley, 18 October 1972; Jitendra R. Sharma to S. Dillon Ripley, 4 January 1973, Box 24, Smithsonian Institution, Assistant Secretary for Science Records, 1963–1978, Record Unit 254, Smithsonian Institution Archives, Washington, DC. (hereafter Smithsonian RU254).
28. Emerald J. B. Rana to Michael R. Huxley, 19 September 1973, Box 24, Smithsonian RU254; John C. Seidensticker to Michael R. Huxley, 2 December 1973, Box 24, Assistant Secretary for Science, circa 1963–1986, Record Unit 329, Smithsonian Institution Archives, Washington, DC. (hereafter Smithsonian RU329).
29. John C. Seidensticker to Michael R. Huxley, 2 December 1973, Box 24, Smithsonian RU329; Peter A. Jordan, Report on Visit to Smithsonian Tiger Project, Royal Chitwan National Park, November 1977, Box 54, Smithsonian RU329.
30. The procedure is described in James L. David Smith, Melvin E. Sunquist, Kirti Man Tamang and Prem Bahadur Rai, 'A Technique for Capturing and Immobilizing Tigers', *Journal of Wildlife Management* 47 (1983): 255–59.
31. John M. MacKenzie, *The Empire of Nature: Hunting, Conservation, and British Imperialism* (Manchester, 1988), 167–99.

32. Russell E. Train, Journal Entry, 6–9 February 1981, Box 36, Russell E. Train Papers, Library of Congress, Washington, DC.
33. John C. Seidensticker to Leonard Carmichael, 20 August 1973, Box 24, Smithsonian RU254.
34. Charles McDougal to Secretary of Forests, His Majesty's Government of Nepal, 8 September 1973, Box 24, Smithsonian RU254.
35. Mishra, *Bones of the Tiger*, 20–22; Benson, *Wired Wilderness*, 99–100.
36. 'Small riot' comes from Hemanta R. Mishra, 'A Delicate Balance: Tigers, Rhinoceros, Tourists and Park Management vs. the Needs of the Local People in Royal Chitwan National Park', n.d. (1981), Box 59, Smithsonian RU329. See also Mishra, *Bones of the Tiger*, 47–67.
37. Jim Corbett, *Man-Eaters of Kumaon* (Oxford, 1944).
38. George Schaller, *The Deer and the Tiger: A Study of Wildlife in India* (Chicago, 1967).
39. On the park expansion, see Mishra, *Bones of the Tiger*, 47. The crucial data is described in James L. David Smith, 'The Role of Dispersal in Structuring the Chitwan Tiger Population', *Behaviour* 124 (1993): 165–95.
40. Ross Simons to Kirti Man Tamang, J. L. David Smith, and Rebecca Troth, 10 November 1976, Box 53, Smithsonian RU329; Ross Simons to Chris Wemmer, 31 August 1976, Box 27, Smithsonian RU254. See also Chris Wemmer to Ross Simons, 3 May 1979, Box 55, Smithsonian RU329.
41. Biswa N. Upreti to Ross Simons, 28 November 1979, Box 55, Smithsonian RU329.
42. Russell E. Train, *Politics, Pollution, and Pandas: An Environmental Memoir* (Washington, DC, 2003), 244.
43. Chris Wemmer, Ross Simons and Hemanta Mishra, 'Case History of a Cooperative International Conservation Program: The Smithsonian Nepal Tiger Ecology Project' (Draft, 1984), Box 59, Smithsonian RU329.
44. John J. Craighead to Jack K. Anderson, 14 April 1969, Box N-196, Yellowstone Archives.

 **PART III**

Nations and Natures

CHAPTER 10

A Revolutionary Civilization

National Parks, Transnational Exchanges and the Construction of Modern Mexico

Emily Wakild

Between 1934 and 1940, Mexican bureaucrats created and administered forty national parks. An average of 20,000 hectares in size, the majority of these parks resided within one hundred kilometres of the nation's capital and contained coniferous forests. The contents of these parks embodied neither wilderness nor distant frontiers but instead marked a civilized combination of accessibility and symbolic nature in the territory recognized by the social-reform-minded government as central to the nation's past. The timing, intention and process of national park creation in Mexico reveals a unique combination of revolutionary social reforms, transnational intellectual exchanges and widespread political incorporation that brought vast numbers of citizens into a growing federal bureaucracy through environmental policy.[1] Tensions existed among rural and urban peoples, scientists, educators and farmers, and national, regional and local interpretations of the parks, but the encompassing ideological revolution and the populist reforms of President Lázaro Cárdenas (1934–40), drew upon national parks as a method of popular incorporation rather than a means of exclusion.[2] By the end of Cárdenas's term, national parks were distributed across seventeen states, including those most densely populated. This result was not coincidental. Mexican national parks were formed out of the crucible of revolutionary reforms that altered the dynamics of citizenship and governance in radical ways, establishing a framework for the expansion of political participation to previously marginalized groups by redistributing millions of acres of land, building rural schoolhouses and fostering union activity.[3] These reforms demonstrated a firm, if sometimes fleeting, commitment to changes that would allow lower-class groups more complete integration into public life, yet parks were demonstrably modern as they did not mark a return to a pre-Columbian wild past but a revolutionary future. Recognition of this confluence of processes and characteristics gives Mexican parks their own place in a dynamic and changing global history that nevertheless led to the adaptation of the national park concept to protect nature worldwide.

National parks in Mexico appropriately exemplify the combination of historical ideas about science, local contestations over land use and international exchanges of expertise that were absorbed and promoted by a burgeoning bureaucracy at a particular moment in time. While Mexicans' revolutionary experience shaped the way they came to rethink the place of nature in both the national imaginary and the national economy, they also drew upon—but did not unilaterally duplicate—global understandings of parks circulating worldwide. By using a recognized worldwide cultural symbol of conservation, Mexicans could internationalize their domestic platform for social reform without compromising their commitment to designing a 'Mexico for Mexicans'. Such a reformulation privileged neither distant wilderness nor exotic wildlife but instead set to designate as national the landscapes that surrounded the heart of the nation's past.

In their own way, each of the forty national parks exemplified the union of a global idea with domestic politics, yet one park highlights the circulation of ideas about nature protection as they became grounded in place. Nestled in the southwestern range of the Valley of Mexico, the seven lakes in the 4,468-hectare Lagunas de Zempoala National Park, located 66 kilometres from the capital and just 15 kilometres off the highway, provides a fitting example of how conserving natural features (such as forests, clean air and water sources) became a strategy for improving the nation.[4] The proximity of the park to the capital and the various potentially beneficial uses of the space made the park a prime example of the ideas of conservation circulating in this period. The vision for the parks held by Cárdenas and the troupe of foresters he employed did not involve evicting resident peasant communities or extinguishing economic activity; rather, park creation sought a compromise between urban and rural groups that combined existing uses under expanding federal authority.

This chapter will provide a short overview of the national context contributing to park creation. It will then briefly chronicle the rise of conservation ideas related to parks and forests with particular attention to how they arose in an international context. Finally, it will address the local effects of these trends in Lagunas de Zempoala National Park.

From *Científicos* to Revolutionary Foresters

In Mexico as elsewhere, the rise of forestry precipitated ideas about national parks. Federal forestry did not originate with the revolution but during the preceding liberal dictatorship. While historians have paid much attention to the role of scientific and positivist thought as promoting Western sensibilities during the rule of Porfirio Díaz, known as the Porfiriato (1872–1911), much less is known about how a similar commitment to rational science influenced the revolutionary social reforms. Several of these men felt certain that their country's wealth would be squandered unless they inspired more urgent attention to the forests that surrounded both national history and daily life in the country's central corridor. This environment garnered the most public notice and largest scholarly attention because it visibly changed before citizens' eyes in the late nineteenth century. The increase in public lighting, railroads and building construction all relied heavily on the logging of coniferous forests mainly found in the corridor of temperate lands in the country's central volcanic axis. Besides lampposts and poles to hold lines, refined products made from tree sap served as sealants and combustibles.[5] The subsequent environmental consequences of deforestation, including erosion, flooding and dust storms, weighed down urban reforms. This meant that attention to forests, and foresters themselves, earned a proportionally dominant position shaping the national conservation agenda.

Miguel Ángel de Quevedo (1862–1946), the first director of the autonomous Department of Forestry, Fish and Game established in 1935, provides the paradigmatic example in this respect.[6] Quevedo was a *científico,* meaning one of the scientifically oriented advisors that made up the oligarchy under Díaz. Along with other *científicos,* he worked to conserve greenery in the quickly modernizing capital city where officials created more manicured gardens, tree-lined avenues and public parks during the Porfiriato than at any other time in the capital's history.[7] Because these larger processes of modernization often involved erasing native influences in favour of European trends, the Porfiriato led to the backlash of the revolution, which sought to elevate rural, traditional people as essential to the core of the Mexican nation.

Quevedo played a major role in fostering elite and scholarly interests on forest issues. He helped start the Central Forest Group (Junta Central de Bosques) in 1908, the first organization dedicated to studying the nation's forests. The group remained active through the presidency of Francisco Madero (1911–13), was driven underground when Victoriano Huerta took power in 1913 and then reconvened as the Mexican Forestry Society in 1923.[8] This group of wealthy, educated men continued to set the agenda for national forestry priorities as long as Quevedo was alive. In 1926, the society published a formal declaration of the eighteen principles that formed the core beliefs of their members. These principles centred on the benefits forests provided and would continue to supply if they were conserved, cared for and replenished. They advocated that all agriculture should be undertaken in the appropriate territory and that forest vegetation should never be destroyed to cultivate food. They believed in the rational harvesting of forest products and that the economics of forestry allowed for logging and cutting, if it was done in a fashion that permitted the trees to regenerate for the future. Finally, these foresters believed that the immense wealth of the forests heightened their duty to ensure that all social groups were instructed in the principle elements of forest economy, to promote the best interests of the nation.[9] In fact, the Forestry Law of 1926 explicitly aimed to foster a cadre of skilled technicians to oversee such actions.[10]

These foresters not only romanticized their social obligations; they firmly viewed their work as fundamentally differing from that of agriculturists. Whereas an agrarian engineer sought the artificial propagation of plants, silvaculturists tended to imitate the cultivation techniques of nature, or so they believed. They saw their work as connected to larger natural cycles including climate, soil and hydrologic regimes as well as wildlife and human habitats. But forests and landscapes full of forests took front stage. Many foresters saw their mission as helping agriculture in the long term by assuring a stable climatic regime and protecting hillsides from erosion. Rather than cultivating for a short-term (one or two season) harvest, foresters looked ahead decades, even centuries, for the realization of their work. Foresters claimed to seek two related but opposed ends: the constant use of the forest and its perpetual conservation. The social effects of forests in elevating the human spirit and protecting aesthetic landscapes weighed in the foresters' minds, and they believed such noble endeavours were incomparable to the work of agriculturists.[11] In their minds, just as fostering a revolutionary society necessitated a long-term investment, so did rescuing the forests.

After the fall of the dictatorship, foresters faced the challenge of transforming social groups of high society into makers of national policy. In the views of Forestry Society members, the only way to make forestry a legitimate and sovereign issue was to get it out from under the thumb of the Ministry of Agriculture. Lázaro Cárdenas stood out as the appropriate politician to adopt some of the priorities of elite foresters and widen national attention towards forest issues. He understood this conflict of bureaucratic interests, and as one of his first acts as president, he created the autonomous Forestry Department, freeing it from the mandates of the Ministry of Agriculture.[12] This act was not an entirely original idea but one that came out of the official party's economic contract with the people: the 1934–40 Six-Year Plan for development. Cárdenas announced the new department on a radio address where he promised that greater federal control over forests did not mean the abstention from the use of wood products, but rather the Forestry Department would study methods for the appropriate use of these natural resources. He also supported the training of salaried technical workers to manage reforestation.

Because of the vast devastation of the forests of the state of Michoacán that occurred while he was governor there, Cárdenas seemed to have a soft spot for trees.[13] At the national level Cárdenas could see that states besides Michoacán suffered from deforestation. The president promised to foster research into gas and other combustibles in order to replace the use of forest-derived fuels.[14] The Six-Year Plan put forth a spectrum of coordinated proposals that included forestry reserves, protected areas, producers' cooperatives and nurseries. Complimentary landscape reforms for agriculture, including communal land parcels, irrigation districts and grazing areas, also emerged. Forestry was seen within a spectrum of productive enterprises, rather than merely conservation for protection alone, and this heritage similarly shaped the view of national parks as also connected to economic and social goals rather than romantic or idealized notions of wild and untamed nature.

Proponents of forestry conservation proposed many strategies, and one of the most popular proved creating national parks to resolve the problem of forest degradation. These parks often protected areas with deteriorating forests as a means to recover the forest and stall future land conversion. Visitors came in droves to the new parks, in part because they were conveniently located, since highly used forests that suffered degradation were most commonly near large population centres. An average of 1,500 visitors came to Lagunas de Zempoala each month in 1938.[15] Parks gave the public a site that belonged to them, yet allowed the federal government to manage particularly crucial areas for long-term benefits. Parks, then, were more than sites of recreation; they served broader economic purposes by maintaining an environmental equilibrium for agriculture. Whether or not the foresters believed that by ensuring stability the main benefit of a forest was to provide for agriculture, the premise of parks as ecological protection fit into the revolutionary promises of land reform made to rural people.

In separating forestry from agriculture, Cárdenas overlooked Quevedo's association with the dictatorship and chose him to head the Forestry Department that created and administered national parks.[16] Quevedo supported revolutionary promises unenthusiastically, but his dedication to science and the diffusion of conservation, as well as a certain amount of self-righteous egotism, convinced him to take the job managing the nation's forests.[17] Notably, and tragically for the support of the parks, the Forestry Department was placed under the control of the Secretary of Agriculture and Hydraulic Resources in 1940 as Cárdenas left office.

International Sources and Exchanges

In addition to fervent planning, overtly nationalist desires derived from the cosmopolitan experiences of the Forestry Society's members and the Forestry Department's employees. Policies developing in the United States influenced Mexican foresters as did those from the long-emulated country of France.[18]

Quevedo trained in France, but not as a forester. He studied mathematics at the Institute Polytechnique in Paris and later graduated from the École nationale des ponts et chaussées as a civil engineer. In addition to training in classes, Quevedo learned scientific thought from people like Louis Pasteur and received practical advice from Paul Laroche, a French engineer working on the Suez Canal. Such experiences shaped Quevedo's management style, where he continually promoted exchanges between his foresters and foreign emissaries, especially once he directed the Forestry Department. Under Quevedo's suggestion, Ángel Roldán, an engineer with the Forestry Department, attended the Congress on Silviculture and Carbon Fuels in Brussels in 1936. In addition to the conference he went on a tour of French, German, Swiss, Austrian, Czechoslovakian and Polish parks and reserves making observations on each and bringing back ideas on how to improve parks.[19]

The proximity to the United States also inspired periodic international exchanges. Quevedo and two associates attended the North American Conservation Conference in 1909, and negotiations for several border parks brought officials from both nations into contact repeatedly in the 1930s.[20] In 1936, Quevedo and his employees Daniel Galicia and Hans Zimmerer toured U.S. parks including Carlsbad Caverns in New Mexico, the Grand Canyon in Arizona and Sequoia National Park in California. These trips gave them the opportunity not only to see the way U.S. national parks were run, but also to exchange ideas and philosophies of park management. In return, several resource managers

Illustration 10.1. Members of the Joint Mexico and United States International Park Commission visiting potential sites of park cooperation: (left to right) George Wright, Dr. Bell, Daniel Galicia, Conrad L. Wirth, Roger Toll, Santos Ibarra and Juan Treviño, Big Bend region of Texas, 1936

from the United States toured the proposed park areas around Mexico City in the spring of 1936.[21] The trips taken by bureaucrats were tangible exchanges of conservation ideas. In addition, there were several attempts to use a theme similar to the U.S. Park Service's 'See America First' campaign as Mexican officials called on their fellow citizens to 'Know Our Mexico'.[22]

While the reverberations and echoes of these European and North American forestry and park management ideas can be seen in Mexico, reformers also looked south and east for inspiration. Quevedo toured Guatemala to foster friendship with the southern neighbour, and he proposed an international peace park to include the Suchiate River crossing from Guatemala to Mexico.[23] Employees of the fishing division of the Forestry Department took an extensive tour of Japan and invited Japanese experts to Mexico to improve the fish cultivation programmes.[24] Japanese experts did not limit their contributions to fish; one Japanese professor sent one hundred cherry trees to be planted in Lagunas de Zempoala National Park. The trees were to help with erosion around the lake, but they also symbolized the exchange of knowledge, friendship and nature between the two countries.[25] Mexican officials came to understand and define their parks vis-à-vis their exchanges with other countries and their desire to compare and comprehend their native situation in tandem with strategies employed elsewhere.

The coalescence of ideas for parks grew out of international exchanges but soon became emphatically Mexican in style. While Mexico's parks came decades after the first U.S. parks, the country was second among its Latin American peers to designate a national park in 1917; Argentina preceded Mexico in 1903, while Chile followed in 1934 and Ecuador in 1935.[26] The significance of the Mexican parks comes less from their comparatively early status and more from their own national context. That the parks are included into the repertoire of revolutionary nature administration—alongside forests, agricultural lands and oil—sets the parks within a radical framework of social design with long-range implications. Placing parks within a revolutionary platform meant the national park idea, as forged in Mexico, provided a redefinition of the national park idea as a piece of a larger social plan promoting political incorporation and integrating rural production. The park vision did not prove separate from broader goals of resource use (in the way parks were divorced from forestry in the United States) nor did it necessarily signify colonial or neocolonial usurpation of resources from local populations (as in many parks in sub-Saharan and Northern Africa).

Federal scientists, engineers and other 'experts' were sent out to determine boundaries of land reform parcels (known as *ejidos*), allocate irrigation works and decide park boundaries. How (and if) these officials obtained the appropriate information to make such decisions became a highly contested matter in rural villages across the country, and many resentful villagers readily articulated their complaints.[27] Certainly for parks, the origination of plans for parks came from outside experts, but because they never gained complete authority, outsiders had to collaborate with local desires to avoid creating irate constituents.

Foresters in general, and Quevedo in particular, supported the use of forest products as long as the integrity of the forests remained intact. In this way, the Forestry Department espoused policies similar to forestry regimes in other countries, especially the U.S. Forest Service under Gifford Pinchot.[28] The major emphasis on rational science and the value of planned exploitation underscored the unique virtues of forests—spaces simultaneously for use and protection with the overall goal of eliminating waste. The major difference in the Mexican case came with the revolutionary context, which constrained foresters from eliminating the position of small-scale users—especially firewood gatherers—whose position as emblematic of the revolutionary cause required their inclusion. Foresters necessarily had to reformulate their position on acceptable uses to accommodate the demands of peasants. Although this inclusion took a patronizing and paternalistic form, it did not breach the commitment to keeping rural people on their land and incorporated into the federal government's growing apparatus.

Parks, and the forests they aimed to protect, proved particularly problematic for the postrevolutionary process of returning land to peasants for agricultural uses. Members of the burgeoning Agrarian Department faced pressure to increase the amount of land redistributed while they feared the resistance of expropriating large and resistant landowners. For many agronomists, forests proved an obvious source of land to redistribute and let peasants clear for fields. Foresters, on the other hand, had no such illusions of turning the nation into a patchwork of farms without forests. They warned sternly against the fallacy that fields would remain fertile without a general climatic system supported by resilient forests. Such a philosophical disagreement about a political programme divided scientific expertise within the federal government and proved possible because President Cárdenas had separated and elevated the Department of Forestry into its own autonomous entity. While the agrarian reform pressures far outweighed the forest supporters, Cárdenas and his administrators' willingness to pursue differing strategies of rural incorporation propelled the state into rural life in heretofore unseen ways that nevertheless remained within the new revolutionary and democratic framework solidified by the Cárdenas regime.

Creating a National Park in a Local Space

The local and national dynamics of park creation proved complicated and situational. While the promotion and publicity for parks showed a benevolent and universalizing interpretation, not surprisingly, the creation of parks proved more contentious. Many federal reformers viewed locals as amateurs at best, and many local residents felt aggrieved by what they viewed as greedy and corrupt outsiders. Despite these disputes, the revolutionary context made one thing certain—the ideal of inclusion precluded centralizing authorities from running roughshod over locals in the interest of national forestry. Ignoring or excluding local requests would undermine the philosophical justification of park creation. This meant federal officials sought acceptance—even if reluctant—to validate their conservation agenda and the broader project of federally managed natural resources. Incentives for acceptance came most readily in the form of promises of development, either through work in producers' cooperatives, surveillance jobs or the like, or through the distribution of material resources such as tree saplings or infrastructure projects. A park promised jobs and security and often brought with it roads and afforestation projects.

The creation of Zempoala National Park exemplifies the process of landscape demarcation, local incorporation and ongoing regulation promoted by federal officials in their rhetoric and many publications. Zempoala was a purely typical park, in the centre of the spectrum of highly successful sites of tourism and parks rejected by local communities. This park was neither exceptional in its popularity nor rare for its local acceptance. The area gradually became embedded with federal authority although local tenancy persisted. The largest lake was declared national property in 1926 as it met the requirements set forth by the federal government for nationalizing water sources.[29] Quevedo selected the site, and the area officially became a national park through a presidential decree on 27 November 1936.

Although the federal presence expanded, it did not move into idle lands. Residents of the closest community to the park, Huitzilac, lived almost entirely off economic activities that drew upon the forests. In keeping with the quest for a spectrum of uses, forest use did not end with the creation of the park. Huitzilac residents had organized themselves into a forestry cooperative in 1929, and they maintained this status once the lands became a park. This gave them incentives and permits for collectively exploiting dead wood by making charcoal. Residents also subsisted from their fields in the area, but many of the areas around the lakes had uneven slopes that made agriculture difficult. Although federal officials imposed the park from the outside, in many ways it converged with the interests of local residents by protecting the forests from clear cutting where residents gathered wood. While the park came to limit the cooperative, it also restricted large, outside paper companies from clearing the land. In this way, the park kept the forest which communities relied upon intact.

Before the designs to create a park, the area was relatively unknown to maps, due to its location on the boundaries between the states of Mexico and Morelos. Mapping the territory set the park apart from the surrounding communities, and placed communities precisely outside the protected zone's boundary. This park delineation attempted to evade property disputes while recognizing the presence of communities in a recognizable natural area. Edmundo Bournet, the engineer in charge of technical inspections and also the acting president of the Mexican Forestry Society, explained that the boundaries were marked by not only taking into account the hydrology and silviculture of the area, but also the topography. He believed such scientific methods successfully outlined the beauty and richness these forests and lakes captured.[30] Bournet's design and the park's creation came on paper, with no fence or wall as a visible manifestation. In this way, the park created few immediate controversies because its creation alone failed to disrupt pasturage or firewood gathering. Instead, the marking of the area included this local space into national geography.

This did not mean the area was conflict free. Subject to the demands of multiple users and increasingly a focus for land reform, the area hosted numerous disputes over land use. The Agrarian Department granted the community Huitzilac an *ejido* out of restituted lands in 1929.[31] Because of an ambiguous delineation, the former property owner complained to the Agrarian Department that the residents of Huitzilac had begun to use the forests that did not belong to them.[32] Two other communities existed slightly more distant from the park boundaries, Tres Marías and Xalatlaco, both of which repeatedly contested Huitzilac's *ejido* boundaries.[33] The area was certainly not conflict free, yet, none of these communities explicitly protested the park's use of lands in their region as residents quickly did with other parks.[34]

Landscapes of agricultural and forest production also transformed into places of recreation for the growing working classes. Zempoala existed near the expanding urban periphery around Mexico City, and city dwellers recognized the convenience and beauty of the park, visiting it eagerly. In addition to the thousands of monthly visitors in the park between 1936 and 1939, various groups used it for nature excursions.[35] The Treasury Department held a retreat for their employees in the park, and the first youth summer camp in Mexico took place there.[36] Some locals observed the popularity of the park and requested rights to concessions to provide food and refreshments to visitors and even to establish a dance floor.[37] Residents of Huitzilac insisted that the reforestation of areas around that park would include fruit trees that they could use as additional sources of income. They also asked that the highway be extended to reach the park and their community.[38] Forestry officials saw the park as a site of restricted nature; local residents viewed the space as a source of multiple economic benefits and park users saw the area as a pleasant place to recreate.

Zempoala also provided an opportunity for federal reformers to educate citizens about the value of both their environmental conservation programme and the legitimacy of the government. To do so, federal officials created a space for experiencing nature and set this apart from areas of rural labour or agricultural production. They then publicized the meaning of this space. To better administer nature and incorporate people, forestry employees simultaneously marked the landscape with their own scientific priorities and attempted to infuse the citizenry with educational campaigns. They labelled the landscape, naming some peaks within the park after Quevedo and Cárdenas, and they physically marked the forests with tangible indicators of governmental authority, such as roads and signs. Marks are meaningless unless their symbolism and power is understood; therefore the complementary process of securing bureaucratic power involved education—or convincing the population that national parks had a purpose that included them.

Yet, scientific foresters of this era were also products of their own revolutionary experience. As critical as they were of certain peasant practices, they likewise sought to limit the large-scale logging enterprises associated with foreign ownership. The hard-fought lessons of the revolution caused even the most liberal scientists to be wary of unfettered exploitation by foreign capitalists and the resentment this triggered in fellow citizens. Cárdenas promoted the belief that federally governed public land subject to a meticulous set of regulations and policies proved the most useful safeguard against such exploitation. At the heart of this system that crept in to dominate federal forestry policy remained scientific knowledge with roots in European cosmopolitanism, but its protective casing was respect for rural livelihoods. In tandem, these forces created Zempoala, a heavily used park that represented a balance between local uses and national demands.

Conclusion

Whether local citizens appreciated opportunities associated with tourism and recreation over primarily extractive industries is unclear. Such compromises and alternatives presage current debates over community-based conservation strategies. What is striking is that both the community and the park persisted throughout the twentieth century, decades before international conservation organizations become interested in devising strategies for keeping residents on lands near parks by engaging them in the protection of natural spaces for remuneration.[39] The system devised in the late 1930s did not prove perfect, but its origins in a period of expanded democratic activity and on the heels of an emphatic claim of the worthiness of rural life meant that national parks had to be defined as spaces of inclusion and compromise, not bastions of wilderness set apart from humanity. Defining parks as places to allow nature to recover, protect flailing forests, conserve local livelihoods and mark landscapes as nationally recognized shaped Mexican parks more so than did adherence to wildlife and game protection or to claims on colonial territory. These attributes made the parks unique and likely helped them to persist throughout the century. The parks have been resilient, retaining their territory amongst burgeoning cities and populations although they are far from naturally 'wild' spaces; they are nature civilized to fit the nation.

Zempoala demonstrates several attributes of the broader national park programme. First, parks proved overwhelmingly popular among a diverse spectrum of constituents ranging from urban workers to foreign tourists. Second, the proximity of the forest to the capital signified the importance of multiple uses and complementarities to the redefinition of a national park in Mexico. Third, reconceptualizing the internationally recognized concept of a national park into the Mexican context ensured that the park would use a global category to promote a revolutionary spirit situated in a local environment. This Mexicanized national park ideal promoted the incorporation of local geographies into a nationwide movement to federalize natural resources. Although the process proved flawed in various ways, especially after the Forestry Department was placed within the Ministry of Agriculture in 1940, the deliberate creation of parks during the revolutionary remodelling of society etched a radical and inclusive meaning into the international concept. This concept is similar to current proposals promoted as innovative.[40]

The park, and the associated forestry programmes, had paternalistic attributes. Rational, modern and scientific knowledge derived from a cosmopolitan understanding of forestry sought to edge out customary systems and skills based on generations of forest use and practical experience in sustaining forest and peasant livelihoods. Yet, this forestry also aimed to displace the one-sided foreign extraction and mistreatment that visibly altered the environment during the nineteenth century, just as the revolution aimed to invert the antidemocratic political regime. Trained under the modernizing and scientific Porfirian programme, engineers such as Quevedo also responded, somewhat reluctantly, to the social reforms of the revolution that shaped their scientific and social goals. While this scientifically based agenda felt the influences of worldwide forestry initiatives, the practitioners of Mexican forest policy were largely products of their experience in both the Porfirian and revolutionary epochs.

National parks also grew out of international exchanges among different nations. Contact with and tours to other countries involved crafting the messages for promotion and collecting useful information for future incorporation into projects and plans. By interacting with other countries on park topics, officials highlighted their achievements and became ambassadors of rational planning and multiple uses of natural resources. Far from direct mimicry of the ideas that sprang out of forestry schools in France or national park development in the United States, Mexican foresters and officials created programmes, meanings and constituents of their own. In pervasive and persistent ways, they were influenced by international developments especially in fostering the appeal of the very concept of a national park, but more consistently the ways parks came to be used and defined were shaped by local circumstances and domestic dynamics of power.

The development of a system of conservation that came to define parks as somewhere between protection and rational use in a not-yet-industrialized country provides a largely overlooked historical artefact. The existence of an innovative park system remains counterintuitive in a place like Mexico that is better known in environmental circles for its smog-ridden megalopolis and environmental disasters.[41] Mexican national parks had many influences, which meant the concept had preexisting comparisons and expectations. Yet, the parks also had a revolutionary context that constrained rational science from designing a system that met the desires of foresters by sacrificing local demands. This type of nation building provides much mediating insight to the history of global parks and how they civilized nature by tying it to the nation.

Notes

1. The literature on the revolution is too immense to list here; for a broader discussion see my book-length study, *Revolutionary Parks: Conservation, Social Justice, and Mexico's National Parks, 1910–1940* (Tucson, 2011). Works most relevant for the Cárdenas period include Mary Kay Vaughan, *Cultural Politics of Revolution: Teachers, Peasants, and Schools in Mexico, 1930–1940* (Tucson, 1997); Alan Knight, 'Cardenismo: Juggernaut or Jalopy?' *Journal of Latin American Studies* 23, no. 1 (1994): 73-107. On the environment, see Lane Simonian, *Defending the Land of the Jaguar: A History of Conservation in Mexico* (Austin, 1995); Myrna I. Santiago, *The Ecology of Oil: Environment, Labor and the Mexican Revolution, 1900–1938* (Cambridge, 2006); Luis Aboites, *El agua de la nación: Una historia politica de México, 1888–1946* (Mexico, 1998); Alejandro Tortolero Villaseñor, ed. *Tierra, aguas y bosques: historia y medio ambiente en el México Central* (Mexico, 1996); Anthony Challenger, *Utilización y conservación de los ecosistemas terrestres de México. Pasado, presente y futuro* (México, 1998).

2. See Ford and Martin, this volume; Mark Dowie, *Conservation Refugees: The One Hundred Year Conflict between Global Conservation and Native Peoples* (Cambridge, MA, 2009); Roderick Neumann, *Imposing Wilderness: Struggles over Livelihood and Nature Preservation in Africa* (Berkeley, 1998); Richard Peet and Michael Watts, *Liberation Ecologies: Environment, Development, Social Movements* (London, 2004); Mark David Spence, *Dispossessing the Wilderness: Indian Removal and the Making of the National Parks* (New York, 1999).

3. On land reform, see Sara Walsh Sanderson, *Land Reform in Mexico, 1910–1980* (New York, 1984); John Gledhill, *Casi Nada: A Study of Agrarian Reform in the Homeland of Cardenismo* (Austin, 1991).

4. Edmundo Bournet to Miguel Ángel de Quevedo, 28 August 1936, Archivo General de la Nación (hereafter AGN): Secretaria de Agricultura y Recursos hidráulicos (hereafter SARH) 1384: 1/157:1.

5. José Juan Juárez Flores, 'Malintzin Matlalcuéyetl: Bosques, alumbrado público y conflicto social en la desarticulación de un etorno ecológico (Puebla-Tlaxcala, 1760–1870)', M.A. thesis, Universidad Autónoma Metropolitana Iztapalapa, 2005.

6. Hereafter, it will be called the Forestry Department. On Quevedo, see Simonian, *Defending*, 67–84; Christopher R. Boyer, 'Revolución y paternalismo ecológico: Miguel Ángel de Quevedo y la política forestal, 1926–1940', *Historia Mexicana* 57, no. 1 (July–Sept. 2007): 91–138; Emily Wakild, '"It Is to Preserve Life, to Work for the Trees": The Steward of Mexico's Forests, Miguel Ángel de Quevedo, 1826–1946', *Forest History Today* (Spring–Fall 2006): 4–14.

7. Ramona Isabel Pérez Bertruy, 'Parques y jardines públicos de la Ciudad de México, 1881–1911', Ph.D. diss., Colegio de México, 2003, 3; Wakild, 'Naturalizing Modernity: Urban Parks, Public Gardens, and Drainage Projects in Porfirian Mexico City', *Estudios Mexicanos* 23, no. 1 (2007): 110–15.

8. Simonian, *Defending*, 79.

9. 'Es preservar la vida trabajar por el árbol: Principios de conservación forestal para todo bien ciudadano y que norman las labores de la Sociedad Forestal Mexicana', *México Forestal* 4, no. 5–6 (1926): 45–49.

10. Secretaría de Agricultura y Fomento, Dirección Forestal y de Caza y Pesca, *Ley forestal y su reglamento* (Mexico City, 1930), 6.

11. Enrique Rodiles Maniau, 9 February 1937, AGN: SARH:1468:21/4325; Julio Prado, *El apóstol del árbol*, vol. 1 (Mexico, 1936).

12. The Agrarian Department, in charge of land reform, was itself freed from the clutches of the reactionary Ministry of Agriculture in January 1934, only a year prior to the creation of the Forestry Department.

13. Simonian, *Defending*, 86.

14. Lázaro Cárdenas, 'Mensaje del C. Presidente de la República, General Lázaro Cárdenas, radiado al pueblo mexicano el 1o. de enero de 1935 en lo concerniente a la creación del Departamento Autónomo Forestal y de Caza y Pesca', *Boletín del Departamento Forestal y de Caza y Pesca* 1, no. 1 (1935): 36–38.

15. Figures compiled from Lagunas de Zempoala visitor logs, 1938, AGN: SARH: 1384: 1/157.

16. John Sherman, 'Reassessing Cardenismo: The Mexican Right and the Failure of a Revolutionary Regime, 1934–1940', *The Americas* 54, no. 3 (Jan 1998): 357–78.

17. Boyer, 'Revolución y paternalismo', 102.

18. Miguel Ángel de Quevedo, *Relato de mi vida* (Mexico, 1942), 4. European and U.S. ideas about conservation have strongly influenced tropical forestry policy, particularly by training foresters. See Donald Worster, *Nature's Economy: A History of Ecological Ideas* (Cambridge, 1994[1977]); Richard P. Tucker, *Insatiable Appetite: The United States and the Ecological Degradation of the Tropical World* (Berkeley, 2000).

19. Ángel Roldán, 'Informe sucinto acerca de los Parques Nacionales de Europa presentado al C. Jefe del Departamento Forestal por el Ing. Forestal Ángel Roldán, Delegado al Congreso de Silvicultura de Brúcelas', *Boletín del Departamento Forestal y de Caza y Pesca*, 31 January 1936, 281–85.

20. Gifford Pinchot, *Breaking New Ground*, commemorative edition (Washington, DC, 1998), 361–72. Information on the proposed border park leans heavily on the U.S., rather than the Mexican experience; see Belinda Sifford and Charles Chester, 'Bridg-

ing Conservation across *La Frontera:* An Unfinished Agenda for Peace Parks along the US-Mexico Divide', in *Peace Parks: Conservation and Conflict Resolution,* ed. Saleem H. Ali (Cambridge, MA, 2007), 205–26; John Jameson, *The Story of Big Bend National Park* (Austin, 1996); Emily Wakild, 'Border Chasm: International Boundary Parks and Mexican Conservation, 1935–1945', *Environmental History* 14 (2009): 453–75.

21. John Coffman to Juan Zinser, 3 June 1936, AGN: SARH 1426:1/1611:1.

22. Octavio Benavides, 'Conociendo a nuestro México: El Parque Nacional "Popocatépetl - Iztaccíhuatl"', *Protección a la Naturaleza,* March 1939, 14–19.

23. Antonio Sosa, 'Un viaje a Guatemala: Segunda Parte', *Protección a la Naturaleza* 3, no. 14 (October 1938): 4–15.

24. *Protección a la Naturaleza,* December 1937.

25. Gilberto Serrato to Daniel Galicia, 12 February 1937, AGN: SARH 1384:1/157:1.

26. Alexander Adams, ed., *First World Conference on National Parks: Proceedings of a Conference Organized by the International Union for Conservation of Nature and Natural Resources* (Washington, DC, 1962), 409.

27. Christopher Boyer, *Becoming Campesinos: Politics, Identity, and Agrarian Struggle in Postrevolutionary Michoacán, 1920–1935* (Stanford, 2003), 3.

28. Char Miller, *Gifford Pinchot and the Making of Modern Environmentalism* (Washington, DC, 2004); Simonian, *Defending,* 76.

29. One such requirement was that the water source be a natural, not a manmade lake. Domingo Diez to Director de Aguas, Tierra, y Colonización, 5 July 1926, Archivo Histórico de Agua: Aprovechamientos Superficiales, 1699:24969.

30. Edmundo Bournet to Miguel Ángel de Quevedo, 28 August 1936, AGN: SARH 1384:1/157:1; Raymond Craib, *Cartographic Mexico: A History of State Fixations and Fugitive Landscapes* (Durham, NC, 2006).

31. See the *ejidal* resolution in the *Diario Oficial,* 7 November 1929 and Archivo General Agraria (hereafter AGA): Huitzilac 24/3120:6.

32. Ángel Entrambasagua to Departamento Agrario, Distrito Federal, 26 October 1937, AGA: Huitzilac 24/3120:5.

33. Alfonso Ruíz Guillen to Departamento Agrario, Cuernavaca, 4 November 1941, AGA: Huitzilac 24/3120:5.

34. Miguel Dehesa to Departamento Forestal, 21 February 1936, AGN: SARH 1384:1/157:1.

35. Lagunas de Zempoala visitor logs, March, April, May 1938, AGN: SARH 1384:1/157.

36. J. Manuel Corona, 20 May 1938, AGN: SARH 1384:1/157:1. Alfredo G. Basurto's report 1 June 1938, AGN: SARH 1384:1/157:1.

37. Luis Rivera Melo to Daniel Galicia, 14 October 1938, AGN: SARH 1384:1/157:1. Galicia denied the request as it was not in keeping with the park decree.

38. Lázaro Cárdenas, interview with Presidente Municipal of Huitzilac, 9 January 1938, AGN: SARH 1384:1/157:1.

39. David Barton Bray, Leticia Merino-Pérez and Deborah Barry, *The Community Forests of Mexico: Managing for Sustainable Landscapes* (Austin, 2005).

40. J. Peter Brosius, Anna Lowenhaupt Tsing and Charles Zerner, eds., *Communities and Conservation: Histories and Politics of Community-Based Natural Resource Management* (Lanham, 2005).

41. Joel Simon, *Endangered Mexico: An Environment on the Edge* (San Francisco, 1997).

 CHAPTER 11

Parks without Wilderness, Wilderness without Parks?

Assigning National Park Status to Dutch
Manmade Landscapes and Colonial Game Reserves

Henny J. van der Windt

The Netherlands is one of the most densely populated countries in the world and has one of the world's most heavily cultivated landscapes. It is famous for its manmade dikes and polders, but not so much for its national parks. Therefore, it could come as a surprise to learn that the Netherlands has twenty national parks, comprising 3 per cent of its land mass, thereby outdoing many countries, including the United States. This raises the question of how the concept of the national park came to be applied in a country such as the Netherlands, which had already been thoroughly cultivated well before the notion was first used. As such, the Netherlands offers a case in point for an analysis of how the concept of the national park was transformed in an environment that – with the exception of the Dutch colonies – apparently lacked wilderness.

Although the term 'wilderness' is strongly connected to the national park concept, the development of national parks cannot merely be understood in terms of 'real, existing' wilderness. Indeed, such terms are mediated by ideological and socioeconomic factors such as romanticism and neocolonialism. Their meanings are closely related to practices and scientific, aesthetic and ethical arguments of diverse social groups.[1] Given its long tradition in controlling nature to withstand the sea and to maximize agricultural production, it is a matter for debate whether and how admiration for wilderness could arise in the Netherlands. In addition, it is likely that – given its colonial history – arguments concerning interhuman relationships and native peoples' rights to 'natural' wilderness arose. Because of this international orientation, one might well expect that it was not just national developments that influenced Dutch approaches.

Accordingly, the first central question of this paper is how the concept of the national park developed in the Netherlands, in terms of its importation from abroad and its national modification at home and in the Dutch colonies. The second central question concerns the arguments and meanings the involved social groups attached to national parks and, more in particular, to wilderness. Finally, these developments will be related to specific conditions in the Netherlands.[2]

Denial and the Miracle of Yellowstone

Despite having been aware of the founding of Yellowstone National Park for some time, no note of the notion of a national park was taken in the Netherlands until much later. During the nineteenth century, very few people engaged with the concept or its underlying ideas.[3] If there was any association between national identity and Dutch landscape, it probably concerned landscapes that were connected with control over nature, for instance, the famous polder the Beemster. After the Haarlemmermeer reclamation, however, a feeling of disappointment arose about the one-sided economic approach adopted in transforming landscapes. As a reaction, artists started painting and describing the beauty of landscapes. Based on their descriptions and naturalists' reports on the indigenous flora and fauna, the Dutch landscape was defined around its waters, heaths, meadows, forests, dunes and sea. Architects and animal activists stressed the importance of a careful treatment of historical buildings and animals, respectively, as an expression of civilization. Most of these movements referred to matters as being part of national heritage and identity.[4] These proposals had barely any effect on state policy; state initiatives in any case were rare in the Netherlands.

Around 1900, the situation changed. First, national organizations were founded, such as the Dutch Organization for Natural History (NNV) (1901), the Dutch Bird Protection Society (Vogelbescherming) (1899), the Dutch Cycling Organization (1883, forerunner of the tourist organization ANWB) and some scientific organizations. Second, new ideas were imported from abroad about bird protection and sustainable forestry. In this context, the famous Dutch botanist Hugo de Vries introduced the American national park concept to the general public.[5] A long list of the characteristics of a national park can be derived from his and earlier descriptions, in which Yellowstone National Park was central, spreading the notion of a Yellowstone model:

1. a reasonably large area
2. with a relatively pristine and unspoiled landscape, with minimal human intervention and use
3. of outstanding scenic beauty with special floral, faunal or geological characteristics, interesting for scientific purposes

4. owned and protected by the state
5. appealing to nationalistic sentiments
6. for explicitly recreational purposes, designed as a park for the enjoyment of the people

The public response, however, was limited. Only the botanists of the Dutch Botanical Society discussed these ideas seriously, along with the more restricted German concept of *Naturdenkmäler* (natural monuments, *natuurmonumenten* in Dutch), echoing the ideas of the German naturalist Wilhelm Wetekamp and botanist Hugo Conwentz. Although some were enthusiastic about the idea of a national park and certainly the protection of the Yellowstone area, Dutch botanists disagreed about the relevance of these German and American ideas, because their main conservation aim was to protect plants, and they considered such ideas too idealistic to appeal to the Dutch.[6]

Some of the botanists, along with representatives of naturalist, artistic, agricultural and scientific organizations, were nonetheless involved in the initiative to found Natuurmonumenten (1905), a special organization for *Naturdenkmäler*. It was headed by scientists, businessmen, teachers and members of the Dutch aristocracy. Its practical aims expressed the involvement of these groups: to conserve characteristic species, communities, landscapes and cultural-historical elements, including estates, rather than wilderness, and to promote the study of nature and small-scale outdoor recreational activities. As one of the founders formulated, 'It is the duty of a civilized nation to conserve parts of nature for posterity, just as buildings, monuments of the past and pieces of art.'[7] A secondary aim was the commercial exploitation of the conserved areas by, for instance, forestry and fishing to cover the costs of their purchase. Natuurmonumenten was only able to establish a few, relatively small natural monuments during the early decades of the twentieth century. The state still was hardly involved in nature conservation, except for the protection of a few small natural monuments by the National Forestry Office.[8]

To some extent, these first conservation aims reflected ideas from abroad. Yet, they also had a typically Dutch flavour: there was hardly any state involvement, no strong nationalistic appeal, no focus on recreation, wilderness or large areas, and generating income from the exploitation of nature reserves was encouraged.

During the early decades of the twentieth century, neither state nor private institutions showed much interest in founding Dutch national parks, although nature conservationists welcomed initiatives abroad.[9] However, a few individuals took up the concept and adapted it in different ways to the Dutch context. In 1911 the nature conservationist Eli Heimans suggested turning the unique pastoral agricultural landscape of the Dutch province of Limburg into a national park.[10] One proposition used strategic arguments: state-owned national parks would be a better means of protecting 'untouched' environments, although the concept itself was considered 'too American' with respect to its aims and scale. Others explicitly underlined its nationalistic dimension and proposed to found a national park in 1913 to commemorate and honour 1813 as the year that the country was liberated from the French. In 1918, an arborist proposed the establishment of a national park with economic significance: a large arboretum. One individual suggested improving nature conservation in the Netherlands East Indies through the introduction of national parks.[11] However, these ideas were not translated into any practical action.

Planning, Estates and Trees

Just as in various other European countries, after 1920 nationalistic feelings became stronger, and the Dutch state partially abandoned its previous non-interventionist and liberal politics. Along with the rapidly deteriorating circumstances for landowners, this led to a new situation with respect to national parks. In addition, foresters, recreational organizations, planning institutions, ecologists and governmental organizations joined the network of nature conservationists. Conservationists suggested introducing a system of physical planning including regional and national parks.[12] The government, in turn, launched a system of regional planning and announced a National Plan, including a list of nature reserves. This planning policy was accompanied by a system of subsidies for nature reserves and the founding of some new institutions. However, it lacked national parks.

After plans for national parks in several other European countries emerged (France, Germany, Italy, Spain, Switzerland and the U.K.), yet more nature lovers and others called for a Dutch response, including members of parliament. It was probably the literary figure Dirk Tinbergen who was the first to publicly launch the idea of an actual national park in the Veluwe region, which was characterized by heath, sand dunes and forests. One year later, in 1928, naturalists suggested that sections of the dunes should become a national park.[13]

Wilderness areas were still barely an issue. On the contrary, during the 1930s, ecologists, who had previously occasionally advocated for untouched nature, started to promote the idea of a seminatural environment rather than wilderness, and they began to advise nature conservationists to manage reserves actively to achieve the most scenic and diverse results. The geographer Louis van Vuuren even argued that a national park should reflect the interaction between humans and nature, i.e., cultural landscapes, not nature's qualities as such.[14]

The Veluwe initiative was directly linked to financial problems of landowners in that region, the changing policies of local authorities and the growing ambitions of Natuurmonumenten. During the early decades of the twentieth century, this organization had purchased several estates in the Veluwezoom area. While many estate owners regarded such areas as unprofitable and tried to sell them, Natuurmonumenten valued these estates for their beauty and their recreational and forestry potential, and thus considered the land profitable enough. In an effort to considerably enlarge its Veluwezoom natural monument, Natuurmonumenten started a public campaign to raise 450,000 guilders to establish what was then called a national park in the centre of the country, which was to be 'for all people in the Netherlands'. Local authorities there attempted to protect natural areas more systematically by introducing local regulations and supporting the initiatives of Natuurmonumenten. In 1930, with the help of a generous gift from a number of nature-loving industrialists, Natuurmonumenten established the first national park in the Netherlands, Veluwezoom (2,200 ha).[15]

The main reasons to use the term 'national park' were that it was considered 'unspoiled', beautiful, useful for recreation 'for all people', a typical expression of Dutch identity and consequently of national importance. Furthermore, although the park was very small in comparison to national parks in other countries, it was the largest area in the Netherlands designated for nature conservation purposes so far.

The second national park initiative concerned an estate close to Veluwezoom, and was probably the most curious one.[16] This De Hoge Veluwe estate was owned by the successful businessman Anton Kröller, who had founded it

Illustration 11.1. National park Veluwezoom, the first national park in the Netherlands, c. 1935.

as a relatively large game reserve in 1909. The area was exclusively used by his family for hunting and forestry. Kröller's wife Helene Müller also planned to build a huge museum of modern art there. In 1932, due to the economic crisis, the Kröller-Müller family realized that they would have to sell the estate, and they decided to work together with a national park committee, recently founded by a group of arborists. Because of a strong decrease in the export opportunities open to arboriculture, these arborists sought a large area in the Netherlands where they could plant their trees temporarily. Taking into account the national economic relevance of arboriculture, they relaunched the idea put forward in 1918 of establishing a large arboretum in a national park. These plans were strongly supported by tourist and forestry organizations but not by the government. The main problem was raising the 1,000,000 guilders needed to purchase the estate. After much difficulty, the money was provided by a rather curious organization linked to the state. The Minister of Finance had direct access to this money and was able to give it to the new national park board, De Hoge Veluwe Foundation, without permission from parliament.

Eventually, the second national park in the Netherlands was founded in 1935 (6,800 ha). Although some ministers were members of the park board, the park was administered independently from the state. Representatives of the Kröller-Müller family were also on the board, but not Natuurmonumenten, it having doubts about arboriculture and the museum.[17] Ironically, the arborists were hardly involved from that point on. Again the term 'national park' was used because the area was viewed as relatively large, a typical expression of Dutch identity – especially the combination of landscape and art – but initially also because of the economic relevance of arboriculture.

The initiative for a third park was taken by Jac. P. Thijsse, an influential board member of Natuurmonumenten, along with officials from the province of North Holland.[18] This province was looking for a way to protect nature and improve recreational opportunities, and in 1941 Thijsse suggested that a national park be established to save the area's typical Dutch dunes. Immediately on the establishment of Kennemerduinen national park (1,200 ha) by the province in conjunction with the cities of Amsterdam and Haarlem and the state in 1950, its director decided to combine considerable recreational activities with nature conservation. He was convinced that this was possible and even desirable.

Before 1950, in general, the aims of the Dutch national parks resemble those of the smaller Dutch nature reserves. However, some elements were more important or completely new, such as hunting, arboriculture, 'massive' outdoor recreation and the exhibition of art, while the study of nature was less important. In the Dutch national park, manmade Arcadian landscapes were central, not wilderness, and private organizations controlled the parks rather than the state.

Colonial Parks

In the 1930s some biologists and leading conservationists still doubted whether the term 'national park' was appropriate for the Dutch situation.[19] The Dutch state, too, was very hesitant in the establishment of a national park. Nevertheless, the Netherlands was one of the signatories of the London Agreement on the protection of flora and fauna of 1933, which proposed to found national parks. However, the Dutch expressed a reservation: The national parks could not be founded in the European part of the empire because it would be too expensive, but the Netherlands East Indies offered excellent conditions for such parks.[20] In practice, however, nature protection initiatives were not easy to realize in this colony as it had differing dynamics to those at home with respect to both the natural conditions and the social networks influencing decision making. In the 1920s leading figures from Natuurmonumenten, in particular the treasurer and vice-chairman Pieter van Tienhoven, became actively involved in international conservation networks, which included scientists and businessmen from Belgium, Switzerland and the United States.[21] As a result, Van Tienhoven founded the Netherlands Commission for International Nature Conservation in 1925. Because of existing connections, the Dutch were very interested in the South African Kruger National Park (1926) and were even involved in the management of Albert National Park in the Belgian Congo (1925).[22] Just as in the United States, the state played a pivotal role in these countries, with wilderness and the exclusion of human influence being the most important issues. Yet, in comparison to the United States, several African parks focused more on wildlife, were more science related and had a less recreational orientation. Albert National Park was in fact a 'scientific reserve' modelled on the Swedish national parks (founded in 1909), which were managed under the supervision of the Swedish Royal Academy of Sciences.[23]

The Netherlands Commission for International Nature Conservation took several initiatives to provide better nature conservation and a Congo-style national park in the Netherlands East Indies.[24] However, they encountered serious problems. First, the commission had to take into consideration the policies of the Dutch and the Netherlands East Indies governments, and also those of the nature conservationists in the colony, the Netherlands Indies Association for Nature Conservation (1912). Second, they had to know the specific legal and natural conditions in the colony. Third, it was far from clear what should be regarded as a national park.

The Netherlands Indies Association was more or less a copy of Natuurmonumenten, using the same term 'natuurmonumenten' and recruiting its members from the upper classes, i.e., planters and colonial officials from forestry and scientific institutions.[25] Nevertheless, there were clear differences from Natuurmonumenten. During the 1920s, the Netherlands Indies Association had only a few hundred members, while Natuurmonumenten had almost 10,000. The Netherlands Indies Association could not rely on the support of teachers, industrialists or members of the nobility, which reduced its options for propaganda and the independent creation of nature reserves on their own, generally being forced to depend on others. Nonetheless, it had good connections with the government.

Partly as a result of its activities, some nature conservation legislation had been introduced in 1916 to enable the founding of natural monuments. By 1922, forty-six such monuments had been created, based on scientific, historical or aesthetic grounds and varying in size from 0.2 to 320,000 hectares.[26] For conservationists in the Netherlands, this was by no means sufficient. They started an offensive by presenting a brochure to improve nature conservation in the Netherlands East Indies.[27] Despite similarities in organization and aims, personal contacts between the Dutch and Netherlands Indies conservationists were often but loose. The offensive thus created many misunderstandings and irritations. For instance, in 1928 when Dutch members of parliament inspired by the brochure asked the responsible Dutch minister to take measures to encourage national parks, and especially a park at the Peak of Indrapoera – the minister replied that he would ask the Netherlands East Indies government to do so. The Netherlands Indies Association was upset, not only because the brochure was written without their involvement, but also because a large park around the Piek van Indrapoera was impossible. This was not the last time that the Dutch conservationists criticized their Netherlands Indies colleagues or took the initiative for new measures. Although the Netherlands Indies Association also wanted to preserve large unspoiled areas, they were not particularly pleased by the repeated requests, as they were convinced that the conservationists in the Netherlands were not capable of adequately judging the situation in the Netherlands Indies. The discussion in the Dutch parliament in 1928 also reveals another important point. The minister responded that the Netherlands East Indies had already more than fifty national parks, illustrating the confusion surrounding the term.[28]

Nonetheless, the Netherlands East Indies government got the underlying message to improve nature conservation legislation and in particular the preservation of big game. In 1932 it introduced new legislation. This resulted in the establishment of twenty wildlife sanctuaries or game reserves varying in size from 198 to 356,000 hectares.[29] According to Netherlands East Indies conservationists, 'Such game reserves or animal reserves are to be compared with what in other countries are called "national parks".'[30] The main problem was to implement the rather complex conservation measures. To a greater extent than in the Netherlands, the colonial government founded nature reserves itself, but because it did not have the capability to govern the whole Netherlands East Indies effectively, implementation and control were very difficult. Furthermore, the maintenance of the colonial community's hunting privileges appeared to be unavoidable. In contrast, the rights and certain habits concerning the appreciation and protection of nature by the indigenous communities were not always recognized and respected. As a consequence, the rising Indonesian nationalist movement regarded this form of nature protection as just another reprehensible colonial policy.[31]

Even after the new legislation of 1932, it was impossible to give full protection to species such as the Sumatran elephant and the Javanese tiger, and the Dutch nature conservationists therefore requested for improvements.[32] New legislation was introduced in 1941, which included new terminology describing the sanctuaries as 'nature parks' and 'nature reserves'.[33] Again the term 'national park' was avoided. As previously noted, for some it was simply a tautology, but this is not the whole story. For instance, the Dutch Minister for Colonies had expressed his fear that additional measures would be necessary, if the term were used, although he was willing to ask the Netherlands Indies government to consider it. Furthermore, Dutch officials regarded the term 'national' not particularly appropriate for a park or a reserve in a colony.[34] This is probably related to the precarious situation in the colony at that time, where Dutch power was decreasing rapidly. Despite this, Dutch conservationists continued to call for better legislation and the creation of national parks, even beyond the independence of Indonesia in 1945.[35] Many years later, the Indonesian government decided to establish about fifty national parks – most of them during the final years of the twentieth century and after international pressure.[36]

In the other large Dutch colony of Suriname, the Netherlands Commission for International Nature Conservation also called for better conservation legislation.[37] More or less the same pattern can be recognized: conservationists in Suriname argued there was no need for Dutch conservationists to intervene, in this case because there were very few human settlements. Again, the Dutch were not convinced and in 1948 published a report calling for the creation of national parks and wilderness areas. This time they were successful, and in 1954 a Nature Protection Act was introduced. The act recognized that establishing protected areas was important for scientific knowledge, recreation and education, as well as for ethical, aesthetical, cultural and economic reasons. Ten nature reserves were founded immediately and four later, including the national park Brownsberg in 1970. The centrepiece of nature conservation in Suriname was only established more than twenty years after independence from the Netherlands, with the creation of the Central Suriname Nature Reserve (1,592,000 ha) in 1998, one of the most pristine reserves in the world.[38]

The Western ideas of national parks and nature conservation were exported to the colonies, and the colonial governments made decisions without the involvement of the local indigenous communities. However, the focus in the

Dutch colonies clearly differed from that in the Netherlands. Whereas in the latter, manmade Arcadian landscapes were central, the idea of wilderness ruled in the colonies. Furthermore, especially in the Netherlands East Indies, the colonial government and colonial conservationists were relatively autonomous from the homeland. The nature conservation networks in the Netherlands and the colonies barely overlapped. Only a few conservationists, particularly Van Tienhoven, were involved in both the homeland and colonial national park initiatives. Compared to the Belgians, who created an institute for Congolese national parks in Brussels, or the British, who exported their aristocratic hunting habits to the colonies,[39] the Dutch colonial institutions developed their own Netherlands Indies style of nature conservation. It is probably for this reason that developments in colonial nature conservation had no noticeable influence on the developments in the Netherlands.

Twenty or More

In the decades after 1945, the government focused on the major national effort to rebuild and develop a productive Dutch landscape that was safe from the sea. Nevertheless, the prewar undercurrent continued with respect to planning practices, nature conservation, recreation and the search for characteristically Dutch landscapes. For instance, conservationists in 1970 presented a map called 'The Landscape of Tomorrow', showing how all landscapes should be protected by law or physical planning.[40]

This national tendency coincided with the internationalization of nature conservation around 1970. In 1969 the Netherlands became a member of the International Union for the Conservation of Nature and Natural Resources (IUCN). In the same year, the IUCN had tried to establish a classification of nature reserves and national parks with the aim of developing a generally accepted and uniform terminology. Inspired by the IUCN and the U.K. national park system, officials from the departments of Nature and Landscape Protection and Outdoor Recreation felt the need to standardize terminology and introduce more national parks to the Netherlands.[41] The term 'national park' was still used rather loosely and applied to all kinds of areas with certain biological, recreational or landscape qualities. In 1970 the first proposal for a system of national parks in the Netherlands was made, which included a list of twelve potential locations. A shorter, yet official list followed shortly thereafter.[42]

Therefore, the support of ministerial officials and the tourist organization ANWB notwithstanding, it came as quite a surprise that the Dutch government decided to found no less than twenty new national parks. The government opted for a new integrated planning and conservation approach, and in 1975 it presented plans for new agriculture–nature conservation relationships, national landscape parks and national parks. Because the IUCN definition was seen as 'too academic' and not entirely adequate for the Dutch context, with its landscapes invariably affected by human contact, a Dutch definition of national park was coined (though officials did not consider it in conflict with the IUCN definition)[43]:

1. an area of at least 1,000 ha
2. including natural terrains, water systems and/or forests with special natural and landscape characteristics and special forms of animal and plant life
3. owned by the Dutch state or an organization with nature conservation aims, and managed according to certain guidelines which are formulated by the state
4. with management aiming for the conservation or development of scientific, landscape and cultural-historical characteristics
5. offering possibilities for study and enjoyment of the beauty and value of the area

Apart from the size and ownership, the interesting divergences of the Dutch definition from IUCN are the natural status (an explicit focus on an untouched ecosystem absent from the Dutch definition), the aim (conservation alone versus development) and accessibility to visitors (welcome under certain conditions versus offering possibilities for enjoyment). In addition, the Dutch definition stipulates that the parks were to represent all Dutch landscapes. It therefore seems that it was more important to represent the Dutch history of human interaction with nature, including the old national parks, than to strictly follow the IUCN definition.

Not all valuable landscapes were labelled as national parks. For large areas (at least 10,000 ha) of great beauty under use by farmers or others, the term 'national landscape park' was introduced. For the most valuable areas, such as the Waddenzee area, other solutions were attempted, based on physical planning or nature conservation legislation.

After the agreement of the Dutch parliament, a long period of park founding followed.[44] Of the twenty new potential national parks listed in the 1975 national report, only twelve were established. Some disappeared from the list, for instance, because the locations were used more intensively than was assumed, while in other cases the areas were not essential to the protection of certain types of landscape. Sometimes, it also turned out that the establishment of a park would simply have been too expensive. Interestingly, five new national parks arose because the areas were more valuable than expected or they were lobbied for by authorities or nature organizations. In many cases it was not easy to achieve consensus. The nature conservationist organizations, that owned large parts of the parks, feared the negative effects of recreation on nature and asked for more specific and prohibitive legislation, while local communities, on the other hand, feared the regulation of all kinds of activities.[45] Later, special boards were introduced for each national park, which included local groups, authorities and owners who would manage the parks.

From the founding of the first 'new' national park, the Frisian island of Schiermonnikoog in 1989, it was almost twenty years before the last was opened, the old fens and water complex of De Alde Feanen in 2006.[46] At that point, 120,000 hectares of the Netherlands were designated as national park, comprising 3 per cent of the entire country and approximately 25 per cent of the country's nature reserves. A cooperative organization was founded in 2005 to coordinate the management and policy of the Dutch parks.[47]

Wilderness in the Parks?

Although the postwar development of national parks seems to be a classic example of the mixture of Dutch consensus decision making and Dutch manmade landscapes, this is only partially true. From 1975 on, internationally oriented ecologists and conservationists, including the WWF, entered the Dutch conservation network, calling for more wilderness areas within national parks and nature reserves such as those in the Veluwe region.[48]

Certainly, national concerns about the disappointing quality of the nature in the parks and their rising costs played a role, but international developments were also influential. First, ecologists worldwide called for the restoration of ecosystems, for networks of large areas to promote the migration of species and for self-regulating ecosystems within these large areas, which would be better for the survival of species. Ecologists took real wilderness situations as their main reference points, some of them explicitly referring to the wilderness in Indonesia. These insights were incorporated into international conservation policy, such as the Europe-wide network of nature reserves. Secondly, the Dutch WWF argued that it was no longer defensible that only the Third World should create large untouched nature parks and wilderness areas. This viewpoint was supported by the large recreational and touring organization ANWB, Natuurmonumenten and several regional and local authorities. There is little doubt that the expected surplus of agricultural land in Europe was also a stimulating factor.[49]

As a result, the so-called ecological restoration or 'nature development' became an important conservation aim in the Netherlands. In 1990 the Dutch government decided to establish a large National Ecological Network, including all national parks, within which they were regarded as the network's 'pearls'. Simultaneously, the state introduced a more systematic nature conservation approach, with specified nature targets for all types of nature reserves, and thus the wilderness-like areas.[50] Woodcutting and hunting were almost completely banned in various national parks. Furthermore, the management aims changed, using so-called ecological references, which are ecological situations from prehuman times or from untouched areas elsewhere in the world.

Several national parks aspired to create new wilderness areas, which were also viewed as excellent nature, ethically, ecologically and aesthetically. Some introduced 'new' wild animals, such as koniks or so called Heck cattle, the former resulting from a programme attempting to breed back the extinct tarpan horse, the latter the result of an attempt to breed back the aurochs. Certainly, hunters, farmers and foresters agitated against what they called new 'romanticism' and some biologists were sceptical about the feasibility of creating wilderness. It was also still considered important to maintain a management regime that would showcase manmade landscapes and to stimulate recreation. However, although the Dutch private Arcadian type of national park predominated, there was more room for a state-regulated wilderness-oriented type of national park.

Illustration 11.2. Koniks in Lauwersmeer national park, c. 2000. This horse species results from breeding programmes that attempt to recreate the extinct tarpan by back breeding.

Concluding Remarks

As has been shown, the role of different social groups, their networks and the meaning of 'national park' changed significantly over time. The concept was originally adopted by biologists, who were mainly interested in certain plants and their habitats. This, along with the absence of an active state policy, probably explains the limited initial interest in national parks. From 1925 on – the moment that foresters, planners, recreational organizations and conservationists formed a more comprehensive network – there was greater interest in national parks. European and African parks appear to have provided the stimulus, but they also prompted different interpretations of the concept of a national park. A coalition of aristocrats, industrialists and conservationists created sufficient financial means to found national parks in the Netherlands while the state gradually played a more active role, becoming aware of the growing need for recreational areas as well as the rapid disappearance of some of the typical Dutch landscapes. Wilderness, one of the essential elements of the American national park, was not really an issue, even for those ecologists involved. Thus, a Dutch type of national park did develop: not owned by the state, utilized for forestry and recreation and regarded as relevant to national identity, landscape history, nature conservation and science, producing a private Arcadian type of park.

In the Dutch colonies a completely different interpretation developed, related more closely to the state-owned, wilderness type of park. Here, colonial biologists, nature conservationists, landowners and the colonial regime were involved, and nationalistic arguments, recreational aims and the need to raise money to purchase areas did not play much of a role. This led to the founding of a number of very large nature reserves in the Dutch colonies, rarely called national parks.

During the 1970s the Dutch government introduced a definition of national parks inspired by – but not a direct copy of – that by IUCN and it formulated the rather radical aim of establishing twenty national parks. The more prominent role of the state made it possible to make a 'rational' selection of areas that were representative of the Netherlands. The establishment of new national parks became an aspect of physical planning, subject to contemporary democratic forms of decision making. Local authorities and stakeholders played a substantial role in the newly formed social networks, increasing the number of recreational areas. At the same time, ecologists became more involved, helping to plan or even create ecologically sound areas of wilderness. The Dutch private Arcadian form of national park was modified, providing more control for the state and local parties, as well as increased areas for recreation and 'new wilderness'.

The notion of a national park appears to be a powerful but flexible concept that inspired various groups. It can be easily combined with different interests such as hunting or forestry, scientific perspectives such as ecosystem ecology, aesthetic perspectives such as beauty or cultural history and ethical perspectives, wilderness or just the opposite, manmade landscapes. Numerous Dutch social groups have influenced the meaning of 'national park'. However, developments at the international level, such as those regarding the colonies, international conventions and the rise of IUCN and WWF and associated ecologists, all left a distinct mark.

The Arcadian type of national park is not absolutely unique to the Netherlands and can be found elsewhere in Europe, for instance in the U.K., Germany and Belgium.[51] However, the association of parks with trade and profit, the bilateral transformation of nature and multiactor decision making can still be regarded as typically Dutch and may explain why the Netherlands has so many national parks. The Dutch notion of the national park is above all a pragmatic one: if there is a lack of wilderness, then it can be constructed, both socially and physically.

Notes

1. Henny J. van der Windt, Jozef Keulartz and Jacques A .A. Swart, 'Nature and Landscape Planning: Exploring the Dynamics of Valuation, The Case of the Netherlands', *Landscape and Urban Planning* 79, no. 3–4 (2007): 218–28.

2. To address these questions, the archives of the national parks Veluwezoom, De Hoge Veluwe and Zuid-Kennemerland and of the Netherlands Commission on International Nature Conservation were examined. In addition, all relevant Dutch national nature policy reports and the yearbooks of Natuurmonumenten and the Netherlands Indies Association for Nature Conservation in the Netherlands East Indies (1905–1950) were consulted, as well as the journals *Album der Natuur* (1870–1900), *De Levende Natuur* (1896–2008) and *Natuur & Landschap* (1946–76), the daily newspapers *De Leeuwarder Courant* (1872–1930), *Het Volk, NRC, Het Vaderland* and *Het Centrum* (1910–45) and the Handelingen of the Staten-Generaal (Parliament). Several representatives of nature conservation organizations were also interviewed.

3. A. W. Stellwegen, 'Eene wonderen wereld van den Yellowstone', *Album der Natuur* (1872): 222–24; G. Doijer van Cleef, 'Het nationale park in de Verenigde Staten', *Album der Natuur* (1887): 45–64. Only one article was published in the newspaper *Leeuwarder Courant* (22 May 1879).

4. Ed Taverne, 'Het betwiste landschap van de Haarlemmermeer', *Bijdragen en mededelingen betreffende de geschiedenis der Nederlanden*, special issue: *Landschap, natuur en nationale identiteit*, 121, no. 4 (2006): 711–26. In the same issue: Wessel Krul, 'De Haagse school en het nationale landschap', 620–49; Leen Dresen, 'Op weg naar een nationaal landschap', 650–79; Willemien Roenhorst, 'De natuurlijke natie', 727–52.

5. Henny J. van der Windt, 'The Rise of the Nature Conservation Movement and the Role of the State: the Case of the Netherlands, 1860–1955', *Jahrbuch für Europäische Verwal-*

tungsgeschichte 11 (1999): 227–51; Hugo de Vries, *Het Yellowstone-park* (Amsterdam, 1905).

6. Laurens Vuijck, 'Iets over de bescherming van de natuurlijke vindplaatsen onzer inlandsche planten', *Nederlandsch Kruidkundig Archief* (1902): 615–22; Jan W. C. Goedhart, 'De verarming der wilde flora en voorstellen om deze tegen te gaan', *Nederlandsch Kruidkundig Archief* (1905): 49–69.

7. Hein W. Heinsius, 'Natuurmonumenten', *Maandblad der NNV* 3, no. 10 (1905): 36–37.

8. Van der Windt, ' The Rise of the Nature Conservation Movement'.

9. W. H. W., 'Het Yellowstone Park', *De Levende Natuur* 13, no. 1 (1908): 15–16; Jacques P. Thijsse, 'Natuurbescherming in de Vereenigde Staten', *De Levende Natuur* 22, no. 1 (1917): 30–32; no. 2 (1917): 71–73.

10. Hans P. Gorter, *Ruimte voor natuur* ('s Graveland, 1986), 319.

11. *Leeuwarder Courant*, 9 June 1913, 11 November 1913; *NRC*, 16 March 1918, 7 December 1912.

12. Hendrik Cleyndert, 'Wat ik zag en hoorde in Amerika', in *Jaarboek Vereniging tot Behoud van Natuurmonumenten in Nederland 1918-1922* (Amsterdam, 1923), 91–107; Hendrik Cleyndert, 'De Staats-parken in de Vereenigde Staten van Noord-Amerika', in *Jaarboek Vereniging tot Behoud van Natuurmonumenten in Nederland 1923-1928* (Amsterdam, 1928), 177–91.

13. *NRC*, 24 April 1928; Handelingen EK 1927–1928, 24 April 1928; *Het Vaderland*, 5 February 1928; *Het Vaderland*, 1 March 1927.

14. Henny J. van der Windt, *En dan: wat is natuur nog in dit land? Natuurbescherming in Nederland 1880-1990* (Amsterdam, 1995), 65–93; Henny J. van der Windt, 'Biologists bridging science and the conservation movement, the rise of nature conservation and nature management in the Netherlands, 1850-1950', *Environment and History* 18, no. 2 (2012): 209–36; Louis van Vuuren, *Een nationaal park in Nederland* (Utrecht, 1933).

15. Natuurmonumenten brochures from 1930 and 1932, Archive Natuurmonumenten, Veluwezoom, no. 999, inv. no. 1730; Jan Drijver, 'Jaarverslag 1930–1931', in *Jaarboek Vereniging tot Behoud van Natuurmonumenten in Nederland 1929-1936* (Amsterdam, 1936), 55–71; Henny J. van der Windt and Elio Pelzers, 'Nationaal Park de Hoge Veluwe', in *Gelderland 1900-2000*, ed. Dolly Verhoeven (Zwolle, 2006), 202–7; Jacques P. Thijsse, 'Jaarverslag 1929–1930', in *Jaarboek Vereniging tot Behoud van Natuurmonumenten in Nederland 1929-1936* (Amsterdam, 1936), 42–54.

16. Elio Pelzers, 'De oprichting van de stichting het nationale park De Hoge Veluwe', *Bijdragen en mededelingen Vereniging Gelre* 82 (1991): 79–88; Henk Beukhof et al., eds., *De Hoge Veluwe: nature and art* (Zwolle, 2005).

17. Correspondence between Thijsse and Tienhoven, Archive Natuurmonumenten, Veluwezoom, nr. 999, inv. no. 1730.

18. Elze F. van den Ban and Jacques P. Thijsse, 'De Kennemerduinen', *Noord-Holland* (1956): 121–33; Evert C. M. Roderkerk, *De Kennemerduinen* (Haarlem, 1975).

19. Jacques P. Thijsse, 'Voor den Imbosch', *De Levende Natuur* 42, no. 8 (1937): 225–32; August A. Pulle, *Mensch en natuur* (Utrecht, 1930).

20. Memorie van Toelichting. Voorbehoud bevoegdheid om toe te treden tot het in Londen gesloten verdrag betreffende bescherming van de fauna en flora. Handelingen TK 1936-1937 400 3.

21. Elio Pelzers, *Geschiedenis van de Nederlandse commissie voor internationale natuurbescherming, de Stichting tot internationale natuurbescherming en het Office international pour la protection de la nature* (Amsterdam, 1994).

22. Marjolein 't Hart and Henk van Zon, eds., *Natuur en milieu in Belgische en Nederlandse koloniën, Jaarboek voor Ecologische Geschiedenis 2009* (Gent, 2010).

23. Instituut der Nationale Parken van Belgisch Congo, *Decreet tot stichting, Instituut der Nationale Parken van Belgisch Congo* (Brussels, 1935).

24. Pieter G. van Tienhoven, 'Internationale natuurbescherming', in *Jaarboek Vereniging tot Behoud van Natuurmonumenten in Nederland 1923-1928* (Amsterdam, 1928), 191-202; Pelzers, *Geschiedenis Nederlandse commissie*.

25. Pelzers, *Geschiedenis Nederlandse commissie*; Peter Boomgaard, 'Oriental Nature, Its Friends and Its Enemies: Conservation of Nature in Late-colonial Indonesia, 1889-1949', *Environment and History* 5, no. 3 (1999): 257-92.

26. Netherlandsch Indisch Staatsblad (NI Stb.) 1916, 278; Paul Jepson and Roger J. Whittaker, 'Internationalisation of Conservationist Values and Their Adaptation in the Netherlands Indies', *Environment and History* 8, no. 2 (2002): 129-72.

27. Archive Nederlandsche Commissie voor Internationale Natuurbescherming (Cie. int. nb), Stadsarchief Amsterdam, nr. 1283, inv. nr. 168; Nederlandsche Commissie voor Internationale Natuurbescherming, *Nature Protection in the Netherlands Indies,* published in English by the American Committee for International Wild Life Protection (Cambridge, 1936).

28. Handelingen EK 1927-28, 9 May 1928. 'Jaarverslag over 1929', in Nederlandsch Indische Vereeniging tot Natuurbescherming, *Verslag over de jaren 1929-1931* (Buitenzorg, 1932); Pelzers, *Geschiedenis Nederlandse commissie*; Cie. int. nb, Stadsarchief Amsterdam, nr. 1283, inv. no. 168. For confusion about the meaning of 'national park': Het Vaderland, 25 July 1936, 'Jaarverslag over 1931', in Nederlandsch Indische Vereeniging tot Natuurbescherming, *Verslag over de jaren 1929-1931* (Buitenzorg, 1932) and Roger Heim, ed., *Derniers refuges: atlas commenté des réserves naturelles dans le monde* (Amsterdam, 1956).

29. NI Stb. 1932, no. 17; Jepson and Whittaker, 'Internationalisation'.

30. Karel W. Dammerman, 'Preface', in *Nature Protection in the Netherlands Indies* (Batavia, 1938).

31. Boomgaard, 'Oriental Nature'; Robert Cribb, 'Conservation in Colonial Indonesia', *Interventions* 9, no. 1 (2007): 49-61.

32. Cie. int. nb, Stadsarchief Amsterdam, nr. 1283, inv. no. 174.

33. NI Stb. 1941, no. 167.

34. Handelingen TK 1934-35, 21-2-1935; Preamble to draft of new conservation legislation, Stadsarchief Amsterdam, nr. 1283, inv. no. 174.

35. The request was formulated by the Nature Conservation Council. Cie. int. nb, Stadsarchief Amsterdam, nr. 1283, inv. no. 174.

36. In practice, environmental protection has not really improved in Indonesia. Interview Herman D. Rijksen (26 May 2008), leading Dutch ecologist in Indonesia during the 1980s and 1990s; Julia Arnscheidt, *'Debating' Nature Conservation: Policy, Law and Practice in Indonesia, a Discourse Analysis of History and Present* (Leiden, 2009).

37. Cie. int. nb, Stadsarchief Amsterdam, nr. 1283, inv. no. 176.

38. Wet van 3 april 1954, houdende voorzieningen tot bescherming en behoud van de in Suriname aanwezige natuurmonumenten (G.B. 1954 no. 26); Surinaams Staatsblad 1998, no. 65.

39. Cribb, 'Conservation'.

40. Gorter, *Ruimte voor natuur,* 328.

41. Wim G. van der Kloet, *Nationale parken en recreatievoorzieningen in Engeland en Wales* (The Hague, 1957); Anonymous, *Nota inzake een systeem van nationale parken en nationale landschapsparken in Nederland* (The Hague, 1971).

42. Wim G. van der Kloet, 'Een programma voor nationale parken in Nederland', *Recreatievoorzieningen* 21, no. 4 (1970): 49–55; Anonymous, *Nota nationale parken.*

43. IUCN definition in Anonymous, *Nota nationale parken* and in Raymond F. Dasmann, *Classification and Use of Protected Natural and Cultural Areas* (Morges, 1973); Interdepartementale Commissie nationale parken en nationale landschapsparken, *Advies van de Interdepartementale Commissie nationale parken en nationale landschapsparken, deel 1: Nationale parken* (The Hague, 1975); Arnold Boer, 'A System of National Parks in the Netherlands', *Parks* 3, no. 1 (1978): 9–12.

44. Interview Arnold Boer (9 April 2008), leading Dutch official for national parks during the 1980s and 1990s.

45. Interview Arnold Boer (9 April 2008). Because national parks have no legal basis and cannot harmonize agriculture and nature conservation, conservationists paid little attention to national parks, see Anonymous, 'Drie "groene nota's"', *Natuur & Landschap* 29, no. 2 (1975): 85–90; for local resistance: Attie Bos and Margreet ter Steege, *Schiermonnikoog: Nationaal Park?* (Haren, 1987).

46. SNP, *Nederlandse Nationale Parken 1975–2006: ontstaansgeschiedenis, feiten en ontwikkelingen* (The Hague, 2007).

47. The cooperative organisation is not very powerful. Approximately 65% of the total area of national parks is managed by state institutions. Ibid.

48. Harm E. van de Veen, *De Veluwe natuurlijk?* (Arnhem, 1975); Van der Windt et al., *Landscape and Urban Planning* 79, 3–4.

49. Van der Windt, *En dan: wat is natuur nog in dit land?,* 200–209.

50. SNP, *Nederlandse Nationale Parken;* Van der Windt et al, *Landscape and Urban Planning* 79, 3–4; Ministry of Agriculture, Fishery and Food Quality, *Structuurschema Groene Ruimte deel 4* (The Hague, 1995). In 2011, the Dutch government decided to make the provinces responsible for the national parks, *Onderhandelingsakkoord decentralisatie natuur,* appendix of a letter of the Ministry of Economic Affairs, Agriculture and Innovation to Dutch Parliament, October 6, 2011.

51. Hans Bibelriether and Rudolf L. Schreiber, *Die Nationalparke Europas* (Frankfurt am Main, 1989); http://www.nationaalparkhogekempen.be.

 CHAPTER 12

Globalizing Nature

National Parks, Tiger Reserves and
Biosphere Reserves in Independent India

Michael Lewis

On 11 June 1972, Indian Prime Minister Indira Gandhi addressed the UN Conference on Human Environment in Stockholm. Gandhi was the only head of state to attend, and she had the honour of giving the last formal address. Her comments electrified the gathered delegates, as she spoke forcefully of the simultaneous need to both preserve nature and address human inequities. In the most memorable section of her address, she asked:

> Are not poverty and need the greatest polluters? For instance, unless we are in a position to provide employment and purchasing power for the daily necessities of the tribal people and those who live in or around our jungles, we cannot prevent them from despoiling the vegetation. When they themselves feel deprived, how can we urge the preservation of animals? How can we speak to those who live in villages and slums about keeping the oceans, the rivers and the air clean when their own lives are contaminated at the source? The environment cannot be improved in conditions of poverty.[1]

Throughout her address, Gandhi linked the need to preserve the environment to the need to pursue greater global equity among the peoples of the world, both within and between nations. She called for a complete rethinking of the basis of civilization, and although it would be hard, the developed and developing world needed 'to change their style of living' and 're-establish an unbroken link with nature and with life.'[2] In another speech given to a much smaller audience in India almost two months earlier, Gandhi made a similar critique and linked the extinction of plants and animals to racism and global inequities among humans: 'Why worry if [a] few tigers and rhinos and a few plant species are wiped out? ... this attitude of mind is the same which regards one species of human being as superior to another.'[3]

In these speeches, Gandhi developed an environmental ethic that equated the abuse of nature with colonialism (species extinctions linked to human racism). Simultaneously, she suggested that international environmentalism was also a legacy of the colonial world in its occlusion of the brutal poverty affecting so many people in the developing world – from the villages and slums to tribal peoples in the jungle. To stay the environmental course would be to perpetuate colonial relationships towards the poor and their environments, but to fail to preserve nature would be similarly exploitative. Thus Gandhi did not claim to aspire to a global (or colonial) standard of civilization and its nature, but rather sought to formulate a new model for civilizing both nature and India. However, her critique of 'civilization' (meaning primarily overconsumption and the exploitation of others) juxtaposed with a call for greater connections to nature did not look like a radically new vision of civilized nature, but rather a postcolonial iteration of earlier uses of nature to critique the worst excesses of modernity without challenging its basic principles. The history of the creation of Indian national parks confirms this.

Between 1972 and 1974, Gandhi provided the public rationale for a people-centred approach to environmentalism that put social justice at its core. To this end, she deputized a national Man and the Biosphere (MAB) committee to investigate biosphere reserves, a new mode of nature preservation supported by UNESCO that included people in its protected areas. But at the same moment, Gandhi led the push for a series of laws and policies that resulted in forming Indian national parks and tiger reserves. These new parks hewed closely to the global national park norm, and seemed oblivious to her socioenvironmental concerns. Ironically, the same leader who had encouraged the world to recognize the moral claims of the poor to the forests in which they lived was a key impetus in the dispossession of many poor forest dwellers in India from their traditional resource base. In looking more closely at these three modes for establishing protected areas, not just Gandhi's contradictions come into focus, but also those of the Indian government as a whole. A postcolonial state that strove to formulate a new relationship between civilization and nature instead found itself soliciting international funding for conservation, building a shared national identity around the tiger, creating national parks that closely followed global models and simultaneously rejecting the rights of either the global community or scientists (whether Indian or Western) to prescribe how to preserve its own nature. Following her call for a new civilization and new relationship to nature in 1972, Gandhi's India instead created a strikingly standard system of national parks that differed from the transnational model most notably in its incomplete implementation.

National Parks

Within three months of Gandhi's 1972 Stockholm address, India passed the Wild Life (Protection) Act (WLP Act). This law established a legal basis for national parks and sanctuaries in India, as well as protecting endangered and threatened species. India already had a handful of national parks controlled by state governments; the new law established a standard federalized legal framework for them. It defined national parks as locations that should have no human presence, nor cattle, nor human uses, and authorized the removal of villagers and tribal peoples living in national parks.

India's national parks, as codified in the WLP Act, were most immediately connected with the global national park movement that flourished in the post-1945 world, particularly in the United States, but also advocated by scientists and NGOs like the IUCN throughout the world. Further, though, India's national parks drew upon long-term indigenous traditions of princely game reserves and nearly a hundred years of British efforts to preserve colonial nature in India.[4] M. K. Ranjitsinh, an Indian bureaucrat and the principal author of the WLP Act, was the grandson of a ruler of a princely state in Rajasthan. Ranjitsinh is insistent that the national park system that he played such a key role in devising was a product of indigenous Indian game reserve practices, not simply a Western overlay onto India. He has written that he grew up listening to family discussions of how best to manage wildlife on their lands. Ranjitsinh had an uncle who successfully reintroduced tigers onto his land and managed them at a stable population in a reserve with people and cattle excluded. Ranjitsinh claims, 'That was the same principle I adopted when I started the cattle compensation scheme in India.'[5] Of course, 'indigenous' Indian practices in the nineteenth and twentieth centuries were not carried out in cultural or political vacuums, and the British raj also provided both a precedent for later national parks and potential models for the rulers of the princely states.

The British Imperial Forest Service was established in 1867; in the Forest Act of 1927 the requirements for establishing a reserved forest were standardized (in many respects along similar lines to the 1972 WLP Act).[6] These reserved forests were in no way national parks, however. The first national park in India was Corbett National Park (at that time called Hailey National Park), established with a special state law on 6 August 1936. This national park was the special project of a local British official concerned about the loss of the forests in that region, and the park was given legal status only within the state of Uttar Pradesh. It did not serve as a national model, and there was little in the way of further development of national parks in India as the Second World War broke out.

Following independence, the Government of India maintained the British forest system, eventually transferring the administrative structure to the Indian Forest Service. In 1952, the central government appointed a Central Board of Wild Life (later the Indian Board for Wild Life) 'to sponsor the setting up of national parks, sanctuaries, and zoological gardens' in order to conserve wildlife as well as to educate Indians.[7] This board did not have a significant impact during its first decade and a half of existence. A number of Indian states established sanctuaries and a handful of national parks between independence and 1972, but they were strictly state, not federal, designations.

Throughout the 1960s, internal and external pressure grew for the central government to formalize and expand a national park system in India. The Indian Board for Wild Life, with support from the private Bombay Natural History Society, released a series of recommendations. These recommendations were strongly influenced by the 1962 First World Conference on National Parks, held in the United States. This conference was organized by the IUCN, and cosponsored by the FAO, UNESCO, the Natural Resources Council of America and the U.S. National Park Service. Delegates from sixty-three nations attended this conference (four from India), and the stated purpose was 'to encourage the national park movement on a worldwide basis'.[8] As the Indian Board for Wild Life reported,

> [The Board] endorses the various resolutions and recommendations made at the First World Conference on National Parks ... in so far as they apply to India, and draw attention in particular to *Recommendation no. 3* which says *inter alia* that 'there is an urgent need to constitute on a world scale a systematic collection of type habitats as varied and representative as possible which could be permanently protected and to serve as standards for the future, and ... that the appropriate status for these type habitats where possible should be that of strict nature reserves.'[9]

As was evident at this conference, national parks were understood as internationally relevant and needed because of their value in preserving habitats and ecosystems. This had not always been the guiding purpose of national parks.

Since its beginning, the US National Park System had a strong recreational component and was linked to American exceptionalism as manifested in spectacular nature. Further, US national parks at least in part enabled the desire of Americans to experience an idealized frontier and thus imagine themselves linked to the key founding myths of the nation.[10] However, by the 1960s U.S. and international conservation organizations were far more focused upon the role of national parks in preserving ecosystems and endangered species of fauna (and less frequently, flora) than explicitly recreational or nationalist goals. This can be seen in the United States in the influential Leopold Report, named after Aldo Starker Leopold (son of the more famous Aldo Leopold). Leopold had been asked to chair a committee considering elk overpopulation in Yellowstone. The committee had taken an expansive view of their task, and had produced a report suggesting management goals for the entire US National Park System. The Leopold Report quoted and referred to the First World Congress on National Parks at several points, and clearly saw national parks as essentially conservation vehicles (and overwhelmingly focused upon large mammals). The most famous line of the Leopold report was its call for national parks to be managed as 'vignettes of primitive America'.[11]

The Leopold Report ended up being the basis for a wholesale shift in the management practices of the US National Park Service – their official park service history refers to it as a 'landmark', and Leopold's influence as 'vast'.[12] This shifting management base for the US National Parks shaped and reflected larger international and scientific trends, and in turn was reflected in the Second World Conference on National Parks, held at Yellowstone National Park, and sponsored by the US National Park Service in collaboration with the IUCN. The theme of the meeting was 'National Parks: Heritage for a Better World'. The national park model that international environmentalists and scientists promoted at Yellowstone was no longer a recreational or nationalistic ideal, but instead a global system of nature protection. They hailed Yellowstone not so much as a geological amusement park (as it had been perceived for much of U.S. history), but instead as a large protected area in which biological processes could occur with minimal human disturbance, and which would ensure the continued survival of threatened species.[13]

The Second World Conference was held in September, the same month that the Indian WLP Act was passed. Both the conference and the new law illustrated the global state of the art in protected area strategy. The Yellowstone conference had been announced in 1969 at the IUCN general meeting, held that year in New Delhi. This 1969 IUCN conference was significant in its own right; it was the starting point for both WWF–India and what would become Project Tiger. Ranjitsinh, as well as many other Indian scientists and bureaucrats, attended both conferences. To Ranjitsinh or any of the attendees at these conferences, the national park model that was being promoted appeared to be less tied to any one nation than to scientific principles of reserve design rooted in population ecology and management practices based upon the exclusion of human resource uses and grazing. Insofar as Yellowstone was hailed as a model (and it was, repeatedly) it was disassociated from the actual history of its establishment in 1872, the 1916 Organic Act that had established the National Park Service and the recreational impulse that had motivated much of its history as a park.[14] The nineteenth-century removal of its human inhabitants by the U.S. military and the park's large size were in neither case done for scientific reasons, but by the 1960s Yellowstone, this accidental eco-park, was reborn as the large nature preserve of the ecologist's dream. The disjuncture between Yellowstone's actual history and how it was promoted in the 1960s and 1970s is significant.

Although Yellowstone was promoted internationally as the gold standard of a large protected ecosystem, the Indian WLP Act was in fact more in line with international standards of reserve design and management than any codified U.S. law. The WLP Act was simultaneously a protected area act (establishing national parks and sanctuaries with legal status) and an endangered species act, establishing lists of species to be protected and restrictions on hunting and trade in animals. The name matters: in India, national parks were formalized in the *Wild Life Protection* Act. The act makes practically no mention of recreation or tourism, other than in stipulating the various bureaucrats in charge of restricting it. Using the IUCN's protected area standards, national parks in India were in the strictest category of preserved land (Scientific Reserves), and Indian sanctuaries, where some grazing and management 'for the improvement and better management of wildlife' was allowed, fit into the category for Habitat and Wildlife Management Areas.[15] In contrast, the vast majority of U.S. national parks fall into the categories for Parks (geared towards recreation and tourism) or Natural Monuments and National Landmarks.

There is no question that the WLP Act combined with a new enthusiasm for creating parks in India and reorganized a significant piece of the Indian landscape. In 1975, three years after the law was passed, there were 5 national parks and 126 sanctuaries in India. By 1985, there were 53 national parks and 247 sanctuaries, and by 1997, 65 national parks and 425 sanctuaries. As of June 2008, there were 97 national parks and 508 sanctuaries in India, covering 4.76 per cent of India's landmass.[16] But these numbers hide a messier reality. A significant number of these sanctuaries and parks have not yet been finally certified by the central government because the state governments (and the state foresters) have not been able to bring the parks into conformity with the requirements of the WLP Act, particularly its insistence on no grazing by cattle (in national parks), no human settlements within parks and no human uses of the minor forest products such as thatch and honey. Even in federally recognized parks, there is significant noncompliance with the law. In 1989, in response to a voluntary government survey, 40 per cent of the national parks claimed to be in full compliance with the law, and only 8 per cent of the sanctuaries.[17] As participation in the survey had been voluntary, we might assume that the noncompliance rates were even higher. A separate 2000 study claimed that a minimum of 3 million people (illegally) lived within these Indian protected areas at that time.[18] The WLP Act, strongly encouraged by Gandhi, did not reflect an environmentalism of the poor or a new model of development. Rather it seemed to be a direct infringement upon the living conditions of poor peoples living in and near these protected areas, an act more in keeping with international protected area standards than local realities. By the 1980s, one in five protected areas in India reported physical clashes between local peoples and forest officers – in some cases even leading to death.[19]

Tiger Reserves

In November, 1972, two months after the WLP Act was passed, the Indian Board for Wild Life released the project proposal for Project Tiger. This plan was an ambitious attempt to save the tiger from extinction by dedicating a subset of the newly formalized national parks and sanctuaries to tiger protection, expanding their size if possible and increasing funding for management in those areas. The project proposal claimed, 'The best method of protection of the tiger is to have large areas of at least 2,000 km², with similar contiguous areas.' With little apparent irony, the report went on to claim, 'The Task Force could not locate many areas as large as 2,000 km² which could be reserved for tiger preservation.'[20] In fact, in the eight tiger reserves that were originally proposed, only one even had the potential of being expanded to that size (although it would have involved increasing the sanctuary's size tenfold, and today it is only 500 km²). All of them, from small to large, required substantial curtailments of human use, including the relocation of people living within the proposed tiger reserves. As the proposal explained, 'It is desirable that small pockets of forest villages should be shifted. In case it is not possible, at least the village cattle ... should be diverted to alternative sites.'[21] The Project Tiger proposal met with governmental and international approval, and Project Tiger was begun in 1973.

Indian national parks and Project Tiger were legal fraternal twins – born at the same moment and in the same social environment, with the same small group of elected leaders, scientists and bureaucrats involved in planning them. Each initiative justified the other – Project Tiger needed parks with strong legal protection in order to be effective, and national parks needed a popular rationale for displacing people and their practices. Both were spurred along by the 1969 IUCN meeting in New Delhi; both were strongly advocated by Indian and international scientists and both were seen as essential parts of a larger national strategy to confront an ecological crisis: the extinction of key Indian fauna.[22] The cheetah and pink-headed duck were gone. Were the Asian lion, Asian rhino, mugger crocodiles, Asian elephant and tiger to follow? Tigers were the charismatic stars of Indian conservation, the species that garnered the most attention and the most money. But they were only one of many endangered Indian species (including birds) that would benefit, theoretically, from this new protected area strategy.

Project Tiger was implemented via Tiger Reserves. These were not new parks, but instead existing national parks and sanctuaries that would be expanded and managed more carefully, with more research, accountability and enforcement. The task force that established Project Tiger understood the tiger to be what we would now call a keystone species. As they explained in their justification for the project, the tiger 'keeps the population of herbivores under control and thereby saves the vegetation from overgrazing and the land from denudation. It also maintains good stock of animals.' The authors believed that by saving the tiger, they would be saving all of the other associated fauna and flora in those forests – in a fit of exuberance, they even claimed that the tiger was 'the best protector of the forest wealth from pilferage', by attacking ne'er-do-wells, we might assume.[23]

Conservationists believed that the tiger was charismatic enough to bring about larger changes in popular attitudes both in India and abroad, and attract interest and money. 'It is a most colourful creature which arouses public attention, brings to life a lifeless forest, makes it thrilling and attracts tourists from world over [sic]', they wrote. The tourist money was mentioned more than once. As they wrote in their project justification, 'In East Africa, for example, the entire tourism revolves around their wildlife, and if properly developed India also can increase its foreign exchange earnings from this source considerably.'[24] There are several pages in the project proposal devoted to planning a tourist infrastructure, including the possibility of camping in tents – 'at your own risk.'[25] In this, the Project Tiger Task Force diverged considerably from the WLP Act, and this has continued to be a point of contention between government officials who want the tiger reserves to make money and scientists and foresters who perceive tourists (and the things local guides do to impress them) as impediments to ecosystem and tiger health. This tension was written into the planning document, as in one paragraph where the writers encouragingly note, after listing spotlights, saltlicks and feedlots, 'The tiger in the centre of a camera view-finder is an ambition of every tourist visiting India. ... Even tiger viewing can be made easy by artificial means.' This is then followed in the very next paragraph by, 'The reserves are also to function as National Parks and therefore, sound principles of park management should be adopted.'[26] Proper management was then specified to mean limited tourist access into the cores of parks, called here 'wilderness zones'.

As it turned out, since national parks and sanctuaries made up the actual space for tiger reserves, and foresters often attempted to make as much of the park a wilderness zone as possible, tourism was quite limited. Travellers to Indian tiger reserves were often struck by the relative paucity of a tourist infrastructure, and the lack of access to tiger habitat. In Corbett National Park and tiger reserve, for example, tourists were not allowed to walk in the park (let alone camp in tents!); they were strictly kept out of the core area. There were a limited number of jeep trips and elephant rides each day, most leaving from the small and basic guest lodge. Although Corbett is an extreme example, tiger tourism in India was a disappointment to those government officials anticipating an Indian safari industry. Only retroactively, planners realized that the lazy-seeming lions of the Serengeti bore little resemblance to the stealthy and secretive tigers. Even elephants in India like to hide in the jungle, and in the absence of intrusive tourist practices, much of India's most spectacular wildlife is difficult to observe on a casual tour.

Although tourism did not develop in Project Tiger as much as had been hoped, Project Tiger was successful in creating the tiger as a national symbol and nationalizing protected nature. The lion was the royal symbol of India from at least the 3rd century BCE and is still found on rupee coins, but in the late 1960s and 1970s the government made a concerted effort to use the tiger as a symbol of Indian nationalism.[27] Unlike the Asiatic lion, restricted by the twentieth century to one small park in western India, tigers were found throughout India. And while lions were associated with Africa in most international environmentalists' minds, no country in the world had as many wild tigers as India. Project Tiger, then, became not just a conservation programme but also a tool for national pride, branding and unification. This was not subtle. The planning document relates, 'Tiger Reserves are situated in eight different states, in different climates, in all the four corners of the country … thus contributing towards the emotional integration of the nation.'[28] The planning document is suffused with nationalism: 'The tiger has become, in a way, a symbol of the whole wild life and nature conservation movement in India today … Project Tiger is essentially an Indian venture, which nonetheless will attract worldwide interest and support.' And then again, later, 'The project is entirely an Indian endeavour.'[29] Tiger nationalism was further manifested in the decision by the Government of India to deny research access to U.S. ecologists who had been involved in helping to plan Project Tiger and had anticipated working on tiger ecology themselves. This occurred in the context of several factors: Indo–U.S. geopolitical relations following the 1971 India-Pakistan War; a bureaucratic power grab by the Indian Forest Service; U.S. military funding of some U.S. ecologists in India and a larger attempt by the Government of India to assert greater control of Project Tiger, to nationalize it, in a sense.[30] If the tiger were to serve as a national symbol to unify the nation, it would not do to have U.S. scientists doing the work. These U.S.-led tiger studies subsequently moved to Nepal, where many of the same disputes about tigers as objects of tourism, as objects of science or as untrammelled wild beasts would play out in a different national context.[31]

Project Tiger was officially launched on 1 April 1973 at Corbett National Park – India's first national park, newly protected under the national law, and now a flagship tiger reserve (though by no means possessing the largest tiger population in India). Other national parks could have been effective choices – Kanha National Park, to the south, had both a larger tiger population and the most intensively studied tigers in India. The Sunderbans National Park to the east had probably the largest population of tigers in India. But none of these other parks had Corbett's relatively long history – the choice of Corbett for this inaugural function was an explicit merging of this new national symbol (the tiger) with India's oldest and most famous national park. And of course, Corbett National Park was named after Jim Corbett, the famed tiger-hunter-turned-tiger-photographer and conservationist, a metaphor, perhaps for the transition that environmentalists hoped the entire world might make.

Subsequent years would see the same problems that plagued national parks causing trouble in the more specialized tiger reserves. Relocations of villagers from core areas in Kanha and Ranthambore did not always work well. Local peoples complained that the government cared more about tigers than people. Forests in tiger reserves were sometimes burned (as at Nagerhole), and villagers sometimes participated in, or refused to stop, tiger poaching – as when Sariska Tiger Reserve was found to have no surviving tigers in 2006. India's famous tiger reserves, then, were not predicated upon an environmentalism of the poor.[32]

Biosphere Reserves

Since the 1968 UN biosphere conference, UNESCO had been building towards the creation of the international Man and the Biosphere Programme (MAB). MAB was launched globally in 1971 and in India in 1972. MAB advocated a new form of protected area known as 'biosphere reserves' that explicitly dealt with how to preserve nature within the context of human communities and uses. Biosphere reserves were a new and improved model for protected areas, with different use zones and people expressly included in the plan – as indicated in MAB's title. At Gandhi's request the Indian MAB committee considered the appropriateness of biosphere reserves for India, leading to their eventual establishment in the 1980s.

Biosphere reserves in India followed a very different trajectory than national parks and tiger reserves. Unlike national parks in the 1970s, there were no international precedents for biosphere reserves – they were a model for a new form of protected area born primarily of scientists' visions for a rational global system of protected areas that incorporated all of the world's biomes and that offered a new way to understand human-nature interactions. The Indian MAB committee was charged at its outset with leading 'a major programme of research in the field of ecology and environment'.[33] Implicit in MAB was the belief that 'ecosystem people', or people dependent upon their local ecosystems for survival, needed to be included in any planning for preserving nature in protected areas.[34] This did not mean that the biosphere reserve proposal supported national parks with people included throughout, but rather proposed a carefully managed buffer zone with human uses allowed surrounding a sacrosanct core area.

After years of planning, thousands of rupees spent on research, and the formal designation by the Government of India of fourteen areas (centred on national parks) as biosphere reserves, the programme has not resulted in any substantive changes in park management in India. For all of the idealism of the planning documents, national parks that are biosphere reserves simply have one more title to their name.[35] The biosphere idea was popular among scientists and some environmentalists in India, though, and national parks and tiger reserves were thought to be insufficient.

The IUCN, UNESCO and the UNEP, as well as many scientists, invested a tremendous amount of energy in proposing this new category of protected area – a new type of national park. T. N. Khoshoo, a Secretary of the Indian Ministry of Environment and Forests, summarized their rationale when he explained that biosphere reserves were needed in India because of their greater size, their lack of tourism and other human disturbances, and most especially biosphere reserves' scientific selection based upon ecosystem concerns, not species conservation or national landmarks.[36] The other factor that Khoshoo did not mention but that is apparent in the many MAB documents was that biosphere reserves were explicitly international in focus – this was a global initiative, not a nationalist one.

Scientists and scientific organizations like the IUCN were the leading advocates for the MAB programme. It was much more carefully based on science than other protected area programmes. The national park model had been born of different concerns, as mentioned with Yellowstone above, often selecting unique, bizarre or spectacular landscapes of national interest and significance. That iteration of the national park model was predicated upon a pre-ecological worldview. Another early iteration, the early game parks in the colonial world, was based upon fears about game depletion, but again was not based upon an ecosystem approach. But by the early 1970s, with the full bloom of the ecological sciences, there was a push for a park system that preserved land selected on a scientific basis as representative ecosystems of different biomes – that was the biosphere reserve system. Biosphere reserves also deemphasized tourism (allowed only in special exterior zones). Scientists also ensured that biosphere reserves were meant to be huge. Based upon island biogeography and population ecology, many scientists were convinced that existing national parks (or tiger reserves, for that matter) were going to prove to be too small for preserving large mammal species and for allowing evolutionary forces to continue to unfold and shape natural systems.

This notion of parks that would be large enough to allow scientists to watch evolution unfold without human intervention or management was key for many scientists. MAB explicitly called for long-term ecological monitoring and research in biosphere reserves. The Indian MAB committee praised India's 'scientific base', but also suggested that even more scientific expertise would have to be developed: 'In the long run, a strong cadre of trained scientists to undertake environmental research in the Biosphere Reserve areas will have to be developed for which the international organizations like IUCN and UNESCO will have to play a key role in terms of arranging training pro- grammes.'[37] As the Indian MAB committee began their work, their budgets were almost exclusively devoted to funding for scientific research. Again, this differed from existing national parks, where the budgets were used for any number of management or tourism objectives. But, ironically, as biosphere reserves ended up using national parks as their core areas, the insistence of sci- entists upon devoting funds to pure research did not endear MAB to govern- ment foresters or bureaucrats in charge of managing the national parks. To the contrary, the complicated management zones of biosphere reserves seemed like a headache both to foresters and local peoples.

Some government officials in India also felt ambivalent about the ramifica- tions of biosphere reserves. MAB was explicitly international. The FAO, UNEP, UNESCO and the IUCN supported MAB. These four organizations ran the conferences for biosphere reserves, oversaw the international network and provided the voluminous written rationales for their use. The IUCN, in detail- ing the special features of biosphere reserves, wrote, 'They form an interna- tional network in which the international character is ensured by an exchange of information and personnel [apparently scientists].'[38] This was the protected area equivalent of a move towards global governance – but a global governance run by scientists. Naming was important – these were not national parks, but biosphere parks. Rather than nationalized nature, this was internationalized nature, preserved not by or for the nation, but in the interest of global hu- manity. And this rubbed some Indians the wrong way. In the mid-1980s T. N. Seshan (then the Secretary of the Environment) decided not to register India's first biosphere reserves in the UNESCO network and stopped scientists who had begun this paperwork.[39] Seshan wanted to explicitly maintain biosphere reserves as an initiative of the Government of India, not an international col- laboration. Further, foresters had little interest in ceding funding and authority to scientists while being asked to manage a larger and more complex protected area. And the scientists and international organizations proposing the bio- sphere reserve idea could do very little to get the Indian government to join them. India would not finally join the international MAB network until the first decade of the twenty-first century, and by then Indian biosphere reserves had a solid institutional history of irrelevancy.

The IUCN wrestled with this issue when debating whether to encourage na- tional governments to pass biosphere reserve laws. They decided against this, for to have a series of national laws governing biosphere reserves would have ultimately nationalized the system and given management authority to the various nation-states rather than the shared international coordinating bodies. As the chairman of the Commission on National Parks and Protected Areas for the IUCN wrote, 'Indeed it is probably better, in general, that there should not be new legislation specifically for biosphere reserves, because this is likely to harden the definition of the term "biosphere reserve" and it would then be likely to assume different forms in different countries, each with the sanctity of law. This has happened, for example, to the term national park.'[40] Yet, in the absence of national laws, not just in India, but also around the globe, biosphere reserves have been largely toothless. With rare exceptions, biosphere reserves are designations with little to no impact on management.

Conclusion

This brief consideration of a particularly active period in Indian environmentalism suggests a few key themes relevant to the larger discussion of the transnational spread of national parks. First, by the late 1960s, the 'national park idea' was unmoored from the nineteenth-century history of national parks and more predicated upon scientific debates about species conservation and management, ideas that would find their culmination in the biosphere reserve model. While the United States continued to play a key role in this process, it was more through scientists such as A. Starker Leopold and his role in national park management than through John Muir or the original U.S. national parks. Second, as has been pointed out in many other historical studies, large, charismatic megafauna are an effective tool of nationalized nature, providing national parks oriented around species such as tigers as a counterpart to more traditional nationalized landscape or historical features. Third, the biosphere reserve story suggests that a nonnationalized protected area system, a truly global system of parks, is still difficult to implement in a world in which each individual park will still be local and still territory claimed by a nation-state (with the exception of maritime or Antarctic spaces). The partial failure of biosphere reserves in India perhaps speaks to the greater power of nationalized nature to effect conservation initiatives and the difficulty of imagining an effective global governance of protected areas.

While the early 1970s were the most eventful period of the twentieth century in the rise of global environmentalism, these examples suggest that the various national environmental initiatives and movements (from clean air acts to new national parks), as they embraced nationalism and nation-state governance, were more successful than the corresponding attempts at truly international environmental initiatives. And this, finally, brings us back to Indira Gandhi. Perhaps the most striking thing about all three of India's protected area initiatives from this formative period is how limited their successes have been. While national parks and tiger reserves exist both on paper and on the ground, as pointed out above, their implementation has been far short of what was imagined in 1972, and biosphere reserves have been even less effective.

Some scholars have seen in this incomplete implementation a 'cunning state, playing on its own presumed weakness,' that escapes accountability from the same national environmentalists and international organizations that pushed so hard for a national park act and tiger reserves in the early 1970s. In this sense, the incompletely implemented WLP Act was always intended to be only partially implemented. The Government of India has even argued before its own Supreme Court that it did not have the necessary resources to enforce the WLP Act throughout the country. Presumably, this then allows the state both to have laws that placate international environmentalists and that allow severe action when the state wants to do so, while still allowing many of the state's poorest citizens to continue to live in, and use, the forest.[41] This 'cunning state', however, simultaneously overestimates the unity of the Indian government, with its diverse state governments and vast bureaucracy, and underestimates the real commitment of many bureaucrats and politicians – including Gandhi – to the policies represented by the WLP Act, Project Tiger and even biosphere reserves. True, the Indian state is capable of displacing people and enforcing laws, even violently, when its leaders decide to do so. However, India's leaders – and by extension, the state – are simply not sure of which policy to pursue. Rather than a cunning state, perhaps the more apt metaphor is the *uncertain* state. There is ample evidence that Gandhi both sympathized with impoverished forest dwellers, and was also concerned that (in keeping with what her conservation advisors would argue) forest dwellers might endanger highly threatened species. Gandhi understood that the national park, with its roots in colonialism, was problematic, but her government never succeeded in developing a viable alternative before her assassination in 1984. Ultimately, of course, it was not Gandhi, nor the government bureaucrats such as Ranjitsinh, who decided the degree of success or failure of these three initiatives, but rather the complex interplay between laws, administrators, local people, international and national NGOs, scientists and historical contingencies. And while her rhetoric at Stockholm soared in positing a new global human-centred environmental ethic, an ethic that was seemingly much closer to biosphere reserves than Project Tiger or national parks, it was her support of nationalist nature parks that has proven most enduring thus far.

Notes

1. Indira Gandhi, 'Man and His Environment', reproduced as Appendix VI, in *Project Tiger: A Planning Proposal for Preservation of Tiger (Panthera tigris tigris Linn.) in India*, ed. Task Force: Indian Board for Wild Life (Delhi, 1972), 109. For contemporary reactions, see Robert Bendiner, 'Third World Ecology: At Stockholm: On Balance an Awareness that Early Concern for the Environment Is Cheaper and Saner', *New York Times*, 26 June 1972, 33.

2. Gandhi, 'Man and His Environment', 113–14.
3. Indira Gandhi, 'Inaugural Address', *Inaugural Function of the National Committee on Environmental Planning and Coordination* (New Delhi, 1972), 4.
4. Mahesh Rangarajan, *India's Wildlife History* (Delhi, 2001).
5. Interview by author with M. K. Ranjitsinh, WWF–India office in New Delhi, 13 July 1998. Transcript on file with author.
6. Ashish Kothari, Pratibhi Pande, Shekhar Singh and Dilnavaz Varisna, *Management of National Parks and Sanctuaries in India: A Status Report* (New Delhi, 1989), 79.
7. 'Biosphere Reserves: Indian Approach', in *First International Biosphere Reserve Congress at Minsk (USSR)* (New Delhi, 1983), 6.
8. 'How it Began', in *First World Conference on National Parks, Seattle, Washington, June 30–July 7, 1962*, ed. Alexander Adams (Washington, DC, 1962), xxxii.
9. E. P. Gee, 'The Management of India's Wild Life Sanctuaries and National Parks', *JBNHS* 64, no. 2 (1967): 340.
10. Michael Lewis, ed, *American Wilderness: A New History* (New York, 2007).
11. A. Starker Leopold, *Wildlife Management in the National Parks* (Washington, DC, 1963); Richard Sellars, *Preserving Nature in the National Parks: A History* (New Haven, 1997).
12. William Sontag, *National Park Service: The First 75 Years* (Washington, DC, 1990).
13. Hugh Elliott, ed., *Second World Conference on National Parks: Yellowstone and Grand Teton National Parks, USA, September 18–27, 1972* (Morges, 1974).
14. Ibid.
15. Shekhar Singh, 'Biodiversity Conservation through Ecodevelopment Planning and Implementation Lessons from India', Working Papers no. 21, South-South Cooperation Programme on Environmentally Sound Socio-Economic Development in the Humid Tropics, UNESCO, 1997, 6.
16. J. S. Kathayat, 'List of Protected Areas', National Wildlife Database Cell, Wildlife Institute of India, Dehradun, June 2008. http://www.wii.gov.in/nwdc/pa_list.pdf, accessed 20 April 2009.
17. Singh, 'Biodiversity Conservation', 9.
18. Tejaswini Apte and Ashish Kothari, *Joint Protected Area Management: A Simple Guide to How It Will Benefit Wildlife and Humans* (Pune, 2000).
19. Rangarajan, *India's Wildlife History*, 114; Michael Lewis, *Inventing Global Ecology* (Athens, OH, 2004); Ross Mallick, 'Refugee Resettlement in Forest Reserves: West Bengal Policy Reversal and the Marichjhapi Massacre', *Journal of Asian Studies* 58, no. 1 (1999): 103–25.
20. Task Force, 'Project Tiger', 14.
21. Ibid., 25.
22. Rangarajan, *India's Wildlife History*, 98–105.
23. Task Force, 'Project Tiger', 7.
24. Ibid.
25. Ibid., 28.
26. Ibid., 26.
27. Mahesh Rangarjan, 'From Princely Symbol to Conservation Icon: A Political History of the Lion in India', in *The Unfinished Agenda: Nation Building in South Asia*, ed. M. Hasan and N. Nakazato (New Delhi, 2001), 399–442.

28. Task Force, 'Project Tiger', 8.
29. Ibid., foreword and 5.
30. Michael Lewis, 'Indian Science for Indian Tigers', *Journal of the History of Biology* 38 no. 2 (Summer 2005): 185–207.
31. See Benson, this volume.
32. Rangarajan, *India's Wildlife History,* 104.
33. C. Subramaniam, 'Introductory Speech', *Inaugural Function of the National Committee on Environmental Planning and Coordination* (New Delhi, 1972), 3.
34. Ramachandra Guha and Madhav Gadgil, *Ecology and Equity* (Delhi, 1995).
35. Lewis, *Inventing Global Ecology.*
36. T. N. Khoshoo, *Environmental Concerns and Strategies* (New Delhi, 1988), 586–87.
37. 'Biosphere Reserves: Indian Approach', 14.
38. Harold K. Eidsvik, *The Biosphere Reserve and Its Relation to Other Protected Areas* (Gland, 1979), 4.
39. Interview by author with R. Sukumar, CES, Indian Institute of Science, Bangalore, 12 and 15 June 1998. Transcript on file with author.
40. Eidsvik, *Biosphere Reserve,* 11.
41. Shalina Randeria, 'Global Designs and Local Lifeworlds', *Interventions* 9, no. 1 (2007): 25.

 CHAPTER 13

Slovenia's Triglav National Park

From Imperial Borderland to National Ethnoscape

Carolin Firouzeh Roeder

Throughout Europe's history, the Alps have served as a topographical divider and unifier alike.[1] On today's map, the southeastern part of the continent's grand mountain range, the Julian Alps, constitutes the meeting point of Italy, Austria and Slovenia. The core area of the Julian Alps is nowadays part of the Triglav National Park, which received its name from the highest peak of the mountain range. Although the park was founded in its current borders only in 1981, the idea to create a protection regime in the Julian Alps reaches back into the late Habsburg period. Due to this *longue dureé*, the Triglav National Park encapsulates the legacy of four political entities: the Habsburg Empire, the Kingdom of Yugoslavia, the Socialist Federal Republic of Yugoslavia and the independent state of Slovenia. Italian and German occupation too shaped its history. During the course of the twentieth century, nature conservation in the Julian Alps served several different political projects. As an amalgam of nineteenth-century romanticist ideas of nature, socialist structures of admin-istration and postindependence reform attempts, the history of Triglav Na-tional Park transcends any standard periodization and categorization. Indeed, it is one of the finest examples to illustrate that the study of national parks demands a departure from the sustained focus on national history. Bringing the three themes of this volume together – empire, networks and nation – this contribution exemplifies how the project of 'civilizing nature' in the Julian Alps reflected tensions inherent to efforts of nation and state building from imperial times to postsocialist independence.

The political dimension of nature conservation is nowhere clearer than in Slovenia. The small state distinguishes itself from the other Alpine countries in not only having begun the process of nation and state building very re-cently but also having experienced Yugoslav socialism and an unusual history of political ruptures. Indeed, it is striking that the idea of a national park in the Julian Alps was appealing enough to survive imperial dissolution, border changes and two world wars. Before nature was 'civilized' in the form of a protected area, the national antagonisms in the bilingual borderlands of the Austrian Empire resulted in the 'nationalization' of nature even without the availability of a nation-state. The Alpine landscape provided resources for a Slovenian nation-building project that unfolded since the late nineteenth century independently of the fact that the nation-state came about only as late as 1991. Over the course of the twentieth century, and increasingly after the Second World War, the Julian Alps with their highest peak Triglav turned into the 'dominant Slovene collective idea and ideology'.[2] Like the Swiss, Slovenian national identity continuously drew on the symbolic power of the Alps and in so doing secured political and public interest in this particular space.[3]

Yet, the history of the national park cannot be reduced to the function it had within the nation-building project. Nature conservation in the Julian Alps and elsewhere in Slovenia took place in response to and as an adaptation of continuously evolving trans-European trends, including environmentalism, scientific advancement and the emergence of a bourgeois leisure society. Concrete conservational efforts were driven by the scientific interest of individual actors who were overwhelmingly polyglot academics educated in Vienna and showed little interest in nationalistic rhetoric. Despite the political ruptures, there was a remarkable continuity in leaders of the conservation movement. Many of them acted within both nongovernmental and state organizations and carried their conservational pursuits from one political framework to the next, each time adapting to new circumstances. While state and societal actors alike drew on the symbolic power of the Alps to mobilize their respective target groups, there was hardly ever a unified consensus on how to manage and protect the very area celebrated as the 'most Slovene' region.[4] Conservation activists continuously competed with local interests and struggled against political inertia. Continuity in the endeavours of individuals was often obstructed by institutional discontinuity. The Triglav National Park as it was established in its ultimate form in 1981 was the result of complex local ownership structures, antagonistic views about scientific and economic values, the adaptation of international conservation regimes, the restraints those regimes imposed and the mobilizing power of national symbols. After Slovenia's independence in 1991, struggles over implementation polarized society and mirrored the conflicting opinions regarding what values should inform state building and policy making: liberal laissez-faire or socialist protectionism, eco-nationalism or internationalism, traditional conservation or sustainable development.

Nationalizing Nature in the Imperial Borderlands

Imperial power and colonial rule frequently provided the framework for nationalizing nature. In this case, the Julian Alps represented one of the bilingual language frontiers of the Habsburg Empire.[5] Towards the end of the nineteenth century, the rising antagonisms between the fragmented Slovene-speaking bourgeoisie, which remained loyal to the monarchy even as it favoured cultural national emancipation, and those who represented 'German' interests did not remain confined to the political circles of the provincial capitals and Vienna. Especially in the rural areas, cultural and social organizations provided a framework for national agitation and polemics in an increasingly polarized political climate.[6] In order to transform vague ideas of national consciousness into a coherent concept, Slovene national activists strove to establish a sense of national unity not only by means of a common language but also by staking out their claims to the land. In the Alps, the mountaineering activities of Alpine societies soon became a form of claiming and nationalizing territory. Steep summits provided the setting for clashing interests between those who fervently supported the Slovene cause and those who either supported German nationalism or refrained from national polemics in the debate. Starting in the 1870s, the organization of mountaineering activities in the Julian Alps as well as in the other Alpine regions of Carniola were initially dominated by the German and Austrian Alpine Club. Despite the diverse political currents of its members, the organization as a whole was loyal to both empires, praising German-Austrian friendship as an expression of German national consciousness.[7] The ideas of pure nature, physical exercise and cultural uplifting connected well with the nationalist rhetoric of that time and reflected both the spirit of Enlightenment and Romanticist ideas of nature.

The activities of the German and Austrian Alpine Club, which indeed regarded itself as a 'mighty patron of the German culture',[8] evoked resistance from those who supported the Slovene national idea and also those who felt discriminated against by the exclusiveness of the organization. The support of the 'German cause' in the 'battle of nationalities' was especially articulated in those chapters active in the bilingual areas of Carniola and Carinthia.[9] The Alpine writer and humorist Janko Mlakar even claimed that the German and Austrian Alpine Club established chapters in these areas 'to make German mountaineers feel at home in our mountains, to convince them that they walk on German soil, on German paths and eat and sleep in German huts'.[10] As a response to what was perceived as the 'Germanization' of the mountains, the Slovene Alpine Society was founded in 1893. The Slovenian mountaineering organization was motivated by the 'heartfelt wish that the Slovenes become better acquainted with the natural beauty of their wide homeland and henceforward appreciate it much more sincerely',[11] and to instil into its audience a sense of 'national nature' was of pivotal importance. The society erected shelters and huts and blazed trails with marks distinct from those of the German-Austrian club. Most importantly, the purchase of the summit of Triglav by the

Slovene priest, mayor and mountaineer Jakob Aljaž constituted both a physical and symbolic claim on the land.

The activities of the Slovene Alpine Society became a decisive element of patriotic agitation in what Hroch calls the formation of an image of the fatherland as a 'psycho-geographical fact'.[12] Alpinist narratives of endurance, conquest and heroism lent themselves particularly well to a 'usable past' for a national historiography still void of a nation-state; the *Kulturkampf* added a national component that secured that the Alps turned into an 'ethnoscape', to use Anthony Smith's term: a space that was regarded as a 'historical unique and poetic landscape, as a decisive influence over historical events and as the witness to ethnic survival and commemoration over the *longue durée*.'[13]

Heimatschutz Ordered by Vienna

The Alpine clubs' preoccupation with nature and its national character, which translated into open conflict in the Julian Alps, was part of a broader social development that was triggered by the emerging concern about the destructive effects of industrialization. The first initiatives to legislate the protection of plants and natural monuments in the Habsburg provinces were taken on the side of the imperial centre and reflected the contemporary concern of German *Heimatschutz* (homeland protection) and *Naturschutz* (nature protection) as first formulated in Prussia by Ernst Rudorff and Hugo Conwentz. This movement of the educated middle class saw in the conservation of cultural landscapes the preservation of Germany's 'national uniqueness'. Subsequently, these ideas took hold in Austro-Hungary and provided the cultural framework in which the first conservationist ideas in the empire were formulated.[14] While Slovene societies would play a crucial role in the conservation efforts in years to come, it was the imperial centre in Vienna that, on behalf of the Austrian *Heimatschutz* movement, provided the initial input.

Taking up Conwentz's concept of *Naturdenkmäler* (natural monuments) in 1903, Vienna ordered all provincial administrations to compile a list of natural monuments they deemed worthy of protection.[15] In Upper Carniola, the administration commissioned seismologist and university professor Albin Belar, who eagerly accepted the task. Although Belar came to the conclusion that there was no immediate danger to the 'natural characteristics' of the province, he believed that a list of 'especially exceptionable places which are remarkable in regard to their landscape features or scientific value' would assist the authorities in preventing potential damage by the population and especially 'industrialists'.[16] Furthermore he recommended the establishment of 'nature protection areas [*Naturschutzgebiete*], so called reserves' which would provide a sample of the geographical diversity of Carniola. Amongst others, he proposed to set aside the Valley of the Seven Lakes below the Triglav. He underlined that although hitherto the valley had been well known to landscape painters, the geological, geotectonic and paleontological characteristics of the Triglav lakes were of extraordinary scientific value and still awaited thorough research. Although Slovene historians would later claim otherwise, Belar's idea neither reflected Slovene national spirit nor visions of a Habsburg or Slovenian Yellowstone.[17] What he had in mind were small protected areas modelled upon a private wilderness reserve established by Prince Schwarzenberg in the Bohemian Forest. This was in accord with Conwentz's ideas of preserving small areas with diverse characteristics in different parts of the country as opposed to the American national park model.[18] In line with the spirit of *Heimatschutz*, Belar suggested that *Heimatkunde* (homeland education) should feature more prominently in primary education and called upon the Alpine clubs and other private organizations to take part in public education. This effort, he assumed, would in turn assist the authorities in their conservation efforts. Yet, despite the general nationalist connotations of the *Heimatschutz* principle, Belar's considerations were not based on concerns about the preservation of cultural landscapes for the sake of the (either Slovene or German) nation but driven by his interest in preserving unique natural spaces for future scientific research.

The authorities' inertia and the absence of legal devices prevented the realization of Belar's proposal. Although the agricultural ministry convened a commission that surveyed the area of the Seven Lakes, interviewed locals and consulted the German and Austrian Alpine Club, which owned a hut at the fifth Triglav Lake, no action followed.[19] In distant Vienna, a bill in the Austrian parliament that was meant to secure funding and a legal framework for the protection of natural monuments was blocked.[20] Renewing its efforts in the midst of the First World War, the central government took a second initiative. Following the Prussian and Bavarian examples, Vienna established an administrative authority for nature protection (Fachstelle für Naturschutz) in 1917. Once again, a letter was sent out to the provinces requesting inventories of natural monuments.[21] The outcome of the war and the dissolution of the empire, however, changed political priorities and institutional regimes. Ties between Ljubljana and Vienna were cut off. The Slovene provinces that now formed the Dravska Banovina of the new Kingdom of Serbs, Croats and Slovenes remained without an authority that could follow up the task.[22]

A 'Laboratory of Science' in Interwar Yugoslavia

Yet, conservation activists in Slovenia did not lose spirit. In the interwar period, the conservation movement was mainly driven by scientists who hoped that a national park would bring advancement and prestige to the new scientific community of the Kingdom of Yugoslavia. Within the Slovenian Museum Society, a Section for Nature Protection and Natural Monuments was established in 1919. In the First Yugoslavia, similar to Germany and Austria but with less support of the bureaucracy, nature protection became the domain of private actors who organized themselves mainly within the framework of the Alpine Society and the Museum Society. In the same year, the Museum Society presented a memorandum to the provincial government that was to be celebrated as a milestone in the national historiography of nature protection. This memorandum proposed the establishment of a protected area in the Julian Alps and several other protective measures.[23] The conservationists were able to congratulate themselves on at least partial success when one of their demands, the protection of endangered plants and animals, as well as of Slovenia's extraordinary karst caves, turned into legal reality. Their endeavours were supported by a helping hand in the bureaucracy: forest engineer Anton Šivic (1879–1963). Educated in imperial Vienna in scientific forestry, he was a pragmatic technocrat and scientist alike who came to serve four political regimes in his lifetime.

The Valley of the Seven Lakes remained in the focus of conservationists. Albin Belar had been correct when he assumed years earlier that both the Church's ownership and the low economic value of the rocky 1,400 hectares of land would simplify its transformation into a reserve. In the absence of any legal framework, a solution had to be found to protect what was seen as a public good but situated on private land while simultaneously catering to the interests of the actors involved: the scientists, the members of the Alpine Society and the Forest Directorate in Ljubljana that acted as an administrator on behalf of the Church. After the Ministry for Forestry and Mining in Belgrade finally gave its approval in 1924, the conservationists of the Museum Society's Section for Nature Protection and the Alpine Society signed a lease agreement with the Forest Directorate with which the first protected area in the Julian Alps was established.[24] For a period of twenty years, the Museum Society's duty was to maintain the 'Alpine Protection Park' while the alpinists were obliged to 'support [its] establishment and maintenance' and promote the park and nature protection among their members and tourists. The alpinists in return were to receive timber and water usage for the construction and upkeep of huts.[25] The Forest Directorate promised full support, as long as no costs were involved, and at the same time retained hunting rights on the grounds. This position of general endorsement without the political will for fully fledged practical support remained a characteristic feature also in postwar socialist Yugoslavia. Furthermore, the Alpine Society established itself as a stakeholder in the park, which secured its influence for years to come. The fact, however, that the protection regime was placed on private ground would lead to similar problems conservationists encountered in neighbouring Austria, where the overwhelming part of protected areas consisted of private property, too.

While the alpinists retained their right to use the area for their purposes, others saw a triumph not of tourism but of science. What had started as an idea under Austrian rule became praised as the 'fulfilment of a cultural obligation' on the part of the new Yugoslav scientific community.[26] Lauded as an 'achievement of civilization', the park was seen as the starting point of demonstrative unity among Yugoslavia's highest cultural institutions, i.e., the three universities and the Academies of Sciences in Belgrade and Zagreb.[27] Among those who endorsed the park as an achievement of science but also as an advancement of civilization was botanist Fran Jesenko (1875–1932), who was responsible for mapping the borders of the new reserve. Jesenko was confident enough to call the little reserve 'Triglav National Park'.[28] The polyglot university professor was inspired by his extensive travels abroad, during which he became familiar with several European national parks.[29] Jesenko envisioned that with the new park, Slovenia would step up to other European countries that already had their national parks, among them former Habsburg territories like Czechoslovakia. Significantly, the parks he had in mind – those of Sweden, Italy, Switzerland, Romania, Germany and the United States – were all situated in nation-states, in Jesenko's eyes appropriate points of reference for comparing Slovenia, which was, after all, still a province of Yugoslavia.

In the 1920s, Yellowstone became a point of reference not only for Jesenko whose vision went beyond Belar's appropriation of Conwentz's small nature reserves. Public interest in America's national parks grew when Yugoslav scientists started to travel to the United States and return from their journeys with pictures and stories. The lectures of botanist Vale Vouk from the University of Zagreb about his 1926 visit to Yellowstone attracted so much interest all over Yugoslavia that he had to repeat them several times.[30] Announcing one of the lectures, the newspaper *Slovenski narod* pointed out that his talk was now of special interest as the 'national nature park' in Slovenia was close to its successful establishment. It was more than a slip in terminology when the newspaper, like Jesenko earlier, applied the term 'national park' to an area that had no official name and was referred to by others as Alpine protection park or Alpine nature park. One the one hand, it rhetorically stressed Slovenia's nationhood; on the other, the concept of a national park implied that the value of the park went beyond scientific use. Something larger was at stake, which allowed mobilizing public support for scientific objectives. Elucidating the concept of conservation to the Slovenian readership of the liberal daily *Jutro*, Jesenko explained that national parks are so called 'because they are in fact owned by the entire nation, which can observe in them how a corner of the homeland is developing according to nature's autonomous grand laws.'[31]

In 1938, the Yugoslav government passed a decree on national parks. This decree gave guidelines for the establishment of national parks and was in its scope never matched by any succeeding federal legislation of socialist Yugoslavia.[32] Yet, while some scientists dreamed about Yellowstone, even the implementation of the protection regime in the small Valley of the Triglav Lakes proved difficult. Local peasants had years of lease on the pastures around the Seven Lakes and were unwilling to make space for science. The conservationists struggled to find a way to keep the cows off the pastures, and their rage about cattle trampling precious specimens of flora even reached the kingdom's capital. The Academy of Science in Belgrade convened an extracurricular session and lobbied the Ministry of Forestry and Mining to prohibit grazing in the park entirely. The authorities acted accordingly and provided a budget for melioration and even put violations of the protection regime under penalty. According to Jesenko, Yugoslav and many foreign scientists as well as nature lovers took this as a sign that the establishment of a national park was a 'done deal'.[33] But the peasants remained resistant and insisted that the mountain pastures were only for grazing livestock and any other use illegal. This was at least how Jesenko portrayed the conflict—local ignorance and fifty cows endangered plant life that was of interest to the entire international scientific world.[34] Little did he know that the conflict between conservationists, local residents and politicians would continue for decades to come.

In the absence of strong institutions, individual private endeavour remained pivotal to the conservation movement in Yugoslavia. Protected areas were not yet regarded as an economic asset on which the existing but infant leisure and tourism industry could capitalize, and scientific interest alone was not sufficient to secure enough political interest to put nature conservation high on the political agenda. The scientists themselves were not keen to promote tourism in a park they would rather reserve as a teaching ground, laboratory and experimental garden for students of science than open it as a playground for weekenders.[35] When Jesenko died in a mountaineering accident in 1932, nobody stepped in to advocate preservation in the face of conflicts with cattle and undisciplined tourists who picked protected flowers and walked off the assigned trails.[36] The efforts of the Society for Natural Science, which was established in 1934 and demanded the significant expansion of the territory in order to come closer to the idea of a national park, remained fruitless.[37]

The beginning of the Second World War meant yet another moratorium on further conservation efforts and virtually nullified the effects of the Alpine Protection Park instituted in 1924.[38] Yet, when Slovenia came under German-Italian occupation in 1941, conservation did not entirely lose its momentum. General Leon Rupnik, a Slovene collaborator who served both the Italian and German occupation regime in Ljubljana, managed to organize a full-fledged bureaucracy run both by apolitical civil servants and fervent supporters of the Nazis.[39] It is difficult to establish what happened during the chaotic times of occupation to conservationist efforts, but Anton Šivič, then serving his third political regime, remained active and, in 1944, published an inventory of natural monuments, including the Alpine park, which he regarded as worthy of protection.[40] In the same year, an advisory working group for the protection and conservation of natural features was established at the Natural Science Museum in Ljubljana, as the 1938 National Park Decree envisioned it. In general accord with national socialist ideology, nature protection remained a relatively unproblematic field of policy.

Nature under Socialism

After the Second World War, the building of socialist Yugoslavia provided new input for conservationist efforts and enabled new forms of conservation and international cooperation.[41] There was an at least formal commitment of the new state to protect nature, articulated already in 1945; there were agrarian reforms, new institutions and a new legal framework: the parameters were set for the further development of the national park project. Furthermore, the nationalization of the Alpine landscape continued, and Triglav, which embellished the coat of arms of the Slovenian Liberation Front, became a symbol that stood not only for the Slovene nation but also for a new social order.[42] Despite all difficulties, drawing on its Habsburg conservation tradition, Slovenia had a head start compared to the other republics. As a result of the war, border changes had brought the entire Triglav massif, including the upper Soča valley, previously part of Italy, under Yugoslav jurisdiction. Conflict continued and years of negotiations between the Institute for Nature Protection (the administration for nature protection on the republic level), local communities, the Ministry of Agriculture and other actors followed. Results were meagre and reflected the particularities of the new socialist country. In 1946, representatives of the natural sciences at the University of Ljubljana sent a note to the Ministry of Agriculture. Hoping that the scheduled agricultural reform would work in their interests, they laid claim to the area where they hoped to erect an Alpine research station. The Institute for Nature Protection supported this proposal. However, torn between the interests of the scientists and the local population, the state was not willing to restrict the rights of the local peasant population that already had to suffer during the war.[43] Generally disposed to renew and even expand the Alpine park, the ministry nevertheless took action. The conservationists in the Institute for Nature Protection, in the meantime, negotiated with local representatives and tried to clarify the confusing ownership situation in the Valley of the Seven Lakes.[44] A coalition of nongovernmental and academic organizations started to map out the future borders of the park that they had desired already in prewar times. In 1958, a law regulating the protection of cultural and natural monuments was passed; one year later a law on national parks followed.[45] Furthermore, a commission for national parks was established at the Republican Executive Council. Yet, the new Triglav National Park as it was declared by the parliament in 1961 was far from what conservationists hoped to achieve.

When in 1969 the IUCN, the World Conservation Union, for the first time provided a definition of what constituted a national park, the Triglav National Park did not even come close to the standard set by the IUCN as it covered only 2,000 hectares and remained relatively open for economic activities. With international standards in mind, further expansion thus remained the goal of the conservationist camp. The opinions of the local population and decision makers were everything but univocal and depended on what developmental future the local community envisaged. While some areas still hoped to profit from the socialist ideal of rapid industrialization, other areas were already catering to the growing tourist sector. The communities around Lake Bohinj, which increasingly depended on tourism after the war, hardly opposed and rather supported the extension of the park. In the Soča Valley, in contrast, locals were afraid that an extension of the park would obstruct the planned construction of three hydroelectric dams that ought to boost industrial development.[46] Yet, the appeal of hydropower was only reduced by the economic crisis that hit the global economy in the early 1970s.[47]

Not only had scientists and conservationists to face local resistance, but from the 1960s discussions about protection categories and management principles, international standards and national realities, adherence and noncompliance became a new bone of contention. The attempts of international organizations to harmonize conservation regulations on a global scale introduced a new level of conflict to Slovenian conservation. In 1959, the federal state had deferred all responsibility of nature protection to the republics, which created very diverse regulations across the country and partially obstructed participation in international regimes that required ratification by the federal parliament.[48] On the federal level, the environmental protection authorities of the republics formed the rather inefficient Yugoslav Union for the Protection and Improvement of the Human Environment (SAVEZ), which never went beyond the role of a debating club.

While collaboration among the Yugoslav republics remained limited, communication with the other Alpine countries proved to be more beneficial. Sharing the common Alpine space as well as joint objectives brought Slovenian conservationists closer to their neighbours than to Belgrade. Nature conservation enabled Slovenia within the framework of Yugoslav federalism to participate in regional and international cooperation projects in a way that imitated the strength and resources available to the federal state. These ties were fostered as early as 1952, when the International Commission for the Protection of the Alps (CIPRA) was founded. As a nongovernmental umbrella organization it provided an institutional framework of conservation in the Alps, enabling various networks and organizations to link across political levels of authority and state borders. In Slovenia, individual efforts rather than strong institutions remained the driving force. Slovenian conservation became closely connected with the name of its first female activist, botanist Angela Piskernik (1886–1967), who had been the director of the Museum of Natural Science in Ljubljana since the end of the war. Stemming from Carinthia, which remained with Austria after the First World War, Piskernik had been the first woman to receive a doctorate in natural sciences from the University of Vienna. Her efforts were respected and internationally awarded – in fact, she seemed to have received more acknowledgement abroad than in Yugoslavia.[49]

Having survived a German concentration camp, Piskernik oriented her efforts from the beginning towards nature protection schemes that entailed a political dimension of reconciliation. In the 1960s, the Austrian and Yugoslav delegations of CIPRA, headed by Piskernik, made efforts to establish a transnational nature park in the Savinja Alps and Karawanks based on the example of the Italian Gran Paradiso National Park and La Vanoise in France. As Piskernik put it, 'Neither water nor flora and fauna know national borders, wind, water and animals carry seeds of plants and fruits over every border drawn by men far into the surrounding.'[50] For Piskernik, the objective behind the bilateral park was not only to accommodate borderless nature but also to build bridges between neighbours. The bilateral park was, however, never realized, perhaps because after Piskernik's death in 1967 her advocacy was missing.

Independently, attempts to enlarge the Triglav National Park continued. With the planned extension, the group of stakeholders grew but the problems remained the same. Strict conservation or more room for tourist development, unspoiled nature or hydroelectricity – a consensus was hard to achieve. It was clear that with the extension of the park to settled land a differentiated system of restrictions had to be imposed. In 1978, a law proposal was put forward by the parliament that envisaged a four-tier zoning system. Eventually, however, much under critique of the Alpine Society, which had its own interests in the park, the proposal passed in 1981 distinguished only two zones of different protection levels that corresponded to the IUCN level II (core) and V (periphery). The legal framework was prepared by the Natural and Cultural Heritage Act, and the special Law on the Triglav National Park extended the park that then demarcated approximately 3 per cent of Slovene territory (83,807 hectares) and comprised twenty-five settlements.[51] Management remained another contested question. A strong lobby group consisted of the hunting authorities whose clientele feared that with the extension of the park their competences in the previous hunting reserve, which then was to constitute large parts of the new park, would be lost. Instead of creating a new authority, the existing administration of the hunting reserve was charged to manage the park while keeping its old function. While this decision was accompanied by fierce debates, this step secured that the park would have a budget rooted in the republican budget – an advantage compared to other Yugoslav national parks that had to rely on self-created revenues. With the budget the park also inherited the trail and lodge network of the hunting administration as well as a functioning administrative infrastructure. Over the course of time, the conservationist ethos came to shape the staff, function and identity of the authority, which was renamed Triglav National Park Public Service (*javni zavod*). Significantly, the trophies in the offices in Bled were crated.[52] Fights about what was allowed and what should be prohibited within the boundaries of the park nonetheless continued to polarize locals, urban owners of weekend houses, local enterprises and politicians, ensuing that the contestation over the park remained a republic-wide public issue.[53]

After Independence: New State, Old Problems

At the onset of the violent dissolution of Yugoslavia, Slovenia declared independence in 1991. Once state and nation building were aligned, the debates about the future development of Triglav National Park brought old conflicts to the fore and opened up new sites of argument. Getting involved in the process of nationalizing nature provided a venue of conversation for state and social actors to discuss the shape of the new state and compete over resources. New transnational agreements such as the Alpine Convention of 1991 and Natura 2000, an EU network of protected sites based on the 1992 Habitats Directive and the 1979 Birds Directive, as well as joint projects like the International Scientific Committee for Alpine Research extended transnational cooperation. On the national level, however, many questions regarding the future of Triglav National Park remained unanswered. Severe debates over the future use of the park polarized politicians, the public and nongovernmental organizations. Discussions about restoring the previous ownership of parts of the park linked conservation to the question of the role and rights of the Church in the post-socialist society and denationalization in general.[54] Traditional conservationists promoting a nonintervention policy clashed with approaches promoting sustainable regional development. Local communities in Triglav National Park once again felt left out of the decision-making process and were partly led by political actors who primarily supported their own private interest. Rivalling factions called upon international conventions, zoning standards and management principles to lend justification to their respective viewpoints. When in 2010, after two decades of debate, a new law was finally passed, the coalition of NGOs that had worked on their own proposal since 2004 complained that the new legal setup would allow unrestrained development and construction, while the mayor of Bohinj, one of the municipalities in the park, argued that the law assured that 'Bohinj will not become wilderness.'[55] Although wilderness was never the core concept behind Slovenian conservation, it remained an anathema in the eyes of parts of the local population.

Yet, the ethnoscape of the Alps not only became a bone of contention in postsocialist Slovenia but also continued to offer symbolic power towards fostering a cohesive national identity outside of the Yugoslav framework. The Slovenian government passed a National Cultural Program in 2008 that stated that the environment is as significant for national and cultural identity as the Slovene language.[56] On the occasion of the twentieth anniversary of the national park in May 2001, Minister of the Environment Janez Kopač declared, 'Our only national park and also the greatest of all our parks at present, it has become a part of our everyday existence in the past two decades, including all of the benefits and problems we have with it and the pride we take in it.'[57] The Triglav National Park is employed by official and private campaigns alike to brand a competitive 'green image' of the country and justify its place among the European states. This is a broader trend of postsocialist countries, which often draw substantially on the aesthetics of their landscapes to foster both internal cohesion and promote the country as an equal member of Europe's postindustrialized community.[58] Over the period of about a century, the significance of the Julian Alps underwent a change in scale from imperial borderlands to the core landscape of independent Slovenia: the local came to stand for the national.

Notes

1. I would like to thank Patrick Kupper, Bernhard Gissibl and Alison Frank for their helpful comments and advice on this contribution. I owe sincere thanks to Peter Skoberne and Jernej Stritih for providing me with invaluable information and sources, as well as to Mimi Urbanc and Primož Pipan from the Anton Melik Institute of Geography in Ljubljana who generously hosted me during my research in Ljubljana in 2010.

2. Tone Strojin, 'Triglav, simbol slovenstva in gorništva', in *Triglav, gora naših gora,* ed. Tone Strojin (Maribor, 1980), 10.

3. For a detailed analysis see Boštjan Šaver, *Nazaj v planinski raj: alpska kultura slovenstva in mitologija Triglava* (Ljubljana, 2005). For the Swiss case see Oliver Zimmer, 'In Search of Natural Identity: Alpine Landscape and the Reconstruction of the Swiss Nation', *Comparative Studies in Society and History* 40, no. 4 (1998): 643.

4. Strojin, 'Triglav', 10. See also Ana Kučan, *Krajina kot nacionalni simbol* (Ljubljana, 1998).

5. For the national movements in the rural language frontiers see Pieter Judson, *Guardians of the Nation: Activists on the Language Frontier of Imperial Austria* (Cambridge, 2006).

6. For details on the Slovene national movement between 1848 and the First World War see Joachim Hösler, *Slowenien. Von den Anfängen bis zur Gegenwart* (Regensburg, 2006), 91–125.

7. Anneliese Gidl, *Alpenverein: die Städter entdecken die Alpen* (Wien, 2007), 319–21.

8. Ibid., 320.

9. Ibid.

10. Janko Mlakar cited in Tone Strojin, *Oris zgodovine planinstva* (Ljubljana, 1978). 6.

11. Fran Orožen and Anton Mikuš, 'Planinski vestnik', *Planinski vestnik* 1, no. 1 (1895).

12. Miroslav Hroch, 'National Self-Determination from a Historical Perspective', in *Notions of Nationalism*, ed. Sukumar Periwal (Budapest, 1995), 70.

13. Anthony Smith, *Myths and Memories of the Nation* (Oxford, 1999), 151.

14. See William H. Rollins, *A Greener Vision of Home. Cultural Politics and Environmental Reform in the German Heimatschutz Movement, 1904–1918* (Ann Arbor, 1997); Friedemann Schmoll, *Erinnerung an die Natur. Die Geschichte des Naturschutzes im deutschen Kaiserreich* (Frankfurt, 2004), esp. chapters 3–4. For the transnational aspects of the *Heimatschutz* movement and American conservationism see Thomas Lekan, 'The Nature of Home: Landscape Preservation and Local Identities', in *Localism, Landscape, and the Ambiguities of Place. German Speaking Central Europe, 1860–1930.* ed. David Blackbourn and James Retallack (Toronto, 2007).

15. The initiative came from the Bohemian Member of Parliament Gustav Nowak who, in 1905, made his third attempt to introduce a bill regulating the preservation of not only cultural but also natural monuments. Although his proposal was rejected and a similar law only passed in 1924, the idea to regulate cultural and natural monuments together would later be picked up by the provisional Partisan government in 1945. Johannes Straubinger, *Sehnsucht Natur: Geburt einer Landschaft* (Norderstedt, 2009), 265.

16. Albin Belar, 'Die Naturdenkmalstelle in Österreich mit besonderer Berücksichtigung des Landes Krain', *Wiener Zeitung*, 9 June 1907, 3. Thanks to Peter Skoberne for sharing this source. For more on Belar see also Peter Skoberne, 'Prispevek poznavanju vloge Albina Belarja na področju varstva narave na Slovenskem', *Annales ser. hist. nat.* 21, no. 1 (2011):97-110.

17. Compare Jože A. Mihelič and Renato Vidrih, 'Dr. Albin Belar', in *Snovalci Triglaskega narodnega parka - ljudje pred svojim časom*, ed. Martin Šolar (Bled, 2006), 22.

18. Compare Lekan, *Nature of Home*, 178.

19. Mihelič, 'Dr. Albin Belar', 20–21.

20. Straubinger, *Sehnsucht Natur*, 265.

21. 'Za varstvo prirodnih spomenikov', *Carniola. Mitteilungen des Museal-Vereins für Krain* 8 (1917): 271–72.

22. 1918–29 Kingdom of the Serbs, Croatians and Slovenes, 1929–41 renamed Kingdom of Yugoslavia.

23. A facsimile of the memorandum is printed in Stane Peterlin, 'Nekaj o zametkih in začetkih varstva narave v Sloveniji', *Varstvo spomenikov* 20 (1976).

24. The park did not cover the entire valley since its northwestern part with the first Triglav Lake was situated outside of the state borders in Italian territory. Angela Pis-

kernik, 'Jahrzehnte dauernde Bemühungen um den Triglav-Nationalpark', in *Gedenkschrift zur Verleihung des Van-Tienhoven-Preises der gemeinnützigen Stiftung F.V.S. zu Hamburg* (Bonn, 1967), 34.

25. Zakupna pogodba [lease agreement], 1924. Document available at http://web.bf.uni-lj.si/students/vnd/knjiznica/Skoberne_literatura/predpisi_zgodovina/tnp_zakupna.pdf.

26. Marko Hafner, 'Alpski varstveni park v dolini Sedmerih jezer', *Geografski vestnik* 1, no. 1 (1925): 62.

27. Ibid., 62.

28. Fran Jesenko, 'Kraljestvo Zlatoroga: Triglavski Narodni Park', *Jutro* 30 June 1926, 11–12.

29. France Planina, 'Profesor Fran Jesenko', *Loški razgledi* 7 (1960): 154.

30. 'Predavanje o krasotah znamenitega Yellowstone National Parka in gorovja Ročk v Severni Ameriki', *Slovenski Narod,* 30 April 1928, 4.

31. The first official use of the term 'national park' was made in 1928 in a proclamation of the Yugoslav royal government, which designated several areas in Croatia, among others the Plitvice Lakes and the Paklenica area in the Velebit mountains. See Fred Singleton, 'Parks and Conservation of Nature in Yugoslavia', in *Environmental Problems in the Soviet Union and Eastern Europe,* ed. Fred Singleton (Boulder, 1985), 186.

32. 'Državna uredba o narodnih parkih', *Službeni list banske uprave Dravske banovine,* no. 71 (1938).

33. Jesenko, *Kraljestvo Zlatoroga,* 12.

34. Ibid.

35. Hafner, *Alpski varstveni park,* 65.

36. Victor Petkovček, 'Profesor Fran Jesenko in Triglavski narodni park', *Proteus* (1973): 393.

37. Anton Šivič, 'O Alpskem naravnem parku pri Triglavskih jezerih', *Proteus* 13, no. 9–10 (1951): 339–46.

38. Fred Singleton, 'The Triglav National Park in the 1980s', *Slovene Studies* 10, no. 1 (1988): 189.

39. Tamara Griesser-Pečar, *Das zerrissene Volk: Slowenien 1941–1946: Okkupation, Kollaboration, Bürgerkrieg, Revolution* (Wien, 2003).

40. Unfortunately, the folder containing Šivič's material regarding nature protection is missing from AS Fond 33 (Landesregierung Laibach 1861–1918), Archives of the Republic of Slovenia. See also Skoberne, 'Prispevek poznavanju vloge Albina Belarja', 102.

41. Proclaimed 1943 as Democratic Federal Yugoslavia, the Federal People's Republic of Yugoslavia (FPRY) was founded in 1946, and renamed the Socialist Federal Republic of Yugoslavia (SFRY) in 1963.

42. Šaver, *Nazaj v planinski raj,* 236.

43. Piskernik, *Jahrzehnte,* 38–39.

44. Ibid., 39.

45. 'Zakon o vrstvu kulturnih spomenikov in naravnih znamenitosti', Uradni list LRS, no. 22 (1958); 'Zakon o nardodnih parkih', Uradni list LRS, no. 6 (1959).

46. Singleton, *Parks,* 190.

47. Fred Singleton, 'National Parks and the Conservation of Nature in Yugoslavia,' manuscript, Fred Singleton Archive, University of Bradford, Box 5, Folder 1, Item 5.

48. In each republic, and from 1974 also in the autonomous provinces, institutes (*zavodi*) staffed with professionals were responsible for nature protection. In addition, Councils for the Protection of Nature were established at the executive organs. While in some republics separate institutions were established for the preservation of cultural and natural heritage, in Slovenia both functions were united in the Institute for the Protection of Monuments (Zavod za spomeniško varstvo), renamed the Institute for the Preservation of Natural and Cultural Heritage (Zavod za varstvo naravne in kulturne dediščine) in 1981. According to Singleton, this might reflect the role of the Slovene Museum Society in the conservation movement, which initially dealt with both cultural and natural heritage. After independence, these tasks were split. See Singleton, 'The Triglav National Park in the 1980s'.

49. Compare Tone Wraber, 'Dr. Angela Piskernik (1886–1967)', *Varstvo narave*, no. 6 (1967): 5–11.

50. 'Poročilo o zasedanju mednarodne alpske komisije (CIPRA) 11. in 12.VI. v Italiji', Archive of the Republic of Slovenia, Fond AS 1982, Box 3, Folder 5.

51. Zakon o naravni in kulturni dediščini [Law on Natural and Cultural Heritage], *Uradni list SRS*, no. 1 (1981); Zakon o triglavskem narodnem parkom [Law on the Triglav National Park], *Uradni list SRS*, no. 17 (1981).

52. Peter Skoberne, interview with author, Ljubljana, 4 August 2010.

53. For some details on the conflicts see Singleton, *Parks*, 190–91.

54. John Cox, *Slovenia: Evolving Loyalties* (New York, 2004), 124.

55. Blaž Račič, 'Dobra osnova za razvoj parka', *Delo* 24 June 2010.

56. Državni zbor Republike Slovenije, 'Resolucijo o nacionalnem programu za kulturo 2008–2011', *Uradni List*, no. 35 (2008): 3384.

57. Ministry of the Environment and Spatial Planning, 'Environment and Spatial Planning Information Bulletin,' (Ljubljana, 2001).

58. The Baltic states of Latvia and Estonia, equally small and successors of a disintegrating state, have likewise incorporated nature and in particular national parks into the wider discourse of national identity in an attempt to distance themselves from their socialist past. See Katrina Schwartz, '"Masters in Our Native Place": The Politics of Latvian National Parks on the Road from Communism to "Europe"', *Political Geography* 25, no. 1 (2006): 42–71; Katrina Schwartz, *Nature and National Identity after Communism: Globalizing the Ethnoscape* (Pittsburgh, 2006); Robert Smurr, *Perceptions of Nature, Expressions of Nation: An Environmental History of Estonia* (Saarbrücken, 2009).

National Parks, Civilization and Globalization

Jane Carruthers

As almost everyone knows, Yellowstone, the renowned national park, was established in 1872. Some have argued that it was a religious, transcendentalist form of land appreciation, others that it was designed to minimize class conflict in a rampantly capitalist new nation and yet others that it was an attempt to prevent the area from becoming another ruined and exploited natural wonder, as had happened to Niagara Falls. Familiarity with this chronology and background goes a considerable way to explaining how and why such a form of land use and its governance came into being in the United States, and the topic has been examined by historians time and again.[1]

However, while many histories of Yellowstone express pride in this 'American invention', only a few have followed how the ideas it unleashed flowed into other parts of the world, generally undergoing considerable transformations and transmutations as they travelled. Given that Yellowstone emanated from a specific place and within a specific social, political and historical context, it is perhaps surprising that 'national parks' have taken root in so many diverse places around the globe, and that the majority of national parks have no connection either to the Yellowstone 'model' or to the United States. This global phenomenon demands historical explanation. Through the diversity of case studies contained in this volume, the argument has been adduced that the propulsion to 'civilize nature' – by bounding it territorially and by globalizing it through nomenclature and international diplomacy – resonated far beyond Yellowstone and US society. Indeed, 'national parks' – wherever they were established and under whatever circumstances they took root – spoke to an era in which they had a part to play in a globalizing world in which 'civilization' and modernity were significant, and in which a specific form of territoriality was appropriate. On the one hand, it was 'the march of civilization', in the form of urbanisation, population expansion and industrialization, that threatened the existence of 'pristine nature' and necessitated a new form of regional (and later, international) governance. These national parks, with their imperative of public access, were to serve as reservoirs for spiritual and recreational renewal for urban, civilized societies. But, on the other hand, as outlined in many of the contributions to this volume, the establishment of national parks was framed alternatively as an achievement of 'civilized' society. Indeed, national parks provided a universalist language that was a marker of national respectability in an increasingly global century. As the flow of ideas around national parks permeated the globe, a variety of scales intersected and interacted. Moreover, as the chapters in this book also amply demonstrate, some national parks were founded in states that considered themselves to be already 'civilized', i.e., advanced, modern and mature (e.g., the Netherlands, Canada, Switzerland), while others (e.g., Australia, Malaysia, Mexico, Slovenia) sought to stake a claim to civilization via the establishment of national parks. Unlike the comprehensive sweep that is world history, the chapters presented here have concentrated on the process of globalization, interrogating and illuminating the networks that connect various parts of the world with each other.

This is a timely and important book because of the present historiographical milieu. Currently there is an emphasis in almost all disciplines on the transnational, as scholars seek to answer questions about how ideas, people, techniques and institutional structures have flowed around the world. We need to question and debate the factors that have been responsible for this wide dissemination, together with the identification of the ideological motors, at institutional and individual levels. This volume provides some thoughts in answering some of these questions using the vehicle of national parks. Of course, the case studies are neither comprehensive, nor perhaps even representative and, as explained in the introduction, there are immense geographical omissions. However, no single volume would be able to encompass the full range that is 'national parks', and the bottom-up approach pursued here links exemplary sites with the broader processes, structures and agents behind a diverse sample of national parks. By doing so, this book aims to contribute to a fresh, topical, and increasingly significant debate in world environmental history: how national parks can illuminate and problematize the web of modern globalization.[2] The contributions included here construe national parks as fundamentally integral to the twentieth-century world, and they do so in two principal ways.

Nations, National Parks and International Nature

First, they have questioned the emphasis on the 'national' and explored the 'international', the 'supranational' and the 'transnational', of national parks. Even in the most critical literature, national parks are not criticized for being 'national' or for incorporating that adjective – they are critiqued for their biodiversity conservation management or for their detrimental effects on neighbouring communities.[3] The word 'national' (or 'nation')[4] is an extremely powerful evocation – even in our age of globalization – and exploring the 'national park' provides an innovative historical window on the tension between state, subnational and international actors. For almost two hundred years the Western ideal of a modern democratic nation, one in which human rights, the rule of law and a universal franchise contribute to good governance, peace and internal stability, has been posited as the ideal. Consequently, national parks, with their name so clearly linked to the nation, carry within their very appellation an aura both of 'goodness' and of civilized modernity in the same way as does the word 'democracy'.[5]

'National park' is an international brand – a brand, it is true, without clear standards and thus open to almost infinite interpretation, but one that is highly suggestive of international acceptability. Nation-states appear to prefer 'national parks' to other names of protected areas, even when some other title – such as 'state park', 'provincial park' or 'wildlife reserve' – would be legally or ecologically more appropriate. The parameters of national parks are not closely regulated by international law or convention, and the club is not exclusive. Large areas, small areas, land or sea, rich or poor biodiversity, as well as varying structures of governance – all are welcomed within the national park community. By contrast, World Heritage Sites are scrutinized in terms of certain standards, internationally regulated and initiated by government agencies. There are *in loco* inspections, the need for management plans and there is even a List of World Heritage in Danger that – in certain circumstances – can lead to international embarrassment for those countries whose names appear on it.[6] There is no such list for national parks. It is an easy option, for all it amounts to is 'a name'.[7] It is an irony that a state can stake its moral worth for effective environmental protection and governance through national parks while neglecting other important places in the national estate or, for example, by refusing to support a climate change reduction protocol, or other more testing forms of biodiversity conservation or regulated sustainable resource use that would be excoriated by the electorate.

Nonetheless, the idea of the 'national' remains contested and unclear in many parts of the world. National parks provide a vehicle around which divided communities may coalesce in a 'national project'. Cases in point include Yellowstone itself and the Kruger National Park in South Africa,[8] and in this volume the contributions of Carolin Roeder and Bernhard Gissibl demonstrate this clearly. Other challenges that illuminate the national with reference to national parks are those countries, particularly in the former Soviet bloc, that still struggle to come to terms with what kind of 'nature' epitomizes their states – i.e., a postcolonial situation. Indeed, the 'national' in regard to protected areas requires further historical unpacking. For example, there is the symbolic use of nature to heal a community after civil violence, the celebration of release from autocratic government[9] and the complexities of nationality in divided societies. Notably, the 'transnational' has also acquired healing powers: recent IUCN-backed attempts to turn the Iron Curtain of the Cold War into a 'European Green Belt' of connected protected areas, and the establishment of transfrontier conservation areas in southern Africa called 'Peace Parks' suggest that nature may equally be harnessed to transnational social and territorial entities with socio- and ecopolitical as well as biodiversity conservation agendas.

Second, this book explores how the complexity of environmental ideas embedded within this extremely broad 'national park' theme have themselves expanded to become part of the web of globalization. In crossing state boundaries, in gaining an international voice through the World Conservation Union (IUCN) and other nonstate actors, in the flow of ideas at the levels of government, nongovernment organizations and between and among individuals, national parks have played a significant role in globalizing nature. This has been a multifaceted process. As explained in many of the foregoing chapters, some national parks are owned by the state, but others are not. Some are situated in urban areas, others rural. Some were established by national governments, others by provinces or regions. Some were the brainchildren of despots or leaders, others of local communities. Management structures vary greatly, as do scientific fundamentals, conservation goals and the degree of public access.[10] Of critical importance is the fact that national parks are established at particular places only at particular times – and for this reason require examination in terms of the specificity of their historical context.

Linking National Parks and Global Environmental Governance

If so many of the world's national parks differ greatly from one another, then the question arises as to why it is important to continue studying them as though they were a coherent institution and why they, and the name, continue to have such a tremendous hold on the public imagination. We argue here that, for historians, it is because they illuminate an aspect of modern world history that is truly significant.

In September 1972, the second World Parks Congress was held in the United States, at Yellowstone, the venue celebrating its establishment as a national park one hundred years previously. As it happened, this congress was to prove a watershed in protected-area philosophy. The first congress, convened in Seattle in June 1962, was billed as a 'World Congress on National Parks', and its purpose was to 'establish a more effective international understanding of national parks and to encourage further development of the national park movement on a world wide scale'.[11] This was not a particularly innovative philosophy, and it signalled the continued leadership of the United States in leading the 'movement'. The Yellowstone Congress was, however, different. The theme, 'National Parks: A Heritage for a Better World', recognized for the first time their global importance as heritage and their potential for social, environmental and economic improvement.[12] It was the 'heritage' element that eventually bore fruit in the establishment of the World Heritage Convention.[13]

More research remains to be done on unpacking the synergy that globalized conservation and sustainability in the 1970s, contextualizing it also against the growth of the modern environmental movement and the idea of 'One Earth' symbolized by the first Earth Day celebration in 1970. This book marks an innovative start in exploring historical connections between the Convention Concerning the Protection of the World Cultural and Natural Heritage (the World Heritage Convention), which was adopted by the General Conference of UNESCO in 1972 at a meeting in Paris, and national parks.[14] The duties of the World Heritage Committee are to identify outstandingly valuable cultural and natural properties that require protection under the convention and to inscribe them on the World Heritage List, to place properties on the List of World Heritage in Danger, to assess threats to World Heritage Sites generally and to determine how the financial resources of World Heritage can optimally be applied.[15] As indicated above, no such regulatory body exists for national parks, and one might argue that national parks are therefore a more useful marker of the flow of ideas transnationally precisely because they are subject to less scrutiny and standardization.

The year 1972 was not only remarkable for the Yellowstone World Parks Congress and the World Heritage Convention; it was also the year in which the United Nations Conference on the Human Environment was convened in Stockholm, just three months prior to the Yellowstone conference. These three conversations in 1972 linked the triad of national parks, nature as heritage and environmental sustainability, within a global perspective. Despite its flaws, the Stockholm conference was a formal acknowledgement of the need for multilateral efforts to deal with transboundary environmental problems. The Declaration of the United Nations Conference on the Human Environment was the first international instrument that recognized the right of people to a healthy environment, but also the first to link injustice with environmental issues. Stark contrasts between the positions of the developed and the developing world, and between globalism and national sovereignty regarding environmental misuse, came to light at Stockholm and were not resolved there. The industrialized nations focused on environmental degradation as a short-term, technically solvable, issue. The developing countries, however, argued that any actions in this regard would merely deal with the symptoms of the crisis and avoid the global root causes, namely, matters relating to the international economy, to international debt and to inequitable access to financial and technological resources. In order to bring these positions closer to each other, further conferences were planned, thus sparking 'the onset of an era of explosive growth in transnational environmental activism'.[16]

The Man and the Biosphere Programme (MAB), another UNESCO initiative, was also launched in 1970 and formally established in 1977. Under MAB a World Network of Biosphere Reserves (WNBR) has come into being, the majority of which have a formally protected area, usually a national park, at their core. The number of biospheres has grown over the decades, and they go a long way to encouraging regional planning and land use that prioritize sustainable livelihoods, scientific environmental research and education.[17]

Linking national parks explicitly with heritage and moral purpose for the future went further in 1982 at the Third World Parks Congress held in Bali and called 'Parks for Development', and in 1992 at the Fourth, in Caracas, titled 'Parks for Life'. In 2003 the Fifth World Parks Congress, the first to be held in Africa, convened in Durban, with the theme 'Benefits beyond Boundaries'. The integration of national parks into the mainstream of global and local community life is now an enduring motif.[18] Dissecting whether this has occurred 'top down' or 'bottom up', e.g., through community-based programmes, particularly in the developing world, is an important area for further research.

In 1992, in parallel with Caracas, representatives of governments, international bodies and nongovernmental organizations met in Rio de Janeiro, Brazil, for the 'Earth Summit', the United Nations Conference on the Environment and Development (UNCED), strongly influenced by *Our Common Future*, the Brundtland Report of 1987.[19] This conference confirmed that environmental concerns had come to have a central place in the agenda of world politics. The enormous media attention, the large number of national and nongovernmental delegations and the five signed agreements (of which the most important were the Rio Declaration and Agenda 21), formally acknowledged the connection between environmental and developmental pressures and accepted the global character of environmental challenges.[20]

A decade after the Earth Summit in Brazil, world leaders and environmentalists gathered in Johannesburg from 16 August to 4 September 2002 for the World Summit on Sustainable Development (WSSD) to review the outcome of the ambitious goals adopted in 1992. This was the largest international gathering ever held in Africa and attracted tens of thousands of delegates from governments, business, NGOs, farmers, indigenous people, the youth, women, trade unions and many other interested people. The output from Johannesburg was less specific than Rio. There was, nonetheless, a generalized recommitment to sustainable development, the assumption of collective responsibility, a common resolve to ameliorate the challenges around poverty and to lessen the division between rich and poor and to replenish and wisely use an impoverished global environment.[21]

Naturally, the historical trajectory from Yellowstone in 1872 to the WSSD in Johannesburg in 2002 and the Fifth World Parks Congress in Durban in 2003 is neither simple nor linear. But one can certainly argue that there is a connection between the conservation of nature (however construed) and the people, not only of a nation but of a wider global community, that Yellowstone inaugurated and its rhetoric both facilitated and perpetuated.

The antecedents of the frenetic transnational activity of the second half of the twentieth century – the IUCN, founded in 1948 as an arm of the United Nations that encompasses states, government agencies and nongovernmental organizations, and the World Wide Fund for Nature (WWF, founded as the World Wildlife Fund in 1961, with the IUCN's support) as the funding arm of the Western conservation movement, with its mission to obtain financial support from the public directly and from big business – are both analysed in depth in this volume. Together with other voluntary international funding agencies, such as the International Foundation for Animal Welfare (IFAW), the Nature Conservancy, the Frankfurt Zoological Society and the Fauna Society, WWF funds projects of particular concern to the countries in which it works and raises money. The consequence has been that a WWF project, for example, the 'Peace Parks' (Transfrontier or Transboundary Conservation Areas) of southern Africa, is promoted in the same region in which IFAW funds elephant conservation efforts in an effort to prevent culling.[22] The global reach and influence of these nonstate actors and their funding structures would merit more research from environmental historians.

Linking Globalization and National Parks

While scholars generally do not question the reality of globalization, there is considerable disagreement around its causes, characteristics and consequences, to which the history of national parks can profitably contribute. Many accounts of globalization focus on its socioeconomic aspects,[23] and attribute the phenomenon to the evolving activities of transnational corporations (TNCs). As an ideology, globalization is associated with – and in large part legitimated by – capitalism and neoliberalism and this too is a theme that resonates through many of the contributions presented here. Commodification, a major theme in global history, is representative of a specific form of world economy, and in this regard there are social scientists who take issue with the modern commercialization of nature and of national parks, that – it can be legitimately be argued – found an early appearance in Yellowstone in 1872.[24]

Historian Anthony G. Hopkins has referred to the exploration of the many facets of globalization as currently 'the most important single debate in the social sciences'.[25] Historians, in particular, are reexamining the history of colonialism and imperialism, and to this literature also the history of national parks can contribute. Scholars have also become more wary of Eurocentric perspectives – of which the 'Yellowstone model' is one – because this may obscure insights into important trends elsewhere in the world. In addition, if globalization is the increasing level of interconnectedness, localization – the distinctive identity of people and particular places – is both a response to it and an outcome of it.

The transnational character of environmental issues poses challenges to the modern state system. As described above, regulations regarding World Heritage, together with the various other binding conventions and agreements that are internationally monitored, may limit state power. In this regard, national parks are in an interesting position, because although they comprise an internationally recognized and respected brand, their declaration, their management, their size and their governance is free from restriction. Despite this lack of commonalities, it seems that a narrative has emerged from the preceding chapters that would suggest that some general aspects of the transnational thread of national parks may now be identified and thus a lively debate about the shape and structure of this fabric may commence.

Conclusion

The complex nature of international structures and ideas and the entangled histories of national parks speak to each other in productive ways. Increasingly, historians are paying more attention to the 'circulations and connections between, above and beyond national polities and societies'. National parks, like transnational history generally, 'mounts a challenge to nation-centric history and even Eurocentric history'.[26] Transnational history is a growing field, perhaps because 'world history' has a worrying span for historians, who are sceptical of stories of progress and triumph.

It is into this historiography of the Yellowstone model with its Western triumphal signature, its evocation of 'good' versus 'evil', that this book ventures with a fresh appraisal of the internationalization of the national park, its chronology, its particularity both to time and place, and yet within the matrix of globalization. We offer here a new perspective on environmental history through the prism of the particular, but far from offering isolated case studies or direct comparisons we have explored how national parks have reflected both global and local agendas. The name allows interested parties to call upon romanticism, patriotism, democracy, modernity, internationalism, economics and cultural heritage in support for national parks. And as the oldest modern form of public landscape and nature protection, the national park is better able than any other institution to demonstrate global trends in conservation thinking over a long period of time. There is much more to uncover on this score.

Notes

1. Cf. Jones, this volume.
2. For an analysis of how environmental history has been construed in both developing and developed countries see Edmund Burke III and Kenneth Pomeranz, *The Environment and World History* (Berkeley, 2009). This book does not, however, concentrate on national parks, as is the case here.
3. The literature on this topic is extensive. See Arun Agrawal and Kent Redford, 'Conservation and Displacement: An Overview', *Conservation and Society* 7(1) (2009): 1–10.
4. Benedict Anderson, *Imagined Communities: Reflections on the Origin and Spread of Nationalism* (London, 1983).
5. Roderick Nash, 'The American Invention of National Parks', *American Quarterly* 22 (1970): 726–35.
6. See the World Heritage website, http://whc.unesco.org.
7. As has often been quoted in this regard, 'When I use a word it means just what I choose it to mean', says Humpty Dumpty to Alice in Lewis Carroll's *Through the Looking Glass.* See, for example, C. Michael Hall and Warwick Frost, 'Introduction: The Making of the National Parks Concept', in *Tourism and National Parks: International Perspectives on Development, Histories and Change,* ed. Warwick Frost and C. Michael Hall (Abingdon, 2009), 3.
8. Jane Carruthers, *The Kruger National Park: A Social and Political History* (Pietermaritzburg, 1995).
9. See, for example, Sandra Chaney and Rita Gudermann, 'The East's Contribution to International Conservation (Part 1)', *Environmental Policy and Law* 40 (2010): 116–23; Sandra Chaney and Rita Gudermann, 'National Contribution to International Conservation (Part 2)', *Environmental Policy and Law* 40 (2010): 179–87.
10. See the IUCN website, http://www.iucn.org/.
11. A. B. Adams, ed., *First World Conference on National Parks* (Washington, DC, 1962).
12. Hugh Elliott, ed., *Second World Congress on National Parks* (Morges, 1974); Mohammed Valli Moosa and Murphy Morobe, 'The Future', in *South African National Parks: A Celebration,* ed. Anthony Hall-Martin and Jane Carruthers (Johannesburg, 2003), 247.
13. See Natarahan Ishwaran, 'International Conservation Diplomacy and the World Heritage Convention', *Journal of International Wildlife Law and Policy* 7 (2004): 43–56.
14. See Wöbse, this volume.
15. See the World Heritage website, http://whc.unesco.org.
16. Ken Conca, 'Stockholm Conference', in *The Palgrave Dictionary of Transnational History,* ed. Akira Iriye and Pierre-Yves Saunier (Houndmills, 2009), 979–80. The *Report of the United Nations Conference on the Human Environment* is located at http://www.unep.org/Documents.Multilingual/Default.asp?DocumentID=97.

    The United Nations Environment Program (headquarters in Nairobi) was created from the Stockholm meeting. In 1971, at Ramsar, Iran, the Convention on Wetlands of International Importance especially as Waterfowl Habitat was concluded, and in 1973 the Convention on International Trade in Endangered Species of Fauna and Flora. The Bonn Convention, officially known as the Convention on the Conservation of Migratory Species of Wild Animals, was concluded in 1979.

17. See the Man and the Biosphere website, http://www.unesco.mab.

18. Moosa and Morobe, 'The Future', 247. See also Adrian Phillips, 'Turning Ideas on Their Head: A New Paradigm for Protected Areas', *George Wright Forum* 20, no. 2 (2003): 8–32; Marc Hockings, Jamison Ervin and Geoffrey Vincent, 'Assessing the Management of Protected Areas: The Work of the World Parks Congress before and after Durban', *Journal of International Wildlife Law and Policy* 7 (2004): 32–42; Geoffrey Wandesforde-Smith, 'The Future of Wildlife and the World Parks Congress', *Journal of International Wildlife Law and Policy* 7 (2004): 1–7.

19. The commission's report, *Our Common Future: World Commission on Environment and Development* (Oxford, 1987), ensured worldwide publicity for the concept of 'sustainable development'.

20. See http://www.cbd.int; http://www.un.org/esa/dsd/agenda21.

21. See http://www.earthsummit2002.org, accessed 30 July 2010.

22. Anthony Hall-Martin and Johann van der Merwe, 'Developing a National Park System', in Hall-Martin and Carruthers, *South African National Parks*, 53. See also the Peace Parks Foundation website, http://www.peaceparks.org; the IFAW website, http://www.ifaw.org; and the Humane Society website, http://www.humansociety.org.

23. For a short introduction to the field see Jürgen Osterhammel and Niels P. Petersson, *Globalization: A Short History* (Princeton, 2005).

24. See, for example, Bram Büscher, 'Seeking "Telos" in the "Transfrontier"? Neoliberalism and the Transcending of Community Conservation in Southern Africa', *Environment and Planning* 42 (2010): 644–60; D. Brockington, R. Duffy and J. Igoe, *Nature Unbound: Conservation, Capitalism and the Future of Protected Areas* (London, 2008).

25. A. G. Hopkins, 'Introduction: Globalization – An Agenda for Historians', in *Globalization in World History*, ed. A. G. Hopkins (London, 2002), 1.

26. 'Introduction', in Iriye and Saunier, *Palgrave Dictionary of Transnational History*, xvii–xviii.

Select Bibliography

Adams, Alexander, ed., *First World Conference on National Parks: Proceedings of a Conference Organized by the International Union for Conservation of Nature and Natural Resources* (Washington, DC, 1962).

Adams, William M., *Against Extinction. The Story of Conservation* (London, 2004).

Adams, William M. and Martin Mulligan, eds, *Decolonizing Nature. Strategies for Conservation in a Post-colonial Era* (London, 2003).

Agrawal, Arun and Kent Redford, 'Conservation and Displacement: An Overview', *Conservation and Society* 7, no. 1 (2009): 1–10.

Agrawal, Arun, *Environmentality. Technologies of Government and the Making of Subjects* (Oxford, 2005).

Ali, Saleem H., ed., *Peace Parks: Conservation and Conflict Resolution* (Cambridge, 2007).

Allsen, Thomas T., *The Royal Hunt in Eurasian History* (Philadelphia, 2006).

Anderson, Benedict, *Imagined Communities: Reflections on the Origin and Spread of Nationalism* (London, 1983).

Anderson, David and Richard Grove, eds, *Conservation in Africa. People, Policies and Practice* (Cambridge, 1987).

Appadurai, Arjun, *Modernity at Large: Cultural Dimensions of Globalization* (Minneapolis, 1996).

Arnscheidt, Julia, *'Debating' Nature Conservation: Policy, Law and Practice in Indonesia, a Discourse Analysis of History and Present* (Leiden, 2009).

Bachmann, Stefan, *Zwischen Patriotismus und Wissenschaft: Die Schweizerischen Naturschutzpioniere (1900–1938)* (Zürich, 1999).

Barth, Boris and Jürgen Osterhammel, eds, *Zivilisierungsmissionen. Imperiale Weltverbesserung seit dem 18. Jahrhundert* (Konstanz, 2005).

Beinart, William and Lotte Hughes, *Environment and Empire* (Oxford, 2007).

Benson, Etienne, *Wired Wilderness: Technologies of Tracking and the Making of Modern Wildlife* (Baltimore, 2010).

Berger, Thomas R., *Northern Frontier, Northern Homeland: The Report of the Mackenzie Valley Pipeline Inquiry*, rev. ed. (Toronto, 1988).

Biel, Alice Wondrak, *Do (Not) Feed the Bears: The Fitful History of Wildlife and Tourists in Yellowstone* (Lawrence, 2006).

Binnema, Theodore and Melanie Niemi, '"Let the Line be Drawn Now": Wilderness, Conservation, and the Exclusion of Aboriginal People from Banff National Park in Canada', *Environmental History* 11, no. 4 (2006): 724–50.

Blackbourn, David and James Retallack, eds, *Localism, Landscape, and the Ambiguities of Place. German Speaking Central Europe, 1860–1930* (Toronto, 2007).

Boomgaard, Peter, 'Oriental Nature, Its Friends and Its Enemies: Conservation of Nature in Late-Colonial Indonesia, 1889–1949', *Environment and History* 5, no. 3 (1999): 257–92.

Brockington, Dan and Rosaleen Duffy, eds, *Capitalism and Conservation* (Oxford, 2011).

Brockington, Daniel, *Fortress Conservation. The Preservation of the Mkomazi Game Reserve, Tanzania* (Oxford et al., 2002).

Brockington, Daniel, Rosaleen Duffy and Jim Igoe, *Nature Unbound. Conservation, Capitalism and the Future of Protected Areas* (London, 2008).

Brockington, Daniel and James Igoe, 'Eviction for Conservation: A Global Overview', *Conservation and Society* 4, no. 3 (2006): 424–70.

Brosius, J. Peter, Anna Lowenhaupt Tsing and Charles Zerner, eds, *Communities and Conservation: Histories and Politics of Community-Based Natural Resource Management* (Lanham, 2005).

Brysk, Alison, *From Tribal Village to Global Village. Indian Rights and International Relations in Latin America* (Stanford, 2000).

Burke III, Edmund and Kenneth Pomeranz, eds, *The Environment and World History* (Berkeley, 2009).

Büscher, Bram, 'Seeking "Telos" in the "Transfrontier"? Neoliberalism and the Transcending of Community Conservation in Southern Africa', *Environment and Planning* 42, no. 3 (2010): 644–60.

Campbell, Claire Elizabeth, ed., *A Century of Parks Canada, 1911–2011* (Calgary, 2011).

Carr, Ethan, *Wilderness by Design: Landscape Architecture and the National Park Service* (Lincoln, 1998).

Carrier, James G. and Paige West, eds, *Virtualism, Governance and Practice. Vision and Execution in Environmental Conservation* (New York, 2009).

Carruthers, Jane, *The Kruger National Park: A Social and Political History* (Pietermaritzburg, 1995).

Catton, Theodore, *Inhabited Wilderness: Indians, Eskimos, and National Parks in Alaska* (Albuquerque, 1997).

Chase, Alston, *Playing God in Yellowstone: The Destruction of America's First National Park* (Boston, 1986).

Chatty, Dawn and Marcus Colchester, eds, *Conservation and Mobile Indigenous Peoples. Displacement, Forced Settlement and Sustainable Development* (New York, 2002).

Chester, Charles C., *Conservation across Borders: Biodiversity in an Interdependent World* (Washington, DC, 2006).

Cioc, Mark, *The Game of Conservation. International Treaties to Protect the World's Migratory Animals* (Athens, OH, 2009).

Cooper, Frederick, *Colonialism in Question. Theory, Knowledge, History* (Berkeley, 2005).

Dorsey, Kurk, *The Dawn of Conservation Diplomacy: U.S.-Canadian Wildlife Protection Treaties in the Progressive Era* (Seattle, 1998).

Dove, Michael R. et al., 'The Global Mobilization of Environmental Concepts: Re-Thinking the Western/Non-Western Divide', in *Nature across Cultures. Views of Nature and the Environment in Non-Western Cultures*, ed. Helaine Selin and Arne Kalland (Dordrecht, 2003), 19–46.

Dove, Michael R., Percy E. Sajise and Amity A. Doolitttle, eds, *Beyond the Sacred Forest: Complicating Conservation in Southeast Asia* (Durham, 2011).

Dowie, Mark, *Conservation Refugees: The One Hundred Year Conflict between Global Conservation and Native Peoples* (Cambridge, 2009).

Dunlap, Thomas R., *Nature and the English Diaspora: Environment and History in the United States, Canada, Australia, and New Zealand* (Cambridge, 1999).

Elliott, Hugh, ed., *Second World Conference on National Parks: Yellowstone and Grand Teton National Parks, USA, September 18–27, 1972* (Morges, 1974).

Evans, Sterling, *The Green Republic. A Conservation History of Costa Rica* (Austin, 1999).

Ford, Caroline, 'Nature, Culture, and Conservation in France and her Colonies 1840–1940', *Past & Present* 183, no. 1 (2004): 173–98.

———, 'Reforestation, Landscape Conservation and Anxieties of Empire in French Colonial Algeria', *American Historical Review* 113, no. 2 (2008): 341–62.

Frank, David John, Ann Hironaka and Evan Schofer, 'The Nation-State and the Natural Environment over the Twentieth Century', *American Sociological Review* 65, no. 1 (2000): 96–116.

Frohn, Hans-Werner and Friedemann Schmoll, eds, *Natur und Staat: Staatlicher Naturschutz in Deutschland, 1906–2006* (Bonn, 2006).

Frost, Warwick and Michael C. Hall, eds, *Tourism and National Parks: International Perspectives on Development, Histories, and Change* (New York, 2009).

Garland, Elizabeth, 'State of Nature: Colonial Power, Neoliberal Capital, and Wildlife Management in Tanzania', PhD diss. University of Chicago, 2006.

Ghimire, Krishna B. and Michel P. Pimbert, eds, *Social Change and Conservation. Environmental Politics and Impacts of National Parks and Protected Areas* (London, 1997).

Gissibl, Bernhard, 'German Colonialism and the Beginnings of International Wildlife Preservation in Africa', *German Historical Institute Bulletin Supplement* 3 (2006): 121–43.

———, *The Nature of German Imperialism. Conservation and the Politics of Wildlife in Colonial East Africa* (Oxford, forthcoming).

Griffiths, Tom and Libby Robin, eds, *Ecology and Empire: Environmental History of Settler Societies* (Melbourne, 1997).

Grove, Richard, *Green Imperialism: Colonial Expansion, Tropical Island Edens and the Origins of Environmentalism, 1600–1860* (Cambridge, 1995).

Guha, Ramachandra, 'Radical American Environmentalism and Wilderness Preservation. A Third World Critique', *Environmental Ethics* 11, no. 1 (1989): 71–83.

Guha, Ramachandra and Madhav Gadgil, *Ecology and Equity* (Delhi, 1995).

Hall, C. Michael and John Shultis, 'Railways, Tourism and Worthless Lands: The Establishment of National Parks in Australia, Canada, New Zealand and the United States', *Australian-Canadian Studies* 8, no. 2 (1991): 57–74.

Hall-Martin, Anthony and Jane Carruthers, eds, *South African National Parks: A Celebration* (Johannesburg, 2003).

Harroy, Jean-Paul, ed., *World National Parks: Progress and Opportunities* (Brussels, 1972).

Harvey, David, *Justice, Nature, and the Geography of Difference* (Oxford, 1996).

Hockings, Marc, Jamison Ervin and Geoffrey Vincent, 'Assessing the Management of Protected Areas: The Work of the World Parks Congress before and after Durban', *Journal of International Wildlife Law and Policy* 7, no. 1–2 (2004): 32–42.

Holdgate, Martin W., *The Green Web: A Union for World Conservation* (London, 1999).

Hopkins, Antony G., ed., *Global History: Interactions between the Universal and the Local* (New York, 2006).

Hunt, Constance, Rusty Miller and Donna Tingley, *Wilderness Area: Legislative Alternatives for the Establishment of a Wilderness Area in the Northern Yukon* (Ottawa, 1979).

Igoe, Jim, *Conservation and Globalization. A Study of National Parks and Indigenous Communities from East Africa to South Dakota* (Belmont, 2004).

Iriye, Akira, *Global Community: The Role of International Organizations in the Making of the Contemporary World* (Berkeley, 2002).

Iriye, Akira and Pierre-Yves Saunier, eds, *The Palgrave Dictionary of Transnational History* (Houndmills, 2009).

Ishwaran, Natarahan, 'International Conservation Diplomacy and the World Heritage Convention', *Journal of International Wildlife Law and Policy* 7, no. 1–2 (2004): 43–56.

Jacoby, Karl, *Crimes Against Nature: Squatters, Poachers, Thieves, and the Hidden History of American Conservation* (Berkeley, 2001).

Jameson, John, *The Story of Big Bend National Park* (Austin, 1996).

Jepson, Paul and Robert J. Whittaker, 'Internationalisation of Conservationist Values and their Adaptation in the Netherlands Indies (Indonesia)', *Environment and History* 8, no. 2 (2002): 129–72.

Kathirithamby-Wells, Jeyamalar, *Nature and Nation: Forests and Development in Peninsular Malaysia* (Honolulu, 2005).

Kopas, Paul, *Taking the Air: Ideas and Change in Canada's National Parks* (Vancouver, 2007).

Kulchyski, Peter and Frank James Tester, *Kiumajut (Talking Back): Game Management and Inuit Rights, 1900–1970* (Vancouver, 2007).

Kupper, Patrick, 'Nationalparks in der europäischen Geschichte', *Themenportal Europäische Geschichte* (2008), http://www.europa.clio-online.de/2008/Article=330.

——, 'Science and the National Parks: A Transatlantic Perspective on the Interwar Years', *Environmental History* 14, no. 1 (2009): 58–81.

——, *Wildnis schaffen: Eine transnationale Geschichte des Schweizerischen Nationalparks* (Bern, 2012).

Lausche, Barbara J., *Weaving a Web of Environmental Law: Contributions of the IUCN Environmental Law Programme* (Bonn, 2008).

Leach, Melissa and Robin Mearns, *The Lie of the Land. Challenging Received Wisdom on the African Environment* (Oxford, 1996).

Leask, Anna and Alan Fyall, *Managing World Heritage Sites* (Amsterdam, 2006).

Lekan, Thomas M., *Imagining the Nation in Nature: Landscape Preservation and German Identity, 1885–1945* (Cambridge, 2004).

——, 'Serengeti Shall Not Die: Bernhard Grzimek, Wildlife Film, and the Making of a Tourist Landscape in East Africa', *German History* 29, no. 2 (2011): 224–64.

Lewis, Michael, ed., *American Wilderness: A New History* (New York, 2007).

Lewis, Michael, *Inventing Global Ecology: Tracking the Biodiversity Ideal in India, 1947–1997* (Hyderabad, 2003; Athens, OH, 2004).

Luard, Nicholas, *The Wildlife Parks of Africa* (London, 1985).

MacKenzie, John M., *The Empire of Nature: Hunting, Conservation, and British Imperialism* (Manchester, 1988).

Maier, Charles S., 'Consigning the Twentieth Century to History: Alternative Narratives for the Modern Era', *American Historical Review* 105, no. 3 (2000): 807–31.

Martin, Brad, 'Negotiating a Partnership of Interests: Inuvialuit Land Claims and the Establishment of Northern Yukon (Ivvavik) National Park', in *A Century of Parks Canada, 1911-2011,* ed. Claire Elizabeth Campbell (Calgary, 2011), 272–301.

Massey, Doreen, *For Space* (London, 2005).

Matheka, Reuben M., 'Decolonisation and Wildlife Conservation in Kenya, 1958-68', *Journal of Imperial and Commonwealth History* 36, no. 4 (2008): 615–39.

Mazlish, Bruce, *The New Global History* (New York, 2006).

Mazlish, Bruce and Akira Iriye, eds, *The Global History Reader* (New York, 2005).

Mels, Tom, *Wild Landscapes: The Cultural Nature of Swedish National Parks* (Lund, 1999).

Meyer, John W. et al., 'The Structuring of a World Environmental Regime 1870-1990', *International Organization* 51, no. 4 (1997): 623–51.

Miller, Char, *Gifford Pinchot and the Making of Modern Environmentalism* (Washington, DC, 2004).

Mitchell, Donald Craig, *Take My Land, Take My Life: The Story of Congress' Historic Settlement of Alaska Native Land Claims, 1960-1971* (Fairbanks, 2001).

Mitman, Gregg, 'When Nature *Is* the Zoo: Vision and Power in the Art and Science of Natural History', *Osiris* 11 (1996): 117–43.

Muir, John, *Our National Parks* (Boston, 1901).

Nash, Roderick, 'The American Invention of National Parks', *American Quarterly* 22, no. 3 (1970): 726–35.

——, *Wilderness and the American Mind* (New Haven, 2001 [1967]).

Nelson, Daniel, *Northern Landscapes: The Struggle for Wilderness Alaska* (Washington, DC, 2004).

Neumann, Roderick P., 'Dukes, Earls and Ersatz Edens. Aristocratic Nature Preservationists in Colonial Africa', *Environment and Planning D. Society and Space* 14, no. 1 (1996): 79–98.

——, *Imposing Wilderness: Struggles over Livelihood and Nature Preservation in Africa* (Berkeley, 1998).

——, *Making Political Ecology* (London, 2005).

van Osten, Richard, ed., *World National Parks: Progress and Opportunities* (Brussels, 1972).

Peet, Richard and Michael Watts, eds, *Liberation Ecologies: Environment, Development, Social Movements* (London, 2004).

Peluso, Nancy Lee, *Rich Forests, Poor People: Resource Control and Resistance in Java* (Berkeley, 1992).

Phillips, Adrian, 'The History of the International System of Protected Area Management Categories', *Parks* 14, no. 3 (2004): 4–14.

Pritchard, James A., *Preserving Yellowstone's Natural Conditions: Science and the Perception of Nature* (Lincoln, 1999).

Rangarajan, Mahesh, *India's Wildlife History* (Delhi, 2001).

Rawson, Timothy, *Changing Tracks: Predators and Politics in Mt. McKinley National Park* (Fairbanks, 2001).

Ritvo, Harriet, *The Animal Estate. The English and Other Creatures in the Victorian Age* (London, 1990).

Rothman, Hal, *Preserving Different Pasts: The American National Monuments* (Urbana, 1989).

Runte, Alfred, *National Parks: The American Experience* (Lincoln, 1987).

Saberwal, Vasant, Mahesh Rangarajan and Ashish Kothari, eds, *People, Parks, and Wildlife: Towards Coexistence* (New Delhi, 2001).

Sandlos, John, 'From the Outside Looking in: Aesthetics, Politics, and Wildlife Conservation in the Canadian North', *Environmental History* 6, no. 1 (2001): 6–31.

———, 'Federal Spaces, Local Conflicts: National Parks and the Exclusionary Politics of the Conservation Movement in Ontario, 1900–1935', *Journal of the Canadian Historical Association* 16 (2005): 293–318.

———, *Hunters at the Margin: Native People and Wildlife Conservation in the Northwest Territories* (Vancouver, 2007).

Santiago, Myrna I., *The Ecology of Oil: Environment, Labor and the Mexican Revolution, 1900–1938* (Cambridge, 2006).

Schmoll, Friedemann, *Erinnerung an die Natur: Die Geschichte des Naturschutzes im deutschen Kaiserreich* (Frankfurt/New York, 2004).

Schröder, Iris and Sabine Höhler, eds, *Welt-Räume: Geschichte, Geographie und Globalisierung seit 1900* (Frankfurt/New York, 2005).

Schwartz, Katrina, *Nature and National Identity after Communism: Globalizing the Ethnoscape* (Pittsburgh, 2006).

Scott, James C., *Seeing Like a State. How Certain Schemes to Improve the Human Condition Have Failed* (New Haven, 1998).

Sellars, Richard West, *Preserving Nature in the National Parks: A History* (New Haven, 1997).

Sheail, John, *Nature's Spectacle. The World's First National Parks and Protected Places* (London, 2010).

Shetler, Jan Bender, *Imagining Serengeti. A History of Landscape Memory in Tanzania from Earliest Times to the Present* (Athens, OH, 2007).

Sievert, James, *The Origins of Nature Conservation in Italy* (Bern, 2000).

Simonian, Lane, *Defending the Land of the Jaguar: A History of Conservation in Mexico* (Austin, 1995).

Smith, Anthony, *Myths and Memories of the Nation* (Oxford, 1999).

Smurr, Robert W., *Perceptions of Nature, Expressions of Nation: An Environmental History of Estonia* (Saarbrücken, 2009).

Sodhi, Navjot S. et al., eds, *Biodiversity and Human Livelihoods in Protected Areas: Case Studies from the Malay Archipelago* (Cambridge, 2008).

Soja, Edward W., *Postmodern Geographies. The Reassertion of Space in Critical Social Theory* (London, 1999).

Spence, Mark David, *Dispossessing the Wilderness: Indian Removal and the Making of the National Parks* (New York, 1999).

Stevens, Stan, ed., *Conservation through Cultural Survival: Indigenous People and Protected Areas* (Washington, DC, 1997).

Tsing, Anna Lowenhaupt, *Friction: An Ethnography of Global Connection* (Princeton, 2004).

Tucker, Richard P., *Insatiable Appetite: The United States and the Ecological Degradation of the Tropical World* (Berkeley, 2000).

Tyrrell, Ian, 'America's National Parks: The Transnational Creation of National Space in the Progressive Era', *Journal of American Studies* 46, no. 1 (2012): 1–21.

Wakild, Emily, 'Border Chasm: International Boundary Parks and Mexican Conservation, 1935–1945', *Environmental History* 14, no. 3 (2009): 453–75.

————, *Revolutionary Parks: Conservation, Social Justice, and Mexico's National Parks, 1910–1940* (Tucson, 2011).

Wallerstein, Immanuel, *European Universalism. The Rhetoric of Power* (New York, 2006).

Wandesforde-Smith, Geoffrey, 'The Future of Wildlife and the World Parks Congress', *Journal of International Wildlife Law and Policy* 7, no. 1–2 (2004): 1–7.

Warren, Louis S., *The Hunter's Game: Poachers and Conservationists in Twentieth-Century America* (New Haven, 1997).

Weiner, Douglas R., *Models of Nature: Ecology, Conservation, and Cultural Revolution in Soviet Russia* (Bloomington, 1988).

West, Patrick C. and Steven R. Brechin, *Resident Peoples and National Parks. Social Dilemmas and Strategies in International Conservation* (Tucson, 1991).

White, Richard, 'The Nationalization of Nature', *Journal of American History* 86, no. 3 (1999): 976–86.

van der Windt, Henny J., 'The Rise of the Nature Conservation Movement and the Role of the State: The Case of the Netherlands, 1860–1955', *Jahrbuch für Europäische Verwaltungsgeschichte* 11 (1999): 227–51.

Wöbse, Anna-Katharina, *Weltnaturschutz. Umweltdiplomatie in Völkerbund und Vereinten Nationen 1920–1950* (Frankfurt, 2012).

Worster, Donald, *Nature's Economy: A History of Ecological Ideas* (Cambridge, 1994 [1977]).

Zellen, Barry Scott, *Breaking the Ice: From Land Claims to Tribal Sovereignty in the Arctic* (Lanham, 2008).

Zimmerer, Karl S., ed., *Globalization and New Geographies of Conservation* (Chicago, 2006).

Notes on Contributors

Etienne Benson is a research scholar in Department II of the Max Planck Institute for the History of Science in Berlin. His research focuses on the history of human-animal relations, the environmental and animal rights movements and the sciences of ecology and ethology. His book *Wired Wilderness: Technologies of Tracking and the Making of Modern Wildlife* (2010) is an account of the invention of wildlife radio tracking and its impact on understandings of wildness and wilderness.

Jane Carruthers is Research Professor in the Department of History, University of South Africa, Pretoria; Research Associate of the Centre for Invasion Biology, Stellenbosch University, and Fellow of the Royal Society of South Africa and Fellow of Clare Hall, Cambridge. She is Chair of the Academic Advisory Board of the Rachel Carson Centre for Environmental History at the Ludwig Maximilian University in Munich and President of the International Consortium of Environmental History Organizations. Her doctoral thesis, *The Kruger National Park: A Social and Political History,* has become a standard reference work at many universities worldwide. She is widely published, and her current research interests lie in the history of the biological sciences and national parks, colonial art, heritage and cartography. She is a member of numerous editorial boards and professional societies.

Caroline Ford is Professor of History at the University of California, Los Angeles. She is the author of two books and is completing a third on the transformation of environmental sensibilities in metropolitan and colonial France in the nineteenth and twentieth centuries. She is the author of 'Museums after Empire in Metropolitan and Colonial France', *Journal of Modern History* (September 2010); 'Reforestation, Landscape Conservation and the Anxieties of Empire in French Colonial Algeria', *American Historical Review* (April 2008), which was awarded the Koren Prize by the Society for French Historical Studies in 2009 and coeditor, with Tamara Whited, of a special issue of *French Historical Studies* on *New Directions in French Environmental History* (Summer 2009). She was awarded a John Simon Guggenheim Memorial Foundation Fellowship for 2011–12.

Bernhard Gissibl is a Postdoctoral Researcher at the Leibniz-Institute of European History in Mainz, Germany. His PhD dissertation, entitled *The Nature of German Imperialism: Conservation and the Politics of Wildlife in Colonial East Africa* has analysed the political ecology of the wildlife conservation regime established in Tanzania under German rule. It has been awarded the Young Scholar's Prize of the German Association of African Studies (VAD) and is currently under review for publication. His research interests focus on the history of conservation, imperial history and human-animal relations in transnational and global perspective.

Melissa Harper lectures in Australian Studies at the University of Queensland. She is the author of *The Ways of the Bushwalker: On Foot in Australia* (2007) and a number of articles on the history of bushwalking. Melissa edited *Symbols of Australia* (2010) with Richard White. She is currently working on a transnational history of early national parks and a history of dining out in Australia since the 1970s. She is the coeditor of the *Journal of Australian Studies*.

Sabine Höhler is Associate Professor of Science and Technology Studies at KTH Royal Institute of Technology in Stockholm. Originally trained as a physicist, her research centres on the modern earth sciences and their perception of global spaces. She authored *Luftfahrtforschung und Luftfahrtmythos: Wissenschaftliche Ballonfahrt in Deutschland, 1880–1910* (2001) and coedited *Welt-Räume: Geschichte, Geographie und Globalisierung* (2005). Recently she finished a book-length study on 'Spaceship Earth' and the discourse on environmental capacity and life support in the 1960s and 1970s. Presently she explores the intersections of ecology and economy in the view of ecosystems as service providers.

Karen Jones is senior lecturer in American and environmental history at the University of Kent, U.K. Her research focuses on the American West, especially national parks, wildlife and the cultural ecology of hunting. She is the author of *Wolf Mountains: A History of Wolves along the Great Divide* (2002), *The Invention of the Park* (2005) and *The American West: Competing Visions* (2009). Karen is currently finishing a monograph on hunting in the nineteenth-century American West for the University Press of Colorado, and is developing further projects on taxidermy in the West, and horses in the frontier army.

Jeyamalar Kathirithamby-Wells formerly held the Chair of Asian History at the University of Malaya, Kuala Lumpur. Currently resident in the U.K., she researches and teaches in Cambridge. She has worked extensively on Southeast Asia during the early modern period and, in recent years, has expanded her research interests to include environmental and conservation history. Apart from publishing numerous articles and monographs, she contributed to the *Cambridge History of Southeast Asia* (1992), co-edited *The Southeast Asian Port and Polity* (1990, with John Villiers) and authored *Nature and Nation: Forests and Development in Peninsular Malaysia* (2005). Among her current interests is a project on nature and nationalism in Southeast Asia.

Patrick Kupper is Senior Lecturer at ETH Zurich. His research focuses on the history of environment, technology and knowledge. He has published on environmentalism, nuclear energy, science and technology, and nature conservation. Over the last few years he has researched the global history of national parks. He authored *Atomenergie und gespaltene Gesellschaft: Die Geschichte des gescheiterten Projektes Kernkraftwerk Kaiseraugst* (2003); *Transforming the Future: ETH Zurich and the Construction of Modern Switzerland 1855–2005* (2010) and *Wildnis schaffen: Eine transnationale Geschichte des Schweizerischen Nationalparks* (2012).

Michael Lewis is Chair of the Environmental Studies Department and Professor of Environmental Studies and History at Salisbury University. Originally trained as a biologist, his research has focused on the global exchange of conservation science ideas and policies. His work has included *Inventing Global Ecology: Tracking the Biodiversity Ideal in India, 1947–1997* (2004), and his edited volume, *American Wilderness: A New History* (2007).

Brad Martin is a PhD candidate at Northwestern University outside Chicago and the Chair of the School of Community Education and Development at Yukon College in Whitehorse, Yukon, Canada. His doctoral research examines the intersection of state conservation and transnational indigenous politics in the circumpolar North. He has published previously on Inuit land claims and the history of the national park system in Canada and is the coeditor of a forthcoming volume on the environmental history of northern Canada. Other current research projects explore the history of oil and gas development in the western Arctic and the cultural politics of aboriginal self-government.

Carolin F. Roeder is a PhD student in Modern European History at Harvard University. She received her MA in East European Research and Studies from the University of Bologna, Italy. Her research interests include Eastern and Central European history, European imperialism, environmental history and the history of science and exploration. Carolin is currently working on her PhD dissertation, a transnational history of mountaineering.

Henny J. van der Windt is Associate Professor at the Science & Society Group of the University of Groningen, the Netherlands. He earned his master's degree in ecology and wrote his doctoral thesis on the social history of nature conservation and ecology. He published about environmental history, social movements, science theatre, sustainable management of coastal zones, the role of ecologists in decision making and the valuation of nature. He is editor-in-chief of the Dutch-Flemish *Jaarboek voor Ecologische Geschiedenis (Yearbook of Environmental History)*.

Emily Wakild is Assistant Professor of History at Boise State University in Idaho. She specializes in the history of Mexico and modern Latin America with a focus on social change, revolution and the environment. Her book, *Revolutionary Parks: Conservation, Social Justice, and Mexico's National Parks* was awarded the Southeastern Council for Latin American Studies Alfred B. Thomas book award. She has been supported by Fulbright-Hays, National Endowment for the Humanities, and National Science Foundation fellowships. At present she is working on a comparative history of transnational conservation and scientific research in Amazonian and Patagonian South America.

Richard White teaches Australian history and the history of travel and tourism at the University of Sydney. His publications include *Inventing Australia*, *The Oxford Book of Australian Travel Writing*, *Cultural History in Australia*, *On Holidays: A History of Getting Away in Australia* and, with Melissa Harper, *Symbols of Australia*. His latest book, coedited with Caroline Ford, is *Playing in the Bush: Recreation and National Parks in New South Wales* (2012). Current research includes a history of tourism to the past in Australia and a history of the cooee. He is coeditor of the journal *History Australia*.

Anna-Katharina Wöbse works as a free-lance environmental historian in Bremen, Germany. She has earned her PhD at the University of Bielefeld in 2011 and has extensively published on media and the environment, human-animal relations, environmental diplomacy and the role of civil society in global environmental governance. Her recently published book *Weltnaturschutz: Umweltdiplomatie in Völkerbund und Vereinten Nationen, 1920-1950* (2012) explores the role of the League of Nations and its successor, the United Nations in the making of global environmental regimes. Currently, she is involved in a research project on the history of global environmental governance at the University of Geneva and she is co-editing a book-length study on the history of the Hohe Tauern-National Park in Austria.

Index